The Origins of Modern Mexico

Laurens Ballard Perry,
General Editor

The State, Education, and Social Class in Mexico, 1880–1928

Mary Kay Vaughan

Northern Illinois University Press   DeKalb   1982

Publication of this book was assisted by a grant from the Publications Program of the National Endowment for the Humanities, an independent federal agency.

Library of Congress Cataloging in Publication Data

Vaughan, Mary K., 1942–
    The state, education, and social class in Mexico, 1880–1928.

    (The Origins of modern Mexico)
    Bibliography: p.
    Includes index.
        1. Education—Mexico—History. I. Title.
    II. Series.
    LA421.V38   370'.972   81–18733
    ISBN 0–87580–079–3   AACR2

Copyright © 1982 by Northern Illinois University Press
Published by the Northern Illinois University Press
DeKalb, Illinois 60115
Manufactured in the United States of America

for my father

Contents

List of Tables

Acknowledgments

A fellowship from the Henry and Grace Doherty Foundation facilitated this study, which first emerged as a doctoral dissertation. At the University of Wisconsin, Stanley Payne, the late John Leddy Phelan, Thomas Skidmore, and Peter H. Smith made valuable comments on the original manuscript. To John Leddy Phelan, I am especially indebted, for while we did not always agree, his sensitivity toward Mexican culture and his insights into the dynamics of Mexican history were critical to my intellectual development. I want to thank Carlos Blanco Aguinaga, John Coatsworth, Enrique Florescano, Nora Hamilton, Friedrich Katz, Albert Michaels, Anna Maria Taylor, and Josefina Zoraida Vázquez, who read all or parts of this work at different stages of its development and provided helpful suggestions for its improvement.

To my colleagues in the Latin American Studies Program at the University of Illinois–Chicago Circle—Otto Pikaza, Renato Barahona, Emilio Pantojas García, Leonardo Ramírez, Juan Valadés, Marc Zimmerman, and the late Rafael Cintrón Ortiz—I owe much for having created an environment in which it was possible to question long-held intellectual assumptions and to begin the process of rethinking problems of societal development. Needless to say, I am aware of the theoretical shortcomings of this study, and I am of course responsible for any errors in fact and interpretation.

I would also like to thank the personnel of the numerous libraries and archives in which I have worked. Especially helpful and patient were the staffs at the Biblioteca de México, the Hemeroteca Nacional, the archives of the Secretaría de Educación Pública, the archives of don Ezequiel Chávez, housed in the Universidad Nacional Autónoma de México, the Archivo General de la Nación, which maintains the archives of the Secretaría de Instrucción Pública y Bella Artes and the papers of presidents Obregón and Calles, the University of Wisconsin and University of Illinois library systems, and the Midwest Center for Research Libraries of Chicago.

Finally, I wish to thank the editors of *Latin American Perspectives* and the Council on International Studies at the State University of New York at Buffalo for allowing me to reprint in this volume material published earlier by them.

M.K.V.

Introduction

Standard histories of public schooling tend to emphasize the role of education in integrating society, increasing production, and facilitating individual social mobility.[1] Historians of Mexican education are no exception: by and large, they have considered the expansion of public schooling to be an important indicator of modernization. Such interpretations often concentrate upon education's role in national integration and the school as a way out of poverty—both nationally and individually.[2] In most of these studies, important questions go unanswered. Into what, for instance, does the school integrate people and how? Who defines the content of school programs and pedagogy? What is the relationship between schooling and the labor market and between schooling and social class? To whom does education offer social mobility? Above all, if public education is a function of the state, what is the relationship between state and society which in turn influences the function and content of education?

Most historians of Mexican education see the Mexican Revolution of 1910 as a progressive movement which introduced full-scale modernization and promised material well-being to the population as a whole. An extensive campaign for public schooling accompanied this process. This interpretation of the Revolution rests upon two important premises which have recently been challenged. First, it assumes

1. See, for example, George S. Counts, *Education and American Civilization* (New York: Teachers College, Columbia University, 1952), pp. 22–23, 327–472; John Dewey, *Democracy and Education* (New York: The Free Press, 1966); Thomas F. Green, *Work, Leisure, and the American Schools* (New York: Random House, 1968), pp. 147–55; James Munroe Hughes, *Education in America* (New York: Harper and Row, 1970), pp. 225–49; Gordon C. Lee, *An Introduction to Education in Modern America* (New York: Holt, Rinehart, and Winston, 1953), pp. 5–17; Max Rafferty, "Today's Challenge in Education: The Public School in our American Heritage," in James C. Stone and Frederick W. Schneider, *Readings in the Foundations of Education: Commitment to Teaching*, 2 vols. (New York: Thomas Y. Crowell, 1971), 2:75–82. For analytical critiques of the integrative and social mobility functions of the school system, see Martin Carnoy and Henry M. Levin, *The Limits of Educational Reform* (New York: David McKay, 1976) and various essays in James J. Shields, Jr. and Colin Greer, *Foundations of Education: Dissenting Views* (New York: John Wiley and Sons, 1974).

2. See, for example, George Kneller, *Education of the Mexican Nation* (New York: Columbia University Press, 1952); Ramón Eduardo Ruíz, *Mexico: The Challenge of Poverty and Illiteracy* (San Marino: Huntington Library, 1963); Josefina Zoraida Vázquez, *Nacionalismo y educación en México* (Mexico: El Colegio de México, 1970).

a decisive rupture in Mexican history between the dictatorship of Porfirio Díaz (1876–1910), which is seen as an oppressive and authoritarian aberration in Mexican development, and the Mexican Revolution of 1910, which is at least implicitly and often explicitly seen as holding out the promise of national liberation. Thus, while historians acknowledge that public schooling began to take shape in the *Porfiriato*, they view this growth as a liberal "candle in the darkness," emphasize obstacles which prevented school expansion, and focus upon the scarcity of schools—especially at the primary level. Most treatments of education in the Mexican Revolution begin with reference to the dearth of schools in Porfirian Mexico and suggest a *tabula rasa* upon which an enthusiastic and innovative crusade for schools was initiated in 1920.[3] In fact, historical data indicate profound continuities in educational policy, programmatic content, bureaucratic structure, and personnel between the pre- and post-revolutionary periods.

Second, contrary to the hopes of its apologists, education has not offered a significant exodus from poverty in the post-revolutionary period. Despite continuous expansion of state schooling since 1920, poverty in Mexico was more pervasive in 1970 than it was in 1950, and social stratification increased in the same period. In 1960, Mexico's coefficient of income inequality was higher than that of any other major Latin American country.[4] Despite rapid industrial growth, the rate of employment generated by industry declined steadily while the rate of population growth increased. Although the educational budget in 1970 was 65 times greater than that of 1910 and although school enrollments had vastly increased, it has been argued that the educational system most effectively serves the already privileged. In 1970, the average level of schooling was only 1.6 years; of 100 children entering primary schools, 65 could not complete their studies.[5] Figures such as these have led one scholar to observe that no major Latin American government has done more for its economic elites and less for the poorest sectors of its population, despite

3. See, for instance, Guadalupe Monroy Huitrón, *Política educativa de la revolución (1910–1940)* (Mexico: SepSetentas, 1975), pp. 7–8, 11–12; David Raby, *Educación y revolución social en México* (Mexico: SepSetentas, 1974), p. 11; Augusto Santiago Sierra, *Las misiones culturales* (Mexico: SepSetentas, 1973), p. 9.

4. Stephen Niblo, "Progress and the Standard of Living in Contemporary Mexico," *Latin American Perspectives* 5 (1975): 111.

5. Fernando Carmona, "El capitalismo de subdesarrollo y la apertura educativa," in Fernando Carmona et al., *Reforma educativa y 'apertura democrática'* (Mexico: Editorial Nuestro Tiempo, 1972), pp. 29–30.

Mexico's being the only Latin American country to undergo a social revolution in the first half of this century.[6]

In seeking to explain what on the surface appear to be contradictions in the Mexican Revolution, a growing body of scholarship has begun to examine the Revolution as part of an ongoing process of societal development. Although there are significant differences in analysis and interpretation among scholars, and although terminology often differs, there are certain assumptions which many appear to share.[7] First, the Revolution is seen as part of an historical process intimately related to the preceding period which, as an era of rapid growth and institutional formation, demands close examination. Second, attention is given to the process of state formation and the role played by the state in facilitating conditions for capitalist development. This state apparatus was created in the *Porfiriato*, reformed, altered, and expanded in the course of the Mexican Revolution.[8] Third, although the emphasis of historians differs, Mexican economic growth in the late nineteenth and twentieth centuries is usually characterized as dependent capitalist growth, which shaped the nature of Mexican society and has limited in varying degrees the possibility for generating widespread material well-being. Although external factors are considered instrumental in shaping Mexico's development, internal factors such as social class, political movements, and the nature of economic production are viewed as also playing a critical role.[9]

Marxist scholars have focused particular attention on the class nature of the Mexican Revolution. Although there is a variety of opinion among them, it is generally accepted that in the Mexican

6. Roger Hanson, *The Politics of Mexican Development* (Baltimore: Johns Hopkins University Press, 1971), pp. 87–88.

7. Recent historiography of the Mexican Revolution is treated in David C. Bailey, "Revisionism and the Recent Historiography of the Mexican Revolution," *Hispanic American Historical Review* 58 (1978): 62–79.

8. See, for example, Lorenzo Meyer, "Historical Roots of the Authoritarian State in Mexico," in *Authoritarianism in Mexico*, ed. by José Luis Reyna and Richard S. Weinert (Philadelphia: Institute for the Study of Human Issues, 1977), pp. 3–19; Nora Hamilton, "Mexico: The Limits of State Autonomy," *Latin American Perspectives* 5 (1975): 80–101; Juan Felipe Leal, *La burguesía y el estado mexicano* (Mexico: Ediciones El Caballito, 1974).

9. See Lorenzo Meyer, *Mexico and the United States in the Oil Controversy, 1917–1942* (Austin: University of Texas Press, 1977), pp. 107–38 on the interaction between internal and external factors in the determination of economic and social policy in the 1920s. See also Enrique Krauze, *Período 1924–1928: La reconstrucción económica*, Historia de la Revolución Mexicana, 23 vols. (Mexico: El Colegio de México, 1977), 10:7–70.

Revolution a modernizing bureaucracy of petit bourgeois or "middle-sector" origin built a state apparatus which created conditions for the emergence of an enlarged owning class while at the same time utilizing and gaining control over the political organizations of the working class and peasantry.[10] Rather than viewing the Mexican Revolution as one in which middle-sector leadership *dissolved* the antagonism between rich and poor, recent scholarship emphasizes the subordination and domination to which labor and the peasantry were subjected by the state in the course of the Revolution.[11] Refinement of the history of the Revolution will come with further investigation of events at the regional level, of popular-based organizations and their relationship to state structures, and of the development of the state apparatus including detailed studies of policy evolution, bureaucratic expansion, and change in specific areas of state activity.

This particular study of education as an area of state activity broadly utilizes the above framework of analysis in an attempt to understand the relationship between the growth of the Mexican state, the growth of capitalism in its dependent form, and the development of an educational apparatus. It assumes that public education is designed primarily to fulfill two functions in modern society: to reproduce the existing social relations of production (in capitalist society, relations subordinating labor to capital) and to increase the productive capacity of society. This examination of educational policy, programs, and bureaucratic expansion between 1880 and 1928 focuses upon aspects of continuity and change in the Porfirian and revolutionary periods. While the theme of continuity between the periods is most important to this study, the essay also stresses changes in educational policy which the Revolution brought about. It emphasizes the ways in which class conflict influenced the evolution of school

10. A considerable body of Marxist analysis has emerged in recent years from work undertaken at the Universidad Nacional Autónoma de México. See Roger Bartra, "La Revolución domesticada: del bonapartismo pequeñoburgués a la institucionalización de la burguesía," *Historia y Sociedad* 6 (1975): 13–29; Arnaldo Córdova, *La ideología de la Revolución mexicana: la formación del nuevo régimen* (Mexico: Ediciones Era, 1973); Juan Felipe Leal, *La burguesía y el estado mexicano* (Mexico: Ediciones El Caballito, 1974), and "The Mexican State, 1915–1973: A Historical Interpretation," *Latin American Perspectives* 5 (1975): 49–79; Manuel Villa, "Discusión de algunas categorías para el análisis de la Revolución mexicana," *Revista Mexicana de Ciencias Políticas* 70 (1972): 25–38.

11. North American scholarship on Latin America was dominated in the late 1950s and the 1960s by the thesis that middle class leadership would dissolve the antagonism between rich and poor through its ability to modernize and industrialize; this thesis is best articulated in John Johnson, *Political Change in Latin America* (Palo Alto, Calif.: Stanford University Press, 1958).

policy and the ways in which school policy aimed at mitigating class conflict. Mass mobilization in the Mexican Revolution was a tremendous impetus for a policy of popular primary schooling, which the Revolution's bureaucrats often regarded as a means of appeasement and social control and as a necessary element in the development of the nation's productive forces. Secondly, bureaucrats within the revolutionary educational apparatus exhibited ideological differences, which illustrated the heterogeneity of the revolutionary bureaucracy as a whole and revealed that it could be sensitive to pressures from the old owning class as well as to those from the popular forces—especially organized peasants and workers. Although the development of a state educational bureaucracy in the 1920s, like that of the state apparatus as a whole, took place within a seldom-questioned capitalist framework, this educational bureaucracy was never fully consolidated in the period and was vulnerable to a series of ideological currents which reflected class conflict in the larger polity and ideological and political divergence within the state apparatus itself. These factors led to a brief radicalization of the Revolution (and of school policy) in the 1930s, which in turn and somewhat ironically contributed to a consolidation of state bureaucracies and greater state control over peasant and worker organizations after 1940.

This essay is not an exhaustive study of education in the period. The study focuses upon the thought of key policy-makers as articulated in their writings and speeches, and upon the relationship between the latter and implemented policies, programs, and texts. The prolific and minutely detailed documents and periodicals of the Porfirian Secretaría de Instrucción Pública and the post-revolutionary Secretaría de Educación Pública facilitate a study of policy and programs. Many elementary school textbooks from the period have been preserved. In addition, Congressional debates, collections of laws and memorials from the central and state governments, school budgets and statistical data on school expansion and enrollments, as well as capital newspapers, were consulted.

This study is limited in scope and points to the need for further investigation. While it is possible to establish the parameters of ideology in educational policy-making and official program content, it is less possible to measure the degree of transfer of such messages in the classroom, and still more difficult to assess the absorption of messages by students. Statistical data and official reports provide some evidence as to the populations reached by the school and some indication of popular response to public education. The same material gives insight into the degree to which official programs were implemented. Future research should examine the relations between local, state, and central governments in schooling and conditions at the regional and local levels. Schoolteachers as a social-political group are especially important. Because the bureaucracy was in its infancy, teachers had considerable leeway in interpreting their instructions and implementing programs. Although Porfirian school curriculum emphasized the need for law and order, we know that many primary teachers played key roles in the movement that was the precursor of the Mexican Revolution and presumably used their classrooms as platforms for organizing.[12] Teachers also played a highly important role in the years of fighting and at the grassroots level after 1920. They were actors in the scenario of class conflict as it was manifest in education: some identified with the old order, others with the new state, and still others with more radical change in the social system.[13] Teachers must be studied in their relationship to political organizations and to the school bureaucracy. The interplay between the teacher and local, state, and federal governments should be analyzed.

Accurate measurement of the absorption of ideology by students involves a complex assessment of the impact of other ideology-creating institutions on the individual at a given time and over a period of time and is extremely difficult to achieve, especially when one is engaged in historical research.[14] The effort to analyze the impact of a single apparatus which interacts with many others is also fraught with methodological problems and inadequate data. Nonetheless, it is perhaps possible through a study such as this one, which focuses on an ideological apparatus of the state, to shed light on the relationship between state and society and facilitate future research and understanding.

Further, though the impact of class conflict upon policy is integral to the thesis, this study deals primarily with policy formulation; opposition to official school policy both from the left and from the right requires more in-depth examination than is possible here. Thus, the development and expression of radical alternatives to official policy are in need of further investigation. Briefly examined here is the Es-

---

12. See, for instance, James D. Cockcroft, "El maestro de primaria en la Revolución mexicana," *Historia Mexicana* 16 (1967): 565–87; see also David Raby, *Educación y la revolución social.*

13. A pathbreaking study of rural school teachers in the 1930s has been done by David Raby, whose work is cited above.

14. For further explanation of the role of ideology and ideology-creating institutions in contemporary society, see Louis Althusser, *Lenin and Philosophy and Other Essays* (New York: Monthly Review Press, 1975).

cuela Racionalista, a model for schooling created by Spanish anarchist Francisco Ferrer Guardia in Barcelona, which became at least in theory part of the platform of most sectors of the Mexican workers' movement between 1912 and 1925. The extent of the acceptance of the Escuela Racionalista, how it was understood and put into practice, its impact upon official policy, expecially in the 1930s, and, in general, the evolution of labor movement thought on education are questions requiring further research and clarification. Similarly, conservative opposition to the school, articulated in the Church-state conflict which broke out in 1926, had significant impact upon individual schools, teachers, families, communities, social classes, and geographic regions, and yet it was not possible within the scope of this essay to investigate this issue in great depth. It is hoped that these areas will be the focus of future study.

Finally, the terminology I have used to describe the Mexican Revolution of 1910 requires explanation. I have called it a national bourgeois revolution. Clearly, capitalism was developing in Porfirian Mexico. The Porfirian state and ruling class fractions strongly encouraged its growth and participated in it. Although precapitalist modes of production persisted, Porfirian Mexico was not predominantly feudal and the Mexican Revolution was not a bourgeois revolution against feudalism. On the other hand, the Mexican Revolution hastened the penetration of capitalism. Although the Revolution was not made by the national bourgeoisie but by various social classes, the revolutionary state operating within a capitalist framework widened the interests and parameters of the Mexican bourgeoisie by reducing the importance of enclave production for foreign markets, adopting nationalist economic policies and industrialization strategies, and successfully dominating the working class and peasantry. That the Mexican bourgeoisie did not succeed in replacing foreign capital or in achieving equity with it but in fact remained subordinate does not, to my understanding, cancel the validity of the term "national bourgeoisie."

Chapter 1
The State and Public School Policy in Nineteenth-Century Mexico

The process of nation-building in Mexico was slow and difficult. At the moment of independence in 1821, ten years of civil war had devastated the country's economy. The flight of Spanish capital and disappearance of the colonial trade network contributed to economic stagnation, while the departure of the Spanish deprived the country of a skeleton of administrative, political, and economic unity. Regionalism, centrifugality, and separatism emerged as obstacles to political unification as the country became the victim of its diversified geography. Above all, the nascent political factions could find no grounds for compromise: persistent deadlock between liberals and conservatives made it impossible to form a viable government which could establish political forms, administrative institutions, and policies to refurbish the economy. The army, hardly a national entity, was politically powerful because of its quartering in the capital and other cities. Although it tended to favor the conservative cause, the military took advantage of the stalemate to spearhead regular revolts on behalf of any opposition group when the incumbent party emptied the treasury and army officers went unpaid. In this weakened position, Mexico was four times invaded by foreign powers between 1828 and 1867. In 1846, the United States took two thirds of Mexico's territory to the north for purposes of continental consolidation, and in 1861 the French used the pretext of Mexico's large foreign debt to establish a would-be American empire through the short-lived monarchy of Maximilian of Austria.

In the bitter aftermath of the U.S. invasion, differences between conservatives and liberals sharpened. The conservatives, often identified with the creole traditions of large mine- and land-owners and the Church hierarchy in central Mexico, despaired of the republican experiment and looked to monarchy to solve the country's ills. They wished to preserve hierarchies and privileges—especially those of the Church, which possessed in land, urban real estate, and banking institutions the major portion of Mexico's wealth. The liberals, in contrast, put forward an Enlightenment program which envisaged a restructuring of state, society, and economy in consonance with principles of individualism and equality before the law. Their vision derived in part from Adam Smith's defense of open competition within a free market and his criticism of state intervention, corporations, and monopolies. The liberals sought to abolish special privileges accruing to institutions such as the Church, whose power over land and capital the liberals wished to destroy in order to open these factors of production to more enterprising and aggressive individuals. They also wanted to break the Church's ideological power by promoting secular and scientific education at all levels. They foresaw the creation of a limited democracy controlled by property owners.

In the years following independence, the conservative statesman, Lucas Alamán, presented an enlightened plan for Mexico's development. Like his counterparts in the nascent North American republic, he had raised tariffs to protect the infant textile industry. To assist industrialists he created a state bank which he hoped to finance through revenues from silver exports. More viable than the liberals' doctrinaire belief in free trade, Alamán's program had its roots in the statist developmental policies of the Spanish Bourbons who had ruled the colony in the eighteenth century. Some of Alamán's conservative colleagues, however, had opposed the Bourbon program and dreamed of reviving or preserving earlier, more medieval Hapsburg traditions. Alamán's political milieu—inclusive of the Church hierarchy—was not so progressive as he. Further, the conservative cause favored a centralized state and so provoked the opposition not only of lawyers and students versed in Enlightenment notions of laissez faire, but of landowners, political potentates, and merchants in northern and coastal Mexico, who preferred the local freedoms promised by the liberals' avowed federalism.[1]

After 1846, the liberal cause was led by creole and *mestizo* politicians from the states who had accumulated discipline and experience in the course of serving in local government. Benito Juárez, for ex-

1. For history of this period, see Josefina Zoraida Vázquez, "Los primeros tropiezos," in *Historia general de México*, 4 vols. (Mexico: El Colegio de México, 1976), 3:1–84. In his "The War with the United States and the Crisis in Mexican Thought," *The Americas* 14 (1957): 164–71, Charles Hale examines liberal and conservative positions after 1846. François Chevalier analyzes the ideologies, contradictions, and economic base of the liberal and conservative tendencies in his essay, "Conservateurs et Libéraux au Mexique: Essai de sociologie et géographie politiques de l'indépendance a l'intervention française," *Cahiers de l'Histoire Mondiale* 8 (1964): 457–74. On the role and position of the Church in this period, see Michael Costeloe, *Church Wealth in Mexico: A Study of the 'Juzgado de Capellanías' in the Archbishopric of Mexico, 1800–1856* (Cambridge: Cambridge University Press, 1967), pp. 1–29.

ample, had been governor of Oaxaca and Melchor Ocampo governor of Michoacán. The new generation of liberals was able to unite Mexico City politicians with regional elements to draft the Constitution of 1857, which declared Church ownership of land illegal. In the ensuing civil war with the conservatives from 1858 to 1861, Church lands—and a large number of indigenous communal properties—were acquired by naturalized foreigners, liberal politicians, military leaders, and provincial potentates, who provided the social basis of support for the liberal cause. In their struggle against the conservatives, the liberals amalgamated makeshift regional armies to form the basis for a new national army. Strong civilian leadership, typified in the politics of Benito Juárez, also contributed to a final victory over the conservatives in 1867. Although they fought with skill and attracted large numbers to their cause, including many indigenous and *mestizo* peasants, the conservatives were permanently discredited by their association with the French invasion of 1861.[2]

When the liberals came to power in 1867, they began nation-building in earnest. Although the foreign debt remained a thorny and unresolved problem, under the presidency of Juárez the first major railroad project was completed and the legal structure for a public school system was drafted. However, Juárez was unable to amalgamate and control the various elements of the liberal power base. A believer in civilian government and faced with very limited state funds, Juárez dismissed many army officers and reduced the military portion of the budget, thereby alienating a key sector of liberal support. Unable to extend his control effectively to the regions, he manipulated clauses in the Constitution of 1857 to intervene in state elections in order to secure the selection of candidates loyal to him. The liberals in Congress remained locked in ideological dispute, which gave rise to factionalism. Juárez died in 1872. His successor, Sebastián Lerdo de Tejada, was even less adept at cementing unity. In 1876, Porfirio Díaz, an Oaxacan *mestizo* who had risen through the

2. For further background on the Reforma and French Intervention, see Walter V. Scholes, *Mexican Politics during the Juárez Regime, 1855–1872* (Columbia: University of Missouri Press, 1957); Francisco Zarco, *Historia del Congreso Extraordinario Constituyente de 1856–1857* (Mexico: El Colegio de México, 1956); Richard Sinkin, "The Mexican Constitutional Congress, 1856–1857: A Statistical Analysis," *Hispanic American Historical Review* 53 (1973): 1–26; Jan Bazant, *Alienation of Church Wealth in Mexico: Social and Economic Aspects of the Liberal Revolution, 1856–1857* (Cambridge: Cambridge University Press, 1971). On indigenous and peasant opposition to the Constitution of 1857, see T. G. Powell, *El liberalismo y el campesinato en el centro de México, 1850–1876* (Mexico: SepSetentas, 1974), pp. 75–100.

ranks of the liberal armies to become a major figure in the defeat of the French, successfully rebelled against the reelection of Lerdo and in the next thirty years instituted a dictatorship, which created structures of a nation-state.

As a military man, Díaz was able to control the army and to turn it into a semi-professional arm of the state. As such, it played an important role in the establishment and maintenance of social order. Díaz' rule accentuated the contradictions which Juárez' tenure had brought to the fore. In order to secure control over the persistently centrifugal regions and the factionalized Congress, he relied upon certain constitutional clauses which gave the Supreme Court the right to intervene in disputed state elections and others which limited voting to incumbent bureaucrats whom the president could name. In what appeared to be a logical response within the liberal political framework to Mexican circumstances, notions of federalism and elective government yielded to centralism, electoral manipulation, and political dictatorship. Sacrificed also was the liberal vision of autonomous economic growth. Where Juárez had anticipated balancing foreign investment in Mexico to foster the emergence of national capitalism, Díaz opted for a more generous policy toward foreign, and especially United States, penetration.[3] He furthered the construction of railroads from the northern border to central Mexico, which encouraged large-scale U.S. investment and trade. It has been argued that in 1876–77, faced with a large debt to the United States and suggestions from the U.S. press and Congress to establish a protectorate over Mexico, Díaz chose an expedient solution that would ward off another foreign invasion—and thus maintain national integrity—while at the same time providing a means of securing internal order (i.e., foreign investment made possible economic opportunities which could be used by the government to co-opt local elites). Although Díaz hoped to counterbalance U.S. penetration with European investment, the latter was not immediately forthcoming, owing, among other factors, to a reluctance in granting recognition to the nation which had executed Maximilian. Even when such investment materialized, Mexico's proximity to the United States contributed to the latter's preponderant role.[4]

---

3. Juan Felipe Leal, *La burguesía*, p. 86, Díaz' negotiations with the United States are described in detail in Daniel Cosío Villegas, *The United States versus Porfirio Díaz* (Lincoln: University of Nebraska Press, 1963).

4. Leal, *La burguesía*, pp. 135–36; Luis González y González, "El liberalismo triunfante," in *Historia general de México* 3:205–6.

In the final analysis, the development of a dependent, neocolonial economy dominated by foreign interests and centered upon primary export industries was probably caused by a variety of factors beyond Díaz' immediate decisions. At the time that the United States and Europe had reached points in their growth when they needed and had the capacity to obtain specific mineral, food, and agricultural products from abroad, Mexico was particularly vulnerable to their domination because fifty years of anarchy had left her without a national economic base or a well-developed capitalist class. This class developed instead in response to opportunities and directions opened by foreigners and hence in large part became dependent on the foreigner for capital, technology, and markets, as well as for ideologies and lifestyles.

The emergence of neocolonialism must to some extent also be linked to the role played in the Porfirian state by the positivists, a group of Mexican intellectuals who supported the dictatorship as a source of order and progress and who were the architects of Díaz' state, his economic and social policies. Mexican positivism was not only a European import—an eclectic mixture of the ideas of Auguste Comte, John Stuart Mill, and Herbert Spencer—its advocates accepted the idea of European and Anglo-Saxon superiority and so believed foreign penetration a necessary vehicle for development. To be sure, many of them were conscious of the threat posed by the proximity and aggressiveness of the United States and hoped to balance foreign interests against one another to preserve a degree of Mexican autonomy, but in the last analysis, the positivists probably did not understand imperialism and the laws of uneven development, which produced an economy in which foreign interests emerged as dominant.[5] The positivists would not have pursued their ideology of foreign superiority to the extent that they did nor would they have had the power they accumulated if Mexico had had a strong, autonomous capitalist class.

In the absence of such a class, the state, administered by the positivists, created the conditions for capital accumulation: the banking, fiscal, and financial structures which facilitated foreign penetration and its amalgamation with local interests; the transportation system and administrative apparatus which allowed trade to flourish.[6] State

5. Leal, *La burguesía*, pp. 80–81.
6. Changes in administration and law to foster economic growth are described in *El Porfiriato: La vida económica*, 2 vols. in Historia moderna de México, ed. by Daniel Cosío Villegas (Mexico: Editorial Hermes, 1965), vol. 1, chap. 3; vol. 2, chaps. 7–9.

agrarian legislation, combined with partiality in the court system, allowed for occupation of public lands and usurpation of ancient village lands by large landowners and contractors, foreign and national. Between 1876 and 1910, thousands of rural Mexicans lost their means of subsistence.[7] This process in turn created the land and labor base for the expansion of large-scale agriculture, infrastructure, mining, and light industry. The state also administered institutions of repression (the army, rural police, etc.) which guaranteed that a particularly violent process of despoliation and exploitation could proceed for many years relatively uncontested by affected groups—principally peasants, artisans, and wage-earners in agricultural, mining, and industrial establishments. The state also laid the foundations for a national school system which was designed to increase the productive capacity of a hierarchical class society while insuring loyalty to the existing social order and nation-state.

Liberal Antecedents of the Porfirian School System

The notion of public education for modernization and social control had always been an element of Mexican liberalism—at least as it was articulated by liberals in power. Following independence, liberal opposition to the Church was based in part on the contention that clerical control of education inhibited the development of a scientific and patriotic ideology, necessary to economic growth and political stability within the liberal framework. More critically, control over education became a question of political power, a question of replacing the Church's ideological domination. José María Luis Mora, early ideologue of Mexican liberalism, wanted a national public school system because he recognized that ideas "fixed in youth" would be defended to death by men in adulthood: the educational system, he said, had to be in consonance with the political system.[8] Liberals were not only concerned with destroying the Church's control over people's ideas and loyalties as a means of transforming traditional Mexico, they tended, as men of property and class, to be contemptuous of the popular sectors. While they viewed an illiterate public as an unreli-

7. See, for example, John Coatsworth, "Railroads, Agrarian Protest, and the Concentration of Landholdings in the Early Porfiriato," *Hispanic American Historical Review* 54 (1974): 48–71.

8. *Escuelas laicas. Textos y documentos* (Mexico: Empresas Editoriales, SA, 1948), p. 63.

able basis for democracy, they also believed that mass education should develop values and attitudes appropriate to their own values and interests. Mora believed that education should better the "moral" condition of the people. His colleague Valentín Gómez Farías told Congress in 1833 that primary schooling ought to be fostered if "we wish good parents, good children, and good citizens who know what their duties are and how to fulfill them."[9]

Influenced by Mora and introduced by Gómez Farías, the short-lived liberal reforms of 1833 were primarily concerned with emancipating higher education from clerical control. The Pontifical University and major Catholic seminaries in the capital were dismantled and replaced by six institutes of higher education which included in their offerings training in law, medicine, engineering, and agriculture. These schools were subject in their staffing and programs to a Dirección General de Instrucción Pública, made up of the country's vice president and other government appointees. The Dirección General was also to set up primary schools, which would teach reading, writing, arithmetic, and political and religious catechisms. To stimulate primary education, the laws projected the establishment of two normal schools—one for men and one for women. Poor children were to receive school supplies to encourage their attendance. No religious personnel were to be permitted to teach in government schools. Although private schools were allowed, private colleges were subject to the rules, criteria, and inspection of the Dirección General.[10]

The reforms of 1833 had scarcely gone into effect when they were abolished by clerical and conservative opposition. They, however, foreshadowed the creation of an over-arching state educational apparatus which began to take shape after 1867. While confined in its jurisdiction to the Federal District and territories, the Dirección General de Instrucción Pública of 1833 had the capacity to rule on all areas of education. This included the right to administer cultural institutions such as artistic monuments, museums, theaters, and libraries. A prolongation of the Spanish administrative tradition, the jurisdiction over culture coincided with liberal concern for refining

9. Carlos Alvear Acevedo, *La educación y la ley: La legislación en materia educativa en el México independiente* (Mexico: Editorial Jus, 1962), p. 62.

10. See Manuel Dublán and José M. Lozano, *Legislación mexicana o colección completa de las disposiciones legislativas expedidas desde la independencia de la república, ordenada por los licenciados*, 11 vols. (Mexico: 1876–1908), 2:570–76.

popular morality. It anticipated a function developed by the Secretaría de Instrucción Pública y Bellas Artes in the *Porfiriato* and expanded on in the Mexican Revolution of 1910.[11]

There were few primary schools in independent Mexico. Liberals favored the Lancasterian mutual system of popular education. This method of drill learning through a hierarchy of student "monitors" under the direction of a single official teacher was also favored for its "utility" by British liberal Jeremy Bentham.[12] Many liberals patronized the founding of the Lancaster Society in Mexico in 1822 and the reforms of 1833 were intended to use its instructional method. Municipal, state, and federal governments provided the Lancaster schools with financial assistance and space in former churches. In 1842, the society became the reinstituted Dirección General de Instrucción Primaria and in a three-year period organized normal training institutes and primary schools in the capital and states. In 1850, the Lancaster schools taught the three r's, Christian doctrine, political catechism, and elements of urbanity, to which were later added geography, geometry, and drawing. The first schools in Mexico to address the question of mass education, they decayed rapidly after 1870 as municipal, state, and federal schools were created in increasing numbers—many of them through absorption of the Lancaster schools.[13]

11. Technically, the Church was responsible for morality in colonial society but the Church itself functioned under the aegis of an over-arching, paternalistic, administrative state. In the eighteenth century, the state exhibited a secularizing, regalist trend in attempting to limit Church power. Correspondingly, in 1786 the Ayuntamiento of Mexico City approved a proposal for the creation of Mexico's first state primary schools. The *escuelas pías*, taught by members of the clergy but administered by the state, aimed at providing primary education to the poor, who could not afford tutors or private schools. The motive was in large part one of moralization or social control. The schools were introduced in the midst of economic crisis when hundreds of rural people, victims of famine, drought, and epidemic, migrated to the capital. The schools were set up to alleviate social tensions caused by so many young people idle and hungry in the streets. Explicitly, they were to reform vices and customs, transforming the poor into law-abiding, respectful, and industrious citizens. See Dorothy T. Estrada, "The "Escuelas Pías" in Mexico City, 1786–1820," *The Americas* 31 (1974): 51–71.

12. Charles Hale, *Mexican Liberalism in the Age of Mora* (New Haven: Yale University Press, 1968), pp. 168–69. The monitor system had also been used in the *escuelas pías* (Estrada, "The 'Escuelas Pías,'" p. 70). For a helpful description of the functioning of the Lancaster schools in Mexico City in the independence period, see Dorothy T. Estrada, "Las escuelas lancasterianas de la ciudad de México, 1822–1842," *Historia Mexicana* 22 (1973): 494–513.

13. Francisco Larroyo, *Historia de la educación comparada en Mexico* (Mexico: Universidad Nacional Autónoma de México, 1948), p. 182.

If early Mexican liberals were concerned with the role of public education in transforming and cementing a new society in consonance with their principles, the second generation of liberals who drew up the Constitution of 1857 exhibited in their debates on schooling at the Constitutional Convention a greater concern with the principles themselves. The Constitution of 1857 contained no specific provisions for the development of public schooling. Only Article 32, dedicated to bettering the intellectual level of Mexicans, stated that laws should improve the condition of hard-working citizens through the creation of technical schools. Debate at the convention centered around Article 18—later Article 3—which declared teaching to be free, in keeping with the principles of individual liberty and the destruction of monopolies, in this case, the Church's alleged monopoly over education. The article also charged the state with determining which professions required titles for their exercise and what requirements had to be met to earn degrees. In presenting the article, Manuel Fernández Soto argued that freedom of teaching would lead to the perfecting of society through development of intelligence, that is, the most gifted minds would come to the fore. Education, he said, was a function of the father of the family: it was his right to delegate this function to whomever he chose and his right alone to keep check on those to whom he had delegated it. In ancient republics, Fernández Soto claimed, the rights of men and families had succumbed before the rights of states; children belonged more to the state than to the family and education was strictly controlled. In democratic republics such as Mexico, he exhorted, freedom of teaching was a necessary consequence of civil liberty. However, he knew that many delegates feared that freedom of teaching would serve as a pretext for clerical undermining of liberal institutions, which could prolong the civil war. Thus, he qualified his position by advocating government selection of textbooks, which should be scientifically current and compatible with the development of democracy.[14] Some deputies responded that liberty of teaching would encourage fanatical and unscientific education as well as charlatanism in the professions. Several called for government inspection of all schools to safeguard science, morality, and public peace.[15] Defenders of the ar-

---

14. Francisco Zarco, *Historia del Congreso*, pp. 713–14, 720.

15. See, for example, ibid., p. 723. Richard Sinkin notes that the delegates in general saw the importance of public schooling to the establishment and maintenance of public order; see Sinkin, "The Mexican Constitutional Congress, 1856–1857: A Statistical Analysis," pp. 1–26.

ticle retorted that against immorality there was no better remedy than the good judgement of families and public opinion, while the government's right to determine what professions required degrees and what requirements had to be met in order to obtain the degree was sufficient bulwark against charlatanism. Ponciano Arriaga thought that it was ridiculous to speak of government inspection in defense of morality: did the government intend to go into homes to monitor the advice which mothers gave to children? Ignacio Ramírez, one of the most militant champions of liberal principle, spoke insightfully against government inspection:

> Governments want inspection because they have an interest that their subjects learn certain materials and learn them in a manner which is in the interests of power; thus they create a purely artificial form of knowledge.[16]

The principle of freedom of teaching was approved by a vote of 69 to 15 and became Article 3 of the Constitution of 1857.

While commitment to freedom of instruction remained basic to a persistent but increasingly weakened strain of liberal thought in the Mexican Congress, liberals in the executive branch of government tended to thrust aside these preoccupations in their assessment of the circumstances blocking the formation of the state: the strength of the conservative-clerical opposition; deepening economic stagnation and mounting foreign debt; foreign invasion; and the centrifugal tendencies of regional oligarchies, armies, and the liberal party itself. Public education was seen as one of several means of achieving unification, order, and growth.[17] Thus, while briefly in power in 1861, President Juárez developed the structural outlines of a public school system. He placed all matters of public, primary, secondary, and professional training in the Federal District under the Secretaría de Justicia y Instrucción Pública. Primary schools would be created in the Federal District. Municipal schools and those run by philanthropic societies would receive federal aid. All would be subject to a single government-determined program and inspection. The federal government would finance teachers to work in small towns in the states which lacked schools. In addition to the three r's, the school program would include morality and a study of the country's fundamental laws. Like the reforms of 1833, the law of 1861 projected the establishment of

16. Zarco, *Historia del Congreso*, p. 723.
17. Josefina Zoraida Vázquez, *Nacionalismo y educación en México*, pp. 54–55; Luis González y González, "El liberalismo triunfante," pp. 174–75, 178.

a normal school. It also anticipated what later became the basis for state inspection of private schools in requiring applicants for professional degrees to take qualifying examinations if they had not attended state schools.[18]

Although this law went by the boards when the conservatives and French forced the liberals out of Mexico City, in 1867, when the liberal victory was final, President Juárez continued his efforts to build a public school system. He set up a commission headed by the positivist Dr. Gabino Barreda to legislate on education from primary school to professional studies. The emerging organic laws of public instruction of 1867 and 1869 and the reglementary law of January 1868 made elementary education obligatory and tuition-free in public schools in the Federal District and territories. Municipalities were required to set up a school for boys and one for girls for every 500 inhabitants. Owners of *haciendas* were urged to establish schools on their properties. Poor children were to be given texts and supplies. To supplement the municipal and Lancaster schools, the federal government would set up four boys' and four girls' primary schools, one night school for male workers and one for female workers. The program would include the three r's, principles of geography, especially of Mexico, instruction in morality and hygiene, and principles of drawing. In night schools, instruction would also be given in notions of the Constitution, rudiments of history (especially of Mexico) and, for men, elementary physics and chemistry applied to crafts. The teaching of religion was not included in the program; in 1874, it was formally abolished and replaced by instruction in morality.[19]

The new laws also established or reformed existing professional schools in law, medicine, pharmacy, agriculture, engineering, commerce, architecture, and the fine arts. The Escuela de Artes y Oficios para Hombres was created to apply contemporary science to traditional trades; in 1871 a similar school was established for women. In secondary education, the laws created a school for women, which operated de facto as a normal school until it was formally converted into such in 1877. The attention of policy makers focused especially on the creation of the Escuela Nacional Preparatoria for men. With a uniform curriculum based on Auguste Comte's interpretation of the physical and social sciences, the Preparatoria was to establish a "com-

18. See Dublán and Lozano, *Legislación*, 9:208; Josefina Zoraida Vázquez, *Nacionalismo y educación en México*, p. 54.
19. See Dublán and Lozano, *Legislación*. 9:215–17.

mon fund of truths" in future directors of Mexican society.[20] In creating this school, Dr. Barreda acted against what he believed to be the causes of Mexican backwardness: disdain for productive labor and rational entrepreneurial behavior which the Spanish colonial heritage had allegedly produced; clericalism which had inhibited the development of a scientific attitude; and liberal preoccupation with abstract principle rather than social realities and the pragmatism necessary to business expansion.[21] The preparatory school would teach men to observe, experiment, and reason without recourse to theology or metaphysics. Like Comte, Barreda believed in a hierarchical social order beyond principles of individual rights in which a team of social engineers would aid captains of industry to insure orderly economic progress.[22] The Escuela Nacional Preparatoria would transform the behavior of a future Mexican bourgeoisie whose acquired skills and ideology would make them effective leaders of economy and state. The idea of using the school to transform behavior patterns in order to effect economic and political modernization, implicit in the thought of Mora and Gómez Farías, became with Barreda a permanent feature of Mexican educational policy.

In 1874, there were 8,103 schools in Mexico, 2,000 of which were private and 117 of which belonged to the Church. From a school-age population of 1.8 million, only 349,000 children—or about one fifth—were enrolled in schools and fewer attended regularly.[23] Although the laws of 1867–69 had made schooling obligatory, they had established no age limit or means of enforcement. They had specified disciplines to be taught, but they had not detailed a primary school program nor the means to carry it out. Further, the laws were only

20. Gabino Barreda, "Carta dirigida al C. Mariano Riva Palacio, Gobernador del Estado de México," 1870, in *Opúscolos, discusiones, y discursos* (Mexico: Imprenta del Comercio de Dublán y Chávez, 1877), pp. 28, 30, 31. For further examination of the relationship between positivism and higher education in Mexico, see Leopoldo Zea, *El positivismo en México: Nacimiento, apogeo, y decadencia* (Mexico: Fondo de Cultura Económica, 1978). See also William D. Raat, "Positivism in Díaz's Mexico, 1876–1910: An Essay in Intellectual History" (Dissertation, University of Utah, 1967), and his "Leopoldo Zea and Mexican Positivism: A Reappraisal," *Hispanic American Historical Review* 48 (1968): 1–18, which offers an informative criticism of Zea's content and method.

21. See, for example, Gabino Barreda, "La instrucción pública," in *Revista Positiva* 1, no. 8 (1901): 265–66, 276, 288, 291–93, 301, 311, 324.

22. Ibid., pp. 308–10. For analysis of the political implications of Comtian positivism, see John Laffey, "Auguste Comte: Prophet of Reconciliation and Reaction," *Science and Society* 29 (1965): 44–65.

23. Larroyo, *Historia de la educación*, p. 241.

applicable to the Federal District and territories. The task of creating a primary school system which was nationwide, obligatory, and uniform in content was carried forward in the *Porfiriato* principally by Joaquín Baranda, Minister of Justice and Public Instruction from 1882 to 1901, and Justo Sierra, head of the educational branch of the Ministry of Justice and Public Instruction from 1901 to 1905, when he became chief of the newly created Secretaría de Instrucción Pública y Bellas Artes, which was responsible for primary, technical, preparatory, professional, and artistic education in the Federal District and territories.

In the process of creating a primary school system, the central piece of legislation from which others emanated was the federal law of primary instruction of 1888. Applicable to the Federal District and territories, it became the model for subsequent state legislation. The law divided primary education into elementary (four years) and superior (two years). It made elementary education obligatory in public or private schools for children between the ages of six and twelve who were healthy and lived within reasonable distance of a school. Children could also be educated at home, although they had to be certified by state examination. Parents who failed to comply with the laws were to be fined or jailed. The law made public schools tuition-free and lay. No religious material could be taught and no minister could teach in them. An official school program, based upon the pedagogy of faculty development then current in the United States and Europe, was detailed. It embraced the disciplines of morality and civics, national language, reading and writing, arithmetic, geometry, elementary notions of physics and the natural sciences, geography and national history, gymnastics and manual skills for girls, to which were later added singing and manual arts for boys.[24]

When Congress passed the law, Joaquín Baranda sent a circular to state governors urging them to adopt it. To insure that they did so, in 1889 and 1890 Baranda called the first two national education congresses. A means of bypassing Congressional opposition to a single national school system by manipulating Díaz' increasingly centralized political apparatus, the conferences agreed on the desirability of a uniform national system of obligatory popular education and adopted the detailed official school program. They also approved the much disputed inspection of private schools to insure the fulfillment of

---

24. See *Ley sobre la instrucción primaria en el Distrito Federal y territorios federales* (Mexico: Imprenta del Gobierno Federal en el Ex-Arzobispado, 1888), pp. 4, 5, 7.

obligatory instruction.[25] Following the congresses, the Mexican states enacted school laws replicating the federal program and began to consolidate, centralize, and expand state school systems. The bureaucratization process also took place at the federal level, although jurisdiction was limited to the capital and territories. In 1908, Justo Sierra refined the 1888 school program in a new law for the capital and territories. He hoped to have this law adopted by the states at the third national education congress which he convened in 1910. This process was cut short by the Mexican Revolution.

Primary Schooling in the *Porfiriato*: Ideology and Program

Justo Sierra emerged as the most eloquent spokesman for state primary education in the period. Prior to 1901, he had assisted Baranda in his promotion of education in Congress, on special commissions, and in national education congresses. In pressuring unsuccessfully in the 1880s for a constitutional reform making instruction obligatory for the nation as a whole, in defending and securing Congressional approval of the comprehensive school program based upon contemporary pedagogy in 1888, in leading education congresses and conferences designed to develop a uniform system in the states, Sierra came to articulate an ideology of schooling consistent with the principles of his predecessors Mora and Gómez Farías but couched within the framework of positivist thought. Although the idea of public schooling was generally supported by politicians in the *Porfiriato*, Sierra's strong position at first encountered some opposition. Certain liberals in Congress still regarded obligatory education as a tyrannical attack on the rights of parents. Some positivists questioned the educability of the indigenous peoples. Simple sceptics doubted that obligatory education was feasible: it would be too costly to implement and enforce.[26] Others believed it was unjust to ask children to learn

25. *Primer Congreso Nacional de Instrucción, 1889–1890* (Mexico: Secretaría de Educación Pública, 1975), pp. 141–43, 160 (hereafter cited as SEP). Among the delegates were many politicians associated with positivism and the centralizing thrust of the Díaz regime, including Rosendo Pineda, representing Baja California; Miguel Serrano, representing Campeche; Porfirio Parra for Chihuahua; Luis E. Ruiz for the Federal District; Francisco Cosmes for Guanajuato; Francisco Bulnes for Morelos; Miguel F. Martínez representing Nuevo León.

26. Even Barreda thought that a national system of obligatory public instruction was impractical because it could not be realized at the time. He said it was typical of the

unnecessary subjects when their basic need was to work in order to eat.[27] Combining a pragmatic scepticism with a heavy dose of social Darwinism, the positivist Francisco Cosmes in 1883 doubted that the school was of any use or interest to the indigenous peoples. It would deprive the family of workers. What did it matter if a child learned to read and write when he would never again hold a book or piece of paper in his hand? Did Sierra really believe that the indigenous peoples "would abandon their labors, their drunkenness, their saints, and their priests, to go to school exclaiming with joy, 'I am going to leave the degradation from which no one has been able to raise me in three and a half centuries of contact with a superior race?'"[28] To each of these arguments, Sierra gave a singular response: obligatory public instruction was necessary to national survival and growth—to the development of production, the unification of the country, and the maintenance of political order. Rejecting the notion that the poor and non-white were congenitally inferior, Sierra believed that the state could intervene to improve society and its members.[29]

Like most of his peers, Sierra was anxious that political order replace the anarchy of Mexico's first half-century of independence. Thus, he legitimized the dictatorship of Porfirio Díaz, who became for him the patron of Mexican progress, the creator of peace and order whose principal concern was to bring Mexico within the orbit of *"los países cultos."* Sierra's defense of a strong state was not without a theoretical base, stemming from his Spencerian view of society as an organism subject to evolutionary laws tending toward progress. Progress involved a process of simultaneous integration and differentiation. In advanced societies, Sierra argued, integration took place through natural laws allowing the state to maintain a policy of laissez faire, but in Mexico, which was a backward, heterogeneous, and incoherent society threatened with internal anarchy and foreign invasion, the central state had to assume the integrating task.[30] Sierra was

---

Mexican lack of pragmatism to legislate laws which could not be carried out but remained fantastic schemes on paper. See Barreda, "La instrucción pública," p. 265.

27. Moisés González Navarro, ed., *El Porfiriato: La vida social*, in Historia moderna de Mexico, ed. by Daniel Cosío Villegas (Mexico: Editorial Hermes, 1957), pp. 547, 552.

28. *La Libertad* 1 (16 Feb. 1883); 1 (1 March 1883).

29. Justo Sierra, *La educación nacional. Artículos, actuaciones y documentos*, Edición ordenada y anotada por Agustín Yañez, vol. 8 of *Obras completas* (Mexico: Universidad Nacional Autónoma de México, 1948), p. 56.

30. Justo Sierra, *Periodismo político*, Edición ordenada y anotada por Agustín Yañez, vol. 4 of *Obras completas*, p. 239. For a fuller analysis of Sierra's theory of state and

one of the first Mexican political thinkers to develop the theory of an "active" state, whose intervention in society was justified on the grounds of society's need to survive and grow in the face of stronger competitors.

To the claims of some positivists that the state ought to limit itself to the role of policeman and dispenser of justice, he countered that the state had to assume functions of tutelage and protection. One such function was public education, the purpose of which was to mold a homogeneous people equipped with values, attitudes, and skills appropriate to modernization. Speaking to the national educational congress in 1890, he said that now that

. . . our life is linked with iron chains to the industrial and economic life of the world, all that there is of centrifugal force in the heterogeneity of habits, languages, and needs must be transformed into cohesion thanks to the sovereign action of the public school.[31]

Education would create national unity and contribute to economic growth. The Mexican people, he told Congress, needed

. . . as a means of their own preservation (a task which becomes more painfully urgent with the gigantic advances of our neighbors) to improve their elements of work to make them more productive; above all, the generating and principal element of the worker himself, and if the way of bettering him is to make him more intelligent, instruction must transform him.[32]

To the classical liberals who believed that freedom of education was a sacred liberal right, Sierra responded that the right of society to survive and prosper conditioned and superceded the rights of individuals within society. The right of the child to the fullness of life, made possible by the general progress of society, denied parents the right to resist schools and made obligatory education an issue beyond debate.[33]

The task of modernization was complex enough, argued Sierra, that the educational role played by the family, customs, and other social institutions had to be supplemented by that of the state, the only institution whose functions embraced the whole of society. The

society and the relationship of the latter to capitalism and social class, see Arnaldo Córdova, *La ideología de la Revolución mexicana*, pp. 46–86.

31. *Primer Congreso*, p. 165.
32. Sierra, *Educación*, p. 167.
33. Ibid., pp. 109, 222–23, 249; *Primer Congreso*, p. 166.

conscience of the collectivity, the state, he wrote, was in a position to apply a uniform direction to the whole.[34] However, the state was not equal in its relationship to the different parts of society. Rather, society was a hierarchy of classes with functions subordinate to that of the capitalist class, accumulator of wealth and generator of work, which the state had to protect.[35] "Here, there is not a class on the move except the bourgeoisie," he said. The singular, dynamic force in society, "it absorbs all active elements of the inferior groups," by which he meant the upper and lower classes, both of which he believed were dominated by superstition and, in the case of the poor, by alcohol. The bourgeoisie assimilated both of these groups, argued Sierra—the first through the budget and the second through the school.[36] While the entrepreneur would create "national conditions for work," the school would form proper habits and attitudes in the labor force. It would convince men that the only solution to poverty was work. "Their intelligence directed by wisdom," men would not so easily succumb to "weariness and disgust." They would learn their place in society:

> Instead of these unlimited desires and unhealthy ambitions which engender only evil passions, [the school] will present them with a smiling future: that of well-being through honorable work.[37]

In distinguishing the new school program of 1888 from the Lancasterian program, Sierra argued that while the latter had relied upon memorization of loosely-hung-together subjects unrelated to real life, the new program formed a coherent system for the development of the human faculties. Its fundamental goal, he said, was to increase society's productive forces through the creation of practical, patriotic individuals conscious of their rights and duties toward society and the state.[38] The program was based on faculty psychology then popular in the metropolitan countries and adapted to Mexico by various pedagogues including positivist Manuel Flores, who taught in Mexico City normal schools, Enrique Rébsamen, Enrique

34. Sierra, *Educación*, p. 223.

35. Justo Sierra, *México social y político*, Edición ordenada y anotada por Agustín Yáñez, vol. 9 of *Obras completas*, p. 131. For analysis of his position on the relationship between class and state, see Córdova, *La ideología de la Revolución mexicana*, pp. 65–76.

36. Justo Sierra, *Evolución política del pueblo mexicano*, Edición establecida y anotada por Edmundo O'Gorman, vol. 12 of *Obras completas*, p. 387.

37. Sierra, *Educación*, p. 25.

38. Ibid., p. 230, 235–37, 239; *Primer Congreso*, p. 168.

Laubscher, and Carlos Carrillo, all of whom began their careers at the Escuela Modelo in Orizaba, Veracruz. The pedagogy had its roots in the theories of Johann Heinrich Pestalozzi (1746–1827), Friedrich Froebel (1782–1852), and Johann Friedrich Herbart (1776–1841). Its intention was to discipline the instincts to develop the intellectual, moral, and physical faculties in a desired direction. The primary school corollary of the positivist curriculum in the Escuela Nacional Preparatoria, faculty development pedagogy, allegedly grounded in a scientific understanding of human behavior and the learning process, proceeded on the assumption that ontogeny recapitulated philogeny. Thus the child should proceed from the concrete to the abstract through observation and experimentation with natural and man-made phenomena. Designed to equip the student with a scientific understanding of the universe and consequent skills for manipulation of the environment, the program was also supposed to develop habits of self-restraint, altruism, discipline, punctuality, and industriousness to create a balance of initiative, order, and harmony in work tasks within a modernizing society.[39]

Central to this nineteenth-century pedagogy was the notion of self-control which was in turn bound up with the ethical system of the capitalist class, who identified it with the process of work, savings, and accumulation. As Ezequiel Chávez, Undersecretary of the Ministry of Public Instruction in the last decade of the *Porfiriato*, wrote, quoting the French thinker Gustave Lebon:

> Man does not begin to leave barbarism . . . until he has learned to dominate his hereditary instincts. . . . An intelligent education in which the needs of the environment create this discipline will convert discipline into a characteristic of the race. No wonder the English take first place in the qualities of character—that of self-control or dominion over oneself.[40]

In the nineteenth century, with the breakdown of the precapitalist order and its institutions of social control, the imposition of disciplinary values on the subordinate classes acquired new importance to the dominant class. Migration, proletarianization, and impoverishment often manifested themselves in an apparent disintegration of family and community life in the nascent working class and the expression

39. For discussion of the link between these pedagogical ideas and the development of industrial society, see Fidel Ortega, *Política educativa* (Mexico: Editorial Progreso, 1967), pp. 26–29, 53–54.

40. Ezequiel Chávez, "Notas," 1914, in Archivo Ezequiel Chávez, Universidad Nacional Autónoma de México (hereafter cited as AEC).

of less repressed social behavior in the public life of streets, parks, taverns, and factories, which sometimes led to violence and provoked the specter of working class political organization and protest. Because the disciplined and consistent labor of workers was necessary to production and capital accumulation, such counterproductive behavior became problematic for the dominant class and was a strong consideration in the promotion of public schooling.[41]

In the Mexican case, both at the beginning of the dictatorship and toward its end, Sierra and others referred to public schooling as an alternative to socialism and worker agitation.[42] Between 1880 and the turn of the century when the repressive capacity of the dictatorship somewhat diminished the level of popular protest, the concern for social control did not abate as modernization changed and accentuated the nature of class differences. Where Mexico City neighborhoods had traditionally housed people from different social strata, they now became segregated along class lines. Parks as well became so defined. The rich stopped going to the Zócalo for their Sunday *paseo* for fear of rubbing elbows with the "prostitutes." The well-heeled did not simply wish to get away from the poor, many had an interest in disciplining them. Thus, concern for the use of alcohol among workers gave rise to a proliferation of anti-alcohol leagues among the more privileged sectors of society, who associated drink with soaring crime rates, poor health, family disintegration, and low worker productivity. The campaign against *cantinas* and *pulquerías* engaged wealthy and politically powerful Mexicans such as Guillermo de Landa y Escandón, president of the Council of Government, who sponsored Sunday festivals for workers and their families to "keep them away from the taverns" and "moralize" them. Similarly, the Mexican Congress argued for days about outlawing the bullfights, the "bloody and barbarous spectacle," which, according to the deputies, lowered the "moral" level of the people, squandered their pesos, and awakened their savage instincts. "From the bulls," maintained Gustavo Baz, "a people like the Mexicans with so little respect for authority only learn to vociferate against it with impunity."[43]

41. For development of this thesis in relation to North American schooling and social reform, see James Weinstein, *The Corporate Ideal in the Liberal State, 1900–1918* (Boston: Beacon Press, 1968), and Joel Spring, *Education and the Rise of the Corporate State* (Boston: Beacon Press, 1972).

42. See, for example, Sierra, *Educación*, p. 114; *El Imparcial*, 13 July 1907.

43. On demographic changes see María Dolores Morales, "La expansión de la ciudad de México en el siglo XIX. El caso de los fraccionamientos," in Seminario de Historia Urbana, *Investigaciones sobre la historia de la ciudad de México* (Mexico: Cuadernos

Underlying the question of moralization was a concern with the productivity of labor and the modernization of a traditional society. Education was not simply a task (as it often seemed for North American educators) of assimilating immigrant groups. The goal was to transform the behavior patterns of an entire population in order to create a modern labor force. Sierra wrote:

> In his *History of Civilization in England*, Henry Thomas Buckle wrote that Spain needed a system diminishing superstition through physical sciences, familiarizing people with ideas of order and regularity, gradually destroying old notions of miracles and habituating the individual to find explanations for human vicissitudes in natural causes rather than supernatural ones. . . . We are like the Spanish and need the same.[44]

In a real sense, Mexican educators were engaged in a process of transferring loyalties from the Church, ideological arm of the colonial order, to the nation-state and its economic base. The new school incorporated many values taught by the Church (submission, restraint, modesty) into a new ideology corresponding to the needs and values of the bourgeoisie. It is not surprising that the Mexican school program proposed to alter precisely those traits which foreign investors identified and criticized in Mexican workers: inertia, fatalism, petty thievery, lack of initiative, lack of foresight and savings, and unreliability in the performance of continuous labor. Like Sierra and most positivists, the businessmen attributed such behavior to 300 years of servitude under the Spanish. While owners and managers appreciated the submissiveness, capacity for endurance in heavy labor, and low wages associated with this legacy, they complained of high absenteeism for which they blamed the excessive number of religious holidays, the drinking away of wages on the weekend with the consequent *San Lunes*, and the tendency of workers to return to the land in planting and harvest seasons. Foreigners with an economic interest in Mexico often expressed hopes that public education would help to increase worker productivity and were quick to praise the Mexican government for its efforts in this direction.[45]

---

de Trabajo del Departamento de Investigaciones Históricas, Instituto Nacional de Antropología e Historia, 1974), p. 80; on propriety in the Zócalo, see Moisés González Navarro, *La vida social*, p. 548; on the concern with alcohol, see *El Imparcial*, 22, 27, 29, 30, 31 Jan., 1 Feb., 21 May 1897; 3, 11, 16, 22 Nov., 13, 16, 26 Dec. 1903; 5, 11, 15 Jan. 1904; 1, 2 July, 15, 21, 22, 25 Aug. 1907; on Congressional attitudes toward "morality," see Moisés González Navarro, *La vida social*, pp. 727–28.

44. Sierra, *Educación*, pp. 256–57.

45. On attitudes toward Mexican workers, see, for example, Evan Fraser Campbell, "The Management of Mexican Labor," *Engineering and Mining Journal* 91 (1911): 1104–

In Porfirian educational policy and programs, the anxieties, needs, and prejudices stemming from the class position and the dependent mind-set of Mexican policy-makers emerged in attitudes of contempt and paternalism toward Mexicans in general and toward the subordinate classes in particular. Educators especially emphasized the school's role in correcting behavioral deficiencies, usually referred to as "vices." At the end of the period, Puebla school authorities expressed such attitudes when they spoke with pride of the progress which they attributed to the school:

> The people of Puebla present a better physical appearance each day. . . . They are losing their prejudices, errors, and rudeness and acquiring habits of morality, economy, and order; they are sympathetic to our propaganda against the vices which unfortunately have dominated our race.[46]

Further, given their experience with political disorder in the years preceding the dictatorship, educators believed the school to be the foundation for social order. A preface on moral education used in many Mexican schools in 1910 stated, for example:

> One will endeavor to inspire a love for work, for the nation, for other people, for justice and truth, and for respect for the law

---

5; Hugh G. Elwes, "Points about Mexican Labor," *Engineering and Mining Journal* 90 (1910): 662; John Hays Hammond, *The Autobiography of John Hays Hammond* (New York: Arno Press, 1972), pp. 132–33; Mark R. Lamb, "Tales of Mountain Travel in Mexico," *Engineering and Mining Journal* 90 (1910): 676; Edwin Ludlow, "The Coalfields of Las Esperanzas, Coahuila, Mexico," *Transactions of the American Institute of Mining Engineers* 32 (1902): 145; James W. Malcolmson, "Mining Development in Mexico during 1902," *Engineering and Mining Journal*, 75 (1903): 35–39; "Mining in Mexico," *Engineering and Mining Journal* 75 (1903): 210; "Mining in Mexico," *Engineering and Mining Journal* 77 (1904): 21–22; Allen H Rogers, "Character and Habits of the Mexican Miner," *Engineering and Mining Journal* 85 (1908): 700–702; E. A. H. Tays, "Present Labor Conditions in Mexico," *Engineering and Mining Journal* 84 (1907): 621–24; A. Tischendorf, *Great Britain and Mexico in the Era of Porfirio Díaz* (Durham, N.C.: Duke University Press, 1961), p. 91; Walter E. Weyl, "Labor Conditions in Mexico," *U.S. Labor Department Bulletin* 7 (1902): 11–14, 18, 91–92. For praise of Díaz's educational policies, see Weyl, "Labor Conditions," pp. 18–21, and Charles F. Lumiss, *The Awakening of a Nation: Mexico of Today* (New York and London: Harper and Brothers, 1898), pp. 9–11, 15, 27. For an interesting and critical discussion of these attitudes and Mexican workers' responses to them, see Rodney Anderson, *Outcasts in their Own Land: Mexican Industrial Workers, 1906–1911* (DeKalb: Northern Illinois University Press, 1976), pp. 68–74.

46. Secretaría de Instrucción Pública y Bellas Artes, *Informes presentados al Congreso Nacional de Educación Primaria por las delegaciones de los estados, del Distrito Federal, y territorios en septiembre de 1910*, 2 vols. (Mexico: Imprenta de A. Carranza e Hijos, 1911), 2:710 (hereafter cited as *ICNEP*).

and constituted authorities. . . . . They will be taught to obey and to sacrifice.[47]

Thus a confluence of the ideas, values, class interests, and social fears of policy-makers produced a school program whose primary messages were work, obedience, and patriotism.

There can be little doubt, however, that in principle the faculty development school program was a progressive step beyond the rote learning of the Lancaster school. In designing the program, Mexican pedagogues made a real effort to correct the deficiencies they attributed to the Lancaster school: reliance upon memorization and texts, divorce of content from daily life, discontinuity in subject matter, and harsh methods of discipline. Had the pedagogues had their way, only a reading text would have been used in the first years of school although more books were assigned and used for history, mathematics, geography, and morality. Arithmetic, formerly learned by memorizing tables, was now taught through problems related to daily life. Distinct subject matter was synchronized and interrelated so that, for instance, in drawing classes, students would illustrate stories from reading exercises and episodes from history or copy specimens from science class. Taught through a method called "lessons of things," science proceeded from the "concrete to the abstract" through "intuitive" learning or observation of flora, fauna, and physical properties such as heat and light. Students were to take excursions into the countryside to gather plants and fruits typical of the area. The conversion of primary materials by man for daily and industrial use was to be emphasized with special reference to local industries. Visits to local factories were often recommended.[48]

Sierra and other pedagogues believed these lessons had an educational rather than a utilitarian end. In drafting the primary school law of 1908, younger bureaucrats like Gregorio Torres Quintero,

47. Ibid., 1:234; 2:83, 180, 355, 653–54.
48. On pedagogical intent, see Enrique Rébsamen, *Método para la enseñanza de la historia en las escuelas primarias elementales y superiores de la república mexicana* (Mexico: Viuda de Ch. Bouret, 1898), pp. iv, 16–17, 32–34; on texts, see ibid., pp. 16–17; *ICNEP* 2:73, 540–41, 612, 708; San Luis Potosí, *Programa detallado de estudios para las escuelas primarias de San Luis Potosí* (San Luis Potosí, 1906), p. 11; on programs, see, for example, *ICNEP* 2:737–85; *Memoria que el Secretario de Justicia e Instrucción Pública Joaquín Baranda presenta al Congreso de la Unión comprende desde el ler de diciembre de 1892 hasta el 30 de noviembre de 1896* (Mexico, 1899), pp. 329–33, 371 (hereafter cited as *MSJIP*); San Luis Potosí, *Programa*, pp. 2–7; *Colección de leyes y decretos del estado de Morelos formado por acuerdo del ejecutivo por el Lic. Cecilio A. Robelo* (Cuernavaca: Imprenta del Gobierno del Estado, 1895) 12:42–48 (hereafter cited as *CLM*).

who were in touch with revisionist European and North American pedagogy critical of faculty development psychology, challenged the "intellectuality" of the Mexican program and advocated more practical content.[49] This train of thought, which gained support in the Mexican Revolution, apparently won concessions in the 1908 law. Rural schools were to include agricultural practice; girls were to cultivate vegetable gardens in addition to doing the sewing exercises prescribed for them in 1888. Moving beyond observation and collection, science classes in 1908 were to include the cultivation of vegetables, plants, and flowers in school plots as well as the raising of domestic animals.[50] In fact, prior to 1908, the official program involved such pragmatic instruction. The national educational congresses of 1889 and 1890 approved training in agriculture, mining, and accounting for primary superior schools. These were made part of the school program in the capital and elsewhere. Puebla required agricultural practice in all primary schools, Jalisco and Chihuahua prescribed it for rural schools, and Guanajuato recommended it in cases in which schools had fields to cultivate. Toward the end of the period, Morelos and Yucatán required such instruction in rural schools.[51] Adult night schools, which were created on a small scale in the capital and in the states, were supposed to be explicitly practical in character with emphasis upon the application of science to local industries.[52]

The Porfirian program attempted to relate content to Mexican economic progress. Pedagogue and geographer Daniel Delgadillo believed that geography teaching should abandon memorization of lists

49. Secretaría de Justicia e Instrucción Pública, "Junta Revisora de la Ley de Instrucción Primaria," 28 March 1905 and 4 April 1905, AEC; see also Miguel Schulz, "Informe sobre la educación pública en México: sus condiciones actuales," 1910, AEC. Criticism of faculty development pedagogy and formalistic logic and psychology became quite common in Mexican intellectual circles after 1900. In education, attention turned toward philosophies of child-centered education and pragmatic learning. In part the trend resulted from the frequent missions of Mexican educators to the U.S. and Europe to study educational systems and pedagogy and to take part in international conferences on the same. See, for example, "Informe rendido a la Secretaría de Justicia e Instrucción Pública por la Sr. Laura Méndez de Cuenca, encargada del estudio de las instituciones escolares de instrucción pública de los Estados Unidos de América," *Boletín de Instrucción Pública* 3 (1904): 381–405.

50. Secretaría de Instrucción Pública y Bellas Artes, *Anuarios escolares de la Secretaría de Instrucción Pública, Educación Primaria, 1910–1911* (Mexico: Tipografía Económica, 1911), pp. 8, 46–65, 71–90.

51. *MSJIP*, p. 376; *ICNEP* 2:52, 324–30, 337–40, 787, 798; Moisés González Navarro, *La vida social*, pp. 587, 590.

52. See, for example, *ICNEP* 2:383–89, 843–44.

of rivers and cities in favor of an integrated, materialist approach to nature as man transformed it. Thus in the school laws, geography instruction was to begin with observation of natural phenomena and their impact on local production. Students then were to examine the natural and man-made means of communication and transportation—especially the railroads—and their commercial linkages of the local area with the nation and the rest of the world. Mexico's production in agriculture, mining, and industry was detailed in the texts.[53] In the laws, the teaching of history also assumed a positivist approach as the indigenous role in Mexican history was relegated to a remote and primitive past and the nation's road to industrial civilization emphasized. In Puebla, teachers were to compare "savage" and "civilized" man to illustrate the importance of transforming customs through "work" and "intelligence."[54] The overwhelming purpose of history instruction was to stimulate patriotism and national unity—to stress that all Mexicans formed a "single great family." Teachers were advised to seize every opportunity to "destroy the spirit of localism."[55]

Most school laws required instruction in political rights and the Constitution in civics classes. However, in the 1908 law for the Federal District, civics and geography teaching were combined in primary elementary schools in such a way that civics lost any reference to the political rights of citizens and concentrated instead on the individual's fulfillment of an assigned economic role in national progress. The teacher was to instill in students good civic sentiments they ought to have toward "order in the area through obedience and discipline."[56] In these renderings, the function of government became almost entirely administrative: the state facilitated progress through insuring order and providing services such as public instruction, security, drainage, hygiene, and transportation. Students were to learn that:

> . . . civics consists in a feeling that one is an element of a society which is working to assure well-being, progress, and the respect of other societies; and that this sentiment ought to give rise to a vital interest for all things concerning the life of society and a vital desire to assist it insofar as one can serve it. They will re-

53. Daniel Delgadillo, *La república mexicana. Geografía elemental* (Mexico: Herrero Hermanos, Sucesores, 1911), pp. 11, 13, 50–67. See also *Primer Congreso*, pp. 132–36; *MSJIP*, pp. 331–32; San Luis Potosí, *Programa*, pp. 4–5, 7; *ICNEP* 2:781, 786, 796; *CLM* 12:43.

54. *ICNEP* 2:780–87.

55. *Primer Congreso*, p. 147.

56. *Anuarios escolares*, p. 105.

member that to fulfill civic duties well it is necessary that each of the individuals who make up the society is a good member of the community and as such contributes to the progress and embellishment of civilization within it and that finally, he is a good Mexican, disposed to interest himself always in the progress of the nation and to contribute to its well-being even if this requires the sacrifice of his life.[57]

Students were to note that within the social hierarchy, all honorable work contributed to the well-being of everyone. The labor of workers was indispensable to the labor of "intellectuals" and vice versa. Finally, students were to be informed of what the state did to those who would not contribute to progress, i.e., those who disturbed the peace or manifested some other "vice."[58]

Despite its hopes of liberating children from the iron discipline of the Lancasterian school, the Mexican program from 1888 onward was authoritarian in prescribed method and content. In Chihuahua, students were to attend class punctually, keep silent, remain composed and orderly in the classroom, and fulfill their duties to their superiors with discipline and respect inside and outside school. They were to maintain in their clothing and manners the decorum befitting educated persons and to conduct themselves correctly in the street; they were forbidden to form groups, talk loudly, throw stones, write on walls, or run. In Puebla, students were subjected to inspections before classes began. Dirty students had to wash and their families were to be informed. When the teacher entered, students were to rise, salute, and stand still until signalled to sit. At all times, they were to sit correctly with their hands together to prevent them from doing mischief the teacher could not see. They were to keep their feet together parallel on the floor and look straight at the teacher to avoid distractions. After the instructor gave the lessons, they were to repeat it through the Socratic question-and-answer method. Although an effort was made on paper to avoid over-reliance on memorization from texts, the application of the question-and-answer method lent itself to memorization of the teacher's lectures. The program's method and prescriptions for discipline in themselves suggested the possibility of a high degree of student passivity—a consequence apparently realized in the program's implementation. Returning from a tour of United States schools in 1905, two Mexican teachers commented in their report to the Secretaría de Instrucción Pública that in physical

57. Ibid., pp. 121–22.
58. Ibid., p. 128.

and natural science instruction in Mexico from the first grades to professional training, students were passive beings obliged to contemplate the results of experiments undertaken by the teacher.[59]

The fundamental purpose of faculty development education was to discipline the instincts. In drawing classes, children copied objects less to stimulate their imagination than to train their powers of observation, imitation, and hand control. Singing was to train the ear, voice, and lungs, to develop correct pronunciation, breathing, intonation, and disciplined group coordination. Sierra hoped that music would stimulate a love for order while "refining the emotions" and polishing manners.[60] Gymnastics consisted of coordinated exercises and marches to discipline the body, correct physical deformities, and enhance the ability to work methodically in a group. Because Sierra accepted nineteenth-century metropolitan notions of the decadence of non-European peoples, he believed that gymnastics would invigorate a sick and anemic race: "We have to regenerate this anemic people who with time will become useless to the *patria*."[61] Team sports, added to the program in the 1908 law, were to correct laziness and other vices. They would develop perception, resolution, and speed, while teaching children how to subordinate themselves to the team and its chosen captain.[62]

According to the German pedagogue Herbart, instruction in morality would repress evil instincts. In the Mexican program, instruction in morality, defined as the "formation of character through obedience and discipline," named as vices those traits counterpro-

---

59. For description of rules of school behavior in Chihuahua, see *ICNEP* 1:417; for Puebla, see *ICNEP* 2:730–32; on the question-and-answer method, see Enrique Rébsamen, *Método para la enseñanza de la historia*, p. 21; on criticism of the Mexican school and its methods, see *Boletín de Instrucción Pública* 4 (1905): 675. In emphasizing the authoritarian aspect of the nineteenth-century Mexican school, it should be pointed out that U.S. and European schools were highly rigid as well. Criticism of the authoritarianism of the nineteenth-century school in general comes from a single shared source, i.e., the revisionist and reformist movement and philosophy of child-centered learning which emerged at the turn of the century. Further, it is possible that formal rulings for behavior in the Mexican classroom related to the absence of rigorous order and lack of state bureaucratic control over teachers and classrooms. See, for example, *Boletín de Instrucción Pública* 3 (1904): 381–405.

60. Sierra, *Educación*, pp. 126, 208.

61. Ibid., p. 198.

62. For descriptions of programs in drawing, singing, and gymnastics, see, for example, San Luis Potosí, *Programas*, pp. 8–9; *ICNEP* 2:323, 775; *MSJIP*, p. 329; *Anuarios escolares*, pp. 125, 163–65; M. Velazquez Andrade, "Proyecto para la creación temporal de un campo de juegos. Acuerdo por lo que se señalen bases para la organización y servicios de un campo de juegos desdiñada a niñas y señoritas," 28 June 1907, AEC.

ductive to the molding of a reliable labor force—ignorance, laziness, lack of savings, lack of punctuality, lack of cleanliness, disorganization of family life, anger, jealousy, and the consumption of alcohol and tobacco.[63] The ethics program had a built-in contradiction: disciplinary values of benefit to an elite in the accumulation of capital tended to compel submission to authority when imposed upon the poor. In the midst of the expropriation of peasants' lands, forced migration to the cities, growing unemployment, unhealthy working conditions, long hours, and scanty pay, the Porfirian program offered those it reached no solution beyond work, self-restraint, and self-correction. Jalisco's adult worker schools were to remind students of the respect they should show toward authority and property and the consequences they faced if they did not.[64]

While Sierra and others made hopeful claims that the school would help to guarantee democracy in Mexico and would mitigate exploitation on the *hacienda* by upgrading the skills of workers, its prescribed content and method legitimized a social structure based upon exploitation and a political system which was not democratic. The program obscured the structural causes of poverty and instead blamed misery on the victim—a method potentially enhancing subordinate behavior. Poverty was the result of laziness, superstition, lack of schooling, lack of perseverance, or some other individual deficiency rather than an integral part of the structure of economy and political power. The consequences of poverty—poor housing and health, alcoholism, disruption of family life, crime, lack of hygiene, illiteracy—became moral vices of which the poor were guilty. In making ignorance a vice and equating it with lack of schooling, the school suggested replacing the authority of popular culture with official knowledge, history, and values, all of which encouraged the emergence of an obedient citizen who would accept the school's messages and the existing social order. Sierra believed that the school could reform the poor by convincing them of their inferiority as an incentive for self-improvement. Then would emerge "from the fog of instinct, the intellectual personality . . . the most solid pedestal of moral progress."[65] Although pedagogues criticized the awarding of prizes for intellectual or "moral" performance, the practice was maintained

---

63. *ICNEP* 1:149, 157, 341–46, 476–79, 490–92, 510–15, 568–73; 2:48, 50–51, 60, 64–65, 111, 115–17, 154–59, 167, 173, 203–7, 211, 213–14, 236–43, 321–28, 336, 339, 344, 359, 462–65, 470, 636–42, 693, 773–74, 831–34.

64. Ibid., 2:345.

65. Sierra, *Educación*, p. 55.

in many states and carried out with fanfare in Mexico City. By the law of 1908, students distinguishing themselves for orderly, punctual, and obedient behavior were to take places of honor at the side of the Mexican flag each morning upon the opening of classes.[66]

In principle, the expansion of the Porfirian school initiated a long process of absorption by the state of family functions—a process which for poor families suggested subordination to the state and reinforcement of feelings of inferiority and inadequacy. The school taught children how to behave at table, in the home, and on visits. In both reading and music classes, it tried to develop "good taste." The often casual organization of the poorer Mexican home was directly attacked in the 1908 law which insisted that the civilly registered marriage formed the only moral union, and which encouraged the child to reform the deficiencies of his family. The food they ate, the clothes they wore, the houses they lived in—all had to be changed in accord with the values and needs of the dominant class. The 1908 law read:

> . . . to attain good health and physical vigor, it is indispensable to modify the diet to which they are accustomed; they must also modify the material conditions in which they live and modify their dress.[67]

Such directives obscured the fact that unequal distribution of wealth in society limited the possibility of making such changes. Instead, such rules encouraged subordination, low self-esteem, and isolation. A particular form of individualism inimical to the development of class solidarity, consciousness, and organization was implicit in this model. Despite the fact that most could not conform to the school's values, the student who failed to do so would believe he had only himself or his family to blame. The student who struggled to conform might feel contempt for and alienation from others within his community or social class who fell short of the school's model. These suggested consequences were not necessarily the intentions of educators but they emerge from the formal program which represented the interests, values, and goals of policy-makers.

Because the Mexican school aimed at social transformation, called "progress" within the positivist paradigm, its thrust suggested an at-

---

66. *Anuarios escolares*, pp. 169–70; on awards ceremonies, see *El Imparcial*, 4, 27 February, 8, 12, 19 March, 8, 25, 27 April 1897; 6 February, 10 October, 16, 23, 25, 29, 30 November, 1, 2, 3, 6 December 1903; 5 February 1904. For criticism of the prize system, see *Boletín de Instrucción Pública* 3 (1904), 384–85.

67. *Anuarios escolares*, p. 124.

titude of rigidity and, to some extent, contempt toward Mexican children in general. Its method and program implied not only a strengthening of existing social hierarchies within the country but of international ones as well. The dependent mind-set of Mexico's dominant class, its feelings of Mexican inferiority and European superiority, made their way into the schools in a contradictory expression of nationalism. In geography classes in primary schools in Mexico City, teachers were to emphasize the importance of European civilization and the significance of other people's efforts to assimilate it. In Campeche, teachers were instructed to emphasize that Chinese society was in decay because it had resisted European penetration. In capital primary schools, students were to learn that it was their duty to work with "harmony and perseverance to develop civilization in our country so that Mexicans can collaborate with greater prestige and success in the progress of the world."[68] Sierra was delighted with the acceptance of the school program by the states in 1890 because he saw it as redeeming Mexico in the eyes of "civilization":

> Then we will have made ourselves worthy of presenting to the eyes of the world a people who work conscientiously to redeem ourselves: then we will merit the words of the great French orator Eugene Pelletan, who in speaking of Latin America in the French Assembly before men who belittled him and belittled us, said, "New generations are rising in Latin America who will transform those societies, because these generations bear the light of hope before them and the thirst for progress in their hearts."[69]

However, it is incorrect to suggest, as revolutionary educators often implied, that the Porfirian program was devoid of national content: this was in fact dominant in history, geography, and literature.[70] One of the primary purposes of singing classes was to promote patriotism through learning Mexican songs. The Porfirian program promoted a contradictory form of nationalism which incorporated a sense of inferiority in relation to the metropolitan powers while at the same time attempting to instill pride in Mexico. Although the Mexican Revolution ushered in a movement of cultural nationalism which

68. For relevant school programs in the capital, see *MSJIP*, p. 369; *ICNEP* 1:485; for Campeche, see *ICNEP* 1:160.

69. Sierra, *Educación*, pp. 198–99.

70. For example, Amado Nervo, *Lecturas mexicanas* (Mexico: Viuda de Ch. Bouret, n.d.), provided biographies and excerpts from the poetry and essays of fifty-eight Mexican writers from the colonial and national periods.

deepened the Mexican content of school programs, this ambiguous form of nationalism did not disappear with the Revolution.

In conclusion, the Porfirian primary school program was consciously and unconsciously designed to assist the development of capitalism in Mexico. Created to train a disciplined and productive labor force in a society in transition, it aimed at transforming traditional values and behavior patterns in the interests of the dominant class, and, in principle, encouraged subordinate behavior in the dominated classes. It was also a program laced with contradictions. It pretended to liberate children from harsh methods of discipline but was in itself authoritarian and repressive. It gave instruction in individual political rights within a constitutional republic but at the same time legitimized the existing class structure and political dictatorship. It strongly promoted the idea of Mexicans as agents of their own economic development and yet it regarded foreign penetration as a necessary, civilizing factor in Mexican growth. While promoting Mexican patriotism, the program encouraged a subservient attitude toward metropolitan culture and society. The general thrust of the program, and its values, goals, and contradictions, were to be carried forward into the Mexican Revolution of 1910 and the subsequent educational system. The continuity between the Porfirian program and the Revolution's program gives the former its central importance, for evidence indicates that in reality the implementation of the official program in the period of the dictatorship was neither widespread nor particularly effective.

Chapter 2
The Limits of Porfirian Schooling

While the primary school program is important in revealing how educational policy-makers wished to use the school to
bring about economic modernization, one is struck by the limited expansion of the primary school system in the period. Between 1895
and 1910, the percentage of the population reading and writing increased from 14.39 percent to 19.74 percent. Both the lack of extension of the school system and the growth which took place require
explanation. The political process of centralization and bureaucratization in education should also be examined, because these laid the
basis for the school system emerging from the Mexican Revolution
and, in the *Porfiriato*, determined the extent to which the official program could be implemented.

The underdeveloped character of the Porfirian public school system is linked to the situation of the neocolonial state operating within
a framework of relative financial scarcity. The economy was typified
by primitive accumulation, or the accumulation of capital through
expropriation of property and the appropriation of cheap labor. Of
the capital thus amassed, a portion was siphoned off by foreign investors. Thus, public funds available for development were not great.
Within the prevailing political ideology, priorities in spending had to
be those judged most critical to the process of private accumulation.
Expenditures on the repressive apparatus, economic development,
and transportation took precedence over public education. Nonetheless, educational expenditures in the *Porfiriato* rose at a faster rate
than public expenditures as a whole. While combined federal and
state expenditures rose in the period from 26,767,224 pesos in 1878
to 126,177,950 pesos in 1910, total federal and state expenditures on
education increased from 1,413,860 pesos to 12,481,363 pesos.[1] The
percentage of the federal budget devoted to schooling increased
from 3.1 percent in 1877–1878 to 6.74 percent in 1910. The states

1. Moisés González Navarro et al., *Estadísticas sociales del Porfiriato* (Mexico: Secretaría
de Economía, Dirección General de Estadística, 1956), pp. 36–38. This figure does not
include municipal expenditures on primary schools.

invested 10.52 percent in education in 1878 and 23.08 percent in 1910. Education became the largest item in state budgets. Primary education absorbed the greater part of school expenditures—67.26 percent in 1878 and 72.08 percent in 1900.[2] Public primary schools more than doubled in the period. They numbered 4,498 in 1878 and 9,541 in 1907. Enrollments more than tripled from approximately 141,178 in 1878 to 657,843 in 1907.[3]

On balance the idea of mass public schooling gained legitimacy in the *Porfiriato*. Porfirio Díaz took pride in the indicators of educational expansion included in his reports to Congress. He attended with great ceremony and fanfare the inauguration of new schools and annual graduation exercises.[4] State governors congratulated themselves on their contributions to the growth of schools.[5] Despite original skepticism as to the feasibility of mass schooling and social Darwinist cynicism as to its potential for redeeming the masses, most positivists as modernizers became not only vocal advocates of the system, they exercised significant control over it through their positions in the federal and state bureaucracies and governments. Ramón Corral, governor of Sonora and a politician closely associated with positivism and with Díaz, saw no incompatibility between mercilessly warring against the Yaqui Indians for control of their land and the rapid creation of public primary schools throughout the state.[6]

However, public expenditures on education reveal an important contradiction. In a period of state centralization, central state expenditures on education were restricted to the Federal District and territories, with no financial assistance provided to the states. This policy fostered glaringly uneven development in education. In 1878, 42.86 percent of the funds spent on education by the federal government and the states were spent by the federal government on the Federal District and territories of Baja California and Tepic. In 1910, the federal government accounted for 55.84 percent of state and federal education expenditures. Although this increase in relative fed-

2. *Estadísticas sociales*, p. 237. Figure includes municipal expenditures. All statistics on primary school expenditures which follow in the tables represent combined municipal and state expenditures.

3. Ibid., pp. 42–45.

4. *El Imparcial*, 23, 25, Nov., 1 Dec. 1903; 5, 6, 29 Feb. 1904.

5. See, for example, position taken by Governor Ahumada of Jalisco in *ICNEP* 2:296, and by Olegario Molina, governor of Yucatán, in *Boletín de Instrucción Pública* 6 (1906–1907): 337.

6. Hector Aguilar Camín, *La frontera nomada: Sonora y la Revolución mexicana* (Mexico: Siglo Veintiuno Editores, 1977), pp. 80–92.

eral school expenditures corresponds to an increased share of federal in relation to state expenditures (71.31 percent of total state and federal expenditures were federal in 1878 and 81.07 percent in 1910), the degree of imbalance is apparent when one considers that federal expenditures were limited to the capital and territories and not shared with the states. In 1878 the federal government spent 1.37 pesos per inhabitant on education in the territories and capital versus 9 centavos spent by the states. By 1910, the differential had risen considerably: the federal government spent 6.92 pesos per inhabitant and the states 36 centavos.[7] This gap between the states and the capital and territories was reflected in primary school enrollments and literacy figures. In 1907, the Federal District and Baja California ranked first and third in percentage of school-age children enrolled in schools (48 percent and 41 percent respectively in public schools) and first and second in literacy (50.21 percent of the Federal District population and 38.97 percent of the population of Baja California were registered as literate in 1910).[8] Higher education, both in quality and quantity, was also strongly concentrated in the capital.

The educational policy of the Mexican state promoted uneven development in schooling, paralleling uneven development in the economy. Those states experiencing increased revenue, reflecting increased economic activity, could afford to expand their public school systems more readily than those with lower rates of revenue increase and economic growth.[9] Rankings in Table 2.1 show a high correlation between state per capita revenue and expenditures on primary education (coefficient of .88). Yucatán, Campeche, Chihuahua, Coahuila,

7. *Estadísticas sociales*, pp. 209–12.

8. The territory of Tepic was less favored. It ranked sixteenth in percentage of children enrolled in public schools in 1907 (23 percent of the children) and twelfth in literacy (22.21 percent of the population).

9. Other indicators of economic growth, such as statistics on urbanization or changes in the labor force, might have been used in addition to state and municipal income. However, urbanization figures in *Estadísticas sociales* seem not to be real indicators of modernization but rather reflect the large number of small traditional population centers in central Mexico. Labor force statistics contained in El Colegio de México, Seminario de Historia Moderna de México, *Estadísticas económicas del Porfiriato: Fuerza de trabajo y actividad económica por sectores* (Mexico: El Colegio de México, n.d. [c. 1964]) are misleading: categories of industrial occupations include many artisans and self-employed craftsmen. See Donald B. Keesing, "Structural Change in Early Development: Mexico's Changing Industrial and Occupational Structure from 1895 to 1950," *Journal of Economic History* 29 (1969): 716–38, for a fuller discussion of this problem. In correlating educational expenditures with revenue and increases in the same, Spearman's rank order correlation coefficient was used in the tables which follow.

TABLE 2.1

State Revenue and Primary School Expenditures in the Porfiriato

Combined Revenue (State and Municipality), 1888		Combined Revenue (State and Municipality), 1907		% Increase in Per Capita Revenue, 1888–1907	Expenditures in Primary Education, 1874		Expenditures in Primary Education, 1907		% Increase in Primary School Expenditures, 1874–1907	
State	Pesos/Capita	State	Pesos/Capita	State	State	Pesos/Capita	State	Pesos/Capita	State	%
Veracruz	4.82	Yucatán	11.51	Yucatán 390	Sonora	.38	Coahuila	1.12	Chihuahua	4,800
Sinaloa	4.44	Campeche	7.24	Tamaulipas 322	Nuevo León	.36	Campeche	1.00	Tamaulipas	2,000
Sonora	3.67	Chihuahua	6.98	Chiapas 268	Sinaloa	.31	Chihuahua	.98	Chiapas	667
Coahuila	3.47	Coahuila	6.66	Aguascalientes 190	Morelos	.27	Sonora	.98	Jalisco	580
Tabasco	3.26	Sonora	6.56	Nuevo León 136	Coahuila	.25	Yucatán	.80	Zacatecas	550
Morelos	3.20	Tamaulipas	5.66	México 136	Tabasco	.25	Tamaulipas	.77	Campeche	456
Campeche	3.16	Tabasco	5.35	Chihuahua 135	Guanajuato	.24	Nuevo León	.68	Durango	430
Chihuahua	2.96	Sinaloa	4.65	Jalisco 132	México	.24	Colima	.61	Yucatán	371
San Luis Potosí	2.63	Colima	4.45	Campeche 129	Guerrero	.22	Sinaloa	.60	Coahuila	348
Zacatecas	2.62	Aguascalientes	4.24	Durango 115[c]	Colima	.21	Durango	.53	Aguascalientes	245
Yucatán	2.35	Veracruz	4.05	Oaxaca 106	Puebla	.20	Tabasco	.52	Colima	190
Colima	2.35	Morelos	4.04	Colima 98	Veracruz	.19	Zacatecas	.52	Oaxaca	167
Puebla	2.15[a]	Puebla	3.64	Coahuila 91	Campeche	.18	Morelos	.51	Sonora	158
Hidalgo	2.10	Nuevo León	3.31	Tlaxcala 87	Hidalgo	.18	Veracruz	.46	Veracruz	142
Guanajuato	1.74	México	2.93	Sonora 79	Yucatán	.17	Hidalgo	.39	Tlaxcala	119
Guerrero	1.58	Zacatecas	2.87	Puebla 69	San Luis Potosí	.17[d]	Aguascalientes	.38	Hidalgo	117
Querétaro	1.49[a]	Hidalgo	2.80	Querétaro 64	Tlaxcala	.16	Tlaxcala	.35	Tabasco	108
Aguascalientes	1.40	Jalisco	2.53	Tabasco 64	Aguascalientes	.11	Jalisco	.34	Querétaro	100
Nuevo León	1.40	San Luis Potosí	2.53	Michoacán 34	Durango	.10	México	.31	Sinaloa	94
Tamaulipas	1.34[a]	Durango	2.47[c]	Hidalgo 33	Querétaro	.09	Puebla	.30	Morelos	89
México	1.24	Querétaro	2.45	Morelos 26	Oaxaca	.09	San Luis Potosí	.28	Nuevo León	78
Michoacán	1.16	Chiapas	2.43	Guanajuato 16	Zacatecas	.08	Oaxaca	.24	Michoacán	71
Tlaxcala	1.15[c]	Tlaxcala	2.09	Zacatecas 10	Michoacán	.07	Chiapas	.23	San Luis Potosí	65
Durango	1.12	Guanajuato	2.01	Sinaloa 5	Tamaulipas	.07	Guanajuato	.19	Puebla	50
Jalisco	1.09[a]	Oaxaca	1.59	San Luis Potosí −3	Jalisco	.05	Querétaro	.18	México	26
Oaxaca	.77[b]	Michoacán	1.56	Veracruz −16	Chiapas	.03	Guerrero	.18	Guanajuato	21
Chiapas	.66[a]	Guerrero	1.25	Guerrero −20	Chihuahua	.02	Michoacán	.12	Guerrero	18

States are listed in ranked order. Notes: (a) Municipal revenue figures for this year were not available and were estimated by averaging the rate of increase or decrease in the same over a five-year period. (b) State revenue figures were not available and were estimated by averaging the rate of increase or decrease in the same over a five-year period. (c) Municipal revenue figures were not available for any year. Ranking was calculated on the basis of state revenue figures only. (d) Figure includes expenditures on private as well as public education for this year, as no breakdown was available. Sources: *Anuario estadístico de la república mexicana*, 1907; *Boletín de Instrucción Pública* 13 (1909–1910); *Estadísticos sociales del Porfiriato*.

Sonora, Tamaulipas, and Tabasco registered the highest per capita revenues in 1907 and spent the most on primary schooling. Correspondingly, the poorest states in 1907—Guerrero, Michoacán, Oaxaca, Guanajuato—spent the least on schools. The table indicates that other factors were also involved. The correlation between increased state revenue and increased educational expenditures is slightly less (.58) than the correlation between revenue and educational expenditures in 1907. Certain states experiencing significant revenue increases such as Yucatán, Aguascalientes, Nuevo León, and México did not increase educational expenditures as rapidly as other states. For example, Chihuahua ranked first in increased educational expenditures and seventh in increased revenue.

A pattern emerges from these statistics, especially when they are combined with figures on enrollments and literacy, contained in Table 2.2. The northern states of Coahuila, Sonora, Nuevo León, Tamaulipas, and Chihuahua were most progressive in education. Because they were among the top states in per capita primary school expenditures in 1878, Coahuila, Sonora, and Nuevo León rank only average in increased school expenditures in the period as a whole. Table 2.2, however, indicates that each of these states ranked high in percentage of school-age children enrolled in school in 1907 (2, 15, 3, 6, and 10, respectively) and in literacy (rankings of 5, 3, 4, 7, and 6, respectively) in 1910. In contrast, Yucatán, which experienced more increased revenue than any state, was fifth in educational expenditures in 1907 and eighth in increased educational expenditures. Yucatán's literacy rate was only average (14). It was eleventh in number of children enrolled in school. The differences between Yucatán and the northern states in education may in part be due to the former's "late start" and the sudden bonanza found in *henequén* (sisal) production for the U.S. market after 1898 (Yucatán ranked fifteenth in educational expenditures in 1874). But the explanation would seemingly also lie in differing modes of production and contrasting attitudes on the part of entrepreneurs and policy-makers. The north was a region of expanding agricultural, mineral, and industrial production based on paid labor. Its often transient labor force moved sectorally between farming, mining, commerce, and industry, and, geographically, between Mexico and the United States. The increase in production and commerce contributed to a rapid process of urbanization and a growing middle class, urban and rural.[10] The essentially capitalist economy

10. Friedrich Katz, "Labor Conditions on Haciendas in Porfirian Mexico: Some Trends and Tendencies," *Hispanic American Historical Review* 54 (1974): 32–35; Barry Carr, "Las peculiaridades del norte mexicano," *Historia Mexicana* 22 (1973): 320–46.

TABLE 2.2

Primary School Enrollments and Literacy Rates

% Increase in Total Primary School Enrollments, 1874–1907	%	% of School-Age Children Enrolled in Public Primary Schools, 1907		% of School-age Children Enrolled in All Primary Schools, 1907		Literacy Rate, 1910	
Chihuahua	838	Tlaxcala	43%	Tlaxcala	47%	Colima	38.90
Coahuila	535	Coahuila	41	Coahuila	47	Tabasco	33.52
Tabasco	392	Morelos	37	Nuevo León	43	Sonora	33.52
Tamaulipas	386	Nuevo León	34	Morelos	43	Nuevo León	32.09
Chiapas	289	Tamaulipas	34	Colima	41	Coahuila	30.63
Durango	273	Colima	32	Tamaulipas	40	Chihuahua	28.16
Sonora	220	Tabasco	31	Jalisco	37	Tamaulipas	26.91
Veracruz	186	Zacatecas	29	Tabasco	34	Aguascalientes	26.11
Querétaro	163	Sinaloa	28	Zacatecas	33	Jalisco	25.02
Michoacán	160	Yucatán	28	Chihuahua	32	Campeche	24.73
Jalisco	158	Chihuahua	26	Yucatán	32	Morelos	23.58
Yucatán	141	Hidalgo	26	Hidalgo	30	Tlaxcala	21.90
Nuevo León	133	México	26	México	30	Sinaloa	21.89
Hidalgo	103	Sonora	25	Sinaloa	29	Yucatán	21.80
Colima	100	Puebla	24	Sonora	28	Zacatecas	19.44
Oaxaca	98	Campeche	23	Puebla	27	Durango	18.29
San Luis Potosí	97	Durango	21	Aguascalientes	27	Veracruz	16.42
Guanajuato	96	Aguascalientes	21	Campeche	26	México	16.36
Sinaloa	88	Veracruz	21	Veracruz	24	Hidalgo	16.13
Guerrero	88	San Luis Potosí	20	Durango	22	San Luis Potosí	16.12
Campeche	76	Jalisco	19	San Luis Potosí	22	Querétaro	15.73
Zacatecas	75	Guerrero	17	Querétaro	20	Puebla	14.96
Puebla	66	Oaxaca	16	Guanajuato	19	Guanajuato	14.46
Morelos	49	Michoacán	13	Guerrero	18	Michoacán	14.21
Tlaxcala	24	Querétaro	12	Oaxaca	18	Oaxaca	9.40
México	20	Guanajuato	12	Michoacán	14	Chiapas	9.12
Aguascalientes	−.9	Chiapas	12	Chiapas	13	Guerrero	8.30

States are listed in ranked order. Estimates of school-age population are based on census figures for 1900. Sources: *Anuario estadístico de la república mexicana*, 1907: *Boletín de Instrucción Pública* 13 (1909–1910); *Estadísticas sociales del Porfiriato*.

of the north was complemented in state governorships by modernizers like Bernardo Reyes of Nuevo León, Ramón Corral of Sonora,
Miguel Cárdenas in Coahuila, Miguel Ahumada and Enrique Creel
in Chihuahua, all of whom were enthusiasts for schools.[11] One sus-
pects that their commitment to education related as well to a desire
to attract North American investors, who deeply penetrated this region in the *Porfiriato*.

In contrast, Yucatán's economy and society were characterized by
the pre-capitalist *hacienda* coexisting with the indigenous community
which served as a source of both land and labor. Yucatán had the
largest indigenous population in Mexico in 1910 (58.94 percent of
the population spoke only indigenous languages). The rapid expansion of *henequén* production here was achieved through the use of
semi-slave labor—local Mayan Indians chained to the *hacienda* through
debt peonage and the rebellious Yaqui Indians and others imported
from central and northern Mexico.[12] Presumably, landowners had
little interest in educating these workers although it is possible that
hacienda schools were built in Yucatán for technical and administrative personnel increasingly associated with the elaboration of this
highly commercial product. Yucatán's economy was in fact characterized by a form of dualism. *Henequén* production created a modern
labor force in the technical and administrative aspects of production,
in transportation and services. This modern labor force coexisted
with the semi-slave labor force of the *hacienda* and benefitted more
than the latter from the school expansion which took place. Not surprisingly, in the *Porfiriato* Yucatán acquired a reputation for pedagogical innovation reflecting the interests of the urban professional
sector.[13]

Figures on revenue and expenditure indicate low levels of growth
and school spending in central Mexico. This sluggishness is also re-

11. Corral's educational policy is discussed in Aguilar Camín, *La frontera*, pp. 80–92;
on Cárdenas, see Ildefonso Villarello Vélez, *Historia de la Revolución mexicana en Coahuila*
(Mexico: Talleres Gráficos de la Nación, 1970), pp. 37, 41, and Samuel Guy Inman,
Intervention in Mexico (New York: George H. Doran, 1919), pp. 66–67; on Miguel Ahu-
mada, see Charles F. Lumiss, *The Awakening of a Nation*, p. 15; on Enrique Creel, see
Alvaro de la Helguera, *Enrique C. Creel. Apuntes biográficos* (Madrid: Imprenta de Am-
brosio Pérez Asensio, 1910), pp. 31, 37, 48–51, 58–59, 61–76, 82–87, 120–55, and
Enrique González Flores, *Chihuahua de la Independencia a la Revolución* (Mexico: Edi-
ciones Botas, 1949), p. 202; on Creel and Corral, see also Ramón Eduardo Ruíz, *The
Great Rebellion: Mexico 1905–1924* (New York: W. W. Norton, 1981), pp. 20–21.

12. Katz, "Labor Conditions," pp. 15–19; Moisés González Navarro, *Raza y tierra: La
guerra de castas y el henequén* (Mexico: El Colegio de México, 1970), pp. 169–225.

13. Moisés González Navarro, *La vida social*, p. 590.

flected in enrollments and literacy rates. Hidalgo, México, Puebla, Aguascalientes, San Luis Potosí, Querétaro and Guanajuato ranked 12, 13, 16, 17, 21, 22, and 23 in enrollments in 1907 and below the national literacy average of 19.74 percent. Notable exceptions to the mediocre record were Tlaxcala, first in enrollments in 1907 and twelfth in literacy (21.90 percent), and Morelos, fourth in enrollments and eleventh in literacy (23.58 percent).

Alejandro Martínez Jiménez has argued that trends in primary education in central Mexico relate to the decline of the municipality adversely affected by state centralization and the expansion of the *hacienda* at the expense of the community.[14] He argues that a municipal impetus to establish schools in the 1870s slowed with the advent of the dictatorship. There is some validity to this thesis. There are notable examples of school expansion in the 1870s. For instance, with the help of the Lancaster Society, General Juan Crisóstomo Bonilla, *cacique* of the Puebla *sierra*, began to build schools in his region in the 1870s until no *pueblo* (village) was without one.[15] However, Martínez Jiménez' argument should be balanced by several factors. One, there are no statistics available for schooling before the 1870s and those available for the 1870s are incomplete and not as reliable as later figures.[16] Municipal schools clearly existed before the 1870s. In the pre-Porfirian period the quality of municipal schools already reflected inequalities of income between municipalities. In the pre-dictatorship period, the primary school of the typically impoverished small municipality consisted of one room starkly furnished with a few worn desks and benches and without texts and other equipment. The schools often functioned sporadically because of the labor demands of local agriculture and because many municipalities could not regularly pay their teachers, who in any case tended to be untrained.[17] As

14. Alejandro Martínez Jiménez, "La educación elemental en el Porfiriato," *Historia Mexicana* 22 (1973): 543–44.

15. In this area of predominantly subsistence farming, the motives of the *cacique* are not entirely clear although some element of social control may have been involved as the patriarch indirectly named and controlled the school teacher, who acted also as the town judge. Evidently the teacher exercised some power and was known as the only *gente de razón* in the town. See *Escuelas federales en la Sierra de Puebla; informe sobre la visita a las escuelas federales en la sierra de Puebla realizado por el C. Subsecretario de Educación Prof. Moisés Sáenz*, Publicaciones de la SEP 15, no. 5 (1927): 83.

16. Statistics in *Estadísticas sociales* for schooling begin with 1878 and are incomplete: data are missing for several states. The Secretaría de Instrucción Pública published statistics for 1874 in its *Boletín de Instrucción Pública* 13 (1909–1910), which are more complete although in some cases private and public school enrollments are combined. Martínez Jiménez bases his argument on these data.

17. T. G. Powell, *El liberalismo*, pp. 40, 54–55.

municipal revenue continued to fall in the *Porfiriato* and was recon-centrated in favor of commercial centers, most states stepped in to assume responsibility for primary education. Such was the case in Morelos. One of the states most deeply affected by *hacienda* expansion at the expense of the village community, Morelos managed to main-tain a good record in public education. As early as the 1870s, the state government began to create means of aiding the poorer municipali-ties in school financing. In the 1890s, Governor Alarcón took a spe-cial interest in developing schooling—in improving buildings, equipment, and teachers' pay.[18] It is possible that his interest in edu-cation rested upon the tension which had developed between the ex-panding commercial sugar plantation economy of this state and its deep communal tradition. Perhaps the conflict between these insti-tutions actually contributed to the maintenance and growth of a rela-tively progressive primary school system. In contrast, the states of Puebla and México did not show as clear an interest in primary edu-cation. Puebla left primary school financing almost entirely up to the municipalities—a gesture reflected in low literacy rates, low en-rollments, and declining primary school expenditures in relation to increased state revenue. The state of México began to subsidize municipal schools late in the period when it became clear that local governments could not pay their teachers. Like Puebla, the state of México's increase in primary school expenditures in the period ranked far below increased state revenue. The question of school ex-pansion and school decline in central Mexico as well as the question of trends in municipal revenue and their impact on primary school-ing require further investigation.[19]

It is clear that the Porfirian school system reflected deepening un-evenness in development between regions and between urban com-mercial centers and rural areas. This inequality can be seen in the ratio of primary superior (grades five and six) to primary elementary

18. *ICNEP* 2:561.
19. On the state of México, see ibid., pp. 382, 385. The question of municipal fi-nancing of schools and fluctuations and trends in municipal revenue requires further investigation for the *Porfiriato* as a whole. For example, in the northern states of Nuevo León and Coahuila, responsibility for primary school expenditures remained largely in the hands of municipalities. These states experienced a fairly steady expansion in pub-lic primary schooling. It is probable that this expansion benefited growing commercial centers at the expense of other areas. For example, in 1910, 52.06 percent of municipal expenditures in the state of Nuevo León were accounted for by the capital of Monter-rey. In Coahuila, the capital absorbed 34.68 percent of municipal revenues (*Estadísticas sociales*, p. 216).

schools (grades one through four). As Table 2.3 indicates, primary superior schools were few in relation to primary elementary schools— an indicator of the hierarchical nature of the school system and its failure to act as a channel of mobility for more than a small fraction of the population. The ratio of primary superior to primary elementary schools was greatest in the capital of the country. Regionally, the ratio was appreciably greater in the north than it was in central or southern Mexico. Puebla had only one primary superior school; México had only five. Primary superior schools in the states were almost always located in the capital or major commercial centers at the expense of smaller towns and rural areas.

TABLE 2.3
Primary Superior Schools in 1910 in Selected States

State	Number of Primary Superior Schools	Number of Primary Elementary Schools
Aguascalientes	3	34
Campeche	4	66
Chihuahua	21	163
Coahuila	62	231
Colima	2	52
Federal District	44	338
Guanajuato	20	207
Guerrero	14	280
Jalisco	27	600
México	5	926
Morelos	2	238
Nuevo León	37	278
Oaxaca	7	553
Puebla	1	1,091

Sources: "Informes de los Gobernadores de los Estados, 1909," AGN, FSIPBA, Legajo 130, Expediente 608; *ICNEP* 1,2.

While it is not clear if state aid to rural municipal schools improved the quality of instruction in the *Porfiriato*, it is clear from officials' reports that rural schools were inferior in instruction to urban schools.[20] The program of the rural school was abbreviated in comparison with the urban program. Its buildings were unhygienic. Its equipment for teaching was inferior. Its teachers remained by and

20. See, for example, *ICNEP* 2:473, 704.

large untrained and very poorly paid. In the Federal District, teachers without degrees were sent to the rural schools while trained teachers were given more desirable positions in the city.[21] Although rural schools in the *Porfiriato* were of inferior quality and were few in number in relation to the population, the allegation of Mexican revolutionaries that no rural schools existed at the time of the Revolution is not supported by statistical evidence.[22] In 1900, of 9,363 primary public schools, 2,013 were coeducational schools, which were usually only created in areas of scarce population. The largest number of these schools were in central Mexico—Hidalgo, Morelos, Puebla, San Luis Potosí, although they were also plentiful in Jalisco, Veracruz, and Oaxaca. In 1900, Tamaulipas had 118 rural schools and 98 urban ones. Zacatecas claimed that its *ranchos* and *haciendas* all had schools although of 251 rural schools in 1910, 15 did not function for lack of buildings and teachers. Jalisco exhorted *hacienda* owners to establish schools at their expense which the state promised to subsidize. Some schools were built on *haciendas* in the period in Jalisco, Morelos, and elsewhere, although most were probably designed to serve skilled and administrative personnel.[23]

Because available statistics on school expansion in the period do not provide a breakdown between urban and rural schools over time, it is not clear to what degree rural schools were a survival of the pre-Porfirian era or a creation of the *Porfiriato*. However, interest in rural schools and in indigenous education seems to have intensified in practice at the state and federal levels in the last decade of the dictatorship. This phenomenon might in part reflect growing recognition of the uneven development in schooling caused by deepening structural disparities in municipal and state income; recognition of the educational needs of a modernizing society, including the skill-development and social-control functions of schooling, may also have been growing. Justo Sierra created 17 new rural schools in the last years of the *Porfiriato*. Nuevo León reported the construction of 24 new rural schools in 1905. San Luis Potosí tripled the number of rural schools beteeen 1906 and 1910.

The need for indigenous education was increasingly acknowledged among the influential despite their persistent prejudices against na-

21. *Boletín de Instrucción Pública* 13 (1909–1910): 187–88.
22. See, for example, Isidro Castillo, *Mexico y su revolución educativa* (Mexico: Editorial Pax-Mexicana, Librería Carlos Cesarman, SA, 1965) 1: 149.
23. Direccion General de Estadísticas, *Anuario estadístico de la república mexicana*, 1900, p. 249; Moisés González Navarro, *La vida social*, pp. 587, 595; *ICNEP* 2:302; *CLM* 12:73–79.

tive Mexicans.[24] In 1910, Miguel Ahumada, then governor of Jalisco, emphasized the importance of bettering the indigenous races through schools. At the national education congress in 1910, Sierra identified the Indian "problem" as central to Mexican schooling.[25] The concern stemmed from several causes. Whereas many had seen the Indian as an obstacle to progress and placed their faith in European and North American immigration, the latter failed to materialize on a significant scale, and it became clear that Mexico would have to rely on her own population for development.[26] Further, incorporation of the indigenous through education was seen as a prerequisite for political stability. Schools built by the federal government among the rebellious Maya of Quintana Roo aimed at pacification.[27] The state had exhausted considerable financial and human resources in its campaign against the Yaqui Indians of Sonora who refused to be marginalized by the modernization process. When in 1906 Governor Creel developed plans not only to educate the Tarahumara of Chihuahua's Sierra Madre but to place them on "homesteading" reservations, it is possible that among his intentions was the desire to avoid indigenous revolt as mining companies rapidly penetrated the Tarahumara region.[28]

Some supporters of Indian education at the end of the *Porfiriato* were fundamentally moved by sympathy for the deterioration of indigenous conditions through the land expropriation process. Often this sympathy recalled an old liberal argument now couched in terms of the modern economy: an increase in well-being and education of the Indian would cause an increase in his needs. The idea of the

24. This issue is discussed at greater length in T. G. Powell, "Mexican Intellectuals and the Indian Question, 1876–1911," *Hispanic American Historical Review* 48 (1968): 19–36, and in Martin Stabb, "Indigenism and Racism in Mexican Thought, 1857–1911," *Journal of Inter-American Studies* 1 (1959): 405–43. See also John A. Britton, "Indian Education, Nationalism and Federalism in Mexico, 1910–1911," *The Americas* 32 (1970): 445–58.

25. *ICNEP* 1:25–26; 2:287.

26. T. G. Powell, "Mexican Intellectuals," pp. 21–23.

27. See *El Imparcial*, 25 Nov. 1903; Secretaría de Justicia y Instrucción Pública, "Datos para el discurso presidencial," April 1901, in Archivo General de la Nación, Fondo de la Secretaría de Instrucción Pública y Bellas Artes, Legajo 7, Expediente 414 (hereafter cited as AGN, FSIPBA).

28. See "Exposición de motivos que presentó el Ejecutivo de Estado sobre civilización y mejoramiento de la raza tarahumara y ley expedida acerca del asunto por la Honorable Legislatura," in Alvaro de la Helguera, *Enrique C. Creel. Apuntes biográficos*, pp. 158–92.

Indian as both producer and consumer was to figure prominently in the educational programs of the Mexican Revolution.[29] However, until June 1911 when the Porfirian regime in its final moments passed a law authorizing the federal government to create rural schools for the indigenous throughout the country, Indian education seemed neglected. The question of language was a principal barrier. Singular efforts to create normal schools to train indigenous teachers failed. Although the proportion of the Mexican population speaking only indigenous languages declined from 16.60 percent to 12.93 percent between 1878 and 1907, the drop may have been due more to economic and demographic factors than to the school.[30]

The overall statistical picture would indicate that comparatively few children were reached by the public school. In assessing who was reached, it was said in the period that public schools served the poor and the lower middle class while the more privileged attended private schools.[31] But it must be asked who among the poor attended public schools. Most peons on *haciendas* or people living in marginal rural areas had little or no access to schools. Although the Lancaster schools in the 1830s had served the urban poor—children of laundresses, domestic servants, street vendors, and petty artisans—the rising cost of living and increased rate of exploitation in the *Porfiriato* probably made it increasingly difficult for poorer children to attend school for any period of time even when schools were nearby.[32] Educators frequently complained of the resistance of *"familias incultas"* to the school and attributed this recalcitrance to the high incidence of child labor.[33]

The school system did not expand in a unilinear fashion. Between 1900 and 1907, public primary school enrollments increased most rapidly in states with significantly expanding revenues and progres-

29. The notion did not originate with the Revolution. Matías Romero, secretary of the treasury and ambassador to the United States under Juárez and Díaz, held that Indian education would increase by millions the productive and consuming population of Mexico. See Matías Romero, *Mexico and the United States* (New York: G. P. Putnam's Sons, 1898), p. 105.

30. *Estadísticas sociales*, pp. 119–21.

31. Gabino Barreda, "Instrucción pública," p. 267; *Memoria que el ciudadano General Bernardo Reyes, gobernador de Nuevo León, presenta al xxiv legislatura del mismo y corresponde al período transcurrido del 4 de octubre de 1903 al 3 de octubre de 1907* (Monterrey: Tipografía del Gobierno del Estado, 1907), p. xxxi; Moisés González Navarro, *La vida social*, p. 577.

32. On Lancaster schools, see Estrada, "Las escuelas lancasterianas," p. 509.

33. For example, see *ICNEP* 2:388.

sive school policies, e.g., Coahuila, Chihuahua, the Federal District, Durango, Yucatán, Tabasco, and Jalisco. For the nation as a whole, public primary enrollments declined by 5.5 percent between 1900 and 1907. Part of the reported decline may be due to inaccurate statistical data: figures for Oaxaca show an extraordinary 78 percent decline in enrollments, from 137,892 to 30,087. The 1900 figure for this state is most likely incorrect. Enrollment declines also took place in the central states of Hidalgo (4 percent), México (7 percent), Michoacán (7 percent), San Luis Potosí (37 percent), and Querétaro (20 percent); in the northwestern state of Sinaloa (18 percent); and in the southeastern state of Campeche (10 percent). Enrollments in Aguascalientes, Guanajuato, and Morelos stayed close to their 1900 level. Some of these states were experiencing significant increases in revenue (e.g., México) while others registered less notable increases (e.g., San Luis Potosí, Morelos, Querétaro). Enrollment declines may have been due to relative neglect in public school policy and/or an increasing rate of exploitation. In the central Mexican states of Hidalgo, México, Morelos, and Querétaro, the number of boys attending school fell while the number of girls increased between 1900 and 1907.[34] Presumably, the labor of male children was more important to families pressed for survival.

Judging from frequent complaints of educators about child labor and its interference with school attendance, one must assume that an effort was made to reach the urban working class and rural sectors. In the north, U.S. mining engineers commented that obligatory school laws had to some extent deferred the age at which boys could be put to work.[35] However, one must conclude from the statistics alone that this effect was not so successful as policy-makers hoped. The principal beneficiaries of the Porfirian public and private schools were the middle strata, which included those associated with more precapitalist forms of production (artisans and small merchants) and those increasingly incorporated into the modern economy and state as administrative, technical, and professional personnel.[36] Those within the middle strata who could afford private education and had access to it probably used the private school system. Although the percentage of private primary schools in relation to all primary

34. Statistics are from *Estadísticas sociales*, pp. 45–47.

35. Allen H. Rogers, in "Character and Habits of the Mexican Miner," *Engineering and Mining Journal* 85 (1908): 701, said that the compulsory education laws had deferred to some extent the age at which boys could be put to work.

36. This point is also argued by Alejandro Martínez Jiménez, "La educación en el Porfiriato," pp. 545–46.

schools dropped from 26 percent in 1874 to 20.94 percent in 1907, between 1900 and 1907 private school enrollments for all levels of schooling increased from 17 percent of all students enrolled in school to 20 percent.[37] Statistics suggest that after a period of being over-shadowed by public school expansion, the private school system was beginning to grow as a consequence of modernization. While Mexico's public school enrollment declined by 5.5 percent between 1900 and 1907, private school enrollments rose by 19 percent. The figures would suggest deepening social stratification and income inequality. Growing private school enrollments indicated increased income for some while static or declining public enrollments indicated deepening poverty for others.[38]

Table 2.4 shows rankings by state in numbers of private and Church schools and percentage increases in private school enrollments between 1900 and 1907. It illustrates a dual tendency in the private school system to reflect traditionalism and low rates of economic growth, on the one hand, and modernization and increasing income, on the other. Private schools were largely concentrated in central Mexico and in states which ranked below average in public

37. According to figures in *Estadísticas sociales*, only 13 percent of all schools were private in 1878. Figures, however, are missing for 17 states. Therefore, I have used data for 1874 reprinted in the *Boletín de Instrucción Pública* 13 (1909–1910). Figures for 1900 and 1907 used here are from *Estadísticas sociales*. According to the latter, in 1900, out of 861,062 students, 146,709 were enrolled in private schools. There is a minor error in calculation in *Estadísticas sociales*. On the basis of their data, the compilers calculate 713,394 public school enrollments when their own figures actually add up to 714,353 (see p. 59). In 1907, 174,880 students out of 848,489 were in private schools. These statistics indicate a 5.5 percent decline in all public school enrollments accompanied by a 19 percent increase in all private school enrollments (see *Estadísticas sociales*, pp. 45, 47, 52, 56, 59).

38. It is possible that some less well-off people were included in Catholic school enrollments as a result of the Catholic Church's strengthening its efforts to reach urban and rural workers in the first decade of the century. However, statistics on the expansion of Church schools between 1900 and 1907 do not indicate the types of schools created nor the types of students recruited. Further, scholars who have examined growing Catholic interest in the "social question" have pointed to an interest in mass education but have not discussed the actual construction or opening of schools and their location. For discussion of the Church's interest in the social question see, among others, Jean Meyer, *La cristiada* (Mexico: Siglo Veintiuno Editores, 1973), pp. 45–47; Alicia Olivera Sedano, *Aspectos del conflicto religioso de 1926 a 1929. Sus antecedentes y consecuencias* (Mexico: Instituto Nacional de Antropología e Historia, 1966), pp. 32–33; Robert Quirk, *The Mexican Revolution and the Catholic Church, 1910–1929* (Bloomington: Indiana University Press, 1973), pp. 17–19; David C. Bailey, *Viva Cristo Rey! The Cristero Rebellion and the Church-State Conflict in Mexico* (Austin: University of Texas Press, 1974), pp. 14–46.

TABLE 2.4
Private and Church Schools

% of Private Schools in Relation to All Primary Schools, 1907[b]		% Increase in Private School Enrollments, 1900–1907[a]		% Increase in Number of Church Schools, 1900–1907[c]		% Church Schools in Relation to All Schools, 1907[b]	
Aguascalientes	52	Sonora	282	Coahuila	1,400	Aguascalientes	17.33
Jalisco	47	Yucatán	207	Sonora	500	Michoacán	16.91
San Luis Potosí	46	Coahuila	102	San Luis Potosí	250	Jalisco	16.41
Guanajuato	45	Zacatecas	101	México	182	Colima	12.70
Querétaro	44	Querétaro	88	Nuevo León	133	Guanajuato	11.32
Durango	33	Tamaulipas	82	Aguascalientes	117	Zacatecas	8.22
Michoacán	31	Nuevo León	82	Tamaulipas	100	Querétaro	6.96
Federal District	30	Aguascalientes	57	Zacatecas	84	Durango	5.30
Chihuahua	23	Morelos	53	Jalisco	63	Coahuila	5.23
Colima	22	Durango	44	Querétaro	60	Campeche	4.76
Nuevo León	21	México	40	Tabasco	50	Chiapas	4.28
Coahuila	20	Jalisco	31	Morelos	38	Morelos	3.97
Tamaulipas	16	Hidalgo	27	Hidalgo	4	Sonora	3.61
Zacatecas	16	Puebla	23	Sinaloa	0	Tabasco	3.61
Veracruz	15	Federal District	21	Chiapas	0	Hidalgo	3.27
Yucatán	15	Sinaloa	16	Michoacán	0	México	3.10
México	13	Chiapas	15	Durango	−11	Oaxaca	2.51
Hidalgo	12	Michoacán	12	Colima	−11	Tamaulipas	2.17
Chiapas	12	Guanajuato	4	Guerrero	−38	Nuevo León	1.70
Sonora	11	San Luis Potosí	3	Veracruz	−40	San Luis Potosí	1.69
Tabasco	11	Tabasco	1	Puebla	−65	Puebla	1.68
Morelos	11	Guerrero	−13	Chihuahua	−78	Guerrero	1.31
Campeche	11	Veracruz	−17			Chihuahua	1.29
Sinaloa	9	Campeche	−20			Yucatán	1.23
Puebla	8	Chihuahua	−43			Veracruz	.61
Oaxaca	6	Oaxaca	−44			Sinaloa	.58
Guerrero	4	Colima	−54				

States are listed in ranked order. Notes: (a) Includes all levels of education. (b) There are no data for Tlaxcala. (c) There are no data for Guanajuato, Tlaxcala, Campeche, or Yucatán. Sources: *Anuario estadístico*, 1900, 1907; *Estadísticas sociales del Porfiriato*.

primary school expenditures, i.e., the relative strength of the private school system corresponded to apathy and backwardness in the public sector. This was certainly the case in Guanajuato, Michoacán, and Agauscalientes. Jalisco (which may be an exception in that its public school expenditures increased 580 percent between 1878 and 1907 although its per capita school expenditures remained below average at the end of the period) actively encouraged the opening of private schools to combat illiteracy and provided such schools with texts, furniture, and supplies.[39] In Jalisco, private schools almost equalled public schools in number and in the capital of Guadalajara, more students attended private than public schools.

The table indicates that Church schools were a small but slowly growing proportion of private schools. Catholic schools were 4.0 percent of all schools in 1900 and 4.80 percent in 1907. They were concentrated in the central states of Guanajuato, Querétaro, Aguascalientes, Jalisco, Colima, Michoacán, and Zacatecas. It is possible that their number is underestimated. Bishop Francis G. Kelley, President of the Catholic Extension Society of the United States, claimed that many private schools established by laymen were actually Catholic schools.[40] Many schools probably operated semi-clandestinely, for several Catholic teaching orders flourished in the period despite the legal ban on them.[41] Although no data has been provided, it has also been suggested that the Church took an aggressive position on school expansion in the first decade of the century when in response to Leo XIII's *Rerum Novarum*, it began to focus on the "social question."

Most states formally adopted the rulings of the Federal District and the national education congress of 1890 regarding inspection of private schools. Although many delegates at the congress felt that the teaching of religion should be abolished from private schools as well as from public institutions, Sierra considered this position extreme. Thus, the congress had recommended that private schools be inspected to see that students learned material comparable to the official program. Should the schools refuse inspection, their students would have to take state-administered examinations. In practice, this

---

39. *ICNEP* 2:209, 260, 293.
40. See testimony of Francis G. Kelley, U.S. Senate, *Investigation of Mexican Affairs*, 66th Cong., 2nd sess., 1919–1920, 2 vols., 2:2680; see also his *Blood-Drenched Altars* (Milwaukee: Bruce Publishing, 1935), p. 401.
41. See Karl Schmitt, "The Díaz Conciliation Policy on State and Local Levels, 1876–1911," *Hispanic American Historical Review* 40 (1960): 516–18.

resolution resulted in the adoption of the official program by most private schools. Although, at certain points, conflicts flared between Church and state over schooling, the attitude of the state toward private schools in general and Catholic schools in particular became quite relaxed. The official position of policy-makers toward Catholicism, the Church, and Catholic schools became an almost aggressively conciliatory one of tolerance for "all beliefs."[42]

Among non-Catholic private schools, the growth of North American Protestant schools, especially in the north of Mexico, is of note. In 1892, Protestants reported having 7,336 students in 7 training and theological schools, 25 boarding schools and orphanages, and 164 common schools. These schools produced a number of participants in the Mexican Revolution at least in part because they served as important institutions for the primary and secondary education of middle-sector individuals.[43] In addition to the Protestant schools, most foreign colonies—urban and rural—had their own schools. Foreign companies had schools for non-Mexican personnel in rural

42. For conflicts with private schools, see Sierra, *Educación*, pp. 346–47; *El Imparcial*, 5 Nov. 1903; *Boletín de Instrucción Pública* 3 (1904): 543. For examples of official conciliation on the part of pedagogues, see instructions to teachers in Rébasamen, *Método para la enseñanza de la historia*, p. 19, and Delgadillo, *La república mexicana*, p. 49. Karl Schmitt, "The Díaz Conciliation Policy," pp. 518–19, points out that attitudes toward Catholic schools varied from region to region. Jalisco subsidized its Church schools. In the neighboring state of Colima in the 1890s, the governor asked that public school teachers introduce the idea of God to morality classes. In 1894, a Catholic publicist claimed that in some regions Catholics were able to live with prohibitions against religious instruction in public schools because many public school teachers in rural areas and small towns were graduates of Catholic normal schools and with the local priest would detain children after school for religious instruction. See Kenelm Vaughan, "What Catholics Have Done for Education in Mexico," *The Catholic World* 59 (1894): 128–29.

43. Deborah J. Baldwin in her "Variation in the Vanguard: Protestants in the Mexican Revolution" (Dissertation, University of Chicago, 1979), p. 100, calculates that 58 percent of the Protestant missions were in the north. She argues (pp. 119–20, 222–25) that ideological and financial considerations determined a Protestant educational focus on the middle strata, including artisans. Protestant missionary Samuel Guy Inman claimed that many revolutionary governors, assistants to cabinet ministers, representatives in foreign countries, army officers, directors of departments of education, and teachers were graduates of Protestant schools in Mexico. See his *Intervention in Mexico*, p. 232, and his testimony in U.S. Senate, *Investigation of Mexican Affairs* 1:6–7. For more detailed accounts of some of these individuals see Baldwin, "Variation in the Vanguard," pp. 284–332. Statistics on Protestant schools used here are from Duclos Salinas, *The Riches of Mexico and its Institutions* (Saint Louis: Nixon Jones Printing Company, 1893), pp. 344–45, and Matías Romero, *Geographical and Statistical Notes on Mexico* (New York and London: G. P. Putnam's Sons, The Knickerbocker Press, 1898), pp. 95–98.

areas. Some mining companies subsidized local public schools while large operations like the Huasteca Petroleum Company, the Mexican Petroleum Company, and the Mexican Coal and Coke Company, built and maintained primary schools for Mexican workers as did a few national concerns like the Compañía Metalúrgica de Torreón, owned by the Madero family of Coahuila.[44]

Organization and Bureaucratization of Public Primary Schooling

Growth of the primary school system, though barely underway in the period, formed part of the process of state expansion, bureaucratization, and political centralization, which was essential to the state's capacity to carry out the official program. Broadly speaking, the process of centralization in education included the absorbing of municipal governmental functions by state governments and informal control of state governments by the central government. At the state level, the process of bureaucratization involved the central administration of schools and the creation of a new civil service of teachers, inspectors, and other officials.

The process of bureaucratization and centralization advanced most at the federal level in relation to the capital and territories. At the federal level, the primary education law of 1888 determined that municipal authorities would continue to administer and finance primary schools with the help of federal subsidies. The municipalities maintained the right to hire and fire teachers, who were required to have normal degrees where possible. The federal government could inspect the municipal schools to insure their compliance with the methods, procedures, and programmatic content of the law. Primary superior schools were to be directly administered by the federal gov-

44. See U.S. Senate, *Investigation of Mexican Affairs* 1:235, 275, 942, 982, 1036, 1405–8, 1759; 2:1949–50, 1976, 2001, 2171, 2398, 2575–77; *Engineering and Mining Journal* 90, no. 14 (1910): 657; and Edwin Ludlow, "The Coalfields of Las Esperanzas," pp. 144–45. Before the U.S. Senate Committee in 1919, several managers of U.S.-owned plantation and lumbering operations in coastal Mexico also stated that they had opened schools for Mexican personnel. These claims seem doubtful as most of these enterprises had relatively few full-time Mexican personnel and relied primarily on contract labor from local jails and most distant regions. One plantation owner in the Campeche jungle was honest enough to admit that he could find no teacher for his proposed school. See U.S. Senate, *Investigation of Mexican Affairs* 1:1345–57, 1376–84, 1696–1700; 2:2205–6.

ernment.[45] The reglamentary law of public instruction of 1891 for the Federal District and territories created Consejos de Vigilancia in each *cuartel mayor* of the capital and in the municipalities of the territories. Consisting of the police inspector and his appointees in the Federal District and of the president of the municipal council and his appointees in the territories, the Consejos de Vigilancia were to insure school attendance and to fine or imprison non-complying parents. The 1891 law also created the Consejo Superior de Instrucción Primaria, a consultative body which was to supervise the scientific direction of teaching, name commissions to observe the operation of the official program in elementary schools, upgrade the instructional methods of teachers, propose texts, and recommend firings of teachers.[46] The council consisted of the Minister of Justice and Public Instruction, the director of the educational branch of the ministry, a representative of municipal government, directors of the capital normal schools and their professors of pedagogy, and three directors of primary schools—one municipal public school, one federal public school, and one private school which accepted the official program.

In 1896, by executive decree, all municipal schools in the Federal District and territories were placed under the jurisdiction of the federal government in order to give public primary education a "single direction."[47] The Consejo de Instrucción Primaria was dissolved and replaced by the Dirección General de Instrucción Primaria, a more directly executive and administrative office charged with providing unity of programs, methods, and texts. The Dirección General was responsible for the hiring and firing of teachers and for appointments to the Consejos de Vigilancia, which it was now to supervise. Positivist Luis Ruiz, first chief of this office, initiated the systematic application of the legal program to capital schools through the development of an inspection system and the convening of teachers' conferences to upgrade methods and content.[48] A system of medical inspection was also introduced. Delegates of the Dirección General were placed in charge of public primary instruction in the territories.

After 1896, educational legislation no longer emanated from Congress but was introduced by executive decree. In 1901, when Baranda retired from the Ministry of Justice, Justo Sierra assumed

45. *Ley sobre la instrucción primaria en el Distrito Federal y territorios federales*, pp. 4, 5.
46. *MSJIP*, p. 327.
47. Ibid., p. 326.
48. Ibid., pp. 351–52; Secretaría de Justicia y Instrucción Pública, "Apuntes para el discurso presidencial," 1899, AGN, FSIPBA, Legajo 7, Expediente 414; see also *El Imparcial*, 1 July 1897; 6 Feb. 1904.

leadership of the educational section of the ministry. In 1902, the Consejo Superior de Educación Pública was created to promote progress and unification in all areas of education. Consisting of directors of major institutions of higher education as well as presidential appointees, most members were associated with positivism.[49] With the creation of the Secretaría de Instrucción Pública in 1905, Justo Sierra greatly expanded the school inspection system and took measures to upgrade the hygiene of school buildings and classrooms. As part of the bureaucratization process, he sought to improve the capital's school system by sending many teachers and bureaucrats to Europe and the United States to study pedagogy and school systems. In 1910, the Sección de Educación Primaria of the Secretaría de Instrucción Pública employed 72 officials—20 regular inspectors, 15 inspectors for special subjects such as gymnastics, music, and languages, 12 medical inspectors, an architect and his assistant.[50]

As earlier indicated, the federally sanctioned program was adopted by representatives of state governments at education congresses in 1889 and 1890. Following the meetings, pedagogues Enrique Rébsamen, Enrique Laubscher, and their students went into the states to assist governments in the development of primary school systems and normal schools in consonance with federal directives. By 1900, most states had passed educational laws similar to those in the Federal District. In the states, as in the capital, the trend was toward state subsidization and administrative absorption of municipal schools. In some states, municipal governments continued to finance primary schools, while control over the program, personnel and teaching methods generally passed to the state government through a Dirección General de Instrucción Pública.[51] In other cases, such as Yucatán, state and municipal governments more evenly split the cost of primary schooling: in 1908, larger cities, such as Mérida and Progreso, paid for most of their own primary schools while the smaller towns received larger state subsidies. The most common situation was to leave

49. The council included Ezequiel Chávez, Porfirio Parra, Alberto Correa, Manuel M. Zamacona, Pablo Macedo, Agustín Aragón, Manuel Flores, Joaquín Casásus, Ramón Corral. See *Boletín de Instrucción Pública* 1 (1903):1–11, 238–40.

50. *Anuarios escolares*, pp. 419–25.

51. The states included Nuevo León, Coahuila, Campeche, Veracruz, and Puebla. See *Memoria que el ciudadano General Bernardo Reyes, gobernador de Nuevo León, presenta al xxiv legislatura*, p. xxiv; *Anuario estadístico*, 1900, pp. 249–50; Secretaría de Instrucción Pública y Bellas Artes, "Gobernadores de los estados remitan datos relativos a la instrucción pública," 1909, AGN, FSIPBA, Legajo 130, Expediente 608; *ICNEP* 2:526–30, 721–26.

the municipal government or the *jefes políticos* of the area in charge of buildings and attendance through Consejos de Vigilancia, while state governments assumed control over content, hiring and firing, and the administration of funds. To this end, state offices of education created inspection systems similar to that in the capital although on a smaller scale. In 1909, for example, Chihuahua and Durango each had four zone inspectors. While this process of centralization and bureaucratization was to be a bone of contention in the Mexican Revolution as local governments tried unsuccessfully to reclaim their autonomy, the development of the school bureaucracy was skeletal and embryonic and by no means insured the implementation of the official school program.[52]

In examining the question of program implementation, the most crucial initial issue was attendance. It is obvious that a relatively small proportion of the school-age population was reached by the school—approximately one-quarter to one-third. Of those enrolled, about two-thirds attended regularly.[53] The key issues here were the existence or proximity of an elementary school, the indifference and sometimes hostility of parents to the alien institution, and, as indicated, the central question of child labor. The federal school regulating law of 1891—imitated in the states—forbade entrepreneurs from hiring children of school age without a primary elementary certificate unless the owner could provide three hours of schooling a day or employed children outside school hours. However, the situation seemed to be one of laxity on the part of local officials and school inspectors in enforcing obligatory schooling laws.[54] In Puebla, by law, *jefes políticos* not visiting at least two schools once a month were to be fined 50 to 100 pesos—a likely indicator that they showed little interest in enforcing attendance.[55] After all, many children presumably worked for local entrepreneurs whom the political chiefs usually served directly or indirectly. The question of attendance obsessed

52. On Yucatán, see *Memoria leido por el C. Gobernador del estado libre y soberano de Yucatán General Octavio Rosado. En el solemne instalación de la décima legislatura constitucional verificada el 1 de enero de 1884* (Mérida: Imprenta de Echanove y López, 1884), p. iv; *Boletín de Instrucción Pública* 13 (1909–1910): 713; on Chihuahua and Durango, see *ICNEP* 1:312, 535. The question of municipal autonomy as an issue in the Revolution requires more investigation. For a discussion of this issue and its relationship to the schools in the state of Sonora, see Camín, *La frontera*, pp. 75–79, 98–102, 203.

53. *Estadísticas sociales*, p. 59.

54. Moisés González Navarro, *La vida social*, p. 587, states that fines were collected in Nuevo León. They were also imposed in the Federal District. See *Boletín de Instrucción Pública* 3 (1904): 543.

55. *ICNEP* 2:726.

Justo Sierra. He tried coaxing children to school by offering food and clothing. In 1905, he suggested increasing the police force.[56] To facilitate the attendance of children who worked, many schools ran on half-time schedules. The latter was a good idea, according to Ezequiel Chávez, Undersecretary in the Ministry of Public Instruction. The factory and school should work together, he wrote: the school would upgrade the child's skills and instill habits of order, discipline, and morality, to offset the influence of the factory which Chávez believed bred a variety of vices and created "a very poor attitude toward life."[57]

Even when children went to school, they were not necessarily taught the full faculty development program. In some instances, the effort to introduce the official program seemed haphazard. For instance, the governor of Michoacán appeared content at first to do little more than send out a series of circulars and pedagogical periodicals to teachers about the new methods and new program.[58] Other states took the process seriously and used a variety of means to introduce the program. They created or upgraded existing normal schools; held teacher conferences—especially in vacation periods; implemented inspection systems; sent teacher study commissions to the capital and even abroad; and circulated many pedagogical periodicals, texts, and teaching manuals.[59] Governor Bernardo Reyes, for instance, sent Nuevo León teachers to Mexico City and abroad to observe schools. His colleague, Miguel Cárdenas, sent a group of Coahuilan teachers to the normal school in Bridgewater, Massachusetts, to prepare for a reorganization of the state school system.[60]

However, evidence suggests that few states fully implemented the prescribed program. For lack of funds and trained teachers, Michoacán did not implement faculty development pedagogy until 1903 and then only in the capital of Morelia. Campeche practiced the old Lancaster monitor methods until 1902. In 1910, only seven of its schools were of "perfect organization." Although Nuevo León authorized simultaneous teaching—or teaching by grades—in the 1890s, over half its schools lacked the necessary space. In order to carry out

56. Secretaría de Instrucción Pública y Bellas Artes, "Junta revisora de la ley de instrucción primaria," 6 April 1905, AEC.

57. Ezequiel Chávez, "La educación de los niños pobres," Sept. 1911, AEC.

58. *ICNEP* 2:572.

59. Ibid., pp. 261, 295, 528–29, 591. Of special importance were guides on teaching methods written by leading pedagogues such as Enrique Rébsamen's *Guía metodológica para la enseñanza de la historia*; for others, see *Anuarios escolares*, pp. 221–22.

60. Samuel Guy Inman, *Intervention*, p. 67.

the program, schools also needed equipment and supplies. In 1884, for example, most Yucatán schools lacked pencils, maps, globes, benches, desks, chairs, and even a place for the teacher to sit. While conditions undoubtedly improved in this state, most states could probably not supply the recommended equipment. The Puebla school law specified that schools have globes, maps, dictionaries, consultative books for each subject area, rulers, compasses, scales, barometers, movable letters, murals for natural history, models of clay and wood, and musical instruments—not to mention pencils, notebooks, texts. Most schools did not have these supplies and many lacked texts. In its entire inventory in 1910, Aguascalientes counted 4 history texts, 268 books on morality, 69 arithmetic primers, 4 primers on political economy, and 10 civics texts. For lack of texts, students in Sonora read the newspapers after the third year of school.[61]

Further, schools were of different categories of organization corresponding to full or partial implementation of the program. Typically, Jalisco's schools were of four classes. First-class schools included primary superior instruction and were few in relation to elementary schools. At the other end of the scale were the fourth-class schools or those of "inferior" organization, which tended to be rural and coeducational with girls and boys attending separately on half-day schedules. As said, the rural schools lacked equipment, space, supplies, and trained teachers.

Where schools existed, the greatest variable in the implementation of the program was the teacher. The inspection system and teacher training were regarded as means of insuring program implementation. Both were incipient in the period although teacher training expanded significantly. Some states like Puebla, Veracruz, and Yucatán had teacher training schools prior to 1890, but most were created after this. In 1907, Mexico had 26 normal schools; some states had two normal schools—one for men and one for women—and others prepared teachers in secondary schools.[62] Morelos, Tlaxcala, and Hidalgo, and the territories of Baja California and Quintana Roo had

61. On Michoacán, see *ICNEP* 2:527; on Campeche, see ibid. 1:136; on Nuevo León, see Moisés González Navarro, *La vida social*, p. 582; on Yucatán, *Memoria leido por el C. Gobernador del estado libre y soberano de Yucatán General Octavio Rosado*; on Puebla, see *ICNEP* 2:708; on Aguascalientes, see ibid. 1:89–91; on Sonora, see Moisés González Navarro, *La vida social*, p. 580.

62. *Estadísticas sociales*, p. 50.

no normal schools but, like other states, sent students to the normal institutes of the capital, which were best funded and developed. In 1887, to complement the Escuela Nacional de Profesoras, the federal government inaugurated the Escuela Nacional de Profesores with a model primary school for teacher practice. The faculty included leading pedagogues Enrique Laubscher, Manuel Flores, Daniel Delgadillo, Lucio Tapia, and others. The women's normal school also acquired a primary school and a model kindergarten. The normal school programs were frequently revised to keep abreast of current European and North American pedagogy and to deepen the practical aspects of teaching itself. In keeping with general educational policy in the period, there was concern that content be adapted to Mexican needs, especially the need to increase production. The Escuela Normal de Profesores taught about Mexico's principal industries, mineralogy, and geology, and opened a workshop in manual arts in 1894. There were 370 normal school students in the capital in 1905. In the country as a whole, normal school enrollments increased from 72 in 1878 to 2,552 in 1907.[63]

Despite the expansion in teacher training, the majority of Mexican teachers lacked degrees in 1910. The Federal District had the best ratio of titled to untitled teachers: 56 percent of its teaching staff had degrees in 1910. Coahuila also had a good record: 85 of its 185 primary teachers had normal degrees in 1910. The more typical situation prevailed in Durango where at the end of the period 77 teachers out of 316 had normal titles. In Campeche, only 14 teachers had normal school training, 106 did not. According to Campeche authorities, the demand for teachers was so great that outside the capital, the first person who came along was hired to teach school. Nor did a normal degree always signify adequate preparation, according to Campeche officials, because teachers trained in the state normal school concentrated more on the upper levels of teaching rather than on the method and content of the primary school faculty development program. Further, there is some evidence that normal schools may have contributed to the spread of liberal opposition to the dictatorship.

---

63. For normal school programs and reforms in the capital, see *MSJIP*, pp. 385–88; Secretaría de Justicia y Instrucción Pública, "Discurso presidencial," 1895, AGN, FSIPBA, Legajo 7, Expediente 414. For enrollments, see *Boletín de Instrucción Pública* 4 (1905): 320–22 and *Estadísticas sociales*, p. 52. These figures do not include students in private normal schools, some of which were Catholic and Protestant. On graduates of Catholic normal schools teaching in public schools, see Kenelm Vaughan, "What Catholics Have Done," pp. 128–29. On Protestants, see Inman, *Intervention*, p. 67.

Teachers did not always perform as the dutiful and neutral civil servants which Sierra and other policy-makers wished to create.[64]

Teachers were in a highly contradictory position within the Porfirian social structure. For one thing, the profession grew in absolute numbers from 12,748 in 1895 to 21,017 in 1910. Proportionally, teachers outstripped the numbers of those practicing other professions by a considerable amount, as Table 2.5 indicates. While the demand for teachers grew, their working conditions, their social prestige, and their wages remained inferior—a fact which may be linked in part but not entirely to the rapid entry of women into the profession. In 1877, Guillermo Prieto said that teachers' wages were on a par with those of taxi drivers.[65] At this time, teachers working for the federal government earned 50 pesos a month, a sum twice as high as that paid by the municipalities. Although the cost of living rose 20 percent between 1885 and 1900 and 25 percent between 1900 and 1910, teachers' wages, even in the Federal District, lagged behind. In 1910, elementary teachers in the capital earned between 54 and 84 pesos a month, depending on whether they had a title, on number of years of service, and on other variables. In the north, where the cost of living was higher, Durango teachers earned between 2.30 and 3 pesos a day in first-class schools in the capital and 1 peso to 1.75 in rural schools. Teachers in the largest cities earned the most. In Torreón, Coahuila, for example, primary superior school directors earned 836 pesos a year while in the small town of Ramos Arispe, teachers received only 197.50 a year. While the directors of primary superior schools in Cuernavaca earned 70 pesos a month in 1896, rural teachers earned 50 centavos a day. Forty centavos a day was the going wage for rural teachers in Guerrero in 1909. These rates can be compared with the national minimum wage for wretchedly remunerated factory work, which was 59 centavos a day in 1910. Although it may be argued that rural teachers earned less because the cost of living was lower in the country, the wage differential also is related to the hierarchical nature of the school system and its promotion of uneven and unequal development. The low wages paid to teachers generally must be explained both in terms of the penury of

64. On the Federal District, see *ICNEP* 1:224; on Coahuila, see ibid., p. 250; on Durango, see ibid., p. 434; on Campeche, see ibid., p. 138. For suggestions of normal school influence on opposition politics, see Camín, *La frontera*, p. 116, and Cockcroft, "El maestro de primaria," pp. 556–87.

65. Moisés González Navarro, *La vida social*, p. 601.

TABLE 2.5
Growth of Professions in the Porfiriato

	1895		1900		1910	
	Total	Number/ 10,000[a]	Total	Number/ 10,000[a]	Total	Number/ 10,000[a]
Teachers	12,748	10.14	15,523	11.44	21,017	13.86
Doctors	2,282	1.80	3,652	1.93	3,021	1.99
Lawyers	3,315	2.66	2,626	2.68	3,953	2.61
Priests	3,576	2.86	3,915	2.97	4,461	3.03

Note: (a) Ratio per 10,000 inhabitants.
Source: *Estadísticas sociales del Porfiriato.*

the budget within the neocolonial state and the fact that schooling was still not deeply legitimized in the society.[66]

In short, the school bureaucracy of the *Porfiriato* was not well enough developed to insure the implementation of the official program. Teachers were not adequately trained. They were not well enough remunerated or provided with other incentives—including social recognition—to perform as loyal civil servants. Nor were they checked through a well-developed bureaucratic chain of command. Thus it is not surprising that these conditions encouraged, on the one hand, absenteeism, apathy, and routine, and, on the other, political insubordination. Some schoolteachers—especially in rural areas— used their classrooms in the *Porfiriato* to preach against the dictatorship rather than to implement the program which legitimized it.[67] Their motives for doing so may be attributed to their objective circumstances, their social awareness, and even their training. In some cases, too, their expectations for upward mobility had been thwarted. Their trade did not put them much above the factory worker or *hacienda* day laborer in terms of wages and placed them well below the miner in certain regions. Proximity to the oppressed probably heightened the teachers' sense of identification with them. Further, as teachers were increasingly appointed by state rather than municipal

66. For teachers' wages in the capital, see *Anuarios escolares*, pp. 251–53; for Durango, see *ICNEP* 1:535; for Coahuila, see ibid., p. 250; for Morelos, see *CLM* 12:73–79; for Guerrero, see *Boletín de Instrucción Pública* 13 (1909–1910): 701–2. The national minimum wage figure is taken from Jorge Basurto, *El proletariado industrial en México (1850–1930)* (Mexico: Instituto de Investigaciones Sociales, Universidad Nacional Autónoma de México, 1975), p. 42.

67. This theme is developed in Cockcroft, "El maestro de primaria," pp. 565–87. Jorge Vera Estañol, a Díaz supporter who was briefly minister of education in the government of Francisco de la Barra in 1911, harangued in 1920 that the Mexican Revo-

authorities, the degree of leverage and autonomy they held at least temporarily in relation to the municipal power structure may have encouraged teachers to voice critical perspectives in the classroom. Thus teachers functioned both as agitators and as organizers. They exercised their acquired intellectual skills and disseminated information to peasants and workers. Otilio Montaño, rural teacher in Anenecuilco, Morelos, helped Emiliano Zapata and his fellow villagers to write the Plan de Ayala in 1911.[68] Juana Gutiérrez de Mendoza, schoolteacher in Guanajuato, taught her miner husband how to read and write, then set up a printing press to assist the miners in their organization and to keep them abreast of working conditions and opposition political activity in other parts of Mexico. A follower of the Partido Liberal Mexicano, precursor opposition party formed in 1906, she later joined the peasant movement of Emiliano Zapata and in the 1920s became a school zone inspector.[69] Luis G. Monzón, later one of Mexico's most outspoken Communists, received his normal school title in 1893 and directed various primaries in his native San Luis Potosí until he was expelled for his activities against the local *cacique*. From 1900 to 1908, he taught in a Sonoran mining town organizing for the Partido Liberal Mexicano. Librado Rivera, normal schoolteacher in San Luis Potosí and a founding member of the Partido Liberal Mexicano, used his classes to expound liberal ideals and to denounce the dictatorship.[70] Not surprisingly, while the growth of opposition politics in the first decade of the century increasingly involved schoolteachers, it coincided with efforts by policy-makers to use the school as an institution of social control, as expressed in Justo Sierra's growing obsession with means of enforcing attendance, his creation of new rural and worker night schools, and the intensified emphasis upon obedience to authority evident in the 1908 school program. A serious but understandable discontinuity had developed in the embryonic bureaucracy of Mexican education.

Other Areas of Schooling

The educational system which emerged in the *Porfiriato* was a hierarchical one. Although in absolute terms, more money was spent on

---

lution had been the work of unsuccessful professionals, underpaid school teachers, and inexperienced students. See Jorge Vera Estañol, *Carranza and his Bolshevik Regime* (Los Angeles: Wayside Press, 1920), p. 14.

68. John Womack, *Zapata and the Mexican Revolution* (New York: A. A. Knopf, 1968), p. 126.

69. *Historia Obrera* 2, no. 5 (1975): 4.

70. Cockcroft, "El maestro de primaria," pp. 569–72.

primary education than any other area of schooling, far more money was spent per student on secondary and higher education. In 1900, 104.79 pesos were spent on each secondary school student and 126.42 on each student enrolled in higher education, compared with 20 centavos spent on each primary school student. Given the penury of the public budget, the reduced number of educational institutions above the primary level, and the general poverty of the majority of Mexicans, the school system allowed for very little social mobility. Most people could not afford to go to school for any period of time, nor were they supposed to do so. In 1900, public secondary school enrollments represented only 1 percent of children attending public primary schools. Professional school enrollments, including those of normal schools, were 1.4 percent of public primary enrollments. The educational system tended to reinforce the existing class relations of society although it appears to have benefited certain sectors of the *petite bourgeoisie.*[71]

In the area of vocational education, the formal training of skilled workers for industry was not taken seriously until late in the period and then primarily in the capital. Although all Mexican states opened night schools where workers (including women and children) could complete their elementary education, basic socialization of the labor force was the main aim.[72] In the first decade of the century, these schools proliferated in the capital as Justo Sierra became more concerned about the discipline, loyalties, and productivity of the working class. In recognition of the skill requirements of an increasingly differentiated economy, Sierra in 1901 divided primary superior schools in the capital into two types—those preparatory for professional schools and those offering basic training in industrial, commercial, and clerical fields. By 1911, there were six of these trade schools in the capital. While offering mobility to some, the dual system, based on the European model, introduced tracking to the already hierarchical school system. It was to become an integral part of Mexico's educational apparatus.

On the whole, state vocational education for manual labor remained underdeveloped in the period. In major industries, skilled workers were at first imported with the approval of the regime: Díaz

71. Calculations of expenditures and enrollments are based on data in *Estadísticas sociales*, p. 60.
72. As one educator put it, they were intended to bring "culture and civilization" to the workers. *ICNEP* 2:123, 132, 223–25.

told foreign entrepreneurs that the presence of foreign workers would educate Mexican laborers.[73] The replacement of foreign skilled workers by Mexican labor was more a consequence of worker pressure, management considerations, and the Mexican Revolution itself than it was the result of public educational policy (see Chapter 6). In the *Porfiriato*, only a handful of states had traditional crafts schools modeled on the Escuela de Artes y Oficios para Hombres, established in Mexico City in 1869 to train artisans in carpentry, iron-working, cabinet-making, plastering, printing, and other trades.[74] To service the growing railroad network, the government in 1890 created a school for machinists. Two years later, this school became part of the Escuela de Artes y Oficios para Hombres, which also added electricity to its curriculum. Although one of the stated purposes of the school was the training of Mexican workers to replace foreign skilled labor, it is doubtful that the school was effective in this. The institution was small in relation to its task. In 1906 it accommodated 360 students and in 1907, 225. Unlike the preparatory and professional schools, it had few if any students from outside the capital. It received fledgling, although apparently growing, government support. Only 2 students were on scholarship in the school in 1902 compared with 12 in the music conservatory; by 1905, the number had increased to 12 in the vocational school.[75] School reports suggested some difficulty in importing up-to-date mechanical equipment; the competency of the staff in new fields of technology was questionable. Students did not readily respond to the new fields. Carpentry continued to be the most popular course: 82 students were examined in this trade in 1906 compared with 7 in mechanics and 6 in electricity courses.[76] On the other hand, students had begun to train in national

73. Diaz told Edward Doheny, head of the Mexican Petroleum Company, to import skilled U.S. workers so that they could transfer their skills to the Mexicans. See U.S. Senate, *Investigation of Mexican Affairs* 1:225. See also testimony of G. W. Bartch, mining engineer, in ibid. 2:2722.

74. By 1907 trade schools of this type had closed in Guanajuato and Oaxaca. One operated in Chihuahua. A naval school in Veracruz trained machinists. There was a school of industrial drawing in Monterrey, Nuevo León. The Escuela Coreccional and Escuela de Huérfanos in the capital also offered instruction in traditional trades.

75. On enrollments, see *Boletín de Instrucción Pública* 6 (1906–1907): 104–6, 947. On scholarships, see Secretaría de Justicia y Instrucción Pública, "Pensiones: varios disposiciones," 1902, AGN, FSIPBA, Legajo 7, Expediente 420, p. 238; *Boletín de Instrucción Pública* 6 (1906–1907): 108.

76. *Boletín de Instrucción Pública* 6 (1906–1907): 115, 974–75. *El Imparcial* confirmed

firms with up-to-date technology. In 1903–4, a group of students worked with sugar milling machinery on Morelos' largest *haciendas*. Others apprenticed with the Fundición de Fierro y Acero de Monterrey, Mexico's first steel company whose owner, Vicente Ferrara, was a strong supporter of the school. By 1905, the government began sending students and staff abroad for training—especially to Germany and the United States.[77]

The increase in vocational school enrollments in Mexico from 420 to 2,062 between 1900 and 1907 was probably due in large part to the influx of women.[78] By 1907, several states had schools like the capital's Escuela de Artes y Oficios para Mujeres, established in 1871 with course offerings in sewing, embroidery, artificial flower-making, cooking, domestic economy, and, increasingly at the turn of the century, commercial and clerical work.[79] Although originally intended for poor women, the Escuela de Artes y Oficios para Mujeres in Mexico City primarily served the middle strata. In 1900, the director noted that its offerings attracted families of the "*clase media*," or that sector of the petite bourgeoisie not engaged in manual labor who were obliged by "misfortune" to seek public education for their daughters in order to spare them "the fate of manual labor."[80] In a period of rapid economic transition, in which the middle strata was particularly vulnerable, the state provided some job training for women forced to work before they married in order to support their

---

this trend. The newspaper claimed that carpentry and iron-working were the most popular courses and that artisans leaving the schools set up profitable shops. Cabinet-making was reported to be one of the best-remunerated trades in Mexico City. See *El Imparcial*, 6 April 1902.

77. On training with Mexican and foreign enterprises, see *Boletín de Instrucción Pública* 3 (1904): 405–17; 6 (1906–1907): 105–7.

78. The increase took place primarily in Mexico City where the number of students rose from 294 in 1900 to 1,894 in 1907. In addition to the trade schools for men and women in Mexico City, the figures for the capital include the agricultural school and military college. Enrollment in the Escuela de Artes y Oficios para Mujeres in 1906 was 1,364 in contrast to 360 students in the Escuela de Artes y Oficios para Hombres; see *Boletín de Instrucción Pública* 6 (1906–1907): 467.

79. See *Boletín de Instrucción Pública* 1 (1903): 206–7; 6 (1906–1907): 4. The state also subsidized the Colegio de la Paz, a trades school originally set up for female orphans and widows by a Basque *cofradía* in 1732. The school's offerings were similar to those of the Escuela de Artes y Oficios para Mujeres. See *Boletín de Instrucción Pública* 3 (1904): 375–78; 6 (1906–1907): 117–25; *El Imparcial*, 25, 27 December 1901.

80. *Boletín de Instrucción Pública* 1 (1903): 482. The tendency to serve the middle strata is also noted by Duclos Salinas, *The Riches of Mexico and its Institutions*, p. 378.

families. The school showed little concern for the plight of poor women who, lacking educational opportunities and skills, were obliged to labor under extremely poor conditions in textile and to-bacco factories. Manual Zamacona, director of the school in the 1890s, stated that he did not want to upgrade the skills and position of women in factories but to prepare them for petty production, i.e., small dressmaking and hat shops, beauty parlors, and catering.[81] The students were apparently more attracted to clerical training. In 1906, courses in typing, stenography, and accounting were most heavily enrolled, although sewing and fashion were also popular.[82]

In contrast to the vocational training of middle-sector women, opportunities for them in professional education were relatively absent. In 1907, only 13 out of 60 preparatory schools admitted women. Although the educational reforms of 1868–69 had created a preparatory school for women in the capital, it soon became a normal school. Primary school teaching became a major feminine outlet in the *Porfiriato*. Of 2,552 students enrolled in normal schools in 1907, 1,998 were female.[83] At the turn of the century, positions as nurses and pharmacists' assistants also opened to them.

In preparatory education in general, enrollments in public and private schools increased by 122 percent from 1878 to 1900, or from 3,375 students to 7,506. Between 1900 and 1907, enrollments dropped 24 percent to 5,728. In 1900, 23 percent of students enrolled in public preparatory schools were studying in Mexico City.[84] Most states had at least two such schools in 1907 although Tlaxcala, Morelos, Sonora, and Baja California had none. These and other states frequently sent students to the Escuela Nacional Preparatoria in Mexico City. The northern states also made use of Protestant schools in Mexico as well as secondary schools in the U.S. Most likely, Mexico's middle strata benefited most from the national school system, since the wealthiest families sent their sons abroad for prepara-

---

81. Zamacona argued that factory labor consumed time, injured women's health and prevented them from receiving culture mentally and morally (Duclos, *The Riches of Mexico and its Institutions*, p. 403). While these statements were in part true, the school did not help those who had no choice but to work in factories. Zamacona's arguments were repeated in 1906 by the new school director, Emilio Rabasa, who stressed the development of trades not requiring capital, machinery, or costly tools. He also promoted clerical training and introduced courses to prepare druggist's assistants. See *Boletín de Instrucción Pública* 6 (1906–1907): 461–68.

82. See, for example, *Boletín de Instrucción Pública* 6 (1906–1907): 388.

83. *Estadísticas sociales*, p. 52.

84. Statistics are from ibid., pp. 27, 59.

tory and professional formation.[85] Notable figures of the Mexican Revolution experienced upward mobility in this manner. For example, José Vasconcelos, who was to become Minister of Education in 1920, came from a modest but ambitious family (his father was a low-level state employee), which sacrificed to send the oldest son to the Escuela Nacional Preparatoria, where he joined other young men of similar background such as Antonio Caso and Martín Luis Guzmán.[86] In the first decade of the century, they found themselves singled out by Justo Sierra and other veteran *Porfiristas* as promising intellectual leadership of their generation.

If normal school enrollments are excluded, students attending Mexican professional schools represented only .6 percent of primary school students in 1907. Between 1878 and 1907, enrollments increased by only 10 percent from 4,881 to 5,370.[87] Like preparatory school students, professional school students were concentrated in the capital (55 percent in 1907) where the schools were best funded, best equipped, and best staffed. Most states offered preparation in the law. Eight had medical schools. Twelve had schools of engineering, and eight offered some kind of commercial education.

Perhaps because commercial education included the training of office managers, accountants, and future foreign consuls, it was defined as professional education. Enrollments in these schools increased rapidly. In Chihuahua, in 1906, Enrique Creel's major educational project was a commercial college for future bankers, accountants, bookkeepers, and other clerical workers to service Chihuahua's burgeoning economy.[88] In 1907, the director of the Escuela Superior de Comercio y Administración in Mexico City claimed that no industry, commercial, railroad, or public office of any importance was without a graduate of this school.[89] However, it is likely that enrollment increases in schools such as these did not take place in the so-called professional track but among part-time students pursuing occasional courses. For example, in the first decade of the century only one-

85. Martha Robles, *Educación y sociedad en la historia de México* (Mexico: Siglo Veintiuno Editores, 1977), p. 68.

86. Although in the category of middle sector, the families of Caso and Guzmán probably had more status than that of Vasconcelos. Caso's father was an engineer and Guzmán's an army colonel.

87. *Estadísticas sociales*, p. 52.

88. See Alvaro de la Helguera, *Enrique C. Creel. Apuntes biográficos*, pp. 82–155, for a description of the project which was never realized.

89. A. Casillas to Secretaría de Instrucción Pública, 21 Dec. 1907, AEC.

quarter of the students at the Escuela Superior de Comercio y Administración were full-time aspirants to careers: most students attended free courses, the most popular of which were English, commercial arithmetic, and typing.[90]

In university education, degrees continued to be concentrated in the traditional areas: in 1904, the capital's professional schools granted 22 degrees in law, 30 in medicine, and only 8 in engineering.[91] Moreover, engineering students tended to pursue civil engineering, which led them into government administration and public works projects rather than into industry or mining.[92] Later, Mexican revolutionaries would argue that the universities had produced a proletariat of bureaucrats and theorists rather than practical men of action, but the problem distressed Porfirian educators as well. The Consejo de Educación Pública, composed of the country's most influential positivists, complained in 1906 that the engineering school's program was too theoretical. It had failed to produce men "capable of solving the complex problems of reality."[93] Foreign companies, they argued, employed foreign personnel because these were more competent. If Mexicans were better trained, they reasoned, companies would hire them because they were cheaper.[94] In his annual report for 1906, the director of the engineering school reported that he had the latest model machinery in some laboratories and was trying to keep the library stocked with North American and European works. While he admitted that the school's program lacked adequate practice, students were making extended visits to industries, mining, and infrastructural operations.[95] By 1911, several students were doing their practice with private firms abroad.[96]

Concern for the practical aspects of agricultural training also were voiced at the turn of the century. The capital's school of agriculture emerged from a period of decadence to modernize the training of *hacienda* administrators, agricultural engineers, and veterinarians. In

90. *Boletín de Instrucción Pública* 6 (1906–1907): 77.

91. *Boletín de Instrucción Pública* 5 (1905–1906): 67–69. In 1910 the ratio was 25, 56, and 13; *Boletín de Instrucción Pública* 17 (1911): 50–51.

92. In 1907, 136 out of 203 studied civil engineering, 23 topographical and hydraulic engineering, 22 mining, 2 metallurgical engineering, and none electricity, a career which had been introduced in 1892. See *Boletín de Instrucción Pública* 6 (1906–1907): 59. Of titles granted in 1904, 4 were in civil engineering and 4 in topography and hydraulics; *Boletín de Instrucción Pública* 5 (1905–1906): 67–69.

93. *Boletín de Instrucción Pública* 6 (1906–1907): 404–5.

94. Ibid., p. 405.

95. Ibid., pp. 59–65.

96. *Boletín de Instrucción Pública* 17 (1911): 594–96.

1910, it had experiment stations in different parts of the country.[97] Several state governors also expressed interest in agricultural educa-\ tion. Enrique Creel subsidized a private agricultural school established in Chihuahua in 1906 which came to serve the northern states. Other states proposed the creation of agricultural schools which never materialized. Olegario Molina in 1904 spoke of the urgent need for such instruction in Yucatán. He later abandoned the project claiming he lacked money, teachers, land, and buildings. Governor Prospero Cahuantzi's proposal for an agricultural school in Tlaxcala also remained on the drafting table.[98]

In 1910, during Mexico's centennial celebrations, Justo Sierra inaugurated the Universidad Nacional, which incorporated the capital's professional schools, museums, and major libraries. It was designed to train the future leaders of Mexico's development. Included within it were the national pathological and bacteriological institutes which studied national diseases in order to develop antitoxins and vaccines. Sierra hoped that these institutes would not only solve national problems but enable Mexico to participate with greater prestige in the process of world science. Also incorporated into the university was the Escuela de Altos Estudios, another Sierra project modeled on the École Normal Supérieure of France. The Escuela de Altos Estudios was to train secondary and professional-level teachers as well as to sponsor research in the exact and social sciences and the humanities.

Like its modest predecessor of 1833, the Secretaría de Instrucción Publica y Bellas Artes assumed responsibility for the direction of Mexican culture. Under its jurisdiction were the Academia de San Carlos, the Conservatorio Nacional de Música, the Museo Nacional de Historia Natural, the Museo Nacional de Arqueología, Historia y Etnología, the Inspección y Conservación de Monumentos Arqueológicos, and the Biblioteca Nacional. As is well-known, the prevailing elite artistic culture of the period—especially that of the capital—fawned before European styles and artists. The middle and upper classes flocked to hear Italian and French opera performed by Euro-

97. Miguel Schulz, "Informe sobre la educación pública en México: sus condiciones actuales," Jan. 1910, AEC; see also *El Imparcial*, 23 Feb. 1897; Secretaría de Justicia y Instrucción Pública, "Pensiones: varios disposiciones," 1900–1901, AGN, FSIPBA, Legajo 7, Expediente 414, p. 238. Sixteen students attended this school on government scholarship in 1900–1901.

98. On Chihuahua, see Francisco R. Almada, *Diccionario de historia, geografía, y biografía chihuahuenses* (Chihuahua: Talleres Gráficos del Gobierno del Estado, 1927), p. 253; on Yucatán, see *Boletín de Instrucción Pública* 3 (1904): 239; on Tlaxcala, see ibid., p. 70.

pean artists. The Escuela de Bellas Artes relied upon neoclassical French models, and the conservatory interpreted Beethoven, Brahms, and so on. That this cultural dependence has emerged as the major theme of Porfirian cultural life is in large part due to the young intellectuals who were to assume the direction of education and culture in the Mexican Revolution. The idea of cultural dependence in the *Porfiriato* forms an important part of the mythology of the Mexican Revolution. It has a basis in reality but has also buried a portion of the cultural activity of the period. The Museo Nacional de Arqueología undertook important beginning work in the field of Mexican history—publishing unpublished manuscripts and compiling bibliographies for the colonial period as well as initiating the restoration of historical buildings. It also undertook archaeological investigation, collected relics, and began to develop and preserve archaeological sites.[99] While this work was not of the scale or quality of the work produced by the Revolution, the *Porfiriato* provided the social order, economic growth, and bureaucratic structure which allowed scientific research on Mexican culture to begin. Further, for the young intellectuals who rebelled against the European overlay, the *Porfiriato* provided the space and structure within which they acquired the intellectual skills and discipline essential to their educational, technical, and cultural production in the Mexican Revolution. The gifted youth privileged enough to attend capital professional schools in the first decade of the century were doted upon by Sierra and other leading positivists who attended their lectures and concerts, published their works, and sent many of them to Europe to study.[100]

Conclusion

In conclusion, in independent Mexico, in the absence of a strong autonomous capitalist class, the state had gradually assumed responsibility for creating the conditions for private capital accumulation. These conditions included the plans for a public school system designed to modernize values and behavior within a capitalist frame-

99. "Informe leido por el Presidente de la República," Sept. 1898; "Informe del C. Presidente," Sept. 1900; Secretaría de Justicia y Instrucción Pública, "Datos para el discurso presidencial," April 1901, AGN, FSIPBA, Legajo 7, Expediente 414; *El Imparcial*, 1, 9 Feb. 1904; 15 Feb., 26 Sept. 1907; 30 July 1908.

100. Judging from the number of public concerts as well as emerging composers and musicians, the music conservatory especially flourished in the first decade of this century. See, for example, *El Imparcial*, 15 Nov. 1903; 23 Jan. 1904; 24 August 1907.

work and to train a hierarchically graded labor force appropriate to economic expansion. These goals were clear both in the statements of policy-makers and in the content of the school programs. However, the educational system was not well developed in the *Porfiriato*. The state had a limited budget, determined by the low level of capital accumulation and the nation's dependent status. Judging from allocation of public expenditures, public education was evidently not a top priority, although school expenditures increased faster than public expenditures as a whole under the dictatorship. This situation related to the historical phase of transition from traditional, precapitalist modes of production to capitalist forms. The greater the level of capitalist growth and social relations, the greater the interest in public schooling as a means of both training and domesticating a hierarchically graded labor force. Thus, those politicians most concerned with public education were those associated with positivism and modernization policies. If Justo Sierra was the most notable example, at the state level there were articulate protagonists of schooling, such as governors Ramón Corral, Bernardo Reyes, Miguel Cárdenas, and Enrique Creel. Similarly, as a consequence of not extending financial assistance for education to the states, public primary schooling tended to expand in areas experiencing rapid economic growth and in regions where capitalist relations of production were predominant, i.e., in northern Mexico.

Politically, the elaboration of a bureaucratic structure for a centralized school system began under the presidencies of Juárez and Díaz, but was incomplete in 1910. The process of bureaucratization and centralization in the Díaz period involved the absorption of municipally controlled primary schools by state governments and federal exertion of authority over state education programs through educational congresses, exchange of personnel (e.g., the remodeling of state school systems by pedagogues associated with federal policy), and informal political linkages, e.g. through state governors like Corral who were closely associated with Díaz and Mexico City positivists. Although programmatic uniformity in primary school programs existed at least on paper after 1890, the system was clearly rudimentary. The federal government legally had jurisdiction only over the Federal District and territories. Although most developed in the Federal District, the school bureaucracy was skeletal and primitive throughout the country. Enforcement of laws of obligatory attendance was lax. The inspection system was poorly staffed and probably functioned inefficiently. Teachers did not form the civil service necessary for strict implementation of the official program. Although the fastest growing professional group in the period, teachers were poorly paid, poorly trained, and socially unrewarded. They tended toward the routine, while significant numbers of them actually used their schools and classrooms to organize against the dictatorship—thus creating a contradiction in the educational system between the intent of policy-makers to use the school as an agency of political discipline and social control and the politically subversive activities of many teachers.

The Mexican public school system tended to mirror the uneven development which characterized Porfirian economic growth. It favored urban over rural areas, those regions experiencing significant increased income over those growing more slowly or registering declining wealth, and it favored, in terms of social mobility, those who benefited from economic growth or those with enough of an edge within the socioeconomic process to take advantage of the school system to advance their position or to avoid downward mobility. Although the primary school system was in large part intended to socialize the working class as well as the middle strata, the demands on labor, the low wages, the rising cost of living, and cyclical shifts in the economy, coupled in many instances with the scarcity of schools, made it difficult for working-class children to attend schools or to attend them for any length of time. Only a small fraction of primary school students went on to secondary or professional schools. Although the school system tended to reflect the existing class structure rather than to mitigate it, there is some indication that the hierarchical school structure provided mobility for numbers of individuals from the petite bourgeoisie. From this sector also was to come the leadership of the Mexican Revolution—the architects of the new state and its educational apparatus. They were to build upon the bureaucratic structure of the Porfirian school system and were to share in profound ways the goals and directions of their Porfirian predecessors.

Although there is an obvious correlation between high levels of literacy and school attendance and areas which generated initial revolutionary activity—e.g., the northern states, the Federal District, and Morelos—there is a serious lack of data to permit any conclusions on this point. The idea that the school served as a liberal candle in the tyrannical darkness runs counter to what modern scholarship has told us about the social functions of schooling. And yet, as indicated, there were real contradictions in this incipient school system. Although policy-makers intended the school to serve as an institution promoting order, teachers were important in organizing to overthrow the dictatorship. We need to know more about their training and who taught them; we need to know when, where, and why they became politically active and when and where their political activity might even have been condoned by local authorities. In general, we as yet know little about what people learned in school, i.e., the relationship between an ideology articulated at the level of official policy and its implementation at the local level. Ironically, parts of the official ideology of the Porfirian school were, as pointed out above, compatible with the modernizing goals put forward by many participants in the Mexican Revolution of 1910. For instance, constitutional government, national integration, and increased production, valued in Porfirian ideology, were important to most revolutionaries of middle-sector or petit bourgeois origin. But the latter did not constitute the only social group participating in the Revolution nor were constitutional government, national integration, and increased production the only goals of the Mexican Revolution. Indeed, we must know much more about the educational background and experience of the Revolution's participants before we can understand fully the relationship between education and the Mexican Revolution of 1910.

Chapter 3
Educational Thought and Policy in the Years of Revolution (1910–1920)

The first decade of the twentieth century brought deepening crisis to Mexico. The cost of food soared owing to the predominance of export agriculture, the inefficiency of the central Mexican *hacienda*, and poor weather conditions. Inflation worsened in 1905 when Mexico's adoption of the gold standard raised the price of imported goods. Economic depression, beginning in the United States in 1907, led to a withdrawal of capital from the country and a shrinkage of export markets. In its wake came a flurry of bankruptcies and rising unemployment. In 1906, workers in the textile, mining, and railroad industries launched major strikes. In Morelos, sugar production increased at the expense of village lands which disappeared at a devastating rate. Between 1895 and 1910, the real wages of rural workers in central and southern Mexico declined by 17 percent. The number and severity of mining accidents in the north seemed to increase—or at least to receive more public attention.[1]

The regime began to recognize contradictions between national development and foreign-dominated growth. The government purchased a majority of stock in the railroads to prevent a possible takeover by U.S. monopolies. A committee appointed in 1904 suggested reforms in the mining code which would retrieve some public control over the subsoil and would make owners responsible for the safety of their workers. From supporters of the regime came criticism of unproductive *hacienda* agriculture. The government responded with confusion to the militancy of industrial workers. At first, Díaz showed himself prepared to abandon laissez-faire gospel for arbitration, then reverted to a policy of repression and nonintervention. In

1. On Morelos, see Womack, *Zapata*, pp. 37–66; on central Mexico, Clark Reynolds, *The Mexican Economy; Twentieth-Century Structure and Growth* (New Haven: Yale University Press, 1970), p. 20; on mining accidents, Ildefonso Villarello Vélez, *Historia de la Revolución mexicana en Coahuila*, pp. 93–94; Ramón Eduardo Ruíz, *Labor and the Ambivalent Revolutionaries: Mexico, 1911–1923* (Baltimore: Johns Hopkins University Press, 1976), pp. 7–8; *El Imparcial*, 13–14 Oct. 1910.

most instances, efforts at reform and redirection were stymied by powerful opposition from vested interests—foreign and national.[2]

The crisis accentuated differences within the Porfirian elite which in turn heightened old divisions between center and periphery, between Mexico City and the states. As Díaz' sixth election approached in 1910, factions within the oligarchy fought to capture the vice-presidential candidacy on the assumption that the 80-year-old dictator would die in the next term. Internecine political struggle carried into the electoral arena broke the tightness of the Díaz political machine and drew into the political sphere the disenfranchised: peasants, workers, and middle-income groups, whose grievances against the regime were much more serious and threatening to the ruling groups than the differences factionalizing them. When oligarchic elements recognized the revolutionary potential of their challenge, they withdrew and left the swelling field of expectation open to Francisco I. Madero, son of one of Mexico's wealthiest families, who dared to challenge Díaz in the 1910 elections. With sufficient national mobilization, Madero forces were able to defeat the dictator by armed force in February 1911 on the principle of effective suffrage and no reelection—the very slogan through which Díaz had come to power 35 years before.

The Mexican Revolution (1910–1917) was an extremely complex event which must here be treated schematically in order to establish a framework for understanding the evolution of educational thought and policy.[3] The Revolution was not a process in which one social class sought to overturn another. Although the Porfirian ruling class

2. On railroads see, for example, U.S. Senate, *Investigation of Mexican Affairs* 1:1787–89; on mining legislation and opposition to it, see Marvin Bernstein, *The Mexican Mining Industry, 1890–1950: A Study of the Interaction of Politics, Economics, and Technology* (Albany: State University of New York, 1964), pp. 78–80; on criticism of the *hacienda*, see Córdova, *La ideología de la Revolución mexicana*, pp. 113–35; on the labor question, Rodney Anderson, *Outcasts in their own Land: Mexican Industrial Workers, 1906–1911*, pp. 129–33, 152–53, 204–6, 215–20, 229–30; for an interesting case study of opposition to proposed reforms, see William K. Meyers, "Politics, Vested Rights, and Economic Growth in Porfirian Mexico: The Company of Tlahualilo in the Comarca Lagunera, 1885–1911," *Hispanic American Historical Review* 57 (1977): 425–54.

3. For recent efforts to place the Mexican Revolution in a theoretical framework, see *Interpretaciones de la Revolución mexicana* by Hector Aguilar Camín et al. (Mexico: Editorial Nueva Imagen, 1979). Recent scholarship on the Mexican Revolution and its implications for interpretation are discussed in David C. Bailey, "Revisionism and the Recent Historiography of the Mexican Revolution," *Hispanic American Historical Review* 58 (1978): 62–79.

lost its power with the disintegration of the state apparatus in 1913–1914, no cohesively organized groups representing clear class interests immediately replaced it. In many ways, the Mexican Revolution was a reaction against consequences of dependent capitalist modernization on the part of various social classes and groups with different goals and interests. The peasants, dispossessed of their lands by advancing large-scale production, often wished to return to an earlier period of small property holdings. Although numerically they made up a large part of the revolutionary forces, as a class they lacked unity and political organization. The working class was relatively small and of recent formation. Ideologically immature, organizationally embryonic, and numerically small, the industrial working class was not in 1910 capable of leading a social revolution although sectors of it were militant in their demands for economic amelioration and political rights. In the course of the Revolution, the working class grew in ideological and organizational sophistication and capacity.

The third constituent group of the Revolution consisted of small-to medium-size rural and urban businessmen and urban professionals and bureaucrats. Varyingly referred to as middle strata, petite bourgeoisie, or middle sector, this social grouping played a preponderant role in the Revolution for two reasons.[4] First, they were numerically and politically important because of Mexico's state of economic growth. Some were survivors of an earlier precapitalist era and beneficiaries of the still largely small-scale nature of production. Many were products of modernization—of an expanding state bureaucracy, increased urbanization and industrialization, and the creation of national and international trade networks. Some had experienced downward mobility as a result of growing concentration of property. Others, who had acquired holdings which began to flourish with market development, saw their possibilities for further expansion blocked by increasing monopolization. Many urban professionals and bureaucrats had had expectations of upward mobility thwarted by the closed nature of the Díaz political machine. Second,

---

4. I am here using the terms "middle sector" and "petit bourgeois" interchangeably. I would include in these categories both the traditional small property owners producing without the use of non-family labor (or a negligible amount of the same), the professional and bureaucratic sectors which expanded with state formation and market growth in the *Porfiriato*, and the medium-size businessmen and farmers, who also benefited from modernization. For further analysis of the role of the middle sectors in the Revolution, see Manuel Villa, "Discusión de algunas categorías para el análisis de la Revolución mexicana," pp. 25–38.

the middle sectors were important to the Revolution because of the relative political weakness of other social classes: the peasantry, the working class, and the temporarily dislodged Porfirian bourgeoisie and their foreign counterparts. In a situation described by one Mexican scholar as a catastrophic balance in which no social class could establish dominion over another, leadership of middle-sector origin emerged from within the revolutionary Constitutional armies which possessed the organizational capacity to fill the power vacuum left by the destruction of the Porfirian state. Ostensibly, this leadership came to constitute a political-military bureaucracy which was "above" and "apart from" social classes but in fact consistently functioned within a capitalist framework.[5]

As a social group, the middle sectors were not ideologically monolithic but rather expressed many of the contradictions classically associated with the petite bourgeoisie. Many wished a return to small property; others had an appreciation of the importance of large-scale production. Some favored continued development of an agro-export economy; others saw the need to expand an industrial base. Some identified with the demands of the peasantry and working class for structural social reforms; others were concerned with their own upward mobility. Some were reluctant to acknowledge state responsibility for social reform and clung to nineteenth-century liberal doctrines of laissez faire. Others strongly advocated such state responsibility. Most were nationalist and favored greater Mexican control over economy and society, but their nationalism varied in degree.

The strategy of political leadership did not emerge full-blown but developed gradually in response to revolutionary conditions and a high level of class conflict. Thus, the Revolution's first leader, Francisco I. Madero, posited a purely political revolution and had little understanding of the social and economic grievances of workers and peasants, many of whom became alienated from his government. Madero relied on the old Porfirian army and its civilian representatives to deal with dissident forces like those of Morelos peasant leader Emiliano Zapata, and so provided the conditions for his own assassination in February 1913 in the coup of Porfirian General Victoriano Huerta. In April 1913 when Venustiano Carranza, governor of Coahuila, called for the formation of a revolutionary army to overthrow Huerta, he also thought in terms of a political revolution which would

---

5. For a discussion of the idea of catastrophic balance and the emergence of a political-military bureaucracy, see, for example, Juan Felipe Leal, "The Mexican State, 1915–1973: A Historical Interpretation," pp. 50–51.

introduce some modernizing reforms but without seriously altering the structure of property. However, the open conflict which developed between the Constitutional armies, headed by Carranza, and the more popular and radical forces led by Zapata and Francisco Villa made it necessary for Carranza to woo both peasant and worker support with promises of some land reform and worker rights. In fact, in the Constitutionalists' defeat of Zapata and Villa, the alliance between the Carranza forces and the organized workers' movement, orchestrated by Sonoran General Alvaro Obregón, was of key importance insofar as it pitted the organized labor movement against the peasants and allowed the Constitutional armies to establish tentative dominion over both workers and peasants. However, the maintenance of such control depended upon the capacity of the Constitutionalists to accommodate popular demands. That Carranza's adhesion to social reform was purely expedient and superficial became clear at the Constitutional Convention convened in December 1916. Carranza's draft was little more than a rewriting of the Constitution of 1857 and so provoked strong opposition from a large group of deputies, who broadly fell into two ideological camps. On the one hand, there had emerged a radical, popular current deeply and primarily concerned with a revindication of the rights of the subordinate classes. Although there was anticapitalist sentiment in this group, they presented no coherent socialist alternative. At the convention, they were led by Francisco Mújica, a young general from Michoacán who was the son of a school teacher. Also among the opposition was a pragmatic, conciliating faction led by General Alvaro Obregón and others from the northern state of Sonora who believed in capitalist modernization but who understood better than Carranza the importance of social reform and an expedient alliance with labor and the peasantry as a means of weakening the old owning class and its foreign allies. These combined forces—the radicals and the pragmatists—insured the incorporation into the Constitution of 1917 of clauses favoring land reform (Article 27), workers' rights (Article 123), and a curtailment of the Church's role in society (Articles 3, 27, and 130). Their nationalism was reflected in clauses limiting foreign participation in the economy and reclaiming the Mexican subsoil for the nation as represented by the state (Article 27).

When Carranza as president from 1917 to 1920 proved inept at restoring economic order or providing reforms to insurgent worker and peasant groups, General Alvaro Obregón mobilized a revolt to prevent Carranza's imposition of a presidential candidate to succeed him. In the 1920s under the presidencies of Obregón and his Sono-

ran colleague Plutarco Elías Calles, the modernizing faction undertook the construction of the new state. Implicitly authoritarian and
centralized, this state would expand upon the role of its Porfirian
predecessor in creating conditions for private capital accumulation,
while at the same time seeking to regulate relations between different
social classes in the interests of capital.[6] An "active" state, it would
seek to correct through new policies and institutions some of the economic and social bottlenecks inherent in the Porfirian model, i.e., the
persistence of precapitalist enclaves, the tendency toward unproductive investment, foreign hegemony over natural resources and the
primary producing sector, concentration of wealth, and neglect of the
exploited classes. The articulated goal of most revolutionary leaders
was the creation of an autonomous national economy capable of generating widespread well-being. It was not possible in the long run to
achieve this goal, as the root of the problem—capitalism in its dependent form—persisted.

Although educational thought and policy reflected conditions of
fluidity and conflict, certain common tendencies were exhibited by
middle-sector revolutionaries in relation to schooling. Universally rejected was Justo Sierra's view of society as an organic hierarchy gov-
erned by "scientific" laws of evolution. In the opinion of educators,
this model had led to a monopolization of wealth inhibiting economic
growth, individual initiative, and material well-being. In its place,
most middle-sector educators envisioned a society based upon individual entrepreneurship, competition, and political democracy. Each
member of society would increase his or her productive capacity and
reap greater benefit from doing so. Universal mass education became
a priority to increase skills and material well-being and to modernize
attitudes for increased production within the context of an increasingly specialized and complex economic structure. Further, education
was to capacitate the citizen for participation in democracy. Both
goals, the revolutionaries believed, called for a more open, pragmatic
pedagogy immediately applicable to the material improvement of
daily life. On the same grounds that Justo Sierra had once dismissed
the Lancasterian school in favor of his faculty development pedagogy,
so revolutionary educators judged the Porfirian school to be authoritarian, theoretical, and divorced from reality. Overall, however, the
goals of Porfirian and revolutionary educators were similar: to elimi-

6. For a developed discussion of the similarities and continuities between the Porfirian and revolutionary states, see Córdova, *La ideología de la Revolución mexicana*, and
Lorenzo Meyer, "Historical Roots of the Authoritarian State in Mexico," pp. 3–22.

nate precapitalist structures and values to allow for a greater development of the nation's productive forces within a capitalist framework; to cement national unity; to preserve social order; and to elevate the "moral" level of the Mexican people.

The contradictions in educational thought revolved around notions of private property and social order. While most middle-sector educators envisioned a society based upon small property, they often overlooked the fact that competition would lead to a reconcentration of wealth. While many spokesmen proposed cooperatives as a safeguard against deepening inequality in a competitive system and/or an active state which would regulate the distribution of wealth and opportunity, most acknowledged the need for large-scale private industry and the subordination of labor to capital. The latter potentially limited the educators' hope that schooling would increase material well-being for all in an equitable manner. This problem was aggravated by the country's scarce resource base and persistent economic dependency, which educators inadequately understood or challenged. Finally, many educators recognized the need for social control over the insurgent peasantry and working class and so contradicted their own commitment to democracy in their implicit and often explicit support for a strong state capable of controlling the masses and establishing social order. In a variety of ways, support for renewed authoritarianism was to make its way into school policies, programs, and methods—especially after 1920.

The Mexican Revolution produced a mandate from mass education far more profound than had existed in the *Porfiriato*. In part, this mandate was put forward by petit bourgeois educators, but it was strongly advocated by the organized popular forces themselves—peasants, workers, and those middle-sector individuals most identified with their interests. Education for improved agricultural production formed part of the program of the Zapatistas. Pancho Villa, who had learned to read and write in Tlatelolco prison in 1912, ordered schools built wherever he went. For many in the days of struggle, books suddenly became a path to emancipation. One day in December 1914 in the Ministry of War, the well-heeled young intellectual Martín Luis Guzmán found semiliterate Villista General José Isabel Robles reading Plutarch's *Lives*. He had sacked it from a mansion in Torreón, he told Guzmán: now he wished he had taken more. Labor leader Rosendo Salazar remembered that in the early years when the printers organized the Casa del Obrero Mundial in the capital, they had longed for education which would help them fight the *burguesía*. In Luis Mendez' tailor shop, Colombian anarchist Juan Francisco

Moncaleano, known as a "Citizen of the World," introduced them to Peter Kropotkin's *Conquest of Bread* and Max Simon Nordau's *The Conventional Lies of Civilization*. Salazar recalled how the Revolution opened Mexico to the ideas of workers' rights. Books on anarchism and socialism began to arrive from South America and Europe.[7]

It is difficult to characterize the general attitudes of the popular forces toward education because these ideas were more dispersed, less articulated in print, and usually less developed than those of the middle strata. It would seem that, in most cases, while the popular forces supported mass education, they were not aware of the ways in which petit bourgeois educators associated with the emerging state wished to use schooling to continue the subordinate status of the dominated classes. Nor did the popular forces articulate clear alternatives to the middle-sector ideology of schooling as it emerged in these early years of struggle. Thus the general weakness of peasants and workers as class forces in the Revolution was paralleled in their approach to schooling. The exception was the organized labor movement's support for the *Escuela Racionalista*, based upon the ideas of Spanish anarchist Francisco Ferrer Guardia.[8] A pedagogy in principle aimed at liberation from bourgeois ideology, it was poorly developed between 1910 and 1920 except in Yucatán where the Partido Socialista, a mass-based movement of peasants and workers, put it into operation between 1918 and 1924. Here it meshed with revisionist North American and European precepts of pragmatic, child-centered learning to produce within the context of a struggle for social reform an apparent integration between the school, material improvement in daily life, political action, and a critical perspective on capitalism. The experience in Yucatán foreshadowed the official *Escuela Socialista* of the 1930s.

This chapter seeks to illustrate the evolution of educational thought in the revolutionary context. It concentrates on intellectuals and officeholders associated with the Constitutional forces whose ideas seem best to illustrate emerging thinking on schooling. Actual policy implementation is less a focus in this chapter because in the

7. On the Zapatistas and education, see, for example, *El Liberal*, 15 Jan. 1915; on Villa, see Vito Alessio Robles, "La Convención de Aguascalientes," *Todo*, 7 Dec. 1950, p. 13; on José Isabel Robles, see Martín Luis Guzmán, "Un ministro de guerra," *El Universal*, 25 March 1927; on the labor movement, see Rosendo Salazar, *Las pugnas de la gleba. Los albores del movimiento obrero en México* (Mexico: Comisión Nacional Editorial, PRI, 1972), pp. 36–37.

8. The *Escuela Racionalista* was endorsed by the Casa del Obrero Mundial, 1912, the Congreso Preliminar Obrero, Veracruz, 1916, the Confederación Regional Obrero de

years of fighting, policy was not consistently implemented. In some places, schools hardly functioned. Important innovations in the capital and states are mentioned, with special emphasis on Yucatán as a study demonstrating the class dimensions of schooling.

Finally, the debates at the Constitutional Convention are examined. Although the delegates did not explicitly address questions of pedagogy or educational philosophy, the debates focused on two questions of importance to the ideology and structure of Mexican schooling. The first was the issue of the Catholic Church, whose influence in education many hoped to eliminate. The most vehement anticlerical delegates belonged to the factions opposing Carranza's draft. These fell into two categories. The vigorous and pragmatic capitalist modernizers from the north, led by the Sonoran faction, associated the Church with Mexican backwardness and individual inertia and superstition. On the other hand, there were delegates closer to the labor and peasant movements who identified the Church more explicitly with exploitation and oppression of the poor. Although elementary, theirs was more a class perspective than an individualistic one. While anticlerical as well, the liberals around Carranza were more tolerant of Catholic education. Because the radical anticlericals carried more weight at the convention than the liberals, they were able to pass clauses drastically limiting the Church's power in education—especially at the primary level.

The second issue in the Constitutional debates concerned jurisdictional control over public schools. Out of respect for the principles of municipal autonomy and states' rights espoused as an antidote to the centralism of the dictatorship, delegates voted to abolish the Secretaría de Instrucción Pública. However, because the convention debates revealed support for a strong central state capable of carrying out modernization and social reform, it is not surprising that when municipalities proved to be too financially weak to handle the costs of schooling, a base of support emerged from a wide range of political groups for the establishment in 1921 of the Secretaría de Educación Pública (SEP), which would enjoy a national jurisdiction far beyond that exercised by its Porfirian predecessor.

México, 1918–1924, the anarchist Confederación General de Trabajadores, and the Communist party in the 1920s. See Salazar, *Las pugnas*, pp. 37, 70–72, 115, 121–22, 148, 202, 205, 300. See *El Liberal*, 1 Oct. 1914. It also received support from agrarian organizations. See, for example, Isidro de Flores, Presidente, Congreso Campesino Agrarista del Estado de Durango, to Calles, 2 Jan. 1925, Archivo General de la Nación, Acervos Presidentes, Ramo Presidentes Obregón-Calles (hereafter cited as ANG, Acervos Presidentes), Expediente 121-E-E-66. See also *Excelsior*, 4 Jan. 1927.

Evolving Educational Thought and Policy in Mexico City, 1910–1920

From the beginning of the Revolution, educational thought contained contradictions. Francisco I. Madero was typical in expressing a naive axiomatic connection between increased knowledge and increased benefits on the one hand and knowledge of democratic rights and their exercise on the other.[9] He assumed these connections without acknowledging the need for structural reforms and property redistribution in an extremely inegalitarian and oppressive society. While similarly refraining from support for such reforms, Alberto J. Pani, Undersecretary of Education in the Madero government in 1912, carried Madero's notions a step further. In reference to a law hurriedly passed by Congress in June 1911, which authorized the federal government to create rural rudimentary schools for the indigenous population, Pani suggested the need for a more pragmatic and technical education in rural areas which would improve local agriculture and industry, especially crafts. His proposal was based upon two assumptions. Such an education would "integrate" peasants as producers into the market economy while expanding national production and exports. It would also serve as a mechanism for social control. If the intellectual level of the "most ignorant" was raised without a corresponding increase in material well-being, Pani argued, education would create a permanent state of discontent:

> It will prepare an open field for the demagogues . . . to preach the agrarian socialism of the Orozco or Zapata variety, i.e., the violent destruction of the landowners.[10]

If rural teachers came from the villages themselves, he reasoned, education would be more effective. This suggestion, as well as his call for the creation of regional rural normal schools, was later incorporated into school policy.

Carrying forward a concern of Sierra's in urban education, Pani, a graduate of the engineering school, favored increased technical

9. See, for example, Francisco I. Madero, *La sucesión presidencial* (Mexico: Librería de la Viuda de Ch. Bouret, 1911), pp. 233–41; *El Partido Nacional Anti-Reeleccionista y la próxima lucha electoral. Su programa, sus trabajos, tendencias, aspiraciones*, March 1910, Archivos de Francisco I. Madero, p. 20.

10. Alberto J. Pani, *La instrucción rudimentaria en la república. Estudio presentado por vía de información al C. Ministerio del Ramo por el Ing. Alberto J. Pani, Subsecretario de Instrucción Pública y Bellas Artes* (Mexico: Secretaría de Instrucción Pública y Bellas Artes, 1912), pp. 20–21.

training to upgrade skills for greater and more complicated production. In 1912, he helped to create the Universidad Popular, Mexico's first university extension program, graced by the cream of the capital's young intelligentsia. Although the latter liked to think that their initiative was original and demonstrative of their concern for the welfare of the *desheredados*, abandoned by the dictatorship, the Universidad Popular can be seen as a continuation of the adult worker schools introduced in the restored republic and developed in the *Porfiriato*.[11] In addition to skill upgrading, the Universidad Popular like the Porfirian worker schools aimed at political domestication and socialization. In fact, the overwhelming thrust of the school was toward disciplining the working class, then in a state of increasing militancy. This approach was clear both in political economy classes and in the use of art to moralize the poor. In their lectures on political economy, Universidad Popular personnel stressed the need for private capital accumulation and argued that wealth had to be concentrated in the hands of a few to be effective for all. To the workers, they preached the work ethic, the need for savings, and the importance of abstaining from alcohol and gambling. Advocates of a classical approach, they held that the price of labor was determined by free market interplay, that worker demands could close an industry, and that strikes were no solution to problems. Workers should restrain their "egotism." In suggesting that workers should depend upon the good will of the employer, who should administer wealth in accord with social needs, the lecturers expressed a desire to create a moral social order in which employers would cease to be "greedy" and would practice "social responsibility." In their suggestion that, as a last resort, workers should rely upon state intervention in labor disputes, they anticipated what was to become part of the ideology of the emerging state.[12]

A somewhat greater understanding of the need to accommodate

11. Most scholars emphasize the innovative and progressive aspects of the Universidad Popular—at least in part because its founders and participants did so. See, for example, John S. Innes, "La Universidad Popular Mexicana," *The Americas* 30 (1973): 110–22; Enrique Krauze, *Los caudillos culturales de la Revolución mexicana* (Mexico: Siglo Veintiuno Editores, 1976), pp. 48–50; Henry C. Schmidt, *The Roots of Lo Mexicano: Self and Society in Mexican Thought, 1900–1934* (College Station: Texas A & M Press, 1978), pp. 73–75; Michael C. Meyer and William Sherman, *The Course of Mexican History* (New York and London: Oxford University Press, 1979), p. 562. The question is further explored in chapter 8.

12. *Boletín de la Universidad Popular Mexicana* 1, no. 4 (1914): 69–70; 2, no. 1 (1916): 9; 2, no. 4 (1916): 175.

the demands of the popular classes was articulated by Felix F. Palavicini, acting official in charge of education (1914–1916) under General Venustiano Carranza. A graduate of Tabasco's Instituto Juárez with a degree in topographical engineering, Palavicini had come to the capital in 1903 where he had accepted a minor post teaching manual arts in the practice school attached to the Escuela Normal de Profesores. In 1906, Sierra sent him briefly to Europe to study vocational school systems. He became involved in the anti-reelectionist movement, supported the candidacy of Francisco I. Madero, and, presumably in recognition for his services, was made director of the Escuela Industrial de Huérfanos in 1912. Elected to the Twenty-sixth Congress during the Madero presidency, Palavicini formed part of the group of deputies known as the *renovadores* who because they remained in Congress following the assassination of Madero were mistrusted by those Constitutionalists who had joined the rebel armies under Carranza. In the summer of 1914 on the eve of the Constitutional victory, Palavicini attached himself to Carranza, who made him responsible for educational policy.[13]

Basically a classical liberal like Carranza, Palavicini understood the need to incorporate certain popular demands for social reform. Thus he admitted the need for workers' rights and some land reform. For him, the most immediate task of the Revolution was to steer an even course between two forces: the Porfirian elite and their foreign counterparts, on the one hand, and the mobilized popular classes on the other. As a member of what he termed the "*clase media intelectual*," Palavicini believed he had been victimized by soaring prices for consumer goods, high rents, shoddy products, and limited career advancement, all of which he attributed, in a fashion customary among middle-sector revolutionaries, to "monopolies." Like many of his peers, he believed monopolies to be the result not of laws of accumulation but of human greed. The elite, he argued, had sacrificed their sense of patriotism and social responsibility to their desire to be rich. They had abandoned the masses to injustice and misery and thus had provoked the uprising.[14] However, Palavicini's attitude toward the abandoned majority was one of fear and arrogance. For Palavicini, Mexico's greatest national problem was "to civilize two-

13. Biographical information on Palavicini is from *Boletín de Educación* 1, no. 1 (1914): 9.
14. Félix F. Palavicini, *Pro-patria. Apuntes de sociología mexicana* (Mexico: Tipografía La Ilustración, 1905), pp. 57–58; Félix F. Palavicini, *La patria por la escuela* (Mexico: Linotipografía, 1916), p. 87.

thirds of the population," whom he referred to as the "deaf, and dumb . . . only heard in explosions of savagery in the fields of Morelos and mountains of Guerrero."[15] He warned of the threat posed to property and the state by an unschooled people:

> Children abandoned to the immorality of the gutter, the filth of the factories, and the temptation of vice, will be the men who form our society of tomorrow, citizens of a people sovereign by law. If we leave this sovereign people to educate itself in the school of misery, they will learn everything which hunger dictates to the minds of the ignorant . . . We will see dreadful passions of hatred and envy develop. Utopians, apostles of anarchy and communism, have preached among the abandoned. . . . Do we want this volcanic passion of envy to spill over with the force of numbers to envelop the model society and covet its future?

> From the pallid lips of wives and mothers will come the first phrases of children . . . in a seething oration of hate . . . They will grow with incongruent impulses without discipline or orientation . . . While the disciples of Max Stirner and Nietzsche await the triumph of a superman . . . a stronger force can emerge from the union of proletarians who organize, form unions, and join hands as a single strong body sustaining the torch which illuminates consciences and the hatchet which breaks their chains. If this force surprises us as enemies rather than allies, we will be the losers.[16]

Thus while some Porfirian spokesmen had once opposed education on the grounds that it would increase the capacity for social revolution, Palavicini illustrated the emerging conviction among petit bourgeois revolutionary educators of the need for education as a mechanism to prevent social protest.

However, he was prepared to accept some structural changes in order to solve the twin problems of monopolization and popular insurgency. He envisioned an economy based upon small property within which schooling would effect economic betterment while educating citizens for an exercise of their duties and rights without injurying the guarantees of others.[17] A fundamental guarantee was that

15. Palavicini, *La patria por la escuela*, pp. 202–3; Félix F. Palavicini, *Problemas de la educación* (Valencia: F. Sempere y Compañia, Editores, 1910), p. 37; *Boletín de Educación* 1, no. 4 (1916): 30.

16. Palavicini, *Problemas de la educación*, pp. 12–14.

17. Palavicini, *La patria por la escuela*, pp. 27–28, 88, 161, 204; Félix F. Palavicini, *Mi vida revolucionaria* (Mexico: Ediciones Botas, 1937), pp. 236–37; Félix F. Palavicini, *Palabras y acciones* (Mexico: n.p., 1919), p. 53.

of property.[18] He advocated land reform to restore illegally usurped *ejido* (communal) lands. Such a reform would create small farmers for participation in the market economy. By teaching the farmer better use of his lands and methods for improving local industries and crafts, education would help the *campesino* to defend himself against the "exploitative instinct" of owners of land and capital.[19] In the urban setting, he believed the problem of poverty would be resolved through the development of small industries. "One hundred small shoe shops using five workers," he argued, "produce more general well-being and greater public wealth than the property of a banker employing 500 workers."[20]

The above thinking revealed weaknesses in the emerging educational paradigm. One, it assumed that simple skill-upgrading among rural producers could free them from domination by local merchants, large landowners, and political power-holders when in fact profound structural reforms dismantling local structures of domination and exploitation were necessary. Second, while Palavicini's vision of a society of small producers was consistent with the still largely artisan status of Mexican industry and the ideals of many of the *petite bourgeoisie*, it was incompatible with the commitment to economic development within a free enterprise framework which implied expansion and concentration of ownership to exploit economies of scale. This contradiction affected both the urban and rural sectors. Palavicini stumbled upon this problem when he confronted urban workers. In the course of the Revolution, increased trade union militancy provoked him to defend capital against the demands of workers. If the "lions" had to be fought, he declared in reference to the monopolists, "we must also protect ourselves against the poisonous insects and coward reptiles . . . the trade unionists." The obligation of the state was to "protect the interests of all classes . . . the property of all citizens" against the excesses of a "few corrupted ones . . . traitors to the sacred interests of the nation."[21] Workers had to learn that capital accumulation was necessary to the creation of employment. He began to alter his position on small- versus large-scale industry. He said:

> The improvement of social conditions . . . will not be achieved through a redistribution of wealth, it will be won through in-

---

18. Palavicini, *Problemas de la educación*, p. 35.

19. *Boletín de Educación* 1, no. 2 (1915): 104; Palavicini, *Problemas de la educación*, p. 43.

20. Palavicini, *Pro-patria*, pp. 42–43.

21. Palavicini, *Palabras y acciones*, pp. 39–43.

creasing the commonwealth, intensifying and perfecting production . . . Industrialism . . . is the master of the modern world
. . . A million pesos used in industry produces another million
each year in workers' wages. What more can the proletariat ask
than that many capitalists establish factories so that their wages
multiply and increase.[22]

In this situation, Palavicini held that the basis for improved wages
was improved productivity, which could be realized through hard
work and schooling.[23]

Three further contradictions emerged in Palavicini's thought
which were characteristic of most middle-sector educators. First, the
notion of economic amelioration through schooling underwent a
change when it affected the propertyless urban worker who could
expect increased benefits only if he performed more efficiently for
the entrepreneur who purchased his labor power. Insofar as this approach admitted to trade unionism at all, the form of unionism compatible with it was one which recognized the coexistence of labor and
capital within a context of subordination of the former to the latter.
Secondly, to make this approach functional, a strong and implicitly
authoritarian state had to be built to regulate relations between capital and labor while repressing more militant sectors of the working
class. Palavicini suggested such a solution when he warned Carranza:
"Before the latent hostility of the proletarian class, the demands of
the revolutionaries, and the disturbances of the demagogues, the
government has to be stronger than ever."[24]

He presented a third contradiction typical of middle-sector educators in his ambiguous attitude toward the United States. This ambi-
guity, implying as it did a continuation of dependency, suggested
limitations on the ability of schooling to generate widespread well-
being. Most middle-sector revolutionaries stood strongly opposed to
growing U.S. domination of Mexico. Yet, middle-sector educational
thought revealed deep admiration for the United States. This admiration stemmed from several factors including the socialization
process of the middle strata. Most had grown up in a period of im-
pressive U.S. expansion; those from the north of Mexico had been
especially exposed to it and were both the most nationalistic and the
most imitative. Middle-sector revolutionary educators also tended to

22. As cited by Palavicini in *Mi vida revolucionaria*, p. 363.
23. Palavicini, *La patria por la escuela*, p. 203; Palavicini, *Palabras y acciones*, p. 89;
Palavicini, *Problemas de la educación*, pp. 14–15, 26, 49, 52, 70, 89.
24. As cited by Palavicini in *Mi vida revolucionaria*, pp. 346–47.

identify in greater or lesser degree with the North American progressive movement, especially in its critique of political machines and industrial monopolies. Palavicini sent teachers to the United States to observe the balance which he believed existed there between economic growth, individual initiative, and political obedience.[25]

Most middle-sector revolutionaries were anti-imperialist in the sense that they sought a renegotiation with foreign capital which would prevent a plundering of natural resources and would submit foreigners to partnership with national capital in Mexican development. Like Sierra and other nineteenth-century thinkers, they underestimated the laws of uneven development. Most held a fragmented and anachronistic vision of the northern neighbor as a nation of hard-working, striving yeomen and failed to see that competitive entrepreneurial capitalism in the United States had yielded at the turn of the century to large-scale corporate organization of financial and business interests, to which the U.S. state responded by expanding its capacity to regulate and defend this structure both at home and abroad.[26] Thus, one dilemma besetting Mexican anti-imperialism was, on the one hand, the increased capacity of the U.S. state to represent United States business interests abroad and hence to force compromises from the Mexicans of benefit to the United States, and, secondly, the uneven partnership between Mexican and U.S. capital owing to the hegemony of the United States in large-scale industrial production and trade.[27] As Palavicini sensed this problem, he noted the need for a strong state capable of negotiating with the United States for better terms of participation; he thus anticipated the emerging model of the active, developmentalist state which would attempt to regulate economic growth in the national interest. He further recognized that the weakness of Mexican industry in relation to its foreign counterparts would require material sacrifices from Mexican workers. "We have a nascent industry which can be great if we

25. *Boletín de Educación* 1, no. 2 (1915): 89.

26. For description of the process of transformation from competitive to monopoly capitalism and growth of the state in the United States, see Weinstein, *The Corporate Ideal*, and Robert H. Wiebe, *The Search for Order, 1877–1920* (New York: Hill and Wang, 1967).

27. For a brief resume of the political and economic role of the United States in the initial years of the Mexican Revolution and the 1920s, see José Luis Ceceña, *México en la órbita imperial. Las empresas transnacionales* (Mexico: Ediciones El Caballito, 1979), pp. 10–22; for a more detailed discussion, see Robert Freeman Smith, *The United States and Revolutionary Nationalism in Mexico, 1916–1932* (Chicago: University of Chicago Press, 1972).

know how to stimulate it," he said. Such stimulus required caution in conceding to workers' demands, he advised.[28]

Further, as in the *Porfiriato*, capital scarcity in the still dependent country required the state's selection of educational priorities. While commitment to mass education was greater than it had been in the *Porfiriato*, priorities in relation to economic growth would lead to a reinforcement of the hierarchical structure of schooling, which implied that the possibility for mobility through the school system would remain limited. While Palavicini favored primary schooling for the majority, he believed higher education should be reserved for the "select minorities."[29] Following Sierra's trajectory and reflecting the need for more specialized labor, educators in the capital expressed an increased concern for technical training, which suggested the simultaneous creation of opportunities for some and the deepening of a tracking system.[30] Palavicini noted that primary industrial and commercial schools created by Sierra were deficient in their technical aspects and had often served as stepping stones to preparatory and university training, thus contributing, according to Palavicini, to an already overstaffed bureaucracy.[31] He moved to make vocational school certificates trade specific and definitive. To further the development of national industry, he converted the Escuela de Artes y Oficios para Hombres into the Escuela Práctica de Ingenieros Mecánicos y Electricistas, designed to train mechanical and electrical engineers as well as electricians, machinists, and auto mechanics. He also founded the Escuela Nacional de Químicas to promote a national chemical industry based on Mexican primary products. Although originally intended to train skilled workers, the chemistry school became a professional school. Not surprisingly, Palavicini stepped up emphasis upon practice and application in other professional schools such as engineering with the explicit end of replacing foreign engineers and construction contractors.[32] Although this expansion in vocational schooling offered mobility to some individuals who could afford to stay in school over long periods of time, it also strengthened the tracking system designed to differentiate the labor force. The

28. As cited by Palavicini in *Mi vida revolucionaria*, pp. 363–64.
29. Palavicini, *Problemas de la educación*, pp. 57–58.
30. For expansion of technical and night schools, see Carranza's presidential reports for 1916–1919 in *La educación pública en México a través de los mensajes presidenciales* (Mexico: SEP, 1926), pp. 187, 193, 197.
31. See, for example, report on the Escuela Industrial José María Chávez, *Boletín de Educación* 1, no. 1 (1914): 107–8.
32. On this trend, see *Excelsior*, 2, 4 Jan. 1920.

proliferation of night schools, where workers could pick up a course in a specific trade, might have assisted some to upgrade their skills on an individual basis. It also testifies to the expansion of schooling in general which occurred simultaneously with the school system's deepening hierarchization.

Innovations in primary education in Mexico City were in keeping with Palavicini's ideas. Educational officials—former Porfirian bureaucrats as well as recent graduates of the capital professional and normal schools—criticized the Porfirian school program as abstract and rigid.[33] They sought a more pragmatic pedagogy which would stimulate individual initiative while responding more effectively to the needs of practical life. They looked for an experimental method through which the student discovered scientific principles rather than absorbing them from teacher or text. To encourage individual development, prizes and awards were abolished on the grounds that they stimulated false vanity and prejudices. Educators wanted a program which would be directly utilitarian, i.e., aimed at increasing agricultural and industrial production. They called for texts which would guide children to the "laborious life of the field and shop." Such texts were also to stress patriotism.[34] To solve the problem of texts being expensive and in short supply and to insure that their content was in accord with official policy, Palavicini initiated the creation of an editorial department, which was to function more fully after 1920.

The stronger commitment to mass education generated by the Revolution also required an upgrading of the position of the school teacher. Not only was this recognition and remuneration a necessary part of an effective public school system, teachers in the Revolution began to demand it.[35] Politicians no doubt responded in part to win their support. Palavicini spoke of teachers' critical role in "*la magna obra renovadora*," which was education.[36] During his tenure a law on merit increases, promotions, and pensions was drawn up and dis-

33. *Informe rendido al C. Venustiano Carranza, Primer Jefe del Ejército Constitucional encargado del Poder Ejecutivo por el Prof. Andrés Osuna, Director General de Educación Pública, referente a los labores del año escolar de 1916* (Mexico: Departamento Editorial de la Dirección General de Educación Pública, 1917), pp. 8–9.

34. On texts, see, for example, ibid., pp. 37–38; *Boletín de Educación* 1, no. 2 (1915): 42–44.

35. See, for example, *Boletín de Educación* 1, no. 4 (1916): 463–72; Ezequiel Chávez, "Informe," Congreso de Maestros, Dec. 1919, AEC. For further examination of teachers, their organization, and demands see David Raby, *Educación y revolución social en México*, pp. 66–69.

36. *Boletín de Educación* 1, no. 2 (1915): 8; 1, no. 4 (1916): 83.

cussed although such legislation was not to be passed until 1929. Palavicini also claimed to have raised teachers' wages although it is
questionable how regularly they were paid in this period. He himself
contributed somewhat to their financial plight in his efforts to return
school control to the municipalities, most of which proved unable to
meet teachers' payrolls.

When Palavicini took office in August 1914, he immediately announced plans to dismantle the Secretaría de Instrucción Pública. He
argued that the ministry had been created especially for Justo Sierra
and had degenerated into a nest of corruption and political favoritism.[37] He further stated that a national ministry which had jurisdiction only over the Federal District and territories had no reason for
existing. Essentially his position reflected the classical liberal politics
of Venustiano Carranza, whose decree of December 25, 1914, established the principle of the self-governing municipality. Although the
Secretaría de Instrucción Pública was not repressed until after the
Constitutional Convention of 1916–1917, Palavicini initiated its dis-
memberment. The rudimentary schools created by the federal government as a result of legislation in June 1911 were turned over to
municipal and state governments. Schools in the territories passed to
military governors. A movement for university autonomy gained mo-
mentum. The scientific institutes were separated from the university
and turned over to the ministries of development and the interior.
The schools of fine arts and music, the museums and national library,
and inspection of monuments were detached from the university and
regrouped under a new Dirección General de Bellas Artes. The former Dirección General de Educación Primaria became the Dirección
General de Educación Pública, responsible for normal and preparatory schools as well as primary schools. A Dirección General de Enseñanza Técnica was established and was to be transferred to the
jurisdiction of the development ministry. However, until April 1917
when it was abolished, the education ministry continued to function
under Palavicini with three departments: the Dirección General de
Educación Pública, responsible for primary, preparatory, and normal
schools; the Dirección General de Enseñanza Técnica; and the Dirección General de Bellas Artes. The university was also subject to the
ministry. This internal structure anticipated that of the Secretaría de
Educación Pública, which was to be created in 1921.[38]

37. Palavicini, *La patria por la escuela*, pp. 44–46; see also articles by B. Vadillo in *El
Sol*, 22, 24 August 1914.
38. This reorganization is generally covered in *La educación pública en México a través
de los mensajes presidenciales*, pp. 184, 196–97, 420–21. See also *Boletín de Educación* 1,

Educational Activity in the States: The Case of Yucatán

While Palavicini's decentralization of education was to be reversed because it was an inadequate solution to what was judged to be a critical national problem, it is important to note the impetus for school construction and reform which came from the states in these years. The latter is not surprising given the mobilization of mass movements at this level and the participation of state school officials and teachers in the revolutionary process. Nor is it surprising that revolutionary state governors sometimes called upon Mexico City educators who had been part of Sierra's bureaucracy to assist in up-grading state school systems.

The first pedagogical congress of Guanajuato, one of several held in the states in these years, met in December 1915. It passed a number of resolutions designed to improve the practical aspect of Mexican education. Preparatory instruction, the delegates suggested, should be experimental in a manner stimulating student inventiveness. They wanted to create elementary schools of agriculture that would train practical farmers in a short period of time. They suggested that *hacienda* owners provide the schools on their properties with land, animals, orchards, and seeds. They asked that agricultural instruction be given by the state agriculture inspectors, while teachers themselves should learn how to teach modern farming techniques. The latter, they recommended, should be introduced to normal school training programs. Trade schools should be opened in industrial centers to train workers capable of competing with those of other countries. Savings banks, cooperatives, and open air playing fields were among the recommendations of the delegates. The importance of parent involvement and support for schooling was discussed. Teachers here had organized study groups to initiate literacy campaigns and "moral" conferences among adults and children. Delegates raised another demand typical of the period: teachers should be better paid.[39] Similarly, the Congreso Nacional de Maestros, meeting in Mexico City in December 1920, approved practical teaching to develop agriculture and industry adapted to local needs and recommended a pedagogy based on the "liberty of the child." Out of this

---

no. 1 (1914): 4–6; 1, no. 2 (1915): 13–14, 21–22, 161–62; 1, no. 4 (1916): 65–66, 189, 277; *El Liberal*, 28, 29 Oct., 1 Nov. 1914.

39. *Boletín de Educación* 1, no. 4 (1914): 455–77.

conference also came the formation of the first national teachers' leagues concerned with improved wages and working conditions.[40] Several revolutionary governors took up the issue of schools. As governor of Coahuila from 1911 to 1913, Carranza himself increased teachers' wages and sent teachers to the capital to study its school system. He expressed a particular interest in expanding industrial education.[41] Gustavo Espinosa Mireles, governor of Coahuila in 1915, was likewise concerned with teachers' wages and their training. He set up night schools for teacher preparation in five urban centers and created the Congreso Pedagógico Coahuilense de Educación Primaria, a body of teachers which would meet annually at vacation time to discuss teaching methods. He accelerated the construction of schools, including those for adults.[42] General Federico N. Montes, governor of Querétaro in 1915, brought Enrique Garduño from the Secretaría de Instrucción Pública to head the state Dirección General de Educación Popular. He raised teachers' wages, built primary schools, and concentrated on upgrading the quality of normal school training.[43] Carrancista governor Elizondo established a normal school in Morelia in 1915 and built over 100 primary schools in Michoacán. His successor, Governor Pascual Ortiz Rubio, founded the Universidad Michoacana by amalgamating existing professional schools and in 1919 called the state's first pedagogical conference. Attended by over 200 delegates from all over Mexico, the conference addressed such topics as the need to create a "single Mexican school" and to better teachers' wages and working conditions.[44] As governor of Sonora, Plutarco Elías Calles built primary schools, increased teachers' wages, and in 1915 founded two industrial schools (one for girls and one for boys) to train the poor (especially orphans of revo-

40. Eduardo Urzaiz, *Congreso Nacional de Maestros* (Mérida: Talleres Tipográficos del Gobierno del Estado, 1921), pp. 5–8, 14–15; *Excelsior*, 1, 13 Jan. 1921 on the formation of teachers' organizations.
41. Ildefonso Villarello Vélez, *Historia de la Revolución mexicana en Coahuila*, pp. 215–16.
42. Ibid., pp. 312–13, 316; Douglas Richmond, "Factional Political Strife in Coahuila, 1910–1920," *Hispanic American Historical Review* 60 (1980): 65. Espinosa Mireles was also a Protestant and thus received praise for his work in education from Samuel Guy Inman, *Intervention in Mexico*, pp. 65–66.
43. *Boletín de Educación* 1, no. 4 (1916): 481–89.
44. See Ezequiel Chávez, "Informe" Congreso de Maestros, Dec. 1919, AEC; David Raby, "Los principios de la educación rural en México: el caso de Michoacán, 1915–1929," *Historia Mexicana* 22 (1973): 555–56.

lutionary soldiers) in agriculture, small industries, commerce, and clerical work. In December 1915, he founded a normal school. In 1919, his successor Adolfo de la Huerta created a preparatory school, which provided an alternative to attending secondary school in the United States. However, in 1920, the director of education in Sonora lamented that pedagogy remained routine, unrelated to the needs of the era or the area and insufficient to correct the persistent "vices" of students, which he defined as dirtiness, lack of punctuality, negligence, inconstancy, squandering, lack of foresight, and lack of dominion over the will. Echoing a sentiment of his peers, he called for a new pedagogy which would cultivate the will of the child, controlling it and utilizing it for the benefit of himself and the collectivity in such a way as to "release energies for production."[45]

A coherent articulation of such an innovative pedagogy came from Salvador Alvarado, Constitutional governor of Yucatán from 1915 to 1918. Like his fellow Sonorans, Generals Obregón and Calles, General Alvarado identified with that faction within the Constitutional armies which more firmly than Palavicini and the classical liberals grasped the links between a strong state, economic modernization, and social reform.[46] During his stay in Yucatán, Alvarado put forward a more comprehensive approach to education than Palavicini's while defining it within a clearer sociopolitical framework. In his program, he anticipated the emerging revolutionary state of the 1920s: a developmentalist state which would attempt to eliminate precapitalist enclaves while creating conditions for development through state intervention in the economy and state regulation of class conflict. Although his program anticipated much of what was to emerge, it was also particularistic and illustrated the fluidity of revolutionary conditions in Yucatán and Alvarado's personal identification with the interests of aspiring commercial farmers of northern Mexico. This association influenced his ideology in a variety of ways: for one thing, it exaggerated his hopes for development through an agro-export economy.

For Alvarado, as for many revolutionaries, personal greed, semi-

45. See M. Quiroz Martínez, *La educación pública en el estado de Sonora* (Mexico: Talleres Gráficos de la Nación, 1920), pp. 10–11, 14, 21–22.

46. Salvador Alvarado still lacks a solid biography. His period as governor of Yucatán is treated by several writers. See especially Moisés González Navarro, *Raza y tierra*, pp. 231–42; Francisco Paoli and Enrique Montalvo, *El socialismo olvidado de Yucatán* (Mexico: Siglo Veintiuno, 1974), pp. 47–49; Berthe Ulloa, *Período 1914–1917. La revolución escindida*, in Historia de la Revolución mexicana, 23 vols. (Mexico: El Colegio de Mexico, 1979), 4:64–86.

feudal economic practices, and state-conceded privileges had produced in the *Porfiriato* a monopolization of wealth in which backward methods of production were related to an underutilization of resources and a brutal exploitation of labor. In his opinion, a small clique of Yucatán sisal growers, through the use of almost slave labor, lived lavishly in league with a North American monopoly which drained Mexican wealth by forcing overproduction to obtain lower prices. While capital left the country, the people remained "slaves in misery without schools, electricity, housing, or markets."[47]

Alvarado advocated state intervention to negotiate more favorable terms for Mexican commerce, to make Mexican investment more productive, and to alleviate misery. Abandoning vague notions concerning the social responsibility of capital, he actively used the state to make wealth responsible to social needs: capital had to fulfill "a social function which the community has a right to demand" through investment in "remunerative business and those of public necessity."[48] Anticipating the idea of the state as regulator of development, he revitalized the Comisión Reguladora de Henequén through which producers sold to the state, which marketed directly to the United States in order to bypass "trusts and intermediary speculators."[49] In Alvarado's judgement, landowners would receive a higher price for their crop which would enable them to increase workers' wages. To insure productive investment, the commission would put its funds into a Compañia de Fomento del Sureste—a joint project of the public and private sectors for modernization of the southeast as a primary export economy. The project involved the development of agricultural and forest products facilitated by state promotion of infrastructure. It postulated an agrarian reform which did not challenge large-scale property but sought to make it more productive through cadastral surveys and tax laws. Redistribution of property

47. See, for example, Salvador Alvarado, *Actuación revolucionaria del General Salvador Alvarado en Yucatán* (Mexico: Costa Amic, 1965), pp. 43, 69–73; Salvador Alvarado, "Carta al pueblo de Yucatán, publicada en *La Voz de la Revolución*, 5 de mayo de 1916, aniversario de gloria para la patria mexicana," in *La cuestión de la tierra, 1915–1917, Colección de folletos para la historia de la Revolución mexicana, dirigida por Jesús Silva Herzog* (Mexico: Instituto Mexicano de Investigaciones Económicas, 1962), pp. 154–55, 170, 202; Hugo Sol, *La reacción de privilegio* (Mexico: Imprenta I. Escalante, SA, 1918), pp. 4–5.

48. Alvarado, *Actuación revolucionaria*, pp. 34–35.

49. Alvarado, "Carta al pueblo," pp. 170–71. A primary interest of the Constitutionalists in Yucatán was the sisal market which was lucrative during World War I. Its proceeds helped to finance the revolutionary cause. See, for example, Paoli and Montalvo, *El socialismo olvidado*, p. 46.

was to be limited to a return of usurped *ejido* lands adjacent to large estates which could serve to supplement the income of sisal workers. Alvarado also proposed the creation of small property through colonization of uncultivated, interior public lands, the owners of which would receive tools and credit from the state. Addressing himself more seriously than Palavicini to the problems of small producers in relation to middlemen and large owners, Alvarado suggested the formation of producer and consumer cooperatives as well as the creation of state buying commissions to facilitate marketing.[50]

Alvarado's social program was predicated upon his strategy of creating an alliance between progressive entrepreneurs and workers and peasants against the traditional owning class and its supporting institutions. In this alliance, the state would act as arbiter between the bourgeoisie and subordinate classes within terms preserving the subordination of labor to capital.[51] In stimulating the organization of rural and urban workers into unions, Alvarado aimed at destroying precapitalist modes of production as well as increasing worker benefits. Unions would act as an impetus to owners to employ more efficient methods of production. He abolished debt peonage and whiplashings and passed Mexico's first labor law, which promised workers the protection of the state in guaranteeing rights of organization and collective bargaining, improvement of conditions, and compulsory state arbitration in disputes with capital.[52] Henceforth,

---

50. For these proposals on agrarian reform and cooperatives, see Alvarado, "Carta al pueblo," p. 170; Alvarado, *Actuación revolucionaria*, pp. 69–73; Antonia Bustillos Carrillo, *Yucatán al servicio de la patria* (Mexico: Casa Ramírez Editores, 1959), p. 161; Antonio Médiz Bolío, *Salvador Alvarado* (Mexico: Secretaría de Educación Pública, 1968), pp. 18–19. A succinct, analytical history of Alvarado's policy on land tenure can be found in Moisés González Navarro, *La raza y la tierra*, pp. 238–46. His attempt to legislate land distribution in a return of *ejidos* was thwarted by Carranza who nullified Alvarado's efforts and those of other state governors on the pretext that any land reform would have to await the establishment of a constitutional government. See Moisés González Navarro, *La raza y la tierra*, p. 242. When Carranza became president in 1917, the National Agrarian Commission prohibited any fractioning of sisal estates in Yucatán; see *Excelsior*, 23 Feb. 1920.

51. See Alvarado, *Mi actuación revolucionaria*, pp. 157–59; see also Paoli and Montalvo, *El socialismo olvidado*, pp. 48–49.

52. The first Constitutionalist governor of the state, Eluterio Avila, had legally abolished peonage in August 1914. However, the persistent shortage of labor obliged him to countermand his reform. Alvarado got around the problem of labor scarcity by contracting with General Calles for the importation of "recalcitrant" Yaqui tribesmen from Sonora. Thus he reverted to the crude methods of labor recruitment associated with the *Porfiriato*—methods which the Revolution so avidly disclaimed. See Moisés González Navarro, *La raza y la tierra*, p. 238.

the state would conciliate relations between owners and workers who were to view each other as "co-participants in progress."[53] Alvarado's reforms aimed at converting pariahs and debt peons into modern workers. He sought to convince entrepreneurs of the increased productivity they could expect from a "free," educated, and organized worker. Higher wages, he further argued, would create an expanding market for consumer goods for the owners of capital.[54]

While Alvarado's conception of the state was corporate (regulation of relations between producers' associations, trade unions, and cooperatives), his sense of individualism was profound. Like nineteenth-century liberals and positivists, he believed that the Spanish heritage of "feudalism" had fostered resignation, disdain for work, and clericalism in the Mexican people. To this heritage, he counterposed the "rugged individualism" of his hero, Teddy Roosevelt, in an attempt to eliminate precapitalist values and structures and to stimulate greater individual initiative for increased production within a competitive system.[55] His abolition of debt peonage on sisal estates, his establishment of contracts for domestic servants, and his advocacy of women's rights to job opportunities and education must be seen within this context. "If all sleeping minds enter into action," he urged, "the propelling work of evolution will be more intense and effective."[56] His anticlericalism followed. He saw the Church not only as antipatriotic and antiscientific as had nineteenth-century liberals, he viewed it as an institution stifling the individual will.[57] Like Sierra, however, Alvarado believed the individual will had to be circumscribed in critical ways: obedience to the Church should yield to obedience to the nation. "Everyone to the factory, shop, and home!" he exhorted, "Let us create the religion of duty!"[58] Education had the dual purpose of awakening initiative and circumscribing it within a new order.

Convoking one of the Revolution's first pedagogical conferences in

53. Salvador Alvarado, *Breves apuntes acerca de la administración del General Salvador Alvarado como gobernador de Yucatán* (Mérida: Imprenta del Gobierno Constitucionalista, 1916), p. 23.

54. Médiz Bolío, *Salvador Alvarado*, pp. 17–18.

55. See, for example, *Boletín de Educación* 1, no. 2 (1915): 245–53.

56. Ibid., p. 252. Médiz Bolío, *Salvador Alvarado*, p. 44. Alvarado was responsible for calling Mexico's first feminist conference in Mérida in 1915, proceedings of which are published in *El Primer Congreso Feminista de Yucatán, convocado por el C. gobernador y comandante militar del estado, Gral. don Salvador Alvarado* (Mérida: Talleres Tipográficos del "Ateneo Peninsular," 1916).

57. Médiz Bolío, *Salvador Alvarado*, p. 67; *Boletín de Educación* 1, no. 2 (1915): 242–43, 249. On anticlericalism, see also Berta Ulloa, *La revolución escindida*, p. 81.

58. Médiz Bolío, *Salvador Alvarado*, p. 67.

1915, Alvarado defined schooling as *the* national problem.[59] In a circular to military officers and *jefes políticos* in the region, he urged them to devote all their energies to insuring that no one remained illiterate. He was the first middle-sector revolutionary leader to articulate a clear indictment of the rigid teaching methods of the Porfirian school from the perspective of progressive, child-centered pedagogy then popular in the United States and Europe. In advancing these ideas which had been current in Mexican pedagogical circles for some time, Alvarado was probably influenced by Gregorio Torres Quintero, Sierra's director of primary education at the end of the dictatorship whom Alvarado brought to Mérida to head the Department of Education, and by more radical individuals within the group of Yucatecan teachers and intellectuals who had kept abreast of pedagogical innovation for many years.[60] Alvarado wrote of the nineteenth-century school:

> Instruction is given exclusively by memory. It is encyclopedic and of absolute character . . . the supreme end is the examination. The school does nothing to develop the judgement, power of observation, will, tenacity, and self-confidence of the child; it does nothing to put him in contact with reality or to prepare him to overcome the obstacles he will encounter in life; to know a vocation, to develop an aptitude, to build character are things which do not preoccupy our pedagogues. The important thing is that the child knows everything but how to work; the education he receives has nothing to do with what he will do in life. It can be said without exaggerating that the Mexican who triumphs in life does so despite the school.[61]

Though he sounded much like Sierra in the latter's description of the old Lancasterian school, Alvarado was judging that Sierra's school had similarly failed. He called for a "practical" education which would convert men into factors of production, in agriculture, industry, commerce, and the arts and sciences. He suggested that schools be out-of-doors, equipped with fields, orchards, workshops, and sports fields. Adopting concepts of metropolitan reformist pedagogy,

59. Ibid., p. 34.

60. Ideas circulating in Yucatecan pedagogical circles are discussed by José de la Luz Mena y Alcocer, who became the leading spokesman for the Escuela Racionalista. See José de la Luz Mena y Alcocer, *La escuela socialista, su desorientación y fracaso, el verdadero derrotero* (Mexico: n.p., 1941), pp. 18, 26–27, 175. He discusses the influence and ideas of Dewey, Key, Montessori, Decroly, Eslander, Desmoulins, and other European and North American educational thinkers.

61. Salvador Alvarado, *Problemas de México* (San Antonio, Tex.: n.p., 1920), p. 29.

teaching in Yucatán was not to be based upon set hours, texts, or oral lessons, but upon "direct observation of the child" as he "learned by doing."[62] The Yucatán law of primary schooling passed in 1918 established education through work in agriculture and local industries. Such preparation encouraging initiative would channel the energies of the child into productive work. The iron discipline of the old school was to be softened on the principle that each child should enjoy the greatest liberty without prejudicing the rights of others.[63]

A man of remarkable energy, Alvarado contributed to the expansion of Yucatán's already relatively progressive school system. His laws of rural education of May 1915 authorized the creation of schools on *haciendas* for all children and adults. A Dirección General de Enseñanza Rural was formed with a corps of inspectors to oversee the development of rural schools. These schools, sustained by a special tax which Alvarado levied, were opposed by many *hacendados*, who joined forces with the clergy and other political conservatives to combat the educational effort. The Church had additional reason for concern. Alvarado made all schools coeducational. He allowed churches to be shut down and turned into educational centers. The archbishop's palatial residence became a normal school. Many religious schools were closed; lay teaching was imposed on private schools, all of which were subject to state inspection.[64]

The buildings and hygienic conditions of urban primary schools were improved and medical inspection made more effective. To increase the number of teachers, Alvarado opened normal high schools and offered good wages to attract teachers from outside the state. In keeping with the search for a more open and pragmatic pedagogy, courses in experimental psychology were introduced in the normal training. Special conferences and summer courses for teachers were held. Recognition of the need to interest parents in the education of their children led to teacher-parent conferences.

Alvarado was interested in vocational education, especially in conjunction with his plan to develop Yucatán's potential as a producer and exporter of agriculture and agriculture-related products. Thus he founded a school of agriculture with an experimental station and

62. See *El Primer Congreso Feminista de Yucatán*, pp. 89–92.

63. *Ley de Educación Primaria* (Mérida: Departamento de Educación Pública de Yucatán, 1918), p. 3; *Reglamento Interior de la Ley de Educación Primaria* (Mérida: Departamento de Educación Pública de Yucatán, 1918), pp. 2, 13.

64. José de la Luz Mena y Alcocer et al., *Informe de la delegación del estado de Yucatán al Congreso Nacional de Maestros* (Mexico: n.p., 1920), pp. 18, 21; *Boletín de Educación* 1, no. 2 (1915): 239–43.

created the Ciudad de los Mayas, an institution modeled upon Booker T. Washington's Tuskegee Institute. Designed to train *campesinos* in techniques of modern farming, the school failed as a result of poor management.[65] The idea, however, was basic to revolutionary education.

Although Alvarado called his overall scheme *"socialista"* and a promise of "wealth for all," his idea of education functioned within the class framework of his overall ideology.[66] Recognition of the need for private capital accumulation in the fledgling and still dependent economy led him to advise workers to moderation, savings, and self-control.[67] As in the case of Palavicini, his program required the selection of priorities in schooling, which in turn suggested an intensification of a hierarchical school system. The creation of technical schools and greater emphasis in higher education on the applied sciences were priorities for modernization which offered mobility to some within the middle strata, but they could not accomplish the social equality which Alvarado promised. His idea of education functioned within a class framework which the school was to legitimize and preserve in its role of insuring order.[68]

As in the *Porfiriato*, the school was expected to produce a behavioral transformation. These expectations revealed a familiar anxiety stemming from a still dependent mind-set. Rather than finding the roots of Mexican economic backwardness in a historical process which was international in dimension, Alvarado blamed it on the Mexicans themselves—on "our apathy, our laziness, and our lack of entrepreneurial spirit."[69] To be as Anglo-Saxon as the Anglo-Saxon was the solution:

> If we the lucky inhabitants of this privileged land keep sleeping, if we are not strong, aggressive, and enterprising in the exploitation of our fabulous wealth, take heed—other races more enterprising, more aggressive, stronger, and more tenacious will come and whether we like it or not, they will take over what is today ours, our lands, our forests, our livestock, our homes; they will be those who have shown more force in the struggle for survival and afterward, our children will shine their shoes

65. José de la Luz Mena y Alcocer, *Informe*, p. 21.
66. Alvarado, "Carta al pueblo," p. 168.
67. Arnaldo Córdova, *La ideologia de la Revolución mexicana*, p. 210.
68. Alvarado, "Carta al pueblo," p. 168–69; Médiz Bolío, *Salvador Alvarado*, pp. 66–67.
69. Salvador Alvarado, *A dónde vamos. Las cinco hermanas* (Mérida: Imprenta de Novela, n.d.), p. 20.

. . . To insure that they do not take advantage of us, I urge that we get out of our inertia, our indifference, our criminal lethargy, in which we have been since the Conquest . . . We will either work to fulfill our mission in the concert of nations or will cede our place to the apt, the strong, the men of will and character.[70]

This self-incriminating analysis placed a large burden on the school. This in turn revealed itself in a tendency toward regimentation, which was to be borne out in later years. Quoting Teddy Roosevelt, Alvarado maintained that although the Romans lacked the culture of the Greeks and the commercial genius of the Carthaginians, they had conquered both through austerity, a sense of duty, and a faculty to command and obey.[71] He was deeply impressed with the Boy Scouts, founded by General Robert Baden Powell, who, like Roosevelt, was a hero of imperial conquest. As an organization promoting sports and citizenship, the Scouts, which he introduced to Yucatán, would transform inactive children into a "powerful falange of energies prepared for struggle and resistance."[72] They would carry "the banner of progress and regeneration of our nation as the highest radiating summit of civilized life."[73] The school's role in inculcating patriotism was to be intensified. "The nation before life itself," declared Alvarado.[74] Each Mexican should dedicate himself to the building of the country: the school would center around the flag. Teachers—soldiers of the "new Cross"—would introduce "civilization to our environment." Alvarado insisted that children be prepared for democracy through the establishment of Repúblicas Escolares, miniature replicas of the federal system of government whose goal it was to develop patriotic discipline.[75]

His strident approach to "morality" recalled Sierra's efforts to reform the poor by condemning the consequences of oppression rather than its source. Alvarado outlawed gambling, bullfighting, cockfighting, and prostitution. By closing the taverns, he created the first dry state in Latin America. Like Sierra and so many Porfirian reformers, he viewed the use of alcohol as racial decadence (the gratification of

70. Alvarado, "Carta al pueblo," pp. 202–3.
71. *Boletín de Educación* 1, no. 2 (1915): 246–47.
72. Alvarado, "Carta al pueblo," pp. 189–90.
73. Ibid., p. 191.
74. Efrén Nuñez Mata, "Salvador Alvarado y la educación nacional," *Historia Mexicana* 11 (1962): 430.
75. Alvarado, "Carta al pueblo," p. 184; Médiz Bolío, *Salvador Alvarado*, p. 57. The experiment did not work effectively in practice.

appetite and lack of restraint) rather than as a response to an unjust social structure.[76] He encouraged middle-class women's groups to "redeem" and "moralize" prostitutes. Sending the unemployed to an agricultural penal colony to convert them into "elements of production and utility," he declared that consuming without producing was a crime and that the Revolution would do away with all vagrancy. Although his moral notions were more generous than Palavicini's insofar as they placed perhaps more hope in the capacities of individuals to improve themselves, they were articulated within a similar class perspective. As in the *Porfiriato*, the transfer of bourgeois values to the poor within this paradigm was condescending and self-interested. It revealed the intent of maintaining the subordinate status of the dominated classes. The process suggested a possible brake on the growth of class consciousness, as those who could not conform to the model might blame only themselves rather than a social structure whose functioning educators either obfuscated or legitimized.

However, such a brake on class consciousness did not occur in Yucatán. The Partido Socialista de Yucatán (PSY) had been formed in 1915 with the encouragement of Alvarado who saw it as a base of support for himself and his program. Founded by elements of the urban sector—railroad workers, teachers, artisans—it became the spearhead for organizing *hacienda* workers and peasants. Gradually, it developed a life of its own. Moving beyond Alvarado's bourgeois-worker alliance, it came to postulate a singular and militant defense of the interests of workers and peasants.[77] When Alvarado was disqualified from the 1918 gubernatorial elections by legalities in the Mexican Constitution of 1917, the party evolved independently under the governorship of Carlos Castro Morales, a member of the PSY. Class conflict deepened as *hacendados* and their supporters tried to sabotage even moderate reforms, furthering the radicalization of the PSY. Within the party the strong leadership of Felipe Carrillo Puerto, a former petty trader and railroad worker who recognized the limitations of Alvarado's strategy, was also critical to the party's independent evolution. Between 1918 and 1924, the PSY mobilized an estimated 72,000 workers into 416 Ligas de Resistencia engaged in a state of civil war not only with Yucatán's owning class, but with the forces of Venustiano Carranza whose adversary campaign, backed by many middle-sector liberals, almost destroyed the party between

76. Médiz Bolío, *Salvador Alvarado*, p. 57.
77. See Paoli and Montalvo, *El socialismo olvidado*, pp. 176–86.

1918 and 1920.[78] In these years, the PSY became perhaps the most developed mass movement in Mexico.[79] Of all the revolutionary movements, it presented the clearest critique of official state education and the best-developed alternative to the ideas of middle-sector school reformers.

The Partido Socialista never became a real socialist party. Its ideological roots were anarchist and reflected the inclinations of artisans, peasant farmers, professionals, and petty traders. The party's vision seemed to be that of a society of small farmers organized into cooperatives freely interchanging with one another and with urban industrial cooperatives organized around the principle of worker control. In 1918, Felipe Carrillo Puerto articulated an ideology of small property.[80] He urged members of the leagues to free themselves from the service and exploitation of others in order to work for themselves. At the time, the party was primarily concerned with transforming the dependent monocrop economy into a self-sufficient one producing the traditional crops of corn and beans.[81] As the party evolved, its program radicalized. The party congress of 1921 agreed upon the need to socialize the means of production in agriculture, industry, and services and called for revision of Articles 27 and 123 of the Constitution in order to abolish private property.[82]

By 1922, when the PSY won state elections, it had accepted the principle of the newly formed Third International on the need for a vanguard party which aimed at the conquest of state power and implementation of proletarian dictatorship.[83] Although between 1922

78. Juan Rico, *La huelga de junio* (Mérida: n.p., 1922), p. 104; Antonio Bustillos Carrillo, *Yucatán*, p. 207; Paoli and Montalvo, *El socialismo olvidado*, pp. 56–58, 107–33; for description of struggle between liberals and socialists, see also *Excelsior*, 23 Feb., 21, 22, 23, 24 May, 4, 5, 6 June, 1920.

79. The most complete study to date of the PSY is the study by Paoli and Montalvo, *El socialismo olvidado*. A different view of the party as one based upon networks of *caciquismo* is put forward by Gilbert M. Joseph, "Mexico's 'Popular Revolution': Mobilization and Myth in Yucatán, 1910–1940," *Latin American Perspectives* 22 (1979): 46–65.

80. Antonio Bustillos Carrillo, *Yucatán*, p. 222; see also pp. 207, 247; Juan Rico, *La huelga*, pp. 62–63; Felipe Carrillo Puerto, "The New Yucatán," *Survey Graphic* 52 (May 1924): 138–42; *Primer Congreso Obrero Socialista celebrado en Motul estado de Yucatán* (Mexico: Centro de Estudios Históricos del Movimiento Obrero Mexicano, 1977), pp. 32–33.

81. See *Primer Congreso Obrero*, pp. 32–33.

82. *Segundo Congreso Obrero de Izamal* (Mexico: Centro de Estudios Históricos del Movimiento Obrero Mexicano, 1977), pp. 55–58, 60.

83. See José Ingenieros, "En memoria de Felipe Carrillo Puerto," *Historia Obrera*, 1, no. 4 (1975): 2–7.

and 1924 the party used the state for the explicit benefit of the oppressed classes, a fully socialist program was impossible to implement given regional and national circumstances. It has been argued that Carrillo Puerto as governor intended to confiscate the sisal estates and that during his tenure, more land was distributed than in any other state with the exception of the *Zapatista* stronghold of Morelos.[84] However, impetus in this direction was stymied by the severe economic crisis in the peninsula created by the crumbling of the sisal market in the aftermath of World War I and by international speculation on the part of buyers like the International Harvester Company.[85] To this obstacle must be added the intense opposition of the local entrepreneurial class and their middle-sector allies who actively combatted the policies of the state government and the very existence of the PSY. Not surprisingly, this opposition came to include Salvador Alvarado who tried to run against Carrillo Puerto in the 1922 elections.

The PSY held power for a brief period because of its own strength at the base and because of an expedient alliance with the national government of Alvaro Obregón (1920–1924). Beseiged by Carranza-backed opposition in 1919 and 1920, the PSY supported Obregón and the Sonoran faction in their movement to unseat Carranza in 1920, although the alliance implied no deep ideological agreement: Obregón shared Alvarado's ideas. Nonetheless, Obregón's support was probably crucial to the PSY—especially because it had no military base of its own.[86] In 1923–24, the nationwide revolt against Obregón led by his former colleague, Adolfo de la Huerta, provided the means by which the forces opposed to the PSY in Yucatán reasserted themselves, assassinated Felipe Carrillo Puerto, and permanently crippled the party.

In its period of radicalization, the PSY was—in the opinion of many contemporaries—the best-organized party in Mexico in de-

---

84. Carrillo Puerto's record in agrarian reform was much better than Alvarado's. During Alvarado's tenure, there were 14 petitions for land donation and approximately 26 per year in the years following. In 1923, Carrillo Puerto distributed 208,972 hectares to 10,727 persons and claimed that the majority of villages had land; Moisés González Navarro, *La raza y la tierra*, pp. 247–50. See also Joseph, "Mexico's 'Popular Revolution,'" pp. 56–57, and "El asesinato de Felipe Carrillo Puerto," *Historia Obrera* 1, no. 4 (1975): 9.

85. *Excelsior*, 3 May 1920, reports severity of economic crisis in Yucatán.

86. This idea is developed by Paoli and Montalvo, *El socialismo olvidado*, pp. 74, 120–62.

fense of rural and urban workers.[87] The Ligas de Resistencia not only carried out strikes on plantations, rent strikes on *ejidos*, and labor actions in the cities, the PSY also created an elaborate structure for mutual defense which was rooted in the daily lives of thousands of Yucatecans. In rural communities, the leagues were made up of local residents responsible for land distribution, production, consumption, marketing, schooling, health, education, and political action. The PSY was financed by membership which kept two-thirds of its dues for local activities and sent one-third to the central organization to provide strike funds, loans in case of bad harvests, and seed funds for cooperatives to other leagues.[88]

The PSY tried to root itself in the cultural life of its members. It sought to awaken consciousness and militancy by encouraging the progressive aspects of popular life and discouraging backward traits which stemmed from and reinforced exploitation and oppression. It emphasized moral restraint from the perspective of the self-discipline necessary for struggle rather than attempting to impose discipline in the interests of another social class. Carrillo Puerto told workers that it was an error to spend their hard-earned wages on alcohol which enriched those interested in keeping the workers backward.[89] Like bourgeois educators, the PSY believed that sports and the arts were outlets for energy and growth. However, they saw art not as a means of civilizing the masses but as a source of affirmation of self and class. Carrillo Puerto wrote:

> Our people are far too sad and must learn to sing and dance not only our own beautiful songs but other and more spritely dances and freer tunes. They have been slaves so long that they have forgotten how to play—slaves do not play. People who play are not slaves.[90]

In Yucatán, in contrast to other areas of Mexico in the 1920s, the Indian heritage was truly emphasized. The PSY conducted meetings and congresses in Mayan, translated the Constitution of 1917 and texts into the native language, revived indigenous culture in dance, crafts, music, and the development of archaeological sites. The quasi-

87. Ibid., p. 114. See Ernest Gruening, "Felipe Carrillo Puerto," *The Nation* 118, no. 3054 (1924): 61.
88. Paoli and Montalvo, *El socialismo olvidado*, pp. 61, 67–69, 91–97, 102, 104; *Primer Congreso Obrero*, pp. 51–55.
89. Juan Rico, *La huelga*, p. 58; see also *Segundo Congreso Obrero*, pp. 46–51.
90. Felipe Carrillo Puerto, "The New Yucatán," p. 141.

socialist tradition of indigenous communal land holding and cooperative work became a unifying factor in a movement of indigenous
peasants, sisal workers, urban artisans, and laborers.[91] Far from imposing their values on the people, the Yucatán middle sectors had to
choose between remaining with the opposition (as many did) or integrating themselves into the PSY. As conflict mounted, the party organized leagues of teachers, doctors, lawyers, journalists, students,
and women. Women's leagues, for example, went beyond those encouraged by Alvarado to organize street vendors, women workers,
and *campesinas* for a general revindication of their rights as women
and as workers. These leagues stood in contrast to the middle-sector-
inspired Casa de Trabajo de la Mujer created by the Blue Cross in
Mérida in 1921 under the slogan of "Charity, Humanity, and Obedience."[92]

The PSY used education to further class consciousness and political
action. Schooling was to make people "know their oppressors" while
developing an understanding that "political liberty is a myth if it is
not based upon economic liberty."[93] At the party congress in 1918,
delegates called for a school which would "confront the reactionary
organizations." Aware of the low level of political consciousness at the
base, they called for a "true socialist school, which will nourish the
popular masses who organize in an atmosphere still saturated with
slavery."[94]

The PSY combined revisionist precepts of "learning by doing"
pedagogy promoted by Alvarado with the ideology of Spanish anarchist, Francisco Ferrer Guardia, whose *Escuela Moderna* in Barcelona
was an alternative to the public school system. Ferrer saw state education in the nineteenth century as a substitute for the Church for
assuring obedience to authority: it sanctioned, he claimed, a monopoly of wealth by a privileged few exploiting a mass of the poor. It
taught children to "obey, to believe, and to think according to the
social dogmas which dominate us."[95] Equipped with a faith in the
original equality and goodness of mankind, Ferrer saw the social Dar-

91. Paoli and Montalvo, *El socialismo olvidado*, pp. 90–91.

92. Juan Rico, *La huelga*, p. 26; Maria Antonieta Rascón, "La mujer y la lucha social,"
in Elena Urrutía, *Imagen y realidad de la mujer* (Mexico: SepSetentas, 1975), p. 159;
Segundo Congreso Obrero, pp. 86–97. On the Cruz Azul, see *Excelsior*, 1 Jan. 1921.

93. *Primer Congreso Obrero*, p. 64.

94. Ibid., pp. 67–68.

95. Francisco Ferrer Guardia, *La escuela moderna* (Barcelona: Imprenta Elseveriana-
Borras Mestres y Ca., 1912), p. 97.

winist precept of competitive struggle for survival as a fabrication used to justify the hegemony of the ruling class (the "fittest," who had survived). In its place, he upheld the naturalness of group cooperation which he believed could be nurtured through education. Strongly anticlerical and antiauthoritarian, his school in Barcelona stressed group action in an open atmosphere of discovery and work, in which the teacher was a simple guide. Prizes and examinations were eliminated, as Ferrer believed they stimulated competition and false individualism. The Escuela Moderna preached not only the need for social equality but an affirmation of the working class. Artificial distinctions between manual and intellectual labor were eliminated. Children were to recognize that the workers, who passed in and out of the school, were doing the positive work of civilization in their production of its wealth, though they went unrewarded for these efforts.[96]

Between 1915 and 1925, the *Escuela Moderna* or *Escuela Racionalista*, as it was more commonly called in Mexico, provided the official pedagogy supported by most sectors of the Mexican labor movement. While information on the actual functioning of rational education is so far scarce, evidence suggests that for most of those attracted to the pedagogy, rational education meant primarily anticlericalism. In Yucatán, the pedagogy appears to have gone beyond anticlericalism per se in part because it was joined with "learning by doing" techniques familiar to Yucatecan reformers, and, moreover, because it became integrated with an ongoing struggle for social justice.[97] When the PSY adopted Ferrer's rational education as the most effective means of propagating libertarian ideals and achieving workers' aspirations, they gave his pedagogy a concrete direction in a collective movement for short- and long-term betterment. Rural schools became an integral part of the quest for land, implementation of modern techniques of cultivation, installation of public services such as sewage, and development of craft production. In certain instances, workers learned in factory schools where technicians demonstrated means of improving the production that workers controlled.[98] Ideological input was distinct from that of the old public school or the emerging public school. At the pedagogical conference following the party congress

96. Ibid., pp. 12, 17–20, 35–36.
97. For a discussion of the meshing of reformist pedagogy with Ferrer Guardia's ideology, see José de la Luz Mena y Alcocer, *La escuela socialista*, pp. 18, 26–27, 175.
98. Juan Rico, *La huelga*, p. 77.

in 1918, the PSY voted to eliminate texts to end "all ideas of cults and submission to powers known and unknown."[99] Libraries of material of "revolutionary criteria" would "awaken the active forces of men in the collective benefit."[100] The party congress in 1919 ruled that in order to guarantee the autonomy of the leagues' schools, workers' organizations were not to accept gifts or donations from "capitalist or official sources."[101] At the party congress in 1921, the principle of rational education was reaffirmed as the basis for unifying the school system and capacitating workers for eventual control of the means of production.[102]

Teachers formed part of the vanguard of the PSY and so had introduced radical ideas into rural communities and schools since the period of Alvarado.[103] However, rational education became official state policy only in 1922 with the election of Carrillo Puerto to the governorship. In its official form, rational education was strongly anticlerical and stressed the social and collective aspects of the Constitution of 1917 (Article 27 on the social utility of property and Article 123 on workers' rights) rather than the liberal and individualistic aspects of the Constitution, which were to be heavily emphasized in official schooling in the 1920s. José de la Luz Mena y Alcocer, a vociferous protagonist of rational education in Yucatán, was appointed official state representative of the new national Secretaría de Educación Pública on the recommendation of Carrillo Puerto. He tried to bring teachers closer to workers and peasants through weekly trips to different parts of the state and discussion sessions with workers' organizations and more radical teachers. Prizes and examinations were abolished. To curb authoritarianism and idolatry, teachers were forbidden to take children to civic, political, or religious functions which satisfied the "vanity" of men to the detriment of "children's rights." Teachers were leveled to one grade with a single wage. School direc-

99. José de la Luz Mena y Alcocer, *La escuela socialista*, p. 192.

100. Ibid., p. 198; see also *Segundo Congreso Obrero*, pp. 86–87.

101. José de la Luz Mena y Alcocer, *La escuela socialista*, p. 23.

102. *Segundo Congreso Obrero*, p. 86.

103. When a pro-Carranza liberal congress was elected in Yucatán in early 1920, one of its first acts was to fire all school inspectors for "propagating socialism" (*Excelsior*, 23 Feb. 1920). By May when Obregón forces helped to unseat the liberals, the Liga de Profesores of the PSY was a prominent force (*Excelsior*, 23 May 1920). Testimonies in U.S. Senate, *Investigation of Mexican Affairs*, also describe teacher radicalism under Alvarado and after; see, for example, 1:880–81.

tors were eliminated; in an open assembly, teachers chose one of themselves to act as director on a rotating basis.[104]

Given the level of class warfare in Yucatán, it is not surprising that while many teachers spearheaded the reforms as militant advocates of the PSY, others opposed them—especially teachers whose positions as directors were threatened. Opponents of rational education were supported from Mexico City by the new Secretaría de Educación Pública (SEP). When a group of school directors resigned in protest against Luz Mena's reforms, José Vasconcelos, national education minister, ordered their restitution, removed Luz Mena, and appointed a new national representative hostile to the reforms. Although proponents of rational education continued to operate by working directly through the governor, the SEP policy indicated the more conservative direction taken by educators at the national level. It is curious that Yucatán was one of the very few states which received no federal aid for schools between 1920 and 1924.

Not a full-fledged socialist movement, the PSY demonstrated the potential for petit bourgeois radicalization when elements of the latter fused with popular movements. The pedagogy and school of the PSY were clearly different in their class nature, content, and goals from the pedagogy emerging as official policy. Further, it should be emphasized that rational education was probably understood generally as anticlerical education. Its function as a social action pedagogy as well as an anticlerical one in Yucatán must be seen within the context of its integration within a militant mass-based movement. While on the basis of present research it is difficult to assess the impact of rational pedagogy elsewhere in Mexico, it is fair to say that a situation similar to that in Yucatán arose in the 1920s in many parts of the country when it became clear that education could not improve people's lives without significant structural reforms. This dynamic led to the radicalization of the Revolution in the 1930s and to the experiment in socialist education, which at its best resembled the earlier Yucatán experience.

Education and the Constitution of 1917

The Mexican Constitutional Convention which convened at Querétaro in December of 1916 included no representatives of the predomi-

---

104. On implementation of rational education from 1922 to 1924, see José de la Luz Mena y Alcocer, *La escuela socialista,* pp. 28, 199–204, 208–11.

nantly rural supporters of Villa and Zapata. Very few representatives of the industrial working class participated. The overwhelming majority of delegates were professionals and military officers.[105] However, worker representatives and many delegates of middle-sector origin could and did in varying degrees identify with the interests of workers and peasants; members of the PSY were among them. The conflict which emerged at the beginning of the convention erupted between the *Carrancista* faction, which included Felix F. Palavicini and other *"Renovador"* deputies, and the somewhat amorphous populism which arose from the floor against the Carranza leadership and its constitutional draft.[106] The opposition articulated itself at first through the floor-elected Constitutional Committee, headed by Francisco Mújica. Whereas the Carrancistas tended to favor a constitution within the classical liberal tradition emphasizing individual rights and political rather than social reforms (e.g. prohibitions against presidential or gubernatorial reelection), the opposition sought explicit

105. Delegates by law had to be associated with the Constitutional cause and those who had served hostile governments could not be elected, i.e., *Zapatistas* and *Villistas*. Peter Smith calculates that 84.9 percent of the delegates were "middle class," 11.4 percent represented the "lower class." See Peter Smith, "La política dentro de la revolución: el Congreso Constituyente de 1916–1917," *Historia Mexicana* 22 (1973): 381. In a more descriptive breakdown, E. V. Niemeyer, Jr., shows among the delegates two miners, one carpenter, one linotype operator, one printer as the only delegates whose occupations involved manual labor. He lists seven school teachers. See E. V. Niemeyer, Jr., *Revolution at Querétaro: The Mexican Constitutional Convention of 1916–1917* (Austin: University of Texas Press, 1974), pp. 265–67. Niemeyer's study provides the best narrative of the convention in English. Standard histories in Spanish are Gabriel Ferrer Mendiolea, *Historia del Congreso Constitutyente de 1916–1917* (Mexico: Biblioteca del Instituto Nacional de Estudios Históricos de la Revolución Mexicana, 1957), and Juan de Díos Bojorquez [Djed Borquez], *Crónica del constituyente* (Mexico: Ediciones Botas, 1938). The best interpretation of the convention from the classical liberal perspective is provided by Félix F. Palavicini, *Historia de la Constitución de 1917*, 2 vols. (Mexico: n.p., 1938).

106. Much of the mistrust of the *Carrancista* faction stemmed from the fact that many of them, like Palavicini, had served in the Twenty-sixth Congress, had accepted Madero's resignation, and had continued to serve under Huerta. The *renovadores* included Palavicini, José Natividad Macías, Pascual Ortiz Rubio, Manuel Rojas, and others. For a full list, see Ferrer Mendiolea, *Historia del Congreso Constituyente*, pp. 50–51. The *renovadores* argued in defense of their position that they had accepted Madero's resignation in order to save his life and had remained in Congress to combat Huerta. For a description of the controversy over the *renovadores* and other deputies, see Niemeyer, *Revolution at Querétaro*, pp. 45–49, and Germán List Arzubide, "La rebelión constituyente," *Historia mexicana* 1 (1951): 227–250. See also *Diario de los debates del Congreso Constituyente*, 2 vols (Mexico: Imprenta de la Cámara de Diputados, 1922), 1:26–40, 53–69, on the question of credentials.

guarantees for redress of *campesino* and worker grievances as well as institutional means of promoting economic modernization within a nationalist context. Although the capitalist framework of Mexican development was not fundamentally contested, the ideological positions expressed were often divergent approaches to social change, ranging from the liberal approach, wary of a restructuring of property relations to an expedient advocacy of socioeconomic reform through state intervention, to a more militant and singular defense of the interests of peasants and workers. Although the Constitutional Congress was to achieve the appearance of unity on many fundamental points, these differences should not be underestimated for they were critically demonstrated in practice as in the case of Yucatán.

The debate over education focused almost entirely upon the Church for reasons which were both circumstantial and ideological. In Carranza's constitutional draft, Article 3 reinstated freedom of teaching as it had been written into the Constitution of 1857 and added that primary education in public institutions would be free and lay. Obligatory primary schooling was included in Article 31 of the draft concerning the obligations of Mexican citizens. Coming at the beginning of the debates, Article 3 provoked a confrontation between liberals and radicals, which was an initial test of strength.[107] The Constitutional Committee rejected Carranza's version of the article and presented an alternative which declared that teaching would be lay in both private and public primary schools, that no religious organization or minister or priest could administer or teach primary school, that private schools could only be established under government supervision and subject to government inspection, and that primary schooling was obligatory for all.

In presenting their proposal, the Committee argued that although Article 3 was part of the constitutional section on individual rights, a right should be restricted when its exercise affected the conservation or development of society. Religious education, said the committee, spiritually deformed the child's conscience and had to be prohibited; the child could not rationally understand its abstract ideals, and these would later express themselves in blind fanaticism. Historically the enemy of democratic institutions, the Church had consistently preached that its interests were above those of the civil power. Despite the laws of the Reform, the clergy, argued the Committee, had recouped its privileged position under the dictatorship: it had reacquired property, absorbed teaching, and opposed the public school.

107. Niemeyer, *Revolution at Querétaro*, pp. 60–61.

This "subjugation" of teaching was preliminary to a "usurpation" of state functions. It thus endangered the conservation of the state and the natural development of society.[108] To this majority proposal, Luis G. Monzón, school teacher and a member of the Committee, added his minority proposal to substitute "rational" for "lay." Arguing that in the nineteenth century the lay school had stopped teaching clerical doctrine but was nonetheless tolerant of it, he claimed that in this era of liberation for Mexico and Latin America, rational education would destroy the lies and errors of Church dogma.[109]

Although Monzón's suggestion anticipated the constitutional reform of Article 3 in 1933 which introduced socialist education, his suggestion seemed superfluous within the context of the strong anticlericalism articulated by the Committee as a whole and reiterated from the floor of the convention. This anticlericalism added a populist tone to the traditional liberal anticlericalism of the nineteenth century; it identified the Church not only with hostility to science and liberal political institutions but with political dictatorship and oppression of the poor.[110] Did the Revolution want to condemn Mexican children, asked Deputy Román Rosas y Reyes, to a life of degradation, servilism, and moral misery?[111] Repeatedly the radicals argued that the state had to protect the underprivileged from the abuses of the privileged minority. Thus the virgin mind of the child had to be protected from the corrupting influence of the Church. In so arguing, the radicals expressed both the perspective of men like Alvarado within whose vigorously competitive capitalist ideology the Church was seen to repress individual initiative and science, and the more working-class perspective of sections of the labor movement and organizations like the PSY which identified the Church with class oppression and exploitation.

Although anticlerical themselves, the classical liberals vigorously protested the proposed Article 3 because it attacked their draft and offended their primary commitment to individual rights. In the opening section of the Constitution on individual rights, no limits should appear, they argued. Allowing the state to limit the freedom

---

108. *Diario de los debates* 1:433.

109. Ibid., p. 438.

110. For background on anticlericalism in the Revolution, see Charles C. Cumberland, *Mexican Revolution: The Constitutionalist Years*, introduction by David C. Bailey (Austin: University of Texas Press, 1974), pp. 215–32; Bertha Ulloa, *La revolución escindida*, pp. 34–39; Barry Carr, *El movimiento obrero y la política en México, 1910–1929*, 2 vols (Mexico: SepSetentas, 1976), 2:96–100.

111. *Diario de los debates* 1:472.

to learn and to teach was tyrannical. To this central issue, they added other arguments to strengthen their position. Such emotional and imprudent Jacobinism would provoke anarchy and civil war, they said. It would bring about a U.S. intervention.[112] Palavicini suggested it could lead to an invasion of Protestantism in Mexican schooling which would be part of the "Yankee conquest."[113] Recalling an argument put forward by Ponciano Arriaga in 1857, Alfonso Cravioto said that the real source of fanaticism was the home. Did the delegates wish to invade the home—destroying rosaries and crucifixes? Would the state prefer to confiscate children at age five? Should Mexicans be forcibly prevented from procreating?[114] Using 1907 statistics on schooling, Cravioto further argued that the Church's influence in education was small and declining in relation to the expansion of public schools. This argument could have little meaning to Francisco Mújica, who came from the heavily clerical state of Michoacán and who in subsequent years would combat not only the clergy's offensive against the lay school but its alliance with *hacienda* owners and foreign investors against land reform and other basic social changes.[115]

To the liberal argument that each individual should enjoy the right to learn and teach, Jesús Lopez Lira, physician from Guanajuato, responded that such principles evolved with time. The liberal creed had maintained that each individual was free to dispose of his person; thus workers had the right to sell their labor at any wage until their strength was completely exhausted. Today, the law protected the worker by placing a limit on his right to dispose of his labor—a limit which involved fixed and maximum hours of work and minimum wages. Out of respect for the rights and weaknesses of children, the

112. For liberal arguments, see, for example, ibid., pp. 439–40, 444, 463–65, 472.

113. Palavicini's allegation was not outlandish. Protestants were prominent revolutionary educators at the federal and state levels. Andrés Osuna, a Protestant minister and former director of education in Coahuila, served as head of the Direccion General de Educación Pública under Carranza in 1916. Moisés Sáenz, director of the Escuela Nacional Preparatoria under Carranza and later undersecretary of education in the Calles government, was a Protestant as was Governor Gustavo Espinosa Mireles of Coahuila. Salvador Alvarado worked with North American Protestants in his education program. Further, in 1914, representatives of various Protestant denominations met in Cincinnati, Ohio, where they developed a comprehensive plan for Mexican education including the creation of agricultural, vocational, and rural teacher training schools. See Inman, *Intervention*, pp. 66–67, 192, 233–39, and Baldwin, "Variations in the Vanguard," pp. 294–301.

114. *Diario de los debates* 1:452–53.

115. See, for example, David Raby, "Los principios de la educación rural," pp. 557–58.

liberty to learn also required limits, he claimed. No one had a right to teach children other than "conquered truths, positive facts, and proven knowledge," which did not include the "lies" and "errors" of the Church.[116]

Because the liberals were also anticlerical and because they understood that the sentiment of the body ran against them, they were willing to allow lay teaching to prevail in both private and public primary schools. However, they argued that the obligation to attend primary school was out of place in Article 3 and unnecessary because it was included in draft Article 31. Further, they said that it was not necessary to forbid the Church or ministers to direct or administer schools because this restriction was contained in Carranza's draft Article 27. Finally, they refused to accept the idea that no minister could teach, as this clause would prevent a member of a religious association from teaching mathematics or French. The Constitutional Committee recessed and returned with a compromise proposal eliminating the clause on obligatory instruction and the prohibition against ministers' teaching. They included the prohibition against the Church's direction of primary schools as they judged the clause in Carranza's draft to be unclear. This revised Article 3 passed by a vote of 99 to 58.

In assessing the political correctness and importance of Article 3 to the history of the Mexican Revolution, it would seem that the classical liberals had a point in calling the anticlericalism of the radicals provocative and exaggerated. In the 1920s, the anticlerical issue and Article 3 in particular were used by the national government in a divisive way which diverted the attention of workers and peasants from substantive issues of social reform into a bloody, internecine battle over religion.[117] On the other hand, in many instances, Church hostility to the lay school and basic social reforms and its complicity with the old owning class were very real.[118] In some form, destruction of the Church's ideological and material power was an integral part of the program of an ongoing bourgeois revolution. Despite debate over means, there was broad agreement on this point among the

116. *Diario de los debates* 1:455–56.

117. See, for example, Barry Carr, *El movimiento obrero* 2:6, 110; Anatoli Shulgovsky, *México en la encrucijada de su historia* (Mexico: Ediciones de Cultura Popular, SA, 1968), pp. 51–60.

118. This was certainly the case in Yucatán. For description of clerical opposition to schools and reforms in Michoacán, see Raby, "Los principios de la educación rural," pp. 555–59.

Mexican revolutionaries. Liberals and radicals alike saw the public school as the primary instrument for destroying traditional Catholic ideology. At the Constitutional Congress, the liberal Alfonso Cravioto claimed that Mexican progress consisted of schools, schools, and more schools.[119]

It has been argued on the basis of quantitative assessment of voting patterns at the convention that the main division between liberals and radicals concerned centralization of the state.[120] Not only did the radicals wish to increase state power in an effort to guarantee *campesino* and worker rights, they believed further that the state should play a strong role in economic development.[121] Radicals supported the creation of institutions such as a central bank as well as state regulation of private property and its use. Article 27 conceded broad powers to the state in the area of property relations to assuage the land hunger of rural Mexicans and to curb the political and economic power of foreigners and the Porfirian owning class. The liberals, on the other hand, were more comfortable with a formula limiting the central state's power. They believed that social reform was more a question of statutory than constitutional law. However, there were contradictions in both camps on the question of the state. Radicals sought safeguards against the reemergence of political dictatorship and so advocated such points as the congressional right to hold special sessions without the approval of the executive and the Senate's right to resolve local political crises instead of the Supreme Court. Liberals on the other hand were frightened enough of anarchy to grant too much in the way of individual rights.[122] At least implicitly, some of their positions suggested the need for a strong state to insure social order as has been pointed out in the case of Palavicini. Further, both liberals and radicals shared a commitment to economic modernization, which would de facto require a determinant role for the central state in a period of economic dislocation and political turmoil in which the state had been destroyed and the capitalist class (national and foreign) temporarily disorganized and alienated. Both factions had come to agree also on the need for social reform even if many approached the question opportunistically. Thus there was probably broader legitimization for the emergence of a strong central state at the Constitutional Convention than seems immediately apparent.

119. *Diario de los debates* 1:455.
120. Peter Smith, "La política dentro de la revolución," p. 372.
121. Niemeyer, *Revolution at Querétaro*, p. 221.
122. Peter Smith, "La política dentro de la revolución," p. 372.

This issue had implications for education. Despite clear consensus in favor of mass schooling, the delegates divested the central state of the little power it had in this area. To be sure, Article 31 made primary education obligatory and Article 123, which limited child labor, required owners of agricultural, mining, and industrial establishments employing over 100 workers to found schools at their own expense. Section 27 of Article 73 authorized Congress to establish professional and technical schools, institutes of fine arts, museums, libraries, observatories, and other institutes of "higher culture" in the states. However, transitory Article 14 abolished the Secretaría Instrucción Pública.

What entity—state or municipality—should henceforth control public education was not made entirely clear by the Constitution. In the debates on municipal autonomy at the convention, there was confusion on the question of jurisdiction over schools. For example, Rodríguez González, a delegate from Coahuila and head of public instruction in that state, argued that since schools had reverted to municipal control as a result of Carranza's December 1914 decree on municipal autonomy, teachers had been subject to undue political pressures from local authorities. Further, if municipalities were to fund education, they should receive, he argued, a fixed percentage of revenue from the state to insure the regular payment of teachers' wages. With some personal interest in the question, Rodríguez González indicated that his main concern was that the state government not lose administrative and supervisory control over public education.[123]

In the next three years, where schools functioned under municipal control, it was agreed that they did not fare well. In the capital, primary schools were turned over to the municipalities while the government of the Federal District took responsibility for technical,

123. *Diario de los debates* 2:1067. Coahuila appears to be a test case for the failure of municipally-controlled education. Carranza as governor had returned schooling to municipal control in financing and in the right to hire and fire teachers. The Dirección General de Educación Primaria of the state had the right to inspect the schools and had control over "technical" direction. See Richmond, "Factional Political Strife in Coahuila, 1910–1920," p. 53, Villarello Vélez, *Historia de la Revolución mexicana en Coahuila,* p. 215. Espinosa Mireles, however, created the Junta Central de Educación del Estado to be in charge of hiring and firing and other aspects of schooling. It included representatives from the Dirección General de Educación Primaria of the state, the director of the Ateneo Fuente, the state's preparatory school, representatives of the state government, the legislature, the normal school, and the municipalities. Meanwhile, the state provided the municipalities with funds for their schools. See Villarello Vélez, *Historia de la Revolución mexicana en Coahuila,* pp. 314–16.

preparatory, and normal education. Under municipal control, the conditions of school buildings rapidly deteriorated, teacher absenteeism soared, and teachers went unpaid for months at a time. In his report to Congress in 1918, Carranza indicated that average attendance in both public and private primary schools in the capital dropped from 92,415 in 1917 to 73,614 in 1918. In May 1918, teachers launched a manifesto announcing a work stoppage until the Revolution fulfilled its primary duty of instructing the people. In the short run, their hopes were unfounded. Although in April 1919, the federal government intervened to assist in the payment of teachers' wages, in May when municipal income was increased by a tax on *pulque*, the federal government withdrew its support. The result was a closing of 191 municipal schools.[124]

Conditions in some states were worse. In 1920, officials in Durango reported that of 277 municipal schools, only 97 were open and 37 of these were in the capital of Parral, which was more fiscally viable than most municipalities. Not only were teachers unpaid, many had been fired as a result of political favoritism at the local level. So bad was the condition of teachers that no one wanted to enroll in the new normal school. In Michoacán, Governor Ortiz Rubio reclaimed state control over the schools because of the negative influence exercised by local *caciques* and *jefes políticos*. In Sonora, the state never relinquished control to the municipalities and therefore could boast increases in the number of schools, in teachers' wages, and in number of school inspectors. The situation in Tlaxcala was perhaps more typical. Municipal bankruptcy had obliged the state government to pay teachers' salaries but because the state government itself was bankrupt, the result was a drastic decline in personnel. Only 15 percent of the school-age population was in school and only the schools in district capitals were adequately furnished.[125]

124. On conditions of schools in Mexico City, see Ezequiel Chávez, "Iniciativa de ley de la creación de la Secretaría de Educación Pública y la federalización de la enseñanza," n.d., AEC; *Excelsior*, 5 April, 24 June 1920; on enrollments, see *La educación pública en México a través de los mensajes presidenciales*, pp. 192–93, 197; on teachers' actions, see *Excelsior*, 6, 12, 14, 15 May 1919; John A. Britton, "Indian Education, Nationalism, and Federalism in Mexico," pp. 455–56; on the closing of municipal schools and the inability of municipal governments to pay teachers' wages, see *La educación pública en México a través de los mensajes presidenciales*, pp. 201–2; *Excelsior*, 5 Jan., 5 April 1920.

125. On conditions in Durango, see "Memoria que presenta los delegados al Congreso Pedagógico de la Ciudad de México acerca de la marcha que en el año escolar de 1919–1920 siguieran las escuelas municipales y particulares del Estado de Durango," 1920, AEC, pp. 2–9; on Michoacán, see Raby, "Los principios de la educación rural,"

When Obregón's military movement overthrew the government of Carranza in May 1920, the capital press assumed without controversy that the Secretaría de Instrucción Pública would be reestablished and that education would in some way be "federalized."[126] Municipal and state poverty had created a climate favorable to advocates of federal action in education, although they faced some resistance from state governments and their school bureaucracies, where interest in educational control had necessarily become entrenched. Advocates of federal action were not lacking in number. Ezequiel Chávez, Undersecretary of Education in the *Porfiriato*, consistently protested the attacks against the institution to which he had devoted many serious years of work. He put forward proposals for a federalization of schooling to whoever would listen.[127] One official who listened and agreed was José Vasconcelos, who had briefly acted as Secretary of Education in the short-lived government of Eulalio Gutierrez in 1914 and 1915.[128] In May 1920, acting Mexican President Adolfo de la Huerta appointed Vasconcelos to be rector of the university to which de la Huerta conceded jurisdiction over those schools then under the control of the Federal District government, i.e. preparatory, technical, and normal schools. In September 1920, a presidential decree stipulated the need for a national educational system with a well-defined and singular direction and judged that the university was in a position to assume the task of creating such a system. Federal District primary schools were to be transferred from municipal to university control.[129] These measures laid the groundwork for the establishment of the Secretaría de Educación Pública and a reform of Constitutional Article 73, Section 27, which would allow for national action in the area of primary schooling.

---

p. 555; on Sonora, see M. Quiroz Martínez, *La educación pública en el estado de Sonora*, pp. 5–10; on Tlaxcala, see C. Rafael Apanga, Gobernador Constitucional del Estado de Tlaxcala, "Informe de la gestión administrativa, comprendida del 1 de abril de 1920 a 31 de marzo de 1921," 8, 25 Oct. 1921, AGN, Acervos Presidentes, Expediente 816-T-35.

126. *Excelsior*, 29 May 1920. Growing support for federalization is discussed in John A. Britton, "Indian Education, Nationalism, and Federalism in Mexico," pp. 454–56.

127. See, for example, Ezequiel Chávez, "Iniciativa," and "Proyecto para la supresión de la Secretaría de Instrucción Pública," 27 Nov. 1914, AEC; "Las escuelas primarias no deben depender de los ayuntamientos. Memoria dirigida al Lic. Vasconcelos," 29 Dec. 1914, AEC.

128. *El Monitor*, 8 Dec. 1914.

129. *La educación pública en México a través de los mensajes presidenciales*, pp. 208, 462–67; *Boletín de la Universidad* 1, no. 2 (1920): 13.

Conclusion

In the *Porfiriato*, the idea of mass public education had growing but still tentative appeal. In the Mexican Revolution of 1910, which was ultimately a national bourgeois revolution, education became a broad-based demand and a political priority important both for modernization and social control. These dual purposes were central to petit bourgeois educational thought, which also sought a pragmatic pedagogy to counteract the allegedly theoretical and authoritarian pedagogy of the Porfirian school. Middle-sector educational thought was laced with contradictions typical of the ambiguities of the petite bourgeoisie and reflective of Mexico's particular stage of economic development. These contradictions especially revolved around the question of small- versus large-scale property and the issue of foreign participation in the economy.

If the Mexican Revolution ultimately benefited the bourgeoisie, among its major participants were peasants and workers defending their own interests, often in conflict with middle-sector strategies. The emphasis of middle-sector official educators upon the social control function of public schooling matched the militance of the exploited classes. Although neither the working class nor the peasantry could control the Revolution, they were mobilized, and through mobilization they grew organizationally and ideologically. Just as they could not win the Revolution, neither could they put forward an alternative ideology of education. Though their vigorous support for education helped to make schooling a priority, the popular forces were not always clear on how the bourgeois state might use education in its own interests. The organized labor movement adopted an alternative pedagogy, the ideas of rational education formulated by Spanish anarchist Francisco Ferrer Guardia. Associated with the strong anticlericalism of the Mexican labor movement in this period, rational education in fact became a serious alternative to bourgeois pedagogy in Yucatán where it was put into practice by the quasi-socialist movement of urban and rural workers and peasants led by the Partido Socialista de Yucatán. Critical of class domination and oppression, rational education in Yucatán served functions of consciousness-raising and peasant and worker mobilization in the struggle for immediate and long-term reforms. In many ways, Yucatán's experiment in rational education, which ended in 1924 with the liquidation of party leadership, anticipated the era of socialist education at the national level in the 1930s. Both grew out of the same dilemma:

the inability of education to improve people's lives without basic reform in the socioeconomic structure of society.

At the 1916–1917 convention which drew up the Revolution's Constitution, debates on schools centered on the role of the Church and reflected the vehement anticlericalism of a faction of the *petite bourgeoisie* and the working class. The issue of the Church's role in education was important insofar as a weakening of the Church's ideological influence was central to a bourgeois revolution. The Constitutional Convention also raised the question of the role of the state in society and the related issue of jurisdiction over education. A basic precept of the Revolution put forward by factions associated both with classical liberalism and with more radical strategies was the idea of the municipality free from state and federal control. This concept, anachronistic within the context of Mexico's recent development, was an expression of animosity toward the dictatorship. The Constitution thus abolished the Secretaría de Instrucción Pública and left responsibility for public education to the municipalities and states. However, most petit bourgeois revolutionaries recognized the need for a strong interventionist state which would attempt to correct the bottlenecks to modernization which the *Porfiriato* had left unsolved: the persistence of precapitalist enclaves; the tendency toward unproductive investment; foreign hegemony; neglect of the working classes, etc. It is not surprising, then, that when municipal and state control of public education resulted in the closing of hundreds of schools due to bankruptcy, it was assumed, in 1920, that the education ministry would not only be recreated but would exercise national jurisdiction.

Chapter 4
Creation of the State and Expansion of Schooling in the 1920s: The Framework

In the 1920s the state apparatus envisioned by Palavicini and Alvarado began to take shape under the leadership of presidents Alvaro Obregón (1920–1924) and Plutarco Elías Calles (1924–1928), pragmatic wielders of power bent upon maintaining control over the Revolution. The task of organizing the new state was monumental. In 1920, Obregón lacked full control over the revolutionary forces: political power was more effectively lodged in the states where civilian and military governors and military zone commanders often vied against one another and correspondingly against the federal government. Some regional power-holders opposed structural change and allied with traditional elites against increasing mass mobilization. Others sided with peasants and workers—sometimes on principle and often as a means of building power bases to be reckoned with at the national level.[1]

The economy had been devastated by civil war. Foreign trade declined, partly because of the depression following World War I but also as a result of United States hostility to the clauses of the Mexican Constitution affecting foreign property: Article 27 reclaimed the subsoil for the Mexican nation and forbade foreign ownership of land within 100 kilometers of borders and 50 kilometers of the coasts. Of particular interest to the North American government and business

---

1. On *caudillos* of the 1920s, see David C. Bailey, "Obregón: Mexico's Accommodating President" in *Essays on the Mexican Revolution: Revisionist Views of the Leaders*, ed. by George Wolfskill and Douglas Richmond (Austin: University of Texas Press, 1979), pp. 92–93; J. W. F. Dulles, *Yesterday in Mexico: A Chronicle of the Revolution, 1919–1936* (Austin: University of Texas Press, 1961), pp. 109–17; Gerrit Huizer, "Peasant Organization in Agrarian Reform in Mexico," in *Masses in Latin America*, ed. by Irving Louis Horowitz (New York: Oxford University Press, 1970), pp. 408–45; Edwin Lieuwin, *Mexican Militarism: The Rise and Fall of the Revolutionary Army, 1910–1940* (Albuquerque: University of New Mexico Press, 1968), pp. 36–39. On specific *caudillos*, see, for example, Heather Fowler Salamini, *Agrarian Radicalism in Veracruz, 1920–1938* (Lincoln: University of Nebraska Press, 1978), and Emilio Portes Gil, *Quince años de política mexicana* (Mexico: Ediciones Botas, 1941).

interests were the security of U.S.-owned oil wells and repayment of Mexico's foreign debt. To obtain diplomatic recognition and access to foreign credit, the Obregón government pursued negotiations with an international banking commission in New York City headed by Thomas Lamont of J. P. Morgan and Company through which the Mexicans arranged to repay a debt of $77.6 million to the United States. The price for U.S. recognition of Mexico, which came in August 1923, was Mexico's agreement not to touch foreign properties on which attempts had been made to remove oil prior to 1917.[2] As part of the accommodation process of the new Mexican state, U.S. recognition proved important in opening up credit to Mexico and in supplying arms to the Obregón government when it faced a major internal revolt in 1923, but the new relationship signified also a de facto retreat for Mexico from the constitutional principle of national control over natural resources, and acceptance of a less than equal relationship between Mexico and the United States.

In a period of inter- and intra-class warfare and economic depression, Obregón and his successor began to establish mechanisms for the creation of order and growth. State bureaucracies emerged in labor, commerce and industry, education, health, agriculture, and social welfare as well as in the traditional areas of finance and public works. The labor bureaucracy, allied with the government-favored workers' confederation, the Confederación Regional de Obreros Mexicanos (CROM), implemented protective legislation, subjected disputes to state arbitration, and organized workers under the aegis of the government while attempting to eliminate independent trade unionism. Class conciliation was basic to Obregón's program. Like Alvarado, he hoped to create harmonious relations between capital and labor.[3]

In seeking to extend control over the peasantry, Obregón utilized the new bureaucracy of education and its rural school as well as the

2. For treatment of the question of foreign debt and oil, see Lorenzo Meyer, *Mexico and the United States in the Oil Controversy, 1917–1942* (Austin: University of Texas Press, 1977), pp. 75–106, and Robert Freeman Smith, *The United States and Revolutionary Nationalism in Mexico, 1916–1932*, pp. 190–228.

3. For a discussion of Obregón's ideology see Córdova, *La ideología de la Revolución mexicana*, pp. 268–305; Narciso Bassols Batalla, *El pensamiento político de Alvaro Obregón* (Mexico: Ediciones El Caballito, 1967), pp. 75–79; and Bailey, "Obregón," p. 86. History of the CROM in this period is covered in Barry Carr, *El movimiento obrero y la política en México, 1910–1929* 1:138–221, and all of vol. 2; see also Jorge Basurto, *El proletariado industrial*, pp. 195–290; Marjorie Ruth Clark, *Organized Labor in Mexico* (Chapel Hill: University of North Carolina Press, 1934), pp. 72–78; Ramón Eduardo Ruíz, *Labor and the Ambivalent Revolutionaries*, pp. 89–93.

National Agrarian Commission. The latter, assisted by the Partido Agrarista organized from the capital and close to Obregón, worked nationally to implement some land reform. Although Obregón confirmed his commitment to the restoration of despoiled lands and the development of small property, his own experience as a successful commercial farmer influenced his preference for large-scale modern agriculture. His definitive granting of only 1,100,117 hectares of land left the agrarian structure of Mexico virtually intact. Obregón used land reform primarily as a political tool: to reward highly articulate and mobilized agrarians whose support he needed, as in the case of the *Zapatistas* of Morelos and the Partido Socialista in Yucatán; to woo *campesinos* away from potential rivals such as Villa in Chihuahua; to increase national and, more specifically, presidential jurisdiction over the regions. As a result of legislation passed in 1921 and 1922, only the president could grant definitive title to land, which might be provisionally distributed by the states with the approval of the National Agrarian Commission. The latter became an arm of presidential policy. However, Obregón's control over the countryside was far from complete: bitter struggles over land reform took place in the regions between opposing political factions of the Constitutional Revolution.[4]

When Obregón turned over power to Calles in 1924, the strength of the state had grown somewhat. In his crushing of the de la Huerta uprising in 1923–24, Obregón eliminated a large portion of disaffected and largely conservative army officers. Calles strengthened this control over the military by making a series of alliances with key state power-holders such as Saturnino Cedillo in San Luis Potosí, Tomás Garrido Canabal in Tabasco, Lázaro Cárdenas in Michoacán, Emilio Portes Gil in Tamaulipas, Joaquín Amaro, Juan Andreu Almazán and others. As Calles' Secretary of War, Amaro initiated what was to be a long process of modernization and bureaucratization of the army as an apparatus at the service of the state. However, the centralization process was far from smooth. The states continued to exercise considerable autonomy. Military rebellions were frequent. The Yaqui Indians, who had originally allied with the Sonoran gen-

4. On Obregón's agrarian ideology and policy, see Linda B. Hall, "Alvaro Obregón and the Politics of Mexican Land Reform, 1920–1924," *Hispanic American Historical Review* 60 (1980): 213–38; see also Córdova, *La ideología de la Revolución mexicana*, pp. 276–87; Bassols, *El pensamiento político de Alvaro Obregón*, pp. 50–51. On agrarian struggles in the regions, see Romana Falcón, "El surgimiento del agrarismo cardenista: Una revisión de las tesis populistas," *Historia Mexicana* 27 (1978): 343; Gerrit Huizer, "Peasant Organization," pp. 446–57; Heather Fowler Salamini, *Agrarian Radicalism in Veracruz*, pp. 36–41.

erals, took up arms once again to defend their lands; Calles' response was swift and brutal. By far the most serious challenge to state power, however, was posed by the *Cristero* rebellion. In 1926, Calles moved to enforce the anticlerical clauses of the Constitution of 1917 and in so doing unleashed a reaction by the Church and lay Catholics which nearly devastated the western states of Jalisco, Michoacán, and Colima. The revolt required a major deployment of troops and funds from the central government. Not until 1929 did the clerical forces acknowledge military defeat.[5]

In order to preserve Sonoran control over the Revolution, Obregón returned to succeed Calles as president in 1928. When the president-elect was assassinated by a clerical fanatic, a crisis occurred in the transfer of power to which Calles responded by forming the Partido Nacional Revolucionario (PNR), which brought regional military and civilian power-holders into a single political organization more firmly under control of the central civilian bureaucracy.[6] Although Calles used the PNR as his personal mechanism for maintaining political power and handpicking a series of presidents until the election of President Cárdenas in 1934, after this phase the importance of the PNR as the centralizing political institution of the Revolution became clearer.

In strengthening the state between 1924 and 1928, Calles developed the notion of a socio-democratic corporate state along the lines defined by Alvarado—a state which would regulate class conflict while simultaneously implementing social reform and creating conditions for private capital accumulation. He promised land reform and education to the rural population, rights and protection to urban and industrial workers. In the first years of his regime, land distribution was more rapid than before and was complemented by proposals to develop transportation, technical assistance, and credit facilities for land recipients. The CROM enjoyed a privileged position in the Secretaría de Industria, Comercio y Trabajo, with CROM

5. Federal-state relations in the period are discussed in Jean Meyer, *Período 1924–1928: Estado y sociedad con Calles*, in Historia de la Revolución mexicana, 23 vols (Mexico: El Colegio de México, 1977) 4:175–98. On government repression of the Yaqui revolt, see, for example, *Excelsior*, 3, 4 Feb., 10, 19 May 1927. The *Cristero* revolt is treated in detail by David C. Bailey, *Viva Cristo Rey! The Cristero Rebellion and the Church-State Conflict in Mexico*, and Jean Meyer, *La Cristiada*; see also Alicia Olivera Sedano de Bonfil, *Aspectos del conflicto religioso de 1926 a 1929. Sus antecedentes y consecuencias*.

6. Juan Felipe Leal, "The Mexican State, 1915–1973: A Historical Interpretation," p. 53.

chief Luis Morones as minister. Aggressively nationalistic when he first came to power, Calles passed new oil legislation which cancelled the compromises of the Obregón government with the oil companies. At the same time, the government created institutions and initiated investments to develop an infrastructure for nationally controlled economic growth. The Banco de México was founded in August 1925 and the Banco Nacional de Crédito Agrícola in February 1926. The government set up commissions to invest in irrigation and road construction as well.[7]

However, the radical aspects of Calles' policies—especially social reform and foreign policy—were curtailed in 1926. The retreat had structural causes. In mid-1926, with simultaneous crises in the international oil and silver markets, the federal government lost revenue and the economy as a whole suffered in a chain reaction of rising unemployment and failing industries and commercial houses. The crisis demonstrated Mexico's extraordinary dependence on foreign trade as a primary exporter and her growing dependence on the United States, which, despite its hostility to nationalist policies, was rapidly increasing investment in Mexico and replacing European investors. In 1926, Mexico was forced to suspend payment on her foreign debt. At the same time, the opposition of the U.S. oil companies to Calles' petroleum legislation and the support which President Coolidge and James R. Sheffield, U.S. ambassador to Mexico, gave to the companies, resulted in a deterioration of relations between the countries and provoked the specter of U.S. military intervention—a move also supported by many U.S. Catholics enraged by the Mexican government's attack on the Church.[8]

This situation demonstrated the power of the United States vis-à-vis Mexico. Although armed intervention was averted, the U.S. assured the preservation of its interests through the offices of a new ambassador, Dwight W. Morrow, a lawyer associated with the financial house of Morgan, a central member of the international bankers' commission responsible for negotiating payment of Mexico's foreign debt. Arriving in Mexico in the fall of 1927, Morrow persuaded Calles to abandon his nationalist oil legislation and to guarantee perpetual rights to properties acquired before 1917. Assisted by U.S.

7. For detailed discussion of Calles' economic policy, see Enrique Krauze, *La reconstrucción económica*, pp. 7–27, 31–76, 134–58.

8. On increasing North American influence in the Mexican economy and on Mexican politics, see Krauze, *La reconstrucción económica*, pp. 29–57, 211–48, 289–92. On deteriorating U.S.-Mexican relations prior to the appointment of Morrow, see Lorenzo Meyer, *Mexico and the United States in the Oil Controversy*, pp. 112–27.

government accountants and economists, Morrow assessed Mexico's ability to pay her debt and suggested economizing measures which included curtailment of land reform and other social investments. However, the retreat from social reform was not caused by U.S. pressure alone; its roots were structural and lay within the ideological parameters of the Mexican Revolution. From the beginning of his term, Calles affirmed his desire to increase private capital investment in Mexico both foreign and national. Fiscal and banking reforms initiated by Finance Minister Alberto J. Pani in 1924 and 1925 were designed to offset the hostility and suspicions of Mexican and foreign capitalists and to create, through the reforms themselves and cooperation with employers' associations, an alliance between the state and private capital. Porfirian financiers collaborated with the government in banking reforms. They also wanted reassurances for the rights of private property and profit accumulation, which meant that they favored an end to radical social reform. Further, many revolutionaries associated with the government were acquiring sizeable fortunes through land concessions and government contracts for infrastructure development which tilted their interests away from reform of benefit to labor and the peasantry.[9]

Thus within the context of a weak and dependent economy operating in a capitalist framework, the government's need to enjoy the confidence of foreign and national capital compromised its commitment to reform benefitting the oppressed. Calles' notion of social democracy based upon class harmony could provide little for the dispossessed. Whereas he decreed the expropriation of 956,852 hectares of land in 1925, the amount dropped to 502,700 in 1926 and 289,933 in 1927. Rights of large landowners to contest peasant land petitions were strengthened. Agrarian militants were forcibly repressed in many areas of the country. State and private investment turned increasingly toward large-scale agriculture at the expense of the *ejido* community and the small owner.[10]

9. On Morrow's influence on Calles' policies, see Krauze, *La reconstrucción económica*, pp. 60–62, 68–69. On Pani's fiscal reforms, see Córdova, *La ideología de la Revolución mexicana*, pp. 351–67. On the growth of fortunes among the revolutionaries, see Córdova, *La ideología de la Revolución mexicana*, pp. 30, 379; Lorenzo Meyer, *Mexico and the United States in the Oil Controversy*, p. 132; and Lieuwen, *Mexican Militarism*, p. 39.

10. Figures on land distribution are from Krauze, *La reconstrucción económica*, p. 62. Agrarian legislation at the state level was in general more partial to large landowners than was federal legislation, in part because revolutionary generals had acquired large tracts of land and so identified with the interests of landowners (see ibid., pp. 112–13). The degree to which land reform was carried out in the period depended upon the

Regarding industrial workers, the CROM consented to abate its demands on employers while expounding an ideology of cooperation between labor and capital in the interests of development. The workers' organization spent much of its time fighting independent unions, especially the anarchist Confederación General de Trabajadores, while attempting to foster centralized control over its affiliate unions for the sake of social peace. In 1925, it abandoned its support for the *Escuela Racionalista* and henceforth worked closely with the state educational bureaucracy. In 1928, Calles stated that workers' politics in Mexico had concluded its stage of struggle and had entered a new phase of "revolutionary" cooperation with capital.[11] At the same time, Calles hoped to use workers' organizations to persuade industry to modernize. He proposed a mixed commission of owners, workers, and government technicians to examine national industry and to suggest where necessary the renovation of existing facilities, which would receive government financial assistance. Although this scheme corresponded to Calles' notion of cooperation between antagonistic groups in the development process under the aegis of the state, his retreat from social reform, continued by the governments which he dominated until 1934, provoked a new level of mobilization and disenchantment within the ranks of labor and the peasantry. This popular agitation in turn brought to the forefront of the PNR the party's more radical wing, whose strength determined a more militant administration under the leadership of Lázaro Cárdenas in 1934. Although Cárdenas ousted Calles and initiated a new period of social reform in Mexico, it is important to note that it came from within the PNR and operated within the established political-economic parameters.

---

strength of the organized peasantry and often the support of the local state governor such as Adalberto Tejeda in Veracruz, Emilio Portes Gil in Tamaulipas, Francisco Mújica and Lázaro Cárdenas in Michoacán; see Heather Fowler Salamini, *Agrarian Radicalism in Veracruz*, pp. 25–40, Portes Gil, *Quince años de política mexicana*, p. 446; Nathaniel and Sylvia Weyl, *The Reconquest of Mexico: The Years of Lázaro Cárdenas* (New York: Oxford University Press, 1939), pp. 79–80; Gerrit Huizer, "Peasant Organization," pp. 447–64. On repression of agrarian militants, see Krauze, *La reconstrucción económica*, p. 127; Huizer, "Peasant Organization," pp. 450–64; Paul Friedrich, *Agrarian Revolt in a Mexican Village* (Chicago: University of Chicago Press, 1977), pp. 78–130. On growing investment in large-scale agriculture, see Krauze, *La reconstrucción económica*, pp. 157, 163.

11. On CROM policy, see Basurto, *El proletariado industrial*, pp. 248–52. On efforts to defeat independent trade unionism, see, for example, *Excelsior*, 3, 4, 5 Feb. 1927. On Calles' explanation of labor's cooperation with capital, see Córdova, *La ideología de la Revolución mexicana*, pp. 327–28.

Creation and Structure of the Secretaría de Educación Pública

Education became a major reform in the 1920s because it was one mandate of the Revolution upon which most agreed and one which did not challenge existing property relationships. It was also an important means of securing loyalty to the new state. Further, it was dramatically catapulted into national prominence by a dynamic intellectual, José Vasconcelos, who upon becoming rector of the university in May 1920 launched an each-one-teach-one campaign, which became a national crusade for schools and culture involving a true cross-section of the population from unemployed school teachers to Cananea miners and Chiapaneco *campesinos* to idle young ladies who taught their servants to read and write.[12] Thus capital educators initiated a project which provoked an interest in schooling on a national basis and a ground swell of support for federal action in the field of education.

With the assistance of the university council, Vasconcelos drew up the proposal that would result in the creation of the Secretaría de Educación Pública (SEP).[13] The legislation involved constitutional reform of transitory Article 14 and a change in Article 73 so as to permit Congress to establish schools at all levels in the states. Although the reform proposal stipulated that the federal government would maintain its own schools and not interfere with the rights of states to create and sustain their own school systems, opposition was anticipated from those most committed to state sovereignty, including teachers and officials with interests vested in state school bureaucracies. For example, while the National Congress of Teachers meeting in Mexico in 1920 unanimously endorsed joint state-federal action in the states, they recoiled at a proposal for a centralization of schooling.[14] Those who supported the creation of the SEP stressed that federal action would not supercede state and local jurisdiction but complement it in areas where the states and municipalities could not

---

12. See *Boletín de la Universidad* (hereafter cited as *BU*) 1, no. 1 (1920): 55–90; 1, no. 3 (1921): 54–88; 1, no. 4 (1921): 37–43. See also *Excelsior*, 19 June 1920; 7 Jan. 1921.

13. He had much assistance. For instance, Ezequiel Chávez served on the council and drew up several federalization projects which probably influenced Vasconcelos although the latter claimed that the final proposal was his own creation. See José Vasconcelos, *El desastre*, in *Obras completas* (Mexico: Librería Mexicanos Unidos, 1957) 1:1225. The final proposal for the creation of the SEP which includes a description of its structure can be found in *BU* 1, no. 1 (1920): 130–43.

14. Eduardo Urzaiz, *Congreso Nacional de Maestros*, p. 5.

afford it. In congressional debates, opinion was overwhelmingly in favor of this type of federal action: supporters continually juxtaposed sovereignty of the states with the sovereignty of ignorance and misery. With the help of strong lobbying by Vasconcelos, the work of Congressional deputies, and the obviously necessary support of President Obregón, reforms of transitory Articles 14 and 73 passed the House in February 1921 and the Senate shortly thereafter.[15]

Vasconcelos then toured a number of states to build support for ratification of the reforms. On these trips to Jalisco, Colima, Aguascalientes, Zacatecas, and Guanajuato, Vasconcelos took with him young Mexico City intellectuals and artists who performed their music or read poetry before gatherings of state officials, teachers, and the cultured *gente decente* or *clase media*.[16] Congressional deputies favoring the reform went along on these trips as did Ezequiel Salcedo, an important member of CROM and chief of the national printing office, who organized support meetings with groups of workers. The trips were designed especially to win over state governors, municipal officials, bureaucrats in state offices of education, and teachers. The creation of the SEP was presented as compatible with their interest in developing education and raising teachers' wages.

In October 1921, Obregón formally created the Secretaría de Educación Pública and named Vasconcelos its first minister. Given the degree of state and municipal bankruptcy, the SEP enjoyed a strong bargaining position in its bid to initiate schooling. Areas of priority were set in rural, primary, and vocational education. The SEP extended its activities to the states in a variety of ways. It directly created and administered its own schools with the consent of the states; it jointly created and administered them with representatives of state and municipal governments; it managed state and federal schools with the help of local subsidies; and/or the federal government provided outright subsidies to the states for the financing of state and federal schools.[17] In the early years, the federal government granted loans and subsidies to state governments requesting aid to pay teachers' wages, repair or complete buildings, purchase pianos, desks, benches, and school supplies.[18] The tendency was, however, toward

15. Congressional debates are reprinted in *BU* 1, no. 4 (1921): 258–320. For Vasconcelos' interpretation of the issue, see *El desastre*, pp. 1225–33, 1258–63.
16. Vasconcelos describes these trips in detail in *El desastre*, pp. 1218–25.
17. *Boletín de la Secretaría de Educación Pública* (hereafter cited as *BSEP*) 1, no. 3 (1923): 187.
18. See, for example, José Ochoa to Obregón, 22 Sept. 1921, Obregón to José Ochoa, 23 Sept. 1921, AGN, Acervos Presidentes, Expediente 816-T-25; Obregón to

greater rationalization and centralization in both expenditure and administration. In each state, the SEP had a delegated representative, who in October 1924 became a director of federal education responsible for directing, administering, and inspecting federal schools in his state. In December 1924, Calles determined that federal money destined for education in the states would be administered only by the federal representative's office and not given in direct subsidy to the states.[19]

When the SEP took shape in 1921, it was divided into three general sections—schools, libraries, and the fine arts. The Department of Schools was responsible for all primary, secondary, technical, and normal schooling. Within it was a section on school hygiene and medical inspection. The Department of Libraries, while reflecting Vasconcelos' personal admiration for the U.S. public library system and his desire to make reading materials available to his countrymen, could also be seen as an extension of nineteenth-century educational policy on a grand scale.[20] Thousands of small libraries were created in the 1920s as cheap editions of European and Mexican literature and works of social science were published by the Editorial Section, originally created by Palavicini and vastly amplified under Vasconcelos. The Department of Fine Arts, also created under Palavicini and reflecting both a tradition in educational policy and the interests of young Mexican intellectuals in national culture, quickly became under Vasconcelos the center of a cultural renaissance in music, the plastic arts, and literature. Independent of these departments were the Departments of Indigenous Culture and the Literacy Campaign, both of which Vasconcelos saw as temporary sections. Like his nineteenth-century predecessors, Vasconcelos viewed indigenous education as incorporation into the dominant European culture and objected to permanent special and separate indigenous schooling.[21]

SEP, 16 Dec. 1921, AGN, Acervos Presidentes, Expediente 121-E-C-6; Figueroa to Torreblanco, 14 Nov. 1922, AGN, Acervos Presidentes, Expediente 241-E-25; Obregón to SEP, 7 May 1923, AGN, Acervos Presidentes, Expediente 121-E-C; Obregón to SEP, 29 May 1923, AGN, Acervos Presidentes, Expediente 121-E-C-14; Obregón to SEP, 18 Sept. 1923, AGN, Acervos Presidentes, Expediente 121-E-C-22; Obregón to SEP, 27 August 1924, AGN, Acervos Presidentes, Expediente 121-E-C-57.

19. Obregón to SEP, 6 Oct. 1924, AGN, Acervos Presidentes, Expediente 121-E-E-96; Calles to SEP, 17 Dec. 1924, AGN, Acervos Presidentes, Expediente 121-E-E-84.

20. In fact, the suggestion for small branch and mobile libraries in the capital may have come from Salvador Hernández Barrón, chief of the Department of Information and Bibliography at the Biblioteca Nacional. He said he was basing his proposals on experiences in Argentina as well as the United States (see *Excelsior*, 28 Jan. 1921).

21. Vasconcelos, *El desastre*, p. 1251.

The Department of Indigenous Culture quickly took up responsibility for the majority of federal schools created in rural areas of the states and so became the most dynamic section of the SEP. Despite the enthusiasm for schools, the work of the Secretaría de Educación Pública was slow and difficult. The seemingly simple task of reincorporating into the SEP the capital's primary schools was expensive, tedious, and complex. Classrooms were overcrowded with 90 to 100 pupils often jammed into one room. The condition of many buildings was hazardous for students—faulty roofing, deteriorating floors, and unsanitary water installations were common.[22] Repairs were expensive, high rents stymied the search for new buildings, and the SEP's limited budget prevented the rapid construction of new schools. In 1924, half the school-age population of the capital was still out of school. By the end of the 1920s, the number of public primary schools in the capital had not returned to its 1907 level although the number of students enrolled had increased.

The SEP also sought to improve supervision over teachers which had broken down in the Revolution. Some teachers on the payroll did not teach at all; absenteeism and lateness abounded; many teachers were without formal training.[23] The SEP rationalized the inspection system to exert more control over teachers, fined them for lateness, fired many, and demoted others while expanding training facilities in the Escuela Nacional de Maestros, which moved to the former Escuela Nacional de Agricultura to provide more pragmatic training in the new "action" pedagogy of "learning by doing." The SEP introduced the latter in 1924 in a move consistent with the pedagogical thought of the Revolution. Medical inspection was revamped to cope with the high level of disease among school children and the unhygienic conditions of the schools. The SEP also introduced a school breakfast program to entice children to attend and to combat the problem of poor nutrition. Although much heralded by Vasconcelos for its novelty and departure from the negligent policies of the dictatorship, this sort of assistance had been traditional in Mexican public school policy although never on such a scale.

As in the case of primary schools, the first task of the office of technical education, which was within the Department of Schools, was to reincorporate technical schools which had passed to the Ministry of

22. On conditions of the schools, see *BSEP* 1, no. 1 (1922): 188–89, 193–94; Vasconcelos, *El desastre*, p. 1228; M. Peralta to Undersecretary, SEP, 9 Oct. 1922, AGN, Acervos Presidentes, Expediente 121-E-E-15.
23. See *Exelsior*, 15, 22 Jan. 1921.

Commerce and Industry in the Carranza period, and to undertake repairs and renovations of existing plant and equipment, which had fallen into disrepair. Proposals were made for the creation of new schools to train skilled workers and engineers for modernization. Women's vocational education was expanded. A few vocational schools, especially in the traditional crafts, were created in the states.

Despite movements toward autonomy, the university remained under the jurisdiction of the SEP in this period. Higher education emphasized pragmatic technical education for modernization, not only by establishing schools like the Facultad de Ciencias Químicas, but also by introducing the study of applied social sciences such as industrial psychology and social work.[24] Simultaneously, much emphasis and publicity was given to cultural production in philosophy, the humanities, and fine arts in part to establish international respectability in arts and letters and in part to begin "defining" Mexico's national identity.

The most innovative area of activity was rural education. Under the Department of Indigenous Culture, "missionary" teachers ventured forth to study the needs and socioeconomic and cultural conditions of different areas, to interest communities in education, and to recruit teachers locally. The rural teachers, who were to constitute a vanguard of the school movement, needed training which was gradually provided by mobile cultural missions offering short courses in a given region in agriculture, crafts, sports, hygiene, and pedagogy. This training was supplemented by the creation of regional rural normal schools, which numbered 16 by 1931. In addition, the SEP offered special summer courses for teachers in Mexico City and issued a variety of pamphlets, periodicals, instructional manuals, and other publications to assist teachers. In the Calles period, the Casa del Estudiante Indígena was created in Mexico City also as a means of preparing rural teachers.

In 1924, Manuel Puig Casauranc, a Calles political appointee, replaced Vasconcelos as minister and initiated a reorganization of the SEP to increase its bureaucratic control and efficiency. This bureaucratization was both a response to the need to economize and an expression of the technocratic and centralizing approach of the Calles government. The creation of an administrative department and an office of statistics reflected the trend. As stated, the SEP sought more control over its delegates in the states who became directors of the federal schools. Their accountability to the central SEP

24. Krauze, *Los caudillos culturales*, pp. 170–71.

office was strengthened by a series of measures stipulating requirements for appointment and promotion, by requiring regular monthly
reports and responses to frequent questionnaires and permanent offices with a secretarial staff and a corps of inspectors to insure the
implementation of policy in the schools.[25] The directors reported to
the new Department of Rural and Outlying Primary Schools and Incorporation of Indigenous Culture, which replaced the old section of
indigenous culture and came to control all federal primary schools in
the states. The old Department of Schools became the Department of
Primary and Normal Schools with focus solely on the capital. A new
section of psychopedagogy and hygiene initiated aptitude and
achievement testing to improve the tracking function of education in
the capital. Technical education became a separate department devoted to modernizing technical training, especially in the capital. A
new office of secondary education created six new schools in Mexico
City.

While the Department of Libraries continued to disseminate literature on a relatively large scale, the fine arts movement was curtailed
in the Calles period. The Office of Anthropology, which was responsible for excavations, archaeological studies, and the National Mu-
seum and had been functioning within the Department of Agriculture,
was reintegrated into the educational ministry where it continued
and expanded not only its excavations but also its studies of contemporary indigenous cultures. A new government radio station under
SEP jurisdiction was used by all government ministries for purposes
of propaganda and education.

In 1928, the SEP had 29 federal directors with 117 inspectors in
the states responsible for 5,930 schools, in addition to the expanded
bureaucracy responsible for education in the capital. However, given
the instability of the state, its meager resources, and the enduring
strength of the regions, the SEP established in these years more a
structure for bureaucracy than the effective functioning of one. The
SEP complained that its federal directors were not always reliable or
effective. Given the rudimentary nature of the inspection system, a
great deal of liberty remained in the hands of teachers and inspectors. Thus, as in the *Porfiriato*, the probability was low that government programs would be enforced to the letter. In a situation of
continuing class conflict and mass mobilization, teachers became a

25. *El esfuerzo educativo en México, 1924–1928*, 2 vols. (Mexico: SEP, 1928) 1:xxxv–
xxxvi; Obregón to SEP, 6 Oct. 1924, AGN, Acervos Presidentes, Expediente 121-E-E-
96.

political force—unionizing for better wages and working conditions, pressuring for greater socioeconomic reform or resisting the reforms put forward. Further, in its self-criticism in 1928, the SEP complained of lack of coordination between the federal and state school systems and specified the need for greater synchronization and federal control.[26]

Ideological Parameters of the SEP, 1920–1928

José Vasconcelos made education a central issue of reform because he was a charismatic mobilizer of people and a serious creator of institutions. He was not, however, a profound social thinker, but rather an aesthetic philosopher and weaver of spiritual utopias.[27] His belief in a nation of craftsmen was almost an emotional reaction against the squalor, greed, and social schisms created by modernization.[28] His socioeconomic thought penetrated not much more deeply. In the Revolution, he scarcely moved beyond his original allegiance to Francisco I. Madero and his hope that a government of honorable men would purge a corrupt and barbarous environment. Although Vasconcelos' *petit bourgeois* origins made him more critical of privilege than was the wealthy Madero, Vasconcelos was an elitist—probably by virtue of his class origins and his education at the Escuela Nacional Preparatoria and the Escuela de Derecho from which he emerged as a star member of the gifted intellectual generation of 1906. He tended to believe in radical principle but to be skeptical of those who acted upon such principles. Thus while he believed in agrarian reform, he considered Zapata a rapist and a bandit. His assessment of Felipe Carrillo Puerto's movement in Yucatán was negative.[29] "We decide the best manner of educating them," he told a university audience in 1920 with reference to the people.[30] His deepest feelings were conservative—a fact revealed by his attitude toward the indigenous people whom he wished to incorporate into European civilization, by his publication and dissemination of the European classics in a coun-

26. *El esfuerzo* 1:xiv–xvi, 7–8, 14–15, 45, 48, 83.
27. Writings on Vasconcelos are extensive although not always profound or comprehensive. Of particular value are José Joaquín Blanco, *Se llamaba Vasconcelos. Una evocación crítica* (Mexico: Fondo de Cultura Económica, 1977), and John Haddox, *Vasconcelos of Mexico: Philosopher and Prophet* (Austin: University of Texas Press, 1967).
28. The theme is further discussed in chapter 8 of this text.
29. Vasconcelos, *El desastre*, pp. 1240–41, 1293–1307.
30. Vasconcelos, *Discursos* (Mexico: Ediciones Botas, 1950), p. 10.

try which was largely illiterate, by his constant appeal to the *gente decente*, by his recruitment of university personnel and Porfirian pedagogues for the new educational bureaucracy, and by his decision not to alter texts but to reprint Justo Sierra's *Historia patria* for use in primary schools.

Like university youth in many Latin American countries at the turn of the century, Vasconcelos had been influenced by the Uruguayan writer, José Enrique Rodó, who had recommended a crusade to civilize and incorporate the "barbaric" masses into "civilization"—a movement in which the Christian spirit of equality would be tempered by a Greek spirit of hierarchy and respect for genius.[31] Vasconcelos initiated in Mexico a crusade linking, in his words, the "working brains" with the "working hands," but one in which he firmly believed the "working brains" should control and orient the "working hands."[32] His model was the early Christian missionary, the only elite European figure who had been capable of reaching the people. The key words of his mobilization were words of hierarchy and paternalism. His teachers were "noble heroes filled with evangelical fervor which had animated the race in the days of Conquest;" they would "redeem" the masses through "work, virtue, and knowledge."[33] They were to respond to the problem of *miseria* with *misericordia*—or pity—in their work among the *humildes*, the *pobres*, the *desheredados*.[34] In fact, the religious symbolism was apt: Vasconcelos' crusade was in many ways an extension of nineteenth-century educators' attempts to replace the Church as the principal ideological institution of society with the public school system. The new school, named the Casa del Pueblo, was to replace the Church as the center of the community.

Despite these predominant tendencies, Vasconcelos facilitated the articulation within the SEP of contradictions inherent in the ongoing revolutionary situation in Mexico. Because middle-income groups to whom he appealed for action were not a social class but a group between the owning class and the dispossessed, in a period of class conflict these people could identify either with the interests of property or with the interests of the dispossessed. A man of tremendous internal contradiction, Vasconcelos himself fanned the flames of potential radicalization in expressing resentment against intellectuals who iso-

---

31. José Enrique Rodó, *Ariel* (Monterrey: Tallenes Modernos de Lozano, 1908), p. 31.
32. Vasconcelos, *Discursos*, pp. 23–25.
33. Ibid., pp. 10–11.
34. Ibid., pp. 12, 33, 35.

lated themselves from social issues. Upon assuming the position of university rector in 1920, he told the audience:

> I do not come before you today to concede honorary degrees on foreigners who visit us or to preside over councils which have nothing to do with our social needs. . . . I have seen French literature taught here while the spectacle of children abandoned in our barrios goes unnoticed—children the state ought to feed and educate . . . I come here as a delegate of the Revolution . . . to invite you to join me in the struggle . . . I do not come to work for the university but to ask the university to work for the people. . . . I call upon you and all of the intellectuals of Mexico to leave your ivory towers to sign a pact of alliance with the Revolution.[35]

On Teachers' Day, he emphasized the superior understanding and services of the elementary teacher over the university professor:

> The source of civilization, you impart knowledge which regenerates men. . . . The teacher and the tyrant are enemies. . . . The liberator and the teacher are one. The teacher knows better than the university professor the causes of justice. From the ranks of our school teachers have come the deputies, governors, ministers of the new government. If the *campesino* put the strength of his hands to the service of social progress, in many instances it was the teachers who awakened his consciousness.[36]

While upgrading the image of the primary school teacher was part of the bourgeois ideology of schooling, identifying the teacher with the cause of social justice in a revolutionary situation probably contributed to the radicalization of some teachers, as did the real possibilities for action opened by the SEP's programs and policies.

Within the SEP in the early 1920s, ideological lines were broadly drawn between urban educators and those involved in rural schooling (especially at the lower levels of the bureaucracy). The more conservative approach characteristic of urban educators resulted in part from the participation of many of them in the Porfirian school bureaucracy and their lack of identification with the popular revolution.[37] These people exercised considerable influence over urban schooling, technical education, texts, programs, the artistic movement, and the definition of rural pedagogy. While most viewed edu-

35. Ibid., p. 9.
36. Ibid., pp. 43–44.
37. Porfirian pedagogues Ezequiel Chávez, Daniel Delgadillo, José María Bonilla, Gregorio Torres Quintero, for instance, collaborated closely with the school program.

cation as a potential source of economic betterment for individuals, they tended to underestimate the need for structural reforms and to view education as disciplining, civilizing, and controlling. Although perhaps overly transparent, the position advanced by a writer in the SEP magazine, *El Maestro*, represented a tendency in this group. In relation to working class agitation, he wrote:

> We must guide them . . . against the terrible anti-social falsities which will soon make the masses fanatic. . . . Everyone must work not for himself alone but for all people who will receive in the future the disastrous consequences of egoistic and perverse acts. . . . Nothing will be realized while Mexicans do not group with the faith of Roman citizens to cooperate in the conservation and prosperity of the state.[38]

On the other hand, rural education appears to have attracted those more interested in structural social change. Perhaps because the Obregón regime wished to co-opt the *Zapatista* movement, two figures allegedly associated with the latter, the engineer Carlos M. Peralta and Guerreran politician Francisco Figueroa, were made chief administrative assistant and subsecretary of education. Although Vasconcelos claimed that they represented *Zapatismo* and agrarianism in the SEP, the radical impulse in rural education seems to have come less from these men and more from educational missionaries and teachers working for the Department of Indigenous Culture.[39] Some of these appear to have been associated with the Partido Agrarista, whose leader, Antonio Díaz Soto y Gama, had also been allied with Zapata. Before Congress in 1922, Antonio Díaz Soto y Gama lashed out against the urban element in the SEP:

> If we want to do good work, we ought to push aside these men who do not love the people, who want to live in dance halls and socialize with classes higher than they. . . . As a sincere friend of Vasconcelos . . . , I say to him, "I hope you as a talented, working man, as a completely revolutionary man, do not vacillate between the Revolution and the reaction, between the city and the country, but that you are in the fields with nature, with intuition, with the future: Leave the past, leave Horace and Virgil, and all those classical authors!"[40]

In September 1922, the first congress of missionary teachers reg-

38. *El Maestro* 1, no. 4 (1921): 363–64.
39. For Vasconcelos' point of view, see *El desastre*, pp. 1268–69.
40. *BSEP* 1, no. 3 (1923): 75.

istered a conflict with urban educators, which crystallized in the following years. The rural school, they argued, should be fundamentally dedicated to improving the life of the rural collectivity, which often necessitated real structural reform. In 1924, when the SEP proposed to incorporate the Department of Indigenous Culture into the Department of Schools, teachers and agrarian groups immediately protested. They saw the Department of Indigenous Culture as more sympathetic to their concerns for socioeconomic change than the more conservative Department of Schools, which one group claimed was controlled by a known Knight of Columbus.[41] In 1928, SEP analysts noted a general difference between rural and urban teachers: the former, newly recruited, of "rude" origin, and socially committed; the latter, graduates of Porfirian Normal Schools, *clase media*, and "socially respectable."[42] The former took avidly to action pedagogy. The latter were somewhat resistant to the reforms. There were of course exceptions: there were conservative and lax teachers in rural areas and political militants in the city schools.

It was the dominant view of the SEP hierarchy in the early 1920s that education could bring about economic remuneration to the individual Mexican while increasing his or her productive capacity and that of the nation. The underlying purpose of the action school was to encourage greater individual initiative while effectively inculcating habits of work and making more productive the relationship between school and economy. Education, wrote the SEP, was to be based on the "twin pillars of intelligent instruction and productive work."[43] There was a contradiction between the pedagogy's goals and the existing social structure which became apparent in both rural and urban education.

In rural education, top officials believed that they could integrate community and market economy in a manner benefiting the community and the nation. Lack of familiarity with rural Mexico and ideological bias helped to shape the judgement of educators that *campesinos* were isolated from the market economy when in fact they were marginalized within it by their meager land resources, technology, and exploitative market relationships. Their marginalized integration had been and continued to be essential to the functioning of a

41. Eduardo Moreno, President, Primer Convención Regional de Querétaro, to Obregón, 23 May 1924, AGN, Acervos Presidentes, Expediente 711-I-8; see also Miguel Segovia to Obregón, 19 May 1924, AGN, Acervos Presidentes, Expediente 711-I-8.
42. *El esfuerzo* 1:38–39.
43. *BSEP* 1, no. 3 (1923): 189; see also ibid., pp. 83–86.

capitalist economy where the *campesino* served as a source of cheap labor and his land as a factor of production. The educators' vision of the *campesino* as "isolated" probably flowed from the nineteenth-century liberal view of the indigenous community as closed, backward, and, as such, an obstacle to progress. Perhaps more confidently than Justo Sierra, many revolutionary educators, because of their vision of a nation of small-holders, postulated a belief in the redeemability and integration of the rural community as a productive unit within the nation. Within this vision, education for skills, behavior modification, and product diversification became a priority. As Vasconcelos said:

> Let us take the campesino under our wing and teach him to increase his production through the use of better tools and methods.[44]

However, rural missionaries and teachers who came face to face with deeply ingrained rural power structures which depended upon *campesino* marginalization often perceived the naivete of the SEP's assumption that simple skill training and the introduction of new products would significantly alter rural life for the better. Though the SEP spoke of the need for land and other reforms, it proceeded as if property redistribution was not a prerequisite for the fulfillment of educational goals. In this behavior, educators reflected not only personal biases—which were often very real—but the relative weakness of their ministry vis-à-vis other organs of the state regarding implementation of structural change. In the absence of structural reform, as a solution to the contradiction between large and small property, the SEP suggested cooperativism through which a community could supposedly pool resources to improve income without augmenting factors of production such as land.

A second contradiction in educational policy and ideology affected the urban working class. Within the philosophy of small-scale production, technical education emphasized upgrading crafts skills to secure better remuneration for individual producers, but it increasingly involved training for modern industrial production and here ran squarely into the inequities between capital and labor. The SEP before 1924 was not particularly friendly to the concept of trade unionism.[45] In vocational and night schools and workers' cultural centers, SEP directives told teachers to emphasize property rights and the resolution of labor conflicts "without prejudicing the interest of the

---

44. Vasconcelos, *Discursos*, p. 12.
45. See, for example, Vasconcelos, *El desastre*, pp. 1268, 1346–70.

collectivity," with special reference to state arbitration.[46] The general approach to civics teaching in texts and programs stressed individual rather than collective and class rights and the rights of private property rather than the Constitutional articles which modified or challenged them.[47]

In the Calles period, changes took place within the SEP which reflected the increasing strength of the state and the emergence of a social democratic ideology. Puig Casauranc was a bureaucrat of the time who lacked Vasconcelos' imagination and eccentric idealism. The liberalism of the 1920s blended easily into the corporatism of Calles which influenced education both ideologically and structurally. With a greater understanding of the task of modernization, educators veered away from schooling for increased production on an individual basis to encourage individual training for a specialized task within a differentiated socioeconomic hierarchy. Moisés Sáenz, Undersecretary of Education in this period, emphasized:

> The vocational principle wishes to say that all men ought to be agents of production within the group in which they live and that education ought to capacitate them definitively to fulfill this function.[48]

Democracy came to mean a united effort for production within a corporate society based on principles of class conciliation and harmony. As Puig Casauranc stated, education would create a "homogeneous collective organization which puts its effort to national development."[49]

Structurally, this change meant a deepening of the selective and hierarchical organization of the school system. To improve the sort-

46. See, for example, *BSEP* 1, no. 1 (1922): 162–63.

47. See José María Bonilla, *Derechos civiles* (Mexico: Herrero Hermanos, 1918), and José María Bonilla, *Derechos individuales* (Mexico: Herrero Hermanos, 1918). The texts are analyzed in chapter 7.

48. As quoted in Francisco Larroyo, *Historia de la educación comparada en México*, p. 338. Sáenz' ideas permeated rural education in the period. They are best expressed in two reports which he made to the SEP in these years: *Escuelas federales en la Sierra de Puebla. Informe sobre la visita a las escuelas federales en la Sierra de Puebla realizado por el C. Subsecretario de Educación, Prof. Moisés Sáenz*, Publicaciones de la SEP 15, no. 5 (1927), and *Escuelas federales en San Luis Potosí. Informe de la visita practiada por el Subsecretario de Educacion en noviembre de 1927*, Publicaciones de la SEP 18, no. 6 (1928) and *BSEP* 7, no. 2 (1928). See also Sáenz, *La educación rural en México*, Publicaciones de la SEP 19, no. 20 (1928). His classic statement on his hopes for the school and explanation for its failures is found in Sáenz, *Carapán* (Morelia: Departamento de Promoción Cultural del Gobierno de Michoacán, 1970). A helpful essay summarizing his educational ideas is John A. Britton, "Moisés Sáenz, nacionalista mexicano," in *Historia Mexicana* 22 (1972): 79–98.

49. *BSEP* 6, no. 3 (1927): 12.

ing out function of education for differentiated economic roles, the SEP introduced testing and tracking. Secondary education with differentiated curricula and vocational, industrial, and agricultural schooling became priorities. The SEP came to be dominated by social engineers, trained in child psychology, industrial psychology, and current pedagogical theory. These trends were influenced by contemporary North American education, which was being reformed and expanded in this period to meet similar ends. SEP personnel participated regularly in U.S. and Pan-American Union seminars and conferences and attempted to adapt programs and methods to their work in Mexico. Moisés Sáenz, a follower of John Dewey trained at Columbia University, provided leadership in this process.

In the cities, the contradictions between education for social betterment and the unequal relationship between labor and capital may have been blunted in part because of CROM's sway over organized workers, but the contradiction between the school's goals and the intact system of domination became acute in rural education. Puig Casauranc clung to the notion of integrating the isolated rural population into the market economy through skill-training and product diversification.[50] The need for land reform was more consistently acknowledged as was the need for increased technical assistance, credit, and other infrastructural support for land recipients and small producers. Cooperatives became more and more popular as an official solution. But the need for land reform was negatively described as securing enough land for the land-hungry through redistribution of unused *hacienda* lands without seriously altering the *hacienda* system. At the same time, Luis León, Minister of Agriculture, emphasized in 1927 the rights of owners to contest *campesino* land claims through juridical procedure.[51] Rural teachers knew that the legal rights of owners in the courts prevented *campesinos* from obtaining good land and often any land at all; meanwhile, the federal government failed to supply promised technical assistance on an adequate scale.[52]

As a result of these contradictions, Puig Casauranc became increasingly concerned about the politicization of rural teachers. In their agitation for social reform, he saw them as "agents of disruption and social dissolution."[53] The Church-state dispute increased the politicization of teachers. The school became a target for attack as *Cristero*

---

50. *BSEP* 5, no. 4 (1926): 7.
51. Ibid., p. 14; *BSEP* 6, no. 3 (1927): 24–35.
52. For lack of cooperation from other government departments, see *El esfuerzo* 1:xiii.
53. *BSEP* 7, no. 3 (1928): 18.

peasants, organized by the National League for Religious Defense, burned down schoolhouses, harrassed and even murdered teachers.[54] Church supporters, often in league with *hacienda* owners, were able to play upon the real and imagined fears of families and communities about the new and alien institution of the school. While many teachers were dogmatically anticlerical, others understood that the *Cristero* revolt was often supported and used by those who opposed basic reforms for the *campesino*. In this conflict, the SEP itself backed off, attempting to steer an even course. It sought to win community loyalties away from the Church while deploring the use of the school as a channel for agitation for social reform. However, mass mobilization grew in the late 1920s and by the early 1930s forced the government to renew its commitment to structural reforms.

Quantitative Indicators of School Policy in the 1920s

Throughout the 1920s, the federal budget was subject to constant crisis due to economic dislocation wrought by revolution, political instability, and armed rebellions. To these factors must be added the weakness of the dependent economy in relation to the world market and the political-economic demands placed upon it by metropolitan powers such as the United States. Although the percentage of the federal budget devoted to education rose above the 7.2 percent allocated by Díaz in 1910, expenditures were lower than original allocations and the educational effort—given its extension and scope—functioned on a shoestring, subject to constant corner-cutting. The goal was to accomplish as much as possible with as little expenditure as possible.[55]

Table 4.1 indicates that expansion in educational spending was not unilinear. The 30,688,465 pesos spent in 1922 was one half of what had been allocated; the 38,591,674 pesos spent in 1923 was reduced by over 10 million pesos in 1924 due to the de la Huerta rebellion.

54. Teachers were not always victims and antagonists of the *Cristeros*. In Jalisco, for instance, they joined both sides of the dispute. While many rural teachers were attacked by the *Cristeros*, many urban teachers joined the Church boycott of public schools (see, for example, *Excelsior*, 4 Feb. 1927).

55. For crisis affecting the educational budget, see for example, Obregón to Figueroa, 14 Oct. 1922, AGN, Acervos Presidentes, Expediente 121-E-E-15; Obregón to SEP, 24 Nov. 1922, AGN, Acervos Presidentes, Expediente 121-E-E-22; Calles to Secretaría de Hacienda y Crédito Público, 17 March 1925, AGN, Acervos Presidentes, Expediente 121-E-E-71.

TABLE   4.1

Federal Expenditures on Education, 1922–1928 (Mexican Pesos)

	Amount Spent	% of Budget
1922	30,688,465	8.9
1923	38,591,674	9.3
1924	25,593,347	9.3
1925	21,970,813	6.0
1926	26,707,729	7.5
1927	25,808,764	7.8
1928	25,800,446	8.0

Note: There is a discrepancy in total budget figures and in educational expenditures for these years. For example, educational expenditures indicated above and the percentage they represent of the total budget for the years 1925 to 1928 were taken from *Noticia estadística sobre la educación pública in México correspondiente al año de 1927* (Mexico: Talleres Gráficos de la Nación, 1929) and *Noticia estadística sobre la educación pública en México correspondiente al año de 1928* (Mexico: Talleres Gráficos de la Nación, 1930). Figures from *Anuario estadístico*, 1930 (Mexico: Talleres Gráficos de la Secretaría de Agricultura y Fomento, 1930) for these years are slightly less, although they represent approximately the same proportions of the indicated federal budgets (7%, 7%, 7%, and 9% of the budgets for 1925 through 1928, respectively).

Sources: *Boletín de la Secretaría de Educación Pública* 1, no. 3 (1923); *Boletín de la Secretaría de Educación Pública* 2, nos. 5 and 6 (1923–1924); *Noticia estadística sobre la educación pública en México correspondiente al año de 1927*; *Noticia estadística sobre la educación pública en México correspondiente al año de 1928*; James Wilkie, *The Mexican Revolution: Federal Expenditure and Social Change Since 1910* (Berkeley: University of California Press, 1967).

Calles' education budgets were generally lower than Obregón's. Alberto J. Pani initiated savings here in 1925 in his rationalization measures designed to meet payments to the New York bankers' commission and to make the Mexican government and economy more attractive to private investors. The 1926–27 crisis in the world market for oil and silver kept a lid on expenditures, while the Church-state conflict required the deflection of funds to the military. To these constrictions should be added the recommendations of Calles' North American advisors to curb social spending. Not until 1943 under President Avila Camacho did proportional educational funding slip as low as it did in the Calles period. In 1931, for example, President Ortiz Rubio spent 13.8 percent of the budget on schools. In 1937, President Cárdenas budgeted 13.6 percent for education.[56]

Priorities in the Obregón years were the repair and construction of school facilities in the capital and expansion of rural and technical education. The building of the new Secretaría headquarters in this

56. James W. Wilkie, *The Mexican Revolution: Federal Expenditure and Social Change since 1910* (Berkeley: University of California Press, 1967), pp. 160–61.

period consumed considerable funds and gave cause for some criticism on spending priorities. In 1922, the SEP budgeted 6,586,000 pesos for repair and construction of buildings in the capital and 1,594,840 pesos for machinery and equipment for technical schools. In 1923, the SEP spent 1,341,350 pesos on building and repairs in the capital, which was the equivalent of 30 percent of its total expenditures in the states.[57] Although technical education expanded mainly in the capital, some vocational training was established in the states with federal funding. Rural schools were created in most states. In June 1923, the Department of Indigenous Culture had 112 missionaries, 578 teachers, and 569 schools with 34,819 students.[58] The heaviest concentration of schools was in the states of central and southern Mexico where agrarian communities were strongest, i.e., Morelos, Puebla, Guerrero, Hidalgo, México, Chiapas, and Oaxaca. The effort in Michoacán, Veracruz, and San Luis Potosí was also notable.[59]

The 1923–24 military rebellion hurt the missionary effort, as it curtailed most activity in education; the number of missionaries fell from 104 in 1923 to 62 in the first third of 1924. The number of rural schools declined from 1,192 to 1,048. Further economizing took place under Puig Casauranc in 1925. To continue the expansion of rural schools on a lower budget, it was decided to hire more teachers at two pesos a day while shifting expenses for school buildings to the villages themselves.[60] Cuts in funding for cultural missions and rural normal schools reduced both the quantity and quality of technical training available to rural teachers. The SEP also closed most of its technical schools in the states except for the Escuela Cruz Galvez in Sonora, the Escuela Industrial of Culiacán, Sinaloa, and the Escuela Industrial in Orizaba, Veracruz.[61] Whereas proceeds from the sale of

57. *La educación pública en México* (Mexico: SEP, 1922) pp. 59–60, 81; Peralta to Undersecretary, SEP, 9 Oct. 1922, AGN, Acervos Presidentes, 121-E-E-15; BSEP 2, nos. 5 and 6 (1923–1924) 682–83. For criticism and defense of the construction of the SEP office building, see Vasconcelos, *El desastre*, pp. 1229–31.

58. *BSEP* 1, no. 4 (1923): 391.

59. See appendix 2.

60. *BSEP* 1, nos. 5 and 6 (1923–1924): 597; Calles to Secretaría de Hacienda y Crédito Público, 17 March 1925, AGN, Acervos Presidentes, Expediente 121-E-E-71.

61. Calles to M. Méndez, 8 Jan. 1926, AGN, Acervos Presidentes, Expediente 121-E-E-50. Three worker craft schools and cultural centers were maintained in Aguascalientes, Jalisco, and Guanajuato. Spending on schools in Sinaloa and Sonora was bound up with the political nexus of the presidents. Later in the period, the Calles government set up industrial schools jointly with state governments in Chiapas and Campeche and workers' cultural centers in Puebla (see *El esfuerzo* 1:500–501).

technical school products traditionally went to the students themselves, they were now earmarked to finance the schools only. Despite protest from parents and students, tuition and fees were introduced for secondary and technical education.[62]

Federal expenditures for education in the states grew from 3,471,135 pesos in 1922 to an average of 7,416,065 pesos in the Calles period.[63] As this amount increased while federal funding for education in general decreased or remained stagnant, figures tend to corroborate the thesis of a centralizing trend in the Mexican state. Table 4.2 shows the number and types of federal schools and their enrollments between 1925 and 1928.

Most of these schools were rural, and, with the exception of 113 schools, they were outside the Federal District. Federal urban primary schools were concentrated in the capital although all states had some such schools. Those with the lowest number of federal urban primaries (between one and four) were states which had had strong primary systems in the *Porfiriato*, e.g., Yucatán, Veracruz, Tamaulipas, Sonora, Durango, Jalisco, and Chihuahua.[64] Federal activity in normal school expansion involved the creation of rural regional normal schools in the states of central and southern Mexico.[65] Despite the increase in the number of federal normal schools between 1925 and 1928, enrollments declined, probably owing to neglect by the federal government. The federal effort in vocational and preparatory education was largely confined to Mexico City. Federal aid to professional education in the states focused upon the Escuelas Centrales Agrícolas, administered by the Department of Agriculture and established by the Calles government in the central states of Guanajuato, Hidalgo, México, Michoacán, and Puebla, and the northern states of Durango and Tamaulipas. The Escuela Particular de Agricultura of Chihuahua also received federal aid.

---

62. The process of taking proceeds from the students to pay for the schools began under Obregón and culminated under Calles. See Obregón to SEP, 16, Sept. 1923, AGN, Acervos Presidentes, Expediente 121-E-E-17; Obregón to SEP, 20 Oct. 1924, AGN, Acervos Presidentes, Expediente 121-E-E-87; Calles, SEP, 23 Dec. 1924, AGN, Acervos Presidentes, Expediente 121-E-E-82. On protests against the imposition of tuition and fees in these schools, see, for example, *Excelsior*, 6, 8 Feb. 1927.

63. *El esfuerzo* 2:266–67; *La educación pública en México a través de los mensajes presidenciales*, p. 223.

64. See appendix 3 for location of federal schools.

65. The schools were built in Guerrero and Oaxaco in the south, Morelos, Hidalgo, Tlaxcala, Puebla, and Querétaro in the center, Michoacán in the west-central region, and San Luis Potosí in the north-central region.

TABLE 4.2

Federal Schools, 1925–1928

	1925		1928	
Type	Number	Enrollment	Number	Enrollment
Kindergarten	31	6,404	59	9,074
Rural Primary	1,900 ⎫	267,900	3,303 ⎫	483,993
Primary	543 ⎭		640 ⎭	
Normal	6	2,826	12	2,011
Preparatory	2	4,891	7	6,529
Professional	11	5,338	18	6,532
Fine Arts	3	2,854	2	2,520

Source: *Anuario estadístico*, 1930.

Table 4.3 shows that while in the course of the Revolution the number of primary schools and enrollments declined (from 12,271 schools with 776,894 students in 1907 to 9,222 schools with 743,896 students in 1920), there were in 1928 16,692 schools with a total enrollment of 1,402,731, an increase over the 1907 figures of 36 percent in the number of schools and 80 percent in the number of students enrolled. Whereas an estimated 27.4 percent of children of school age were enrolled in 1907, a reported 46 percent were registered in 1928. While private primary school enrollments declined in the years of fighting, they increased rapidly in the 1920s although not as rapidly as public schools. Accounting for 20 percent of all primary schools in 1907, private primaries were 17 percent of the total in 1928. Their enrollments declined from 19 percent of students in 1907 to 12 percent in 1928—a phenomenon due to the larger proportion of poor students entering public schools as a result of the Revolution. The growth in the private school system can be explained in terms of its importance to the middle and upper sectors of society and the impetus provided to private schools by the Church-state struggle.

By and large, federal expansion in education was more vigorous than that of states and municipalities. While overall school enrollments increased by 81 percent from 1907 to 1928, state and municipal enrollments increased by only 32 percent. Federal enrollments were up by 674 percent. Between 1907 and 1928, the number of state primary schools increased by 7 percent while the number of federal schools rose by 525 percent. Table 4.4 shows that the number of state and municipal primary schools increased at a slower rate than did federal primary schools between 1925 and 1928.

TABLE 4.3
Primary Schools and Enrollments, 1907–1928

	1907	1920	% Increase 1907–1920	1928	% Increase 1907–1928
Number of Primary Schools	12,271	9,222	−25%	16,692	36%
State and Municipal	9,113	8,161	−10	9,751	7
Federal	631	—[a]	—	3,943	525
Private	2,527	1,061	−58	2,998	18
Enrollments	776,894	743,896	−4	1,402,731	81
State and Municipal	567,252	679,897	8	750,410	32
Federal	62,501	—	—	483,993	674
Private	147,141	72,460	−51	168,328	14

Notes: [a] In 1920, formerly federal schools had reverted to municipal and state control.
Sources: *Estadísticas sociales del Porfiriato, Anuario estadístico*, 1930; *La educación pública in México*, 1922.

TABLE 4.4
Comparative Expansion in Public Primary Schools, 1925–1928

Primary Schools	1925	1926	% Increase 1925–1926	1927	% Increase 1926–1927	1928	% Increase 1927–1928
Number							
State and Municipal	9,178	9,778	6.5%	9,855	7%	9,751	−1%
Federal	2,443	3,266	34	4,000	22	3,943	−1
Enrollments							
State and Municipal	704,532	758,186	8	740,346	2	750,410	1
Federal	267,900	356,439	33	397,159	11	483,933	22

Source: *Anuario estadístico*, 1930.

However, Table 4.5 shows that state activity in education was uneven. Certain states experienced an overall decline in their school systems and enrollments throughout the period 1907 to 1928, notably Campeche, Chiapas, Guerrero, and Querétaro. By 1928, these states had a high proportion of federal schools in relation to state schools. While many state school systems suffered during the years of fighting, some states actively promoted schooling in these years—e.g., Yucatán, Sonora, Puebla, Jalisco, Coahuila, and, to a lesser extent, Michoacán. In several cases—notably Coahuila, Jalisco, Puebla, Sonora, and Yucatán—the expansionary impulse disappeared after 1920. In Yucatán, this decline followed the assassination of Felipe Carrillo Puerto and the repression of the PSY. In Jalisco, the negative figure may be associated with disturbances caused by the Church-state conflict.

Whether following a trend begun in the Revolution or recovering from losses suffered in the years of fighting, certain states were aggressive in primary school policy in the 1920s, particularly Chihuahua, Guanajuato, Durango, Hidalgo, México, Michoacán, Oaxaca, Sinaloa, Tabasco, Tamaulipas, Tlaxcala, Veracruz, and Zacatecas. Although Morelos and San Luis Potosí closed a number of state schools in this period, they gained in enrollments. Because both Tamaulipas and Veracruz experienced serious declines in enrollments in 1928, out of step with expansion through 1927, figures for 1927 may be more representative. Tamaulipas registered a 59 percent increase in state primary school enrollments from 1920 to 1927 and a 94 percent increase from 1907 to 1927. Veracruz experienced a 70 percent enrollment increase from 1920 to 1927 and a 55 percent increase for the period as a whole. Accordingly, 1927 figures lower the federal to state primary school ratio to 12 percent for both states.[66]

Several of the education-minded states had populist governors in the 1920s who furthered the development of schooling at the state level—politicians such as Francisco Mújica and later Lázaro Cárdenas in Michoacán, Emilio Portes Gil in Tamaulipas, Adalberto Tejeda in Veracruz, Tomás Garrido Canabal in Tabasco. In Michoacán between 1920 and 1922, Mújica gave one half of the state budget to education, doubled the minimum wage for teachers and paid them punctually. The rural normal schools established during Mújica's tenure became the model for those subsequently created by the federal government in other states.[67] A militant advocate of agrarian and worker reform,

66. Departamento de Estadística Nacional, *Anuario estadístico*, 1930 (Mexico: Talleres Gráficos de la Secretaría de Agricultura y Fomento, 1930), p. 248.

67. Raby, "Los principios," p. 562.

TABLE 4.5
Trends in State Primary School Systems as Measured by Numbers of Schools and Enrollments, 1907–1928

% Growth in State Primary Schools 1907–1920	% Growth in State Primary Enrollments 1907–1920	% Growth in State Primary Schools 1920–1928	% Growth in State Primary Enrollments 1920–1928	% Growth in State Primary Schools 1907–1928	% Growth in State Primary Enrollments 1907–1928	% of Federal to State Primary Schools 1928	% of Federal to State Primary Enrollments 1928
Sonora 120	Yucatán 243	Tabasco 436	Tabasco 665	Sonora 166	Tabasco 193	Campeche 76	Campeche 613
Coahuila 100	Sonora 223	Durango 278	Oaxaca 227	Tabasco 120	Oaxaca 164	Chiapas 72	Chiapas 552
Aguascalientes 56	Puebla 85	Oaxaca 275	Chihuahua 164	Yucatán 85	Durango 161	Guerrero 68	Guerrero 277
Jalisco 53	Jalisco 47	Veracruz 154	Sinaloa 131	Chihuahua 74	Yucatán 152	Querétaro 66	Querétaro 231
Puebla 36	Coahuila 41	Chihuahua 145	Durango 93	Tamaulipas 69	Chihuahua 83	Colima 65	Colima 149
Yucatán 11	Nuevo León 34	Tamaulipas 143	Aguascalientes 88	Aguascalientes 60	Sinaloa 75	San Luis Potosí 59	Morelos 125
Michoacán 5	Tamaulipas 23	Sinaloa 93	Morelos 68	Oaxaca 59	Michoacán 73	Tabasco 57	San Luis Potosí 108
Guanajuato 2	Colima 18	Michoacán 93	Michoacán 66	Michoacán 45	Puebla 58	Morelos 49	Tlaxcala 68
Nuevo León −7	Aguascalientes 11	Zacatecas 37	Sonora 64	Puebla 41	Coahuila 50	Coahuila 45	Guanajuato 67
Colima −13	Campeche 9	México 31	Veracruz 49	Sinaloa 34	Zacatecas 36	Zacatecas 42	Zacatecas 63
Campeche −14	Michoacán 3	Guanajuato 29	Hidalgo 45	Guanajuato 18	Nuevo León 35	Aguascalientes 39	Aguascalientes 57
Chihuahua −16	Chihuahua −5	Tlaxcala 19	Yucatán 38	Veracruz 14	Aguascalientes 22	Hidalgo 37	Hidalgo 57
Hidalgo −16	Guanajuato −8	Aguascalientes 10	Puebla 33	Durango 13	Guanajuato 18	México 36	México 56
Sinaloa −27	Veracruz −9	San Luis Potosí 8	Tlaxcala 21	Hidalgo 11	Hidalgo 7	Nuevo León 33	Nuevo León 54
Tamaulipas −28	Hidalgo −16	Yucatán 3	Nuevo León 16	México −13	México −5	Tlaxcala 33	Tamaulipas 47
Chiapas −35	Sinaloa −21	Morelos −3	Guanajuato 1	Nuevo León −15	Veracruz −7	Michoacán 32	Michoacán 42
Tlaxcala −36	México −28	Hidalgo −4	Querétaro −9	Jalisco −16	Jalisco −17	Durango 28	Durango 36
Oaxaca −41	Chiapas −29	Jalisco −10	Jalisco −13	Tlaxcala −24	Tlaxcala −21	Guanajuato 26	Coahuila 33
México −42	Durango −30	Nuevo León −12	Coahuila −15	Chiapas −32	Tamaulipas −22	Oaxaca 25	Oaxaca 31
Tabasco −50	Guerrero −36	Puebla −13	Tamaulipas −16	Morelos −34	Morelos −26	Jalisco 19	Jalisco 29
Durango −51	Tlaxcala −40	Guerrero −17	Zacatecas −24	Guerrero −35	Chiapas −30	Puebla 16	Puebla 28
Zacatecas −52	San Luis Potosí −46	Sonora −27	San Luis Potosí −32	Coahuila −40	Sonora −41	Veracruz 15	Veracruz 22
Guerrero −55	Oaxaca −53	Querétaro −32	Colima −34	Zacatecas −55	Querétaro −46	Chihuahua 14	Chihuahua 18
Veracruz −57	Querétaro −55	Chiapas −34	Chiapas −55	Colima −67	San Luis Potosí −52	Sinaloa 12	Sinaloa 17
Querétaro −59	Zacatecas −59	Colima −67	México −72	Querétaro −70	Colima −68	Sonora 5	Sonora 16
San Luis Potosí −61	Tabasco −66	Campeche −70	Campeche −74	San Luis Potosí −73	Guerrero −72	Tamaulipas 3	Tabasco 14
Morelos −70	Morelos −72	Coahuila −74	Guerrero −75	Campeche −75	Campeche −75	Yucatán 1	Yucatán 3

States are listed in ranked order. Table does not include former territories of Baja California, Tepic, or Quintana Roo. Sources: Calculations are based on data in *Anuario estadístico*, 1930; *La educación pública in México*, 1922; *Boletín de Instrucción Pública* 13 (1909–1910).

Mújica clearly saw the school as an agent of structural change. However, the use of the school by state governors probably varied. School expansion could have been viewed as a means of satisfying or even stimulating demands for reform from the support base of politicians or as a means of controlling and expanding their base of support. The question requires further studies of regional politics and the relationship of the latter to education in the 1920s.

Table 4.6 shows that areas with the largest percentage of children enrolled in school still tended to be those which had led in the *Porfiriato*, e.g., the Federal District, Morelos, Tlaxcala, Nuevo León, and Coahuila. The states that had experienced the most rapid increases in enrollments were, with the exception of Durango and Sonora, in central and southern Mexico, for example, Campeche, Morelos, Michoacán, San Luis Potosí, Yucatán, Guanajuato, Aguascalientes, and Puebla. With the exception of Morelos and Yucatán, these states had had poor school records in the *Porfiriato*, thus indicating that the Revolution had prompted state and/or federal initiative which offset the Porfirian tendency for school enrollments to reflect state income and wealth. Chiapas was an exception: the most backward state in 1907, it remained so in 1928 and had actually experienced an enrollment decline of 3 percent. The decline in enrollments in Jalisco and Colima probably reflected the intensity of the *Cristero* rebellion in 1928 and the closing of schools. The figure for Tamaulipas in 1928 is, as indicated, perhaps misleading: this state claimed to have 63 percent of its children enrolled in school in 1927. The small increase in enrollments in relation to school-age population in Veracruz merits examination because this state was progressive in educational policy after 1920. If 1927 figures are used, the percentage of children enrolled is still only 29 percent. The poor record of Veracruz in increasing enrollments probably reflects a variety of factors, including a substantial deterioration in the school system between 1907 and 1920, a relatively small amount of federal assistance in relation to population after 1920, and a population increase of 28 percent between 1900 and 1928 in contrast to a national population increment of 10 percent.[68]

The number of primary school teachers (public and private) increased from 19,542 in 1920 to 32,657 in 1928.[69] Although the federal government made efforts to raise teachers' wages, most federal rural teachers earned only 2 pesos a day in 1928. In 1928, the average

68. *Anuario estadístico*, 1930, pp. 205–7.
69. *La educación pública en México* (1922); *Anuario estadístico*, 1930, p. 208.

TABLE 4.6

Percentage of School-Age Population in Primary School (Public and Private), 1907–1928

1907		1928		% Increase 1907–1928	
Federal District	59%	Morelos	99%	Durango	145%
Coahuila	47	Federal District	90	Sonora	136
Tlaxcala	47	Yucatán	70	Campeche	135
Morelos	43	Nuevo León	66	Morelos	130
Nuevo León	43	Sonora	66	Michoacán	129
Colima	41	Campeche	61	San Luis Potosí	127
Tamaulipas	40	Coahuila	61	Yucatán	119
Jalisco	37	Tlaxcala	61	Guanajuato	116
Tabasco	34	Aguascalientes	58	Aguascalientes	115
Zacatecas	33	Chihuahua	56	Puebla	104
Chihuahua	32	Puebla	55	Oaxaca	100
Yucatán	32	Sinaloa	55	Sinaloa	90
Hidalgo	30	Durango	54	Chihuahua	75
México	30	México	51	México	70
Sinaloa	29	San Luis Potosí	50	Federal District	68
Sonora	28	Tabasco	49	Guerrero	61
Aguascalientes	27	Zacatecas	48	Nuevo León	53
Puebla	27	Guanajuato	41	Querétaro	45
Campeche	26	Hidalgo	37	Zacatecas	45
Veracruz	24	Oaxaca	36	Tabasco	44
Durango	22	Tamaulipas	36	Coahuila	30
San Luis Potosí	22	Colima	34	Tlaxcala	30
Querétaro	20	Michoacán	32	Hidalgo	23
Guanajuato	19	Guerrero	29	Veracruz	8
Guerrero	18	Jalisco	29	Chiapas	−3
Oaxaca	18	Querétaro	29	Tamaulipas	−10
Michoacán	14	Veracruz	26	Colima	−17
Chiapas	13	Chiapas	10	Jalisco	−22

States are listed in ranked order.
Table does not include the former territories of Baja California, Tepic, and Quintana Roo.
Sources: Calculations based on data in *Boletín de Instrucción Pública* 13 (1909–1910); *Anuario estadístico*, 1930.

teacher employed by the federal government earned 2,254 pesos a year, compared with 848 pesos paid by the states.[70] Wages varied from state to state. In Chiapas, for example, teachers earned an average of 378 pesos a year, or just over a peso a day. In Tamaulipas, teachers earned an average of 4 pesos a day.[71] The federal government occasionally defaulted on teachers' pay; default was very common in the states. The latter often requested emergency loans or subsidies from the central government to meet payrolls. The situation gave rise to rapid unionization and frequent teacher strikes.[72] Not surprisingly, many teachers came to favor federalization, as the SEP was believed to be a more reliable employer.

As Table 4.7 indicates, in post-primary education the system opened to absorb more people. Primary enrollments increased by 81 percent between 1907 and 1928; secondary school enrollments were up by 177 percent as were normal school entrants. The increase in the number of technical school students was even greater and reflected the Revolution's commitment to modernization.[73] Professional school enrollments rose by about 81 percent. While there is little doubt that the Revolution's school system expanded at all levels, closer examination of the above figures indicates how much the system continued to reflect social class structure. Many children dropped

---

70. *Anuario estadístico*, 1930, pp. 205, 208.

71. Ibid.

72. On inability to pay wages and requests to federal government for assistance, see, for example, José Ochoa to Obregón, 22 Sept. 1921; Obregón to Ochoa, 23 Sept. 1921; Virgilio González to Obregón, 10 July 1922, 9 Sept. 1922; Obregón to González, 14 Sept. 1922; Obregón to Hortensia Beltrán, 25 Dec. 1922; Asociación de Maestros Tabasqueños to Obregón, 27 Dec. 1922; D. Ocaña del Angel C. to Obregón, 31 Jan. 1923; Obregón to D. Ocaña del Angel C., 1 Feb. 1923; Garrido Canabal to Obregón, 25 April 1923, AGN, Acervos Presidentes, Expediente 816-T-25; Adalberto Rios to Obregón, 9 May 1922, AGN, Acervos Presidentes, Expediente 813-D-34; Figueroa to Torreblanca, 14 Nov. 1922, AGN, Acervos Presidentes, Expediente 241-E-25. See also Sáenz, *Escuelas federales en la sierra de Puebla*, pp. 85–86. On teachers' strikes in response to inability to pay wages, see *Excelsior*, 15, 17, 20, 23 Nov.; 5, 18 May 1927.

73. Although Table 4.7 indicates a 312% increase in technical school enrollments between 1907 and 1928, the figures are unreliable. The 1907 enrollment figures included those in agricultural, mining, and military training schools and did not include several vocational schools in the states or primary superior technical schools in the capital. The 1928 figures are specifically limited to technical, industrial, commercial, and crafts schools. They include primary superior technical schools and exclude the schools of agriculture, chemical sciences, and engineering which are classified under professional education. However, while it is difficult to assess precisely the percentage of expansion in enrollments in technical-vocational education in the period, it is evident that the expansion was significant.

TABLE 4.7

Growth in the Post-Primary School System, 1907–1928

	1907	1928	% Increase, 1907–1928
Secondary-Preparatory			
Number of Schools	60	86	43%
State	41	32	
Federal	1	7	
Private	18	47	
Enrollments	5,782	16,024	177
State	—	6,694	
Federal	—	6,529	
Private	—	2,801	
Technical-Vocational			
Number of Schools	10	255	2,450
State		36	
Federal		35	
Private		184	
Enrollments	9,984 [a]	41,132	312
State		7,578	
Federal		26,998	
Private		6,556	
Normal			
Number of Schools	26	72	177
State		39	
Federal	2	12	
Private		21	
Enrollments	2,552	7,059	177
State		4,441	
Federal	333	2,011	
Private		607	
Professional			
Number of Schools	21	55	161
State		21	
Federal		18	
Private		16	
Enrollments	5,370	9,763	81
State		2,806	
Federal		6,532	
Private		425	

(a) Does not include private school enrollments.

Source: *Estadísticas sociales del Porfiriato, Anuario Estadístico*, 1930.

out of school in order to work to support their families. In 1928, only three-quarters of those enrolled at the beginning of the school year remained in school at the year's end. The number of primary students pursuing secondary education in 1928 was 1 percent. Three percent went on to vocational schools. Only .7 percent of those enrolled in primary schools went on to pursue professional studies. The post-primary school system cost both time and money. A large portion of new secondary and technical schools were private and available only to those who could afford them. Federal public secondary, technical, and professional schools also charged tuition and fees.

Higher education continued to be biased in favor of the capital. Fifty-two percent of all preparatory school students studied in Mexico City in 1928 as compared with 23 percent in 1907. In some cases, the number of state preparatory schools had declined in the Revolution and in no case, except for Chiapas, which built two new preparatory schools in the 1920s, and the Federal District, which opened six new schools, did states increase the numbers of these schools although enrollments grew to some extent. Fifty-four percent of all vocational school students were concentrated in the capital in 1928. Training in skilled work for modern industry was offered almost exclusively in the capital. Vocational training in the states involved the traditional arts and crafts and the agricultural schools which became a major focus of Calles' policy. The capital's share of professional school students had declined slightly between 1907 and 1928 from 54 to 51 percent of all professional school students.

The rural school system was definitive for most who attended it. For some it was circular: a few graduates would go on to rural regional normals or to the agricultural schools, and then return to teach school. Although these options were justified within the ideology of a nation of small-holders, the ideology was basically in contradiction with economic trends and with government policy in areas other than education. Students in rural normals and agricultural schools were supposed to be children of small farmers, but only 59 percent were of such background in 1928.[74] This discrepancy was in keeping with Calles' growing commitment to large-scale modern agriculture at the expense of the small farmer.

Conclusion

In the 1920s, the Mexican revolutionary state began to emerge under Presidents Obregón and Calles: an implicitly centralized, develop-

74. Ramón Eduardo Ruíz, *Mexico: The Challenge of Poverty and Illiteracy*, p. 107.

mentalist state which would at once eliminate precapitalist obstacles to growth, limit foreign participation in the economy in the interests of national autonomy, stimulate modernization through diverse forms of investment and fiscal incentives, and provide socioeconomic reform for the working class and peasantry. A class-conciliating state, the Mexican government sought to control the subordinate classes through the formation and/or co-optation of class organizations and the creation and action of government bureaucracies in labor, agriculture, health, and education. However, the central state initiated its tasks in a context of weakness vis-à-vis internal and external forces.

In 1920, political power was more effectively lodged in the states where regional power-holders were often protective of their control and sometimes harbored presidential ambitions. In the course of the decade, the central government gained considerable, although not full, control over the states through a variety of measures, e.g.: eliminating recalcitrant generals through suppression of military rebellions; professionalizing the army; making opportunities for investment available; creating informal alliances with regional power-holders; and finally, forming the Partido Nacional Revolucionario.

Mexican development was also constrained in the 1920s by the legacy of a dependent export economy, which had been further debilitated by civil war. Because the Mexican Revolution chose the capitalist road of development, it considered few options and operated within the parameters of the dependent structure it had inherited. Its bourgeois class weakened and alienated by the Revolution, Mexico looked to foreign capital for assistance. The United States, which had emerged from World War I as the leading creditor nation, refused to recognize Mexico or to extend credit to her until the Mexican government arranged to repay its foreign debt and agreed not to implement Constitutional clauses prejudicing foreign holdings in Mexico. Such an accommodation was made by Obregón in August 1923. At the beginning of his term, Calles took a more radical position than his predecessor on foreign holdings and reform for the masses, but factors inherent in the political-economic structure led him to abandon his militancy: a dual crisis in the international oil and silver markets in 1926, hostility to nationalist legislation from U.S. oil producers and the State Department, rapprochement with the Porfirian owning class and the growth of a neocapitalist class among the revolutionaries themselves. The climax of this process of accommodation came in 1927 with the arrival of U.S. Ambassador Dwight W. Morrow, who became Calles' mentor in most areas of policy. The political-economic parameters of the revolutionary state thus limited the nation's ability to control its own economy as well as its commitment to structural reforms benefitting the oppressed. Because in the 1920s the central government had not secured full control over the regions, the working class, or the peasantry, mobilization of popular forces grew as the government's commitment to reform ebbed.

Education became a major bureaucratic task of the central state because it performed functions of national integration while providing skills and values necessary to modernization. A mass demand of the Revolution, education was a reform which did not threaten existing property relations while it potentially assisted the federal government in securing support and exercising social control. In its bid to create schools in the states, the federal government was in a strong position because of the revolutionary mandate for schools and because of the bankruptcy of many state and municipal governments. In contrast to its Porfirian predecessor, the new Secretaría de Educación Pública had national jurisdiction which it exercised mainly in rural education. Most state systems already had a number of urban primary schools, at least at the elementary level. Federal assistance to technical, preparatory, and professional education was limited mainly to the capital. Some vocational schools were created in the states, including schools established by the Ministry of Agriculture.

The politics of the SEP reflected diverse middle-sector approaches to education within the context of class conflict. Throughout the 1920s, the dominant element in the SEP tended to consider the school a panacea for backwardness and poverty; it stressed the disciplinary and skill-upgrading aspects of schooling, and played down the need for structural reforms such as land distribution, full-scale technical assistance, and other means of weakening the local power structures which kept peasants marginal. In principle, the policymakers believed in a rural sector of small-holders, but in fact their own ideologies and priorities, as well as the government's overall lack of commitment to widespread structural reforms, led the educators to act as if the school alone could solve the problems of poverty and inequality. In contrast, many rural missionaries and teachers, who in their enthusiasm for education as social betterment came up against recalcitrant local power systems, became critical of SEP policy and turned to mobilizing villages for land distribution and other forms of challenge to local elites.

Federal education budgets in the 1920s were limited by the persistent structure of dependency, the dislocation caused by civil war, and continued political instability which required the diversion of funds for military purposes. Much of the education budget was used to repair buildings in the capital. Federal assistance to the states offset the Porfirian tendency for school expansion to reflect economic wealth: federal primary education policy in the 1920s favored rural over urban areas and central and southern Mexico over the more growth-oriented northern region. It did so in part because these were the areas neglected by Porfirian policy, but, moreover, because these were regions of agrarian communities from which had emanated the strongest demands for reform. However, the scantiness of the federal budget for rural education showed up in low wages, inadequate technical training for teachers, and the foisting of responsibility for building and maintaining schools on to the villages themselves.

As federal initiative surpassed that of the states, a centralizing trend emerged with regard to bureaucratic control and the quantity and rate of school expansion. Even so, some states were aggressive in primary school policy, the reasons for which require further investigation at the regional level. As a result of combined federal and state action, the percentage of school-age children enrolled in primary schools increased from 27.4 percent in 1907 to 46 percent in 1928. The post-primary school system also grew principally as a result of federal action. It, however, served those with the time and money to continue their education. Because of its slim budget, the revolutionary government introduced fees and tuition to these schools. Higher education also continued to be biased in favor of urban areas and the capital, although the federal rural normal and agricultural schools were an exception.

Chapter 5
Action Pedagogy in Mexico in the 1920s

Middle-sector educators in the years of the Revolution looked for a pedagogy which would increase the productive capacity of their countrymen and would enhance the well-being of the individual and that of the nation. It is not surprising that they found ideas and models in the United States, whose political-economic system Mexican educators most admired despite their avowed nationalism. Action pedagogy, formally introduced in 1923, drew heavily from the ideas of John Dewey in particular and from North American educational thought and practice in the Progressive era more generally. It is important to establish the context within which the North American reform movement took place, for while notably different from the Mexican context, the North American experience had important implications for the Mexican case.

One must clarify first the contextual problems with which North American school reformers grappled. The problem they defined for themselves at the turn of the century was the disappearance of a yeoman society; the emergence of large-scale industrialization; and the corporate organization of capital which manifested itself socially in the rise of antagonistic social classes and a chaotic mushrooming of the city.[1] Most urban educational reformers accepted the new order of society as progressive and saw in the school a means of adjusting people to it. The reformers were concerned both with the school's ability to serve the expanding economy and with its role in the resolution of social conflict. "The new thought," writes one scholar of the period, "predicated unity upon a perfect meshing of society's parts, a frictionless operation analogous to the factory under a pure scientific management."[2] John Dewey said:

---

1. Such has been the thesis of much recent research on U.S. education at the turn of the century. See, for example, Joel H. Spring, *Education and the Rise of the Corporate State*; Marvin Lazerson, *Origins of the Urban School: Public Education in Massachusetts, 1870–1915* (Cambridge: Harvard University Press, 1971); Colin Greer, *The Great School Legend* (New York: Basic Books, 1972).

2. Robert Wiebe, *The Search for Order*, p. 154.

The real question is one of reorganization of all education to meet the changed conditions of life . . . accompanying the revolution in industry.[3]

Dewey's pedagogy of learning by doing had three components. First, with the decline of the rural community, in which children learned habits of industriousness and obedience in the process of cooperative work, school learning had lost its relationship to the concrete problems of daily life. For Dewey, the school had to form within the student "the habits of realizing for himself and in himself the nature of the practical situation in which he will find himself placed."[4] In practice, the Dewey project method, through which children might investigate, for instance, the cause of typhoid in a neighborhood and eliminate it through a sanitary disposal of garbage, combined pragmatism with the internalization of habits of discipline, work, order, and cooperation. Second, Dewey wished to recreate within the school a sense of community and common purpose that had, in reality, disappeared from society. Third, he believed that by learning the totality of the production process in its historical evolution, the future worker would learn the social value of his or her individual task. The school would interpret the intellectual and social meaning of his or her work. While the idea of learning by doing was a method applicable in widely different social contexts, the critical question was how the school defined community and the social value of work.

Although Dewey wished to impress on the worker the social importance of his job, at the same time the pedagogue accepted a productive order that denied the worker any control over the content, execution, and product of his labor. The introduction of Taylorism or scientific management at the turn of the century had broken down the individual craftsman's control over specific processes in factory production and had changed his labor into detail work monotonously repeated and controlled from above.[5] The consequence was alienation, of which Dewey was aware.

3. John Dewey and Evelyn Dewey, *Schools of Tomorrow* (New York: E. P. Dutton, 1962), p. 189.

4. John Dewey, "Teaching Ethics in the High School," *Educational Review* 6 (1893): 316.

5. See Harry Braverman, *Labor and Monopoly Capital: The Degradation of Work in the Twentieth Century* (New York and London: Monthly Review Press, 1974), pp. 85–152; Raymond Callahan, *Education and the Cult of Efficiency* (Chicago: University of Chicago Press, 1962), pp. 21–40.

How many of the employed are today mere appendages of the machines which they operate! This . . . is certainly due in large part to the fact that the worker has no opportunity to develop his imagination and his sympathetic insight as to the social and scientific values found in his work.[6]

In fact, alienation was not the consequence of the worker's ignorance but of an expanding industrial system in which control and decision-making were increasingly being vested in a small group of owners of capital. In school systems in the United States, the potential richness of Dewey's suggestion was being leeched away, as emphasis fell on the individual's specialized contribution to production and the internalization of habits of work, cooperation, and subordination to authority.[7]

This centralizing of production coincided with the expansion of the United States' governmental apparatus and bureaucratization of the U.S. school system. In major cities, businessmen and professionals led campaigns to wrest control of schools away from neighborhood wards. Although urban reformers in taking over the schools spoke of removing corruption in school administration characteristic of ward politics, in the end, communities lost the control they had enjoyed over their own neighborhood schools; authority over the school system came into the hands of school boards consisting largely of businessmen and professionals who presided over an expanded bureaucracy immune from community input. One of the reformers' purposes was to socialize the urban working class to make it "orderly, moral, and tractable."[8] Use of the school as a way to mitigate class conflict was often quite explicit. Senator Wadsworth of New York declared that compulsory education existed to "protect the nation against destruction from forces operating within it. It is to train the boy and girl to be good citizens, to protect against ignorance and dissipation," and to prevent the possibility "that these people of ours should be divided into classes."[9] In many cities, reformers tried to make the school a community center offering programs compatible

6. John Dewey, *School and Society* (Chicago: University of Chicago Press, 1963), p. 180.

7. Callahan, *Education and the Cult of Efficiency*, pp. 27–28; see also Spring, *Education and the Rise of the Corporate State*, pp. 55–61, 105–7.

8. Michael B. Katz, ed., *Education in American History* (New York: Praeger Publishers, 1973), p. 46. On the reform movement, see William Issel, "Modernization in Philadelphia School Reform, 1882–1905," in ibid., pp. 187–97; Herbert Gintis and Samuel Bowles, *Schooling in Capitalist America* (New York: Basic Books, 1976), pp. 188–90.

9. As quoted by James Weinstein, *The Corporate Ideal in the Liberal State*, p. 134.

with the interests, needs, and values of the reformers themselves. Athletic programs and clubs offered youth alternatives to gangs and delinquency while instilling discipline and upgrading potential productivity. Adult evening programs performed a variety of functions from citizenship training to the improvement of women's home cooking, which was believed to be an answer to removing men from saloons and a necessary contribution to the molding of a healthy labor force.[10] While the motives of reformers were often humanitarian and in their own perception benign, when examined within the larger socioeconomic context, the school was being designed to replace and uproot social forms inimical to the interests of capital, with which the reformers in varying degrees identified.

The consequence of the urban reform movement was a school system which imposed alien models on existing communities and penetrated community and private life. Although student government and Parent-Teacher Associations proliferated in the period, they were intended not as channels for participation in decision-making, but as channels for socialization, designed to teach specific behavior patterns such as cooperation, subordination to authority, initiative only within a circumscribed framework, conformity, and loyalty to the school system and to the larger society. One scholar has argued that the bureaucratization of the U.S. school system contributed to the erosion of democracy in a real sense; in place of grass-roots initiative, organization, and participation, it encouraged dependency upon institutions.[11]

An equally important purpose of the school reform movement was to improve the school's capacity to train individuals for a modernizing economy. Testing, vocational guidance and training, differentiated curricula, class sections, and tracking were introduced to help the schools classify students for specialized slots in a complex industrial organization. In an effort to apply concepts of scientific management to education, educators often saw students as "raw material"; teachers became "workers" subject to time sheets and efficiency rating scales. Ellwood P. Cubberley, Dean of the Stanford University School of Education, called the schools "factories" shaping raw materials into "products to meet the various demands of life."[12] According to a student of this reform movement, the consequences of the application of scientific management techniques to education included a routini-

10. See Spring, *Education and the Rise of the Corporate State*, pp. 63, 68–72, 78.
11. Ibid., pp. 152–54.
12. Callahan, *Education and the Cult of Efficiency*, pp. 45–51, 58–62, 85–90, 97.

zation of learning, increased class size, a reduction in the number of teachers and in student-teacher contact hours. The movement also had a depressing effect upon the capacity of public education to encourage creativity, innovation, and critical thought.[13]

Although the introduction of testing—and the differentiated curricula, class sections, and tracking which accompanied it—was ostensibly designed to fit individuals into places in the economy most compatible with their abilities, it has been argued that testing itself both derived from and reinforced existing class differences and that its value was less its sorting out of individual talent and more its obfuscation of class differences through the promotion of an ideology of meritocracy. Education experts who developed tests infused them consciously and unconsciously with their own prejudices, values, and goals. In the testing movement, groups of people were believed to have certain characteristics—usually according to class, race, ethnic group, and sex; they were treated as if they had these characteristics and then tested to prove that they did.[14] University of Chicago professor Frank Freeman, a leader in the testing movement, called it an adjustment to "the inequalities of life . . . with the least possible friction."[15] As a contemporary scholar has written, intelligence testing became a rationale for a stratified society: it nurtured in children the idea that intelligence was the basis for the distribution of wealth in society and that only the individual was responsible for his success or failure.[16]

While testing and tracking led to hierarchical divisions within the schools and within the school system, student government and activities were encouraged to develop a spirit of common purpose and cooperation as well as practice in applied civics. As these activities fostered cooperation, they also bred conformity and social reward for playing by the school's established rules. Student governments were never allowed real decision-making powers within the schools. Democracy came to be redefined as one's specialized contribution to a

13. Ibid., pp. 84, 102, 163.

14. Clarence J. Karier, *Shaping the American Educational State, 1900 to the Present* (New York: Macmillan Free Press, 1975), pp. 7, 9, 138–63, 191–94, 233–34; Gintis and Bowles, *Schooling in Capitalist America*, pp. 30–33. Further articles on the testing movement can be found in Clarence Karier et al., *Roots of Crisis* (Chicago: Rand McNally, 1973).

15. Frank Freeman, "Sorting the Students," *Educational Review* 68 (1924): 170.

16. Gilbert B. Gonzalez, "The relationship between Progressive Educational Theory and Practice and Monopoly Capital," Occasional Papers, No. 1, Program in Comparative Culture, University of California-Irvine, Calif., 1976, pp. 44–45.

preestablished socioeconomic organization, the fundamental logic of which was never questioned. Democracy came to be viewed as

> . . . a means of social organization which allowed everyone to do what he was best able to do. Education was to fit the individual for a social position that would allow for his maximum contribution to society. . . . Unification was that part of the ideal of democracy that brought men together and gave them "common ideas, common ideals, and common modes of thought, feeling, and action that made cooperation, social cohesion, and social solidarity."[17]

The U.S. school reform movement was part of the expansion of the state which accompanied the rise of large-scale corporate production. State expansion was necessary to facilitate the smooth functioning of an increasingly complex economy growing nationally and internationally (e.g., new monetary institutions, the proliferation of business law, regulation of commerce, defense of United States business interests abroad) and as a means of reducing class conflict (through labor legislation, welfare programs, unemployment compensation, co-optation of working class parties and organizations, and schooling). In this process, educational reform was designed to serve a double function: increasing the productivity of the economy through filtering out a labor force; and imbuing the population with values, beliefs, and behavior patterns compatible with the existing social system. The expanded state was effective in fulfilling its functions in large part because of a rapid and sustained accumulation of capital, supported in the nineteenth century by a vast internal empire and in the twentieth century by the collapse of European hegemony and increasing United States penetration of world markets.[18] This process created the material affluence which allowed for the expansion of the state, its ideological apparatus, its welfare programs, etc. It also made possible—with the very real exception of the Depression of the 1930s— the relatively consistent opening of employment opportunities, which was indispensable for legitimizing the ideology of social mobility and social contribution put forward by the North American educational system.

But Mexican educators were operating within a different set of problems. Dependent capitalism had characterized recent economic expansion in Mexico; the capital accumulation process had been subordinate to the interests of foreigners whom it had disproportion-

17. Spring, *Education and the Rise of the Corporate State*, p. 110.
18. Weinstein, *The Corporate Ideal in the Liberal State* p. 253.

ately rewarded. The production process was still largely one of petty organization, and much of the large-scale production was foreign controlled. Nonetheless, the task which Mexican policy-makers set for themselves was modernization and increased production within an economy which Mexicans would more firmly control. They were naturally attracted to North American methods and theories of schooling: they associated the pedagogy of learning by doing with an increased capacity to work and produce. In part, their preoccupation with the filtering out function of education led them, like the North Americans, into testing, tracking, and the deepening of the hierarchical structure of the school system. But the growth of such a system also derived from the scarcity of capital in the dependent economy. Within a production system based on private accumulation, a large portion of which continued to be siphoned abroad, the state had to select spending priorities. The relative poverty of the state and its scarce allocation of resources for education influenced the creation of a stratified educational system which did not offer significant opportunity for social mobility to large numbers of people. Social mobility was also limited by the nature and form of economic expansion determined by the system of dependent capitalism: the economy could neither absorb nor reward large sectors of the population to the degree anticipated by educators. Further, Mexican educators confronted perhaps a more explosive situation of class conflict than did their North American counterparts. The Mexican Revolution destroyed the state apparatus of legitimization and repression while mobilizing masses of people to fight for their basic needs, which were often in conflict with the class interests defended by the state. This situation meant that school policy-makers would consciously try to use the school as a mechanism for legitimizing the new state. However, the relative weakness of the new state, the newness of its bureaucracy, and the scarcity of its resources would make this effort in schooling in an era of continuing popular unrest more tentative and less penetrating than it was in the United States in the same period.

Action Pedagogy in Mexican Urban Education

In their attraction to North American theories and methods, Mexican educators exhibited a still dependent mind-set. Rather than analyzing Mexican economic backwardness in structural and historical terms, they blamed it on behavioral deficiencies of the Mexican. To develop their argument, they often depended upon European and North

American spokesmen. In a letter to Vasconcelos, one intellectual quoted Gustave Le Bon, the nineteenth-century French defender of European racial superiority, and argued that Mexican backwardness was due to "sterile idleness, enervating inactivity, and laziness" imbedded in the Mexican character.[19] Not suprisingly, this kind of racial categorization was often specifically directed toward the indigenous people and the working class. Maximino Martínez, teacher and pedagogue, published a book in 1919 in which he called for a new pedagogy which would raise the cultural level of a degenerate race while repressing "savage violence."[20] The Mexican worker was miserable because he was profligate; the Mexican Indian was weak because he consumed too much *pulque*. Martínez called for a pedagogy which would result in greater productivity.[21]

In introducing the action school, two officials of the SEP quoted Le Bon: while the Latins had a theoretical educational system, the Anglo-Saxon system of practical schooling had produced engineers and geniuses.[22] In their admiration for the pragmatic and hard-working Anglo-Saxon, the educators were aware—as had been Sierra—of the need to emulate to their own advantage. Gregorio Torres Quintero, Porfirian pedagogue and SEP bureaucrat, insisted: "We have to adopt the competitor's system in order to survive."[23] Spokesmen for the SEP emphasized the role the action school would play in increasing the productive capacity of Mexicans to develop a Mexican-controlled economy.[24]

The SEP introduced learning by doing techniques as a means of inculcating habits of work, making work itself directly relate to society, and strengthening the productive capacity of society. In an explanation of the action school, Eulalia Guzmán, an SEP official, stated:

> The two principal foundations of the new school are the observation and experience of the students as a means of developing individual effectiveness and work in common and cooperation

19. *BU* 1, no. 4 (1921): 370.

20. Maximino Martínez, *El estado actual de la educación pública en México* (México: Talleres Gráficos de la Escuela Industrial de Huérfanos, 1919), p. 14.

21. See statement of Martínez at the Congreso del Niño, 1921, in *Memoria del Congreso del Niño* (Mexico: El Universal, 1921), p. 262.

22. Salvador Lima and Marcelino Rentería, "La escuela de acción," *Educación* 2, no. 4 (1923): 242.

23. Gregorio Torres Quintero, *La escuela por la acción y el método de proyectos*, Publicaciones de la SEP 6, no. 18 (1925): 6.

24. Lima and Rentería, "La escuela de acción," p. 247.

in social life as a means of awakening a spirit of fraternity and mutual service which is the preparation of a future social order.[25]

Prizes, punishments, verbal rote learning, and regular schedules were to be dropped. Children would learn through group activity related to gardening, carpentry, animal care, etc. Texts were made optional except for history and geography classes. Children were to become active and the teacher a passive guide, although Guzmán was careful to say that the teacher was passive in "appearance only."[26]

The *Bases para la organización de la escuela primaria conforme al principio de la acción*, published by the SEP in 1925, argued that action pedagogy would internalize habits of work. Behavioral internalization was a far better guarantee than the coerced obedience to external authority characteristic of the nineteenth-century school. Spontaneous, natural action "freely" developed would insure that students were not repulsed by work as serious and formal routine; rather they would receive the impression that "work is the source of pleasure."[27] Recognition of the aptitudes of individual children and the channeling of them into projects would lead to maximum performance. As children would advance at their own speed, the attractiveness of work would eliminate apathy and disorder. The pedagogy would simultaneously reduce class conflict by justifying the individual's "place" while encouraging group cooperation. In an explanation of the new school, two educators, Salvador Lima and Marcelina Rentería, argued that through channeling the will and energy, the school would bring about "accommodation and habituation."[28] It would eliminate "fantasy" and accustom the child to expect what he could reasonably receive from the social system. A poor child, they wrote, could not afford a banquet. While encouraging individual "aptitudes," the school would at the same time foster a spirit of cooperation to "eliminate hostility, always ready to present itself in diverse forms in the social struggle."[29]

The new pedagogy was not easily put into practice in Mexico's urban school system. Although model urban primary schools were cre-

---

25. *BSEP* 2, nos. 5 and 6 (1923–1924): 294–95.
26. *Ibid.*
27. *Bases para la organización de la escuela primaria conforme al principio de la acción*, Publicaciones de la SEP 1, no. 8 (1925): 18, 34–36.
28. Lima and Rentería, "La escuela de acción," pp. 297, 305.
29. Ibid., p. 299; *BSEP* 2, nos. 5 and 6 (1923–1924): 295.

ated by the SEP in the states, it is not clear that action pedagogy took significant root in cities outside the capital. Even in the capital, the problems were many. The reform was introduced in the midst of the military uprising against Obregón which resulted in the state's defaulting on the payment of teachers' wages. The teachers consequently were busy organizing into unions. Many teachers trained in the old methods did not take enthusiastically to the reform proposal. Further, their possibilities for introducing the project method in overcrowded and underequipped urban classrooms were somewhat limited. Moreover, teachers received minimal and often contradictory instruction from school inspectors on how to implement the new methods. Quickly, teachers lined up in favor of or against the reforms, but the confusion about what they meant and how they were to be practiced continued for several years. One teacher in 1925 deplored "the state of chaos which prevails from the diverse ways in which the vague and nebulous ideas put forward in books, pamphlets, and periodicals are interpreted."[30]

Under these conditions, the SEP circumscribed the apparent openness and spontaneity of action pedagogy with a series of programmatic rulings which indicated the SEP's preference for social order and increased production. Texts were reinstituted. Evidently the writing of new texts to complement the new pedagogy was not a priority. One of the restored readers was *Adelante*, written by Porfirian pedagogue Daniel Delgadillo and full of the repressive values of the Porfirian school. "The child who is obedient and has good will is rewarded," claimed the text. "The nation must be loved before anything else so that for others there is time and a way."[31] In 1925, the introduction of U.S.-inspired standardized tests to measure general I.Q. and achievement in individual disciplines suggested a subordination of student initiative and action to group norms. As in the United States, the introduction of testing resulted in a return to rote methods of learning. Poor performance on the tests led to a restoration of traditional classroom methods of teaching arithmetic and reading. In 1926, Moisés Sáenz told a conference of school directors

30. *BSEP* 5, no. 2 (1926): 21. For teacher resistance to the reform, see also *El esfuerzo* 1:160–61.

31. See Daniel Delgadillo, *Adelante*, 2nd ed. (Mexico: Herrero Hermanos, 1920). In this text, which is further discussed in chapter 7, virtues of obedience and respect, work and study, order and cleanliness, patriotism, etc., were juxtaposed to vices of ignorance and laziness, disorder and dirtiness, disobedience and ingratitude, egoism, avarice, anger, and cruelty, in such a way as to leave little room at all for the more spontaneous values of initiative, discovery, creativity, etc., associated with child-centered learning.

that experimental pedagogy was a luxury for Mexico and objected to the use of the project method at the expense of mastering the three r's. "Reading is reading and tables are tables," he said.[32]

The action school notion of civics contradicted the theory that action should arise from perception of problems from the immediate environment. Civics programs in the action school delineated a somewhat narrow sphere for social action: the formation of leagues for the protection of plants, trees, minors, animals, the sick, and the poor. Rather than being an exercise in democratic decision-making, student government became a means of socialization to internalize "discipline, firmness of will, and the desire to realize the good." Service to the school became synonymous with service to the country. The goal of civics was to awaken patriotism and "sympathy in our social institutions and faith in their efficacy in achieving the common good."[33] In 1925, a school calendar was introduced to institutionalize patriotic festivals ranging from the births and deaths of national heroes such as Hidalgo, Juárez, Morelos, and Madero to other important national dates such as Independence, the battle of Puebla, and the beginning of the Mexican Revolution. As in the *Porfiriato*, this calendar was to supplant the calendar of the Church. At the same time, educators became enthusiastic about the formation of Boy Scout troops as a means of creating patriotism, citizenship, and discipline.

In 1925, a morality code was introduced to Mexico City public schools which suggested a definition of democracy as the citizen's specific contribution to development from his allotted place in the socioeconomic hierarchy. Probably introduced to counteract clerical criticism of the "immorality" of the lay school, the code defined morality in a secular sense of patriotism and individual productiveness. The eleven lengthy laws that students were to memorize, recite, and practice concerned self-control, work, health, trust, and cooperation. The law of trust postulated: "Our country will be great as its inhabitants have greater confidence in one another." Children vowed to feel no envy for those who received greater rewards from the system. Under the law of cooperation, they repeated: "In so far as we learn to work better in cooperation the prosperity of the country will be

---

32. SEP, *Memoria de los trabajos realizados en la Junta de Directores de Educación Federal, verificada en la ciudad de México del 24 de mayo al dos de junio de 1926* (Mexico: Talleres Gráficos de la Nación, 1926), p. 30. On restoration of traditional methods, see, for example, *BSEP* 6, no. 1 (1927): 171; 6, no. 6 (1927): 40–54.

33. *Bases*, pp. 36, 39.

increased." They promised to be joyful in work as the lack of joy depressed other workers and made work tedious. Under the law of loyalty, they promised as good Mexicans to obey the laws of their country.[34]

In 1926, the SEP created a National Savings Association for children to which each student had to contribute five centavos a week. Part of the banking reform of the Calles era, its ideological importance was undoubtedly greater than its financial impact. The bank was to serve

> . . . as an appropriate means to assure the economic independence of individuals and to form in them love for the country. . . . [it is] the practical school for the teaching of savings, economy, and cooperation . . . and the recognition of the value of money as a factor of well-being and progress.[35]

The teacher, who was to see that deposits were made daily, was to be assisted by a Children's Savings Association, divided into committees. The association would teach children the civic virtues of discipline, justice, mutual respect, subordination, and obedience to the law. They were to learn the importance of sacrificing individual interests to benefit the interests of the collectivity.[36] The savings association conformed to Calles' concept of social democracy, which obscured structural inequalities and uneven access to wealth. It was intended, he said, to demonstrate

> . . . the existence of a great social force dispersed among the weak who in their majority can take admirable forms thanks to unity, economy, cooperation, and collective savings.[37]

Perhaps a testimony to his mistaken idealism, parents protested the obligatory savings programs on the grounds that it was a sacrifice they could ill afford.[38]

Mexican priorities led logically to tracking. The SEP created six secondary schools in the Calles period for preparation for university, teacher, and upper-level technical training. Modeled on the U.S. high school, the Mexican secondary school emphasized the ideology of specialized contribution to the production process. As indicated earlier, admission to these schools required tuition payment and pay-

34. *BSEP* 4, no. 7 (1925): 100–110.
35. *BSEP* 6, no. 4 (1927): 64–65.
36. *BSEP* 7, no. 3 (1928): 103.
37. *BSEP* 6, no. 4 (1927): 68.
38. Ibid., p. 67.

ment of examination fees. Because of the small number of schools, students were admitted according to their test scores. Within the schools, classrooms were differentiated on the basis of student scores, which, according to one school director, seriously depressed the slower students and affected their performance.[39] As in the North American high school, unity was to be created through extra-curricular activities including intra- and inter-school sports. The purpose of student government was to encourage cooperation with the school. It would also "help the administration to know the feelings and thinking of students in relation to their problems."[40] A series of clubs and committees formed to develop discipline, unity, and notions of public service.[41]

From the secondary school civics program emerged both the concept of the good citizen as "he who usefully contributes in an active and intelligent way to the community in which he lives" and a detailed explanation of the new corporate state as a class-conciliating and socially protective institution to which people owed loyalty. Under the heading of health, children learned of the efforts of the state to eliminate disease, to regulate working hours, to protect against industrial accidents, and to upgrade housing through building codes and inspection. In relation to the protection of life and property, students studied the police and court systems and the nature of contracts and titles. Under the topic of wealth, they learned about employers' and workers' associations, their collaboration for modernization, and the role of the state as regulator of economic growth in commerce, transportation, fiscal matters, and relations between labor and capital. They were encouraged to visit the offices of workers' and employers' associations, the Ministry of Industry, Commerce, and Labor, and the State Board of Conciliation and Arbitration.[42] The government became an over-arching paternalistic institution to which the citizen contributed through his particular economic and social function. As in the *Porfiriato*, the idea of democratic choice or citizen participation was less important than the concept of an administrative state which serviced development and individual needs.

Parents reacted to the extension of schooling with some hostility. They were not only obliged to send their children to school punctually or to provide a written excuse, they had to pay for texts and

39. *BSEP* 6, no. 3 (1927): 379.
40. *BSEP* 6, no. 5 (1927): 84.
41. *BSEP* 6, no. 6 (1927): 223, 231–32, 236–39.
42. *BSEP* 7, no. 3 (1928): 310–23.

equipment which the SEP could not afford. When teachers asked students to supply funds for festivals, teachers' trips, and equipment, parents often objected.[43] Suspicious of shots and vaccinations and the reactions they caused, enough parents withheld their children from school to require a demonstration experiment in which the children of government ministers were publicly vaccinated against scarlet fever and diptheria. As indicated earlier, the National Savings Association provoked the greatest parental protest, for it drained hard-won wages from working people for purposes unknown and foreign. The public, observed the SEP, believed it was one more exaction to exploit parents.[44] When secondary and vocational schools began to require tuition and fee payments, parents also raised their voices in protest.[45]

The state tried to counteract opposition by winning parent support for the school through the formation of parents' clubs and mothers' leagues modeled after the United States PTAs.[46] Like the PTA, these organizations were designed not to give parents a role in school management and decision-making but to solicit their moral and material support for the school, the policy and content of which was already defined. Like their U.S. counterpart, they intended to penetrate family life as well in order to reform it in consonance with the values and goals of social reformers. In 1926, the SEP sent a circular to parents spelling out the rights of children to be well-fed, clean, healthy, educated, and loved; the SEP specified conditions within the home necessary for realizing these rights.[47] Part of a larger state effort to reconstruct family life in accordance with new priorities, the implications of this penetration of private life will be discussed in greater detail in Chapter 6.

Action Pedagogy in Rural Education

Rural education in Mexico, as it was conceived and articulated by top policy-makers in the 1920s, illustrated a situation of dependent capitalism where resources are drawn from the hinterland to metropolis in a process controlled by the metropolis; i.e., rural education was

43. *BSEP* 4, no. 6 (1925): 25–26.
44. *BSEP* 6, no. 4 (1927): 67–68.
45. *Excelsior* 6, 8 Feb. 1927.
46. See, for example, *BSEP* 4, no. 8 (1925): 23–24; 4, nos. 9 and 10 (1925): 166; 6, no. 4 (1927): 180–81; 7, no. 4 (1928): 317; 7, no. 8 (1928): 7–12.
47. *BSEP* 5, no. 5 (1926): 74–76; see also *BSEP* 5, no. 1 (1926): 5–8.

something which the city imposed upon the countryside. This imposition was not only literal and objective, in that the central state developed schools in rural Mexico, it was ideological as well. Although
policy-makers in the early 1920s shared a desire to create a yeoman
society in rural Mexico which seemed to coincide with the peasants'
struggle to defend their communities against the encroachment of
large-scale agriculture, the policy-makers' goals and visions for rural
Mexico derived from an urban framework. These goals grew out of
nineteenth-century liberal ideology, which was at odds with several
important factors in rural life. Top officials believed in individual
competition and ownership within a market economy, whereas many
rural communities still rested upon communal landholding practices.
From the educators' perspective the communal aspect of rural life
was either nonexistent or an obstacle to market integration and increased production. Related to this misconception was a desire to impose urban middle-class standards of propriety on rural communities,
which were often viewed as primitive, backward, and savage. An even
more important contradiction was structural. The rural community
in the late nineteenth century had suffered a brutal attack as advancing capital encroached upon its land and mineral resources, while
drawing from it reserves of cheap labor. Peasants struggled in the
Mexican Revolution to stave off annihilation of the community. While
many educators identified with this struggle in their attachment to
the idea of a small-producer economy, they accepted the laws of a
free market economy and were employees of a state which was in the
process of reconsolidating its relationship with large-scale capital. Although the viability of the community depended on massive structural reforms providing adequate land, capital, inputs, and market
outlets, i.e., in essence, destruction of local structures of domination,
the state did not effectively provide supports. In this situation, the
educational bureaucracy began to take sides. As rural missionaries
and teachers became sensitized to rural needs, many became more
political and adamant in their demands for structural reforms. Top
officials in the SEP, on the other hand, tended to support the central
state's needs for order over reform.

Despite reiteration of the need for structural reforms by policy-
makers both in the Vasconcelos and Puig Casauranc periods, it is
clear that in their approach to rural schooling, they operated according to a paradigm which attributed the problems of rural life to character and behavior rather than to local structures of political power
and economic wealth. Thus, the Casa del Pueblo was to destroy customs of "vice" and "violence" arbitrarily assigned to rural people. The

school was to create instead concepts of "solidarity, respect for others, and the desire to elevate oneself by honorable means"—as if such values did not exist.[48] Educators often saw rural life as an obstacle to progress, a behavioral anachronism, rather than a consequence of marginalization and oppression. A missionary in Chiapas in 1923 described the "vices" of the "degenerate" race as love for liquor, extreme ignorance, and "apparent negation of ideals." "Their culture is completely null," he wrote. "They live like savages."[49] As *campesino* life was thought to be impractical, superstitious, and wasteful, it was often believed that the introduction of the "secrets of intelligent life" and notions of "rationality" would repair it.[50] What was "rational" was modern market behavior: initiative, competition, enterprise, increased skills and production, and consumption through the market place. The school would create

. . . efficient individuals who work intelligently in the evolutionary process of our race, ceasing to be the millstone round our necks which they are today.[51]

The document creating the rural missions stated:

The Indians form over one-half the Mexican population. They will be an important factor of production when they emerge from their present conditions.[52]

Within this ideological framework, educators often underestimated or overlooked the intricacies of local power structures and rational peasant responses to them. For example, although the SEP delegate among the Otomí in Hidalgo noted that monopolization of irrigated land rendered most *campesinos* poverty stricken, he emphasized their lack of enterprise and backward methods of production. Although their wages on *haciendas* had risen from 50 to 75 *centavos* a day, he noted that they responded by working less or drinking their earnings. For him, a key task of the school was to stimulate a spirit of enterprise. In part, this could be accomplished, he argued, through creating new consumer needs, i.e., for soap, furniture, etc.[53] Moisés Sáenz came to a similar conclusion in a visit to San Luis Potosí in 1927:

48. *BSEP* 1, no. 4 (1923): 394–96, 400, 435–36, 439.
49. *BSEP* 1, no. 3 (1923): 453.
50. *BSEP* 1, no. 4 (1923): 439.
51. *BSEP* 1, no. 3 (1923): 456.
52. *BSEP* 2, nos. 5 and 6 (1923–1924): 606.
53. *BSEP* 1, no. 3 (1923): 458–61.

The custom of these *campesinos* is to work two or three days, passing the rest of the week in idleness. This is especially true of the farmers and to a lesser extent of the mine workers. In the latter case, I was informed that the non-working days were obligatory given an excess of labor but for those involved in rural work, the days of idleness cannot but indicate a serious laziness made possible by lack of needs.[54]

Production for market and for direct use (household goods, clothing) and a resulting increased capacity to consume market goods became a central concern for the SEP. But often overlooked in this preoccupation was how to secure stable and lucrative market outlets as well as how communities were to produce goods, given a restricted resource base and a local power structure which usually determined what was produced, marketed, and consumed, and at what prices.

Some missionaries and teachers were more incisive about rural conditions. Among the Tarahumara in Chihuahua, the school inspector noted that the indigenous people had been reduced to poverty when the Porfirian government declared their land public and open for sale. Local *mestizos* had seized the best lands, foreign and national mining companies had grabbed the subsoil and forced the Tarahumara into the barren mountains where they tended a few goats. In this situation, given the lack of a resource base, the introduction of new skills and products to make or cultivate would have little impact. Further, a teacher among the same people noted the "very serious obstacles" to change posed by the local power structure:

> The Indians are true slaves of the *hacienda* owners and on occasion of the municipal president and auxiliary judge who frequently force them to labor on public works without paying them a cent . . . the situation of the Indian is painful and a cruel sarcasm to the meaning of civilization.[55]

He also noted that the indigenous had neither farms nor livestock on any profitable scale because the *mestizos* and whites robbed their cattle and crops, while local merchants cheated them on what they produced. In an area of Nayarit, the cultural mission observed that foreigners monopolized the land at the expense of small farmers who were obliged to labor with their children in sugar mills for a miserable wage at long hours, and were not compensated when the cylinders

54. *BSEP* 7, no. 2 (1928): 255.
55. *BSEP* 1, no. 4 (1923): 444.

crushed their arms. In northeastern Michoacán, the school zone inspector in 1923 reported that child labor, as well as social control, was so important to the American Smelting Company that the latter in league with local authorities threatened to fire parents who sent their children to school.[56]

Educators tended to believe quite naively that a schooled people would be one free from political tyranny, and yet local structures of domination persisted in many areas which were hostile to community needs. In a municipality of San Luis Potosí, visiting SEP officials asked a local officer how he was elected. "In truth, señor," he responded, "I was imposed." "Better put," said the SEP visitor, "you were named." "Maybe so," replied the local judge, "Señor Castillo named me." He then explained that Señor Castillo was an influential rancher in the area.[57]

The local power structure, which was integrated socially, politically, and economically, had to be broken down by political action if change benefitting the communities was to be effected. Not surprisingly, in several areas, local potentates were outright hostile to the establishment of schools. In some areas, teachers and communities succeeded in challenging aspects of exploitation and oppression—for example, eliminating forced and unpaid labor, company store tickets, excessive taxes, and other burdens on *campesinos*. In other instances, they assisted peasants in their struggle for land against the organized opposition of *hacienda* owners. Agrarian villagers and the rural teachers who defended them were attacked on a fairly consistent basis in the zone of Tacámbaro, Michoacán, by *bandoleros* in the pay of landowners. In Acayucán, Veracruz, in 1927, the cultural mission took up the struggle against local *hacienda* owners who had stopped village land petitions in the courts. The cultural mission directly pressured the president in Mexico City to resolve the petitions and to demand that this be done immediately to forestall an alliance between landowners and a foreign company. In appealing directly to the president and urging a rapid solution before state engineers received unappealable orders in favor of the landowners, the cultural mission recognized the complicity between the agrarian court system and the local power structure.[58]

56. On the Tarahumara, see *BSEP* 1, no. 4 (1923): 444–46; *BSEP* 6, no. 3 (1927): 99–101. On conditions in Nayarit, see *BSEP* 6, no. 6 (1927): 120–21. On Michoacán, see Raby, "Los principios," pp. 565–66.

57. *BSEP* 7, no. 2 (1928): 183.

58. On hostility to the school expressed by local elites, see, for example, the appeal to President Calles by Leandro González, president of the municipal council of the Ranchería of Salto de los Saldos in protest against the local *hacendado*'s closing of the

However, at the higher levels of the SEP, there was an overemphasis upon skill-upgrading and a relative de-emphasis of the need for structural reforms. Ideological biases of educators and pressures on SEP policy from other state ministries were responsible. The attention to skills stemmed both from the assumption that *campesinos* were poor because they were technically backward and from the desire to increase production within a small-producer framework. Thus, rural schools taught agriculture, livestock, and bird-raising, fruit and vegetable conservation, and small crafts such as soap-making, ceramics, weaving from local products like *ixtle* and palm, tanning and carpentry. One of the major problems in skill-upgrading was teacher training. Traveling cultural missions providing short courses for teachers on various subject areas and regional rural normal schools were designed to supplement pamphlets on soil improvement, agriculture, and crafts issued by the SEP. Neither the cultural missions nor the rural normals were adequately staffed or financed to cope with the task in an effective way. In the Calles period, more support went to the Department of Rural Schools, which was an administrative unit, than to the Office of Cultural Missions. Rafael Ramírez, head of the missions, complained that his was one of the most neglected sections of the ministry. Scarce funds limited its ability to attract qualified personnel and to cover the necessary territory. Lack of cooperation from other SEP departments and from government bureaucracies in health, industry, and agriculture, often led to the failure of missions. In 1926, in addition to being severely understaffed, the missions' skills training was not necessarily adaptable to local needs. Each of 11 missions had teachers of education, hygiene, and sports, but remaining personnel indicated both a degree of specialization sometimes inappropriate to local needs and a general shortage of trained personnel. Only one mission had a teacher of agriculture. Four had instructors in small industry; two in carpentry, one in soap-making, another in bee raising, and another in fruit-conservation. The rural normal schools were also understaffed, underequipped, and unhygienic. One rural normal director commented on the difficulty of developing small industries when primary materials were too expensive and market outlets absent. The absence of suitable market outlets was a general problem for rural schools.[59]

---

school, González to Calles, 4 Feb. 1927, AGN, Acervos Presidentes, Expediente 241-E-E-20. On teachers' participation in agrarian struggles in Michoacán, see Raby, "Los principios," p. 588. On the cultural mission and school in Acayucán, Veracruz, see *BSEP* 6, no. 6 (1927): 115.

59. For articulation and analysis of the problems faced by the Office of Cultural Missions and rural normal schools, see Rafael Ramírez, "Memoria crítica de la actu-

Often the skills taught were of little use as they were based on urban tastes unrelated to local needs or resources. The first cultural mission concentrated on the elaboration of perfumes and cosmetics exotic to rural life. The making of hair creams and shoe polish for people who were barefoot or in sandals testified to a certain obtuseness on the part of educators. The failure to make direct and viable improvements in rural life sometimes resulted in community apathy. In Campeche, parents refused to allow their children to attend agricultural classes; they said they knew how to farm better. The educators' obtuseness sometimes played into the hands of local power structures hostile to the Revolution. For instance, in a village in Veracruz, landowners not only stirred up opposition to the school by calling it a bed of godless Protestantism bent upon destroying churches and a center for conscripting people into the army, they claimed that the soap the school made was too expensive, its other industries useless, and its conserved fruits poisonous.[60]

The educators wished the school to be the center and orienting point of community life. In addition to introducing economic programs, the school was to teach values and behavior patterns compatible with the educators' own notions of propriety. The first mission in Hidalgo in 1923 was to see that residents

... modify their customs, acquire other forms of work or perfect those they have and receive suggestions for new and superior forms of life.[61]

Moisés Sáenz wrote that the rural school was

... a socializing agency where primitive life demands that the school take responsbility and functions from hygiene to eating habits. Above all, the school has to teach these creatures how to live.[62]

The teacher was a civilizer, who introduced proper customs to the community. Thus, the school was preoccupied with such issues as the

---

ación de la Dirección de Misiones Culturales desde 1926, año de su fundación, hasta la fecha 1928," 14 August 1928, Archivos de la SEP (hereafter cited as ASEP); "Datos acerca de las misiones culturales," n.d., ASEP, pp. 2–3; "Correspondencia de la Dirección de Misiones Culturales, 1926," ASEP.

60. For products elaborated by the first cultural missions and the rural schools, see, for example, *BSEP* 2, nos. 5 and 6 (1923–1924): 121, 125. On community apathy, see, for example, *BSEP* 7, no. 2 (1928): 202–3, 228, 238, 276. On Campeche, see *BSEP* 6, no. 3 (1927): 89. On landowner opposition in Veracruz, see *BSEP* 6, no. 6 (1927): 116.

61. *BSEP* 2, nos. 5 and 6 (1923–1924): 122.

62. Moisés Sáenz, *La educación rural en México*, p. 24.

use of soap and bathing habits, the modification of dress styles, comb-
ing and cutting of hair, the use of shoes, beds, and furniture, as well
as abstention from the consumption of alcohol. While financing and
upkeep of the school fell upon local residents themselves organized
into committees of education, SEP directives insisted that the committees should support the school without having any decision-making power in school programming. This cultural aggression was not
always the case. Teachers were often sympathetic and active in defense of community needs. For instance, in Acayucán, Veracruz,
where schools were intimately linked to the local struggle for land,
communities and teachers created the Centro Cultural Malinche to
affirm and preserve the indigenous culture through song, theater,
painting, and crafts. As in Yucatán in the same period, this cultural
affirmation was integrated into an ongoing struggle for material improvement.[63]

In addition to the relationship between teacher and community,
the relationship of both to local authorities was important. If local
authorities were friendly to both teacher and community, the opportunity for real improvement through education was greater. If local
authorities were hostile, the result was often a struggle between the
school sensitive to community needs and the local power structure.
However, even when local or state authorities favored the school, the
degree of meaningful change taking place depended to some extent
upon why and for what purposes local authorities supported it. Thus,
rural schools in the sierra of Puebla were supported by the local *cacique*, who also continued to maintain tight control over local governments: this arrangement may explain the failure of these schools to
improve rural conditions in any significant way. In San Luis Potosí,
also, there is some suggestion that regional power-holder Saturnino
Cedillo used the creation of schools as a means of building support
and that those most favored were his own military colonies, i.e., his
own troops. On the other hand, a less self-interested and more radi
cal politician like Francisco Mújica as governor of Michoacán saw the
school as an agency of structural social change and supported the
militancy of teachers and villages.[64]

63. On the preoccupation with teaching proper customs, see Sáenz, *Escuelas federales
en la sierra de Puebla*, pp. 3, 23, 36, 39, 40, 55, 63, 93–94; see also Esperanza Mendieta
de Nuñez Mata, *Carta a una maestra rural* (Oaxaca: Talleres Tipográficos del Gobierno,
1931) pp. 9ff. On the affirmation of indigenous culture in Veracruz, see *BSEP* 6, no. 6
(1927): 118. On the affirmation of indigenous culture in Michoacán, see *BSEP* 2, nos.
5 and 6 (1923–1924): 607.

64. On friction between the school and local authorities, see *BSEP* 7, no. 2 (1928):
213–20, 239–43. On the relationship between schools and Cedillo's military colonies,

Within the SEP hierarchy itself, an ideological commitment to small production and an unwillingness to challenge property relations led to an emphasis upon cooperatives and savings associations as the principal means of improving rural life. Viewing cooperatives as a happy medium between "capitalist egotism" and "socialism," an SEP pamphlet noted that cooperatives had diminished rural agitation in Hungary. Because large landowners were unwilling to increase production, according to this publication, the burden fell upon small producers. Educators saw cooperatives as mechanisms for the inculcation of "rational" market behavior. Instilling habits of order, discipline, and morality, cooperatives "teach us to produce honorably, eliminating thievery, banditry, alcohol . . . " Further, the SEP argued, "in this way, they will know well the place which corresponds to them as members of a social group and a well-organized state."[65] Many educators believed that cooperatives were an adequate means of combatting unequal market relationships. The Casa del Pueblo document stressed that they would make

. . . agricultural, industrial, and commercial activities more effective, requiring less effort from each member and resulting in better remunerated work . . . in such a way as to enable them to struggle advantageously with the already established capitalist or merchant.[66]

This document naively suggested asking local merchants and landowners to provide seed money for cooperatives, when in fact it was in the interest of the latter to obtain the lowest possible price for *campesino* produce. To function effectively, cooperatives needed a solid resource base in land, funding, inputs in machinery, tools, fertilizers, and seeds, as well as viable market outlets. The latter required effective, large-scale government support. Four *ejido* credit banks were created in the Calles period to provide such assistance while the SEP itself tried to create a cooperative marketing network with outlets in state capitals and Mexico City for crafts and other products. Neither of these efforts was adequately funded or pursued. In the absence of significant structural change and government support, cooperatives often became a substitute for real change. They emphasized maximum use of existing resources within an extremely unequal structure

---

see Calles to SEP, September 1924, AGN, Acervos Presidentes, Expediente 121-E-C-57. On Puebla, see Sáenz, *Escuelas federales en la sierra de Puebla*, pp. 87–89. On Mújica, see Raby, "Los Principios," pp. 558, 562–63.

65. *Resultados morales del cooperativismo*, Publicaciones de la SEP 6, no. 14 (1925): 43–45.

66. *BSEP* 1, no. 4 (1923): 429–30.

of resource distribution. Given such inequality, it is not surprising that the school cooperative in a town in San Luis Potosí raised just enough money on its harvest to buy a gas lamp for the school. The above should not suggest that cooperatives did not function or, even, in some instances, enjoy relative success—especially when linked with land reform, infrastructural development, market access, or a preexisting adequate resource base. In Texcoco, enterprising teachers and residents persuaded the Dirección de Ferrocarriles to establish a stop in their area as a necessary point for market transport. They installed electricity and irrigation works. Teachers and school inspectors formed a cooperative through which they bought a truck to transport the school harvest.[67]

Whether or not schools functioned to improve rural life depended upon a variety of factors including the local resource base, the relationship between teacher and community, and the relationship of the latter to local and state authorities. Of major importance also was the contradiction between the school's promises and goals, as articulated by the SEP itself, and the level of government support forthcoming. Moisés Sáenz commented on this problem following an extensive tour of San Luis Potosí. He worried that the enthusiasm he found in some villages might turn to disillusionment,

... given the probability of official inconstancy, the poverty of the budget, and the possible ossification of the educational doctrine of today.[68]

The contradiction became more acute as the Calles government retreated from social reform. Growing frustrations of many teachers with rural conditions, their attempts to root themselves in rural needs, and their perception of the structural obstacles to meaningful change contributed to their deepening politicization. In January of 1927, at a national teachers' conference, the delegate from Coahuila argued that current action pedagogy did not respond to social needs, that it had been only a superficial change instituted by capital politicians to forestall effective reform. He argued in favor of the *Escuela Racionalista* which he claimed responded to needs and was capable of overcoming servility, religious prejudices, and other manifestations of oppressed behavior to create a society founded on "collective and socialized work.[69]

67. *BSEP* 4, no. 9 (1925): 244–45.
68. *BSEP* 7, no. 2 (1928): 265.
69. "Congreso de Maestros," 4 Jan. 1927, AGN, Acervos Presidentes, Expediente 728-E-33.

Not all rural teachers gravitated toward the pedagogy of rational education nor were all rural teachers part of the growing radical current, but those who were found some network of communication through the cultural missions and the rural normal schools, as well as teachers' associations, trade unions, and agrarian leagues. As the cultural missions radicalized through their own rural experience and tended to propagate progressive ideas to the teachers whom they instructed, it is probably no accident that the Department of Cultural Missions was underfunded and neglected by the SEP in the Calles period, nor is it surprising that its chief, Rafael Ramírez, whose original position on rural education could hardly be distinguished from the dominant ideology, became a strong proponent of socialist education in the 1930s.

The highest levels of the SEP responded with alarm to the deepening politicization of rural teachers. Puig Casauranc deplored the rise in "militant politics which signifies a perturbing influence for this undertaking of serenity and enthusiasm, abnegation, and sacrifice."[70] The situation worsened in the Church-state dispute as teachers and communities were forced to take sides. *Cristero* peasants in the west stoned and burned schools, attacked teachers, and chased them out of communities.[71] Other teachers and communities actively fought the *Cristeros*. The SEP's response was to attempt to use the school to win the loyalty of the community to the state. Given the retreat of the state from social reform, the latter effort resulted in narrowing the school's role in the community according to SEP policy in Mexico City. In directives, the school's social action was to be limited to anti-alcohol and anti-gambling campaigns, hygiene crusades, the formation of savings associations and cooperatives, and the celebration of patriotic holidays.[72] Puig Casauranc referred to Alberto J. Pani's 1913 concern for averting "dissolving Zapatismo" through the school. He added:

> The child educated in our rural schools has, if the teacher manages to implant in his conscience disciplinary values, the correct and just notion of his duties and rights and far from being a disruptive element will be a notable factor of advance and development in his community when he is an adult.[73]

He continued, "We must . . . examine the problems of Mexico within

70. *BSEP* 5, no. 2 (1926): 12.
71. *BSEP* 6, no. 4 (1927): 53–54, 330; 6, no. 6 (1927): 257, 275, 282, 313.
72. See, for example, *BSEP* 6, no. 3 (1927): 75–82; 6, no. 6 (1927): 260.
73. *BSEP* 6, no. 3 (1927): 11–12.

the context of how the government and the Mexican family are trying to solve them."[74]

In conclusion, action education in Mexico was designed to increase production and productivity within a framework which broadly must be defined as capitalist, although policy-makers perhaps disagreed over support for small-scale or large-scale property as the basis for development. Action education, as it was defined and delineated by top policy-makers in the SEP, had only limited potential for effecting real change at the base, because of: the need to insure social order; the ideological biases of leading educators; the decision to build a hierarchical school system; the relative weakness of the SEP vis-à-vis other ministries; and the priorities for expenditures selected by the central state which did not include strong emphasis on structural reform benefitting the oppressed. To these strictures at the central state level must be added the relative weakness of that state in relation to local and regional power structures.

On the other hand, the school had been viewed as a vehicle for social change by most educators, in the politically fluid situation prevailing in the 1920s. In this time of a still weak central state and its bureacracy, of local-state-federal power struggles, and of movements for structural change at the base, teachers became a political force helping to mobilize rural communities in favor of reforms, and in so doing aggravated the dominant SEP position while demonstrating its lack of viability.

74. Ibid., p. 13.

Chapter 6
Ideology in Vocational Education in the 1920s

Educators in the Revolution were concerned with vocational training for economic growth and as a means of counteracting foreign hegemony. Within a capitalist framework such as that chosen by the Mexican state, technical education may assist capital accumulation in a variety of ways. On the one hand, it contributes to the training of an increasingly specialized labor force. At the same time, technical education can act as a brake on the development of class consciousness and organization. This will work insofar as such schooling articulates an ideology legitimizing the subordination of labor to capital, breaks the solidarity of class by offering workers a channel for individual upward mobility, and duplicates a process of increasing hierarchization in the division of labor within production.

The division of labor in Mexico included a sexual division. Increasingly in the period under study, technical training for modern industry was reserved for men, while women's vocational schooling was designed to remove them from factories and to return them to the home. In the home their principal economic role involved the reproduction of labor on a daily and generational basis, i.e., caring for husbands who worked in the paid labor force and raising children who would become the future labor force. The primary ideological role of women in the home was the reproduction of the social relations of production, instilling within the family, values and beliefs conducive to the subordination of labor to capital.

Vocational Education for Men

When the Escuela de Artes y Oficios para Hombres opened in 1869, there seemed to be a congruence between the establishment of the school and the goals of artisans who through their mutualist organizations had made known both their interest in contributing to national progress through increased production and their desire for education as a means of increasing their capacity to produce.[1] How-

1. See René Ortiz Peralta, "Las posiciones ideológicas de la Convención Radical Obrera," *Historia Obrera* 1, no. 2 (1974): 10–14; José Villaseñor, "El Gran Círculo de Obreros de México," *Historia Obrera* 1, no. 4 (1975): 32.

ever, economic growth in the *Porfiriato* began to undercut the position of the artisan in the economy and to threaten him with proletarianization as new factories began to undersell the individual producer's product. Consistently, Porfirian educational policy focused less on the artisan's vocational development than it did on trying to provide rudimentary training and the inculcation of disciplinary values in the nascent working class and the broadly defined middle sectors who were to occupy supervisory positions in the economic hierarchy. As the industrial working class grew at the turn of the century, so did the interest of educators in workers' night schools, new primary schools, and the enforcement of laws of obligatory attendance. Again, the focus was less on industrial skills and more on the internalization of habits of work and discipline.

Sierra, however, had been concerned with meeting the labor requirements of an increasingly complex society, and to this end, had divided primary superior education into commercial, industrial, and preparatory training in 1901. Correspondingly, educators wished to introduce training for modern industry—especially for railroads, transportation, and the electrical industry as evidenced by new classes in the Escuela de Artes y Oficios para Hombres. They hoped this training would help to replace foreign skilled labor prevalent in certain industries. However, until the final years of the regime support for technical education was fledgling enough to indicate a general acceptance of dependence on foreign technology and know-how.

The replacement of foreign by Mexican skilled workers was less the consequence of state policy and more the result of worker pressure and management considerations. By the 1890s, Mexican workers had assumed skilled jobs on the railroads as mechanics, boilermakers, steamfitters, brakemen, firemen, and carpenters.[2] North Americans monopolized positions as foremen, conductors, and engineers. The Order of Railway Conductors, made up largely of Texans, was particularly protective of its jobs and contemptuous of Mexican labor. In 1908, the Gran Liga de Empleados del Ferrocarril launched a strike demanding the Mexicanization of the railroads. Although the government responded to their demands by encouraging

2. Mario Gil, *Los ferrocarrileros* (Mexico: Editorial Extemporaneos, 1971), p. 41. Edward N. Brown, railroad engineer who supervised construction on the Mexico City-Laredo line and later came to head the nationalized railways, told the U.S. Senate Investigating Committee in 1919 that between 1890 and 1912 he had trained 15,000 to 18,000 skilled Mexican workers in on-the-job training schools. Evidently, the schools had paid very low wages to Mexican apprentices, many of whom left to go into mining, smelting, and factory work. See U.S. Senate, *Investigation of Mexican Affairs* 1: 1791–93.

a Mexicanization of personnel on the government-controlled lines, it was not until 1913 when the U.S. workers went on strike in defense of their jobs that Mexican workers in large numbers moved in to replace them.[3]

In the mining industry, Mexican workers were trained for skilled jobs because they were more available than foreigners and would work for less. As in other industries, foreigners continued as foremen, master mechanics, engineers, and superintendents. The Green Consolidated Copper Company of Cananea, Sonora, employed an unusually large number of Americans. When Mexican workers struck here in 1906, they protested pay inequalities, their lack of access to better jobs, and the behavior of particular U.S. foremen. Their strike opened the way for a Mexicanization of personnel: the foreign portion of the labor force at Cananea dropped from 40 percent in 1906 to between 13.8 percent and 12.9 percent in 1912.[4] When foreigners left in large numbers during the Mexican Revolution, more Mexicans took over skilled and supervisory jobs—handling the railways, trams, power stations, and mechanical installations in mines and factories.

In the Mexican Revolution, middle-sector educators were concerned with technical education for modern industry in order to replace foreign personnel and to serve other areas of economic activity in which foreigners had not been dominant, such as some areas of construction, or fields which were new, like automobile mechanics. They also stressed the traditional crafts and small industries. Their attraction to the latter may be traced to their own petit bourgeois

3. On railroad workers, see Gil, *Los ferrocarrileros*, pp. 41, 53–58, 61–66; Ramón Eduardo Ruíz, *Labor and the Ambivalent Revolutionaries*, pp. 15–20; Anderson, *Outcasts in Their Own Land: Mexican Industrial Workers, 1906–1911*, pp. 90–91; U.S. Senate, *Investigation of Mexican Affairs* 1: 1791–93; 2: 2840–44.

4. On Cananea strike and aftermath, see Ruíz, *Labor and the Ambivalent Revolutionaries*, p. 21, and Dwight Woodbridge, "Labor Data on a Northern Mexican Mine," *Mexican Mining Journal* 17, no. 1 (1913): 348–49. See also Marvin Bernstein, *The Mexican Mining Industry*, p. 58. Of primary consideration to mineowners in employing Mexicans was their cheapness in relation to foreign labor. The differential was increased by payment of foreign personnel in gold and of Mexican workers in silver. See, for example, Hugh Elwes, "Points about Mexican Labor," *Engineering and Mining Journal* 90, no. 14 (1910): 662. Mining company supervisors also argued that Mexican labor was more tractable than North American labor. One of the major attractions of investment in Mexican mining after 1900 was labor agitation in the United States. See James W. Malcolmson, "Mining Development in Mexico during 1902," *Engineering and Mining Journal* 75 (1903): 35–39; "Mining in Mexico," *Engineering and Mining Journal* 75 (1903): 210; "Mining in Mexico," *Engineering and Mining Journal* 77 (1904): 21–22.

backgrounds and to the importance of the small-holder ideology in the Mexican Revolution.

Though he supported small industry, Felix F. Palavicini's major thrust in vocational education in the Carranza period was training for modern industry. He converted the Escuela de Artes y Oficios para Hombres into the Escuela de Ingenieros Mecánicos y Electricistas to train machinists, electricians, auto mechanics, and mechanical and electrical engineers. He created the Escuela Nacional de Químicas for the development of a national chemical industry based on Mexican primary materials. Policy-makers in the 1920s pursued the modernizing strategy. Staff for the expansion of technical schools was scarce, but the college of engineering and the vocational schools themselves had produced a core of technocrats and educators, among whom the most highly placed were engineers Roberto Medellín, chief of technical schooling under Vasconcelos, and his successor Miguel Bernard. In 1922, Medellín proposed the creation of five new technical schools aimed at increasing national control over industry. A railroad workers' school was to contribute to the growth of industry and commerce through an expanded communications network: the school would train mechanics, machinists, brakemen, engineers, conductors, telegraph operators, etc. Similarly, a textile school was planned to improve the competitive capacity of that industry in relation to foreign counterparts by training skilled labor. A school for construction workers would assist engineers in expanding the national building industry. The Escuela de Artes Gráficas would prepare printers and photographers for an industry judged to be foreign-dominated because of the lack of qualified Mexican labor. The Escuela Normal de Tecnología would graduate industrial arts teachers for the country as a whole as a means of expanding and upgrading the quality of technical education nationwide.

An equally important consideration in vocational education was the need to discipline the labor force politically. In reference to the proposed textile school, Medellín said:

> The lack of technical knowledge in textiles means that workers procure their economic betterment only asking for an increase in wages; but they do not try to increase their productivity at work. This makes them toy in a vicious way with the progress of business and to demand concessions frequently impossible to concede. . . . Until today the workers have remained completely isolated, receiving no more counsel than that of false apostles who promise them immense benefits and inculcate in them exalted ideas which maintain a spirit of discord between them and

capital. Nothing has been done to channel the social movement on a correct path. In the textile school, the workers, in addition to receiving the technical instruction they greatly need, will receive instruction on the social question adequate to producing harmony between their interests and those of the nation; this in itself is sufficient to justify the establishment of the school, since it is clear that throughout the world the social question is of great interest and demands urgent attention.[5]

The training of a hierarchically organized work force imbued with discipline and loyal to the employer and in turn enforcing such discipline and loyalty in other workers was seen as a basic goal of the school:

The foundation of this school is a great step on the road to progress for our textile industry, benefitting the industrialists who will be able to have directors, masters, and skilled workers in their labor force which will increase the efficiency and consequently the remuneration of the latter. For the nation as a whole, it will contribute to the formation of an element of order and progress.[6]

Neither the textile workers' school, nor the railroad school, nor the teacher training institute were built, probably due to financial limitations and to political pressures on the state. Before Congress in 1922, for example, representatives of the railroad workers' union—an organization independent of the CROM—objected to the creation of the railroad training school on grounds similar to objections put forward by the United States American Federation of Labor to the expansion of vocational training in the United States.[7] The Mexican workers argued that the state, in usurping craft masters' functions of training journeymen and apprentices, would break the power of the union while preparing a reserve army of surplus labor which could be used to break strikes. The railroad workers asked that the school respond to the needs of existing railroad workers, be located near their work sites, and be controlled by the workers themselves who best knew their trade. They further asked that employment opportunities be created before the vocational schools were constructed. Liberals in Congress, including José Vasconcelos, argued that craft unions were "feudal" and limited the mobility of workers; public edu-

5. *BSEP* 1, no. 1 (1922): 203.
6. Ibid.
7. *BSEP* 1, no. 3 (1923): 28–31. See also Gintis and Bowles, *Schooling in Capitalist America*, p. 193.

cation, they insisted, was a progressive tool which provided equal opportunity for all.[8] Vasconcelos also suggested that the union was incompetent to control technical education as it lacked sufficient command of the scientific theory behind production.

The workers' protest and the educators' response shed light on the nature and purpose of vocational training, which could and in many instances did replace craft union control over work. As elsewhere, vocational training became an adjunct to scientific management.[9] When the state assumed control of industrial training, it sanctioned labor's subordination to capital and promoted in the schools a fundamental anti-union and individualistic ideology. It is probable that Mexican technical education in this period was designed to assist in breaking the power of independent craftsmen while subordinating them to superiors within an expanding organization of corporate production. The Escuela de Maestros Constructores trained master workers to "cooperate effectively in the realization of work directed by engineers and architects"; this included being able to take orders and precisely execute them.[10] The Escuela de Ingenieros Mecánicos y Electricistas aimed at training skilled workers and masters who would subordinate their work to orders from engineers. In a mystification of this relationship, the school's director said:

> The intellectual and physical workers should march together united and constitute a single family: the workers of humanity.[11]

Complementing the notion of hierarchy was the school's initial appeal to individualism; education promised the individual betterment and mobility rather than class solidarity and action. The textile workers' school was a hope for

> . . . the multitude of youth who live in scarcity with badly remunerated work since they will be able in little time to become distinguished workers and independent industrialists.[12]

This approach created the impression not only that class action was unnecessary but that mobility depended on individual ability, perseverance, and education—an idea basic to the bourgeois ideology of

8. *BSEP* 1, no. 3 (1923): 33–39.

9. For a fuller discussion of the impact of scientific management upon work and workers, see Harry Braverman, *Labor and Monopoly Capital: The Degradation of Work in the Twentieth Century*, pp. 142–52.

10. *BSEP* 1, no. 1 (1922): 205, 211.

11. *BSEP* 6, no. 2 (1927): 56.

12. *BSEP* 1, no. 1 (1922): 203.

schooling. In fact, technical education could offer mobility to only a small sector of the population, dependent upon factors such as location, family income, and previous education. Technical schools were urban and located primarily in Mexico City; within the city, accessibility was a determining factor in enrollments. When the SEP closed a vocational school in a working-class neighborhood in 1927 and offered to transfer students to another school, workers protested on the grounds that their school had been well located to allow them to study at night.[13] Further, technical schooling was open to those who had completed primary elementary or primary superior school and who had the leisure time to attend, which meant that they were relatively well-off, with families who would support them while they went to school. This sort of restriction prevailed because of Mexico's socioeconomic structure and the financial limitations of public spending coupled with priorities for spending. Fees and tuition for technical schools were introduced by the Calles government in its effort to save money. Furthermore, given the large number of students seeking technical training, the government decided to introduce entrance examinations rather than to build more schools. This policy prejudiced the less prepared who were often the less prosperous students.

In Mexico City, vocational schooling probably served the middle strata. Even in this group, training was graded to award those with a higher income. In the Escuela Nacional de Mecánicos y Electricistas, a mechanical or electrical engineer had to support himself or be supported for a seven-year instructional period. The training period for a master craftsman and skilled worker in the same school was two years. The Escuela Superior de Administración y Comercio offered a longer period of training for relatively high-level positions in accounting in commercial and government offices, while several other schools offered two- to three-year programs for lower-level clerical positions in secretarial work and bookkeeping. On the other hand, the SEP made an effort to institute night courses in all schools to open opportunities for working people. Probably owing to material circumstances, most students pursued an occasional course at night rather than taking full-career programs either in the evening or daytime. It is not clear what impact these courses had upon their wages or job classifications.

In the schools, the initial appeal to individualism was redefined to emphasize the need for sacrificing individual or class interests to society's interests: cooperation, specialization, and subordination be-

13. *BSEP* 6, no. 1 (1927): 134.

came key values in classroom organization and behavior, in program content, and in extracurricular activities. Luz Vera, who had taught in the Universidad Popular and remained active in technical and women's education, stressed the need for social peace and cooperation at the opening of an industrial school in Puebla:

> Neither teachers nor students should forget that the school is not for the satisfaction of narrow interests. . . . The school is an institution of human interest: in it men and women are formed, not just workers. It is not enough to be skilled in making an object if the school is not made a true social and cultural center in which each student feels his responsibility to the collectivity in which he lives, so that his acts are channeled to procure the well-being of the society to which he belongs. Contemplating that we owe to each person with whom we deal daily, from the workers who bring us fuel to the scientist who gives us knowledge, we can measure the responsibility which weighs on us and the needs we have to cooperate doing the part we are called upon to perform.[14]

The school became a microcosm of the larger society and an experimental laboratory for future participation in that society. An ideology of incorporation stressing cooperation and loyalty was perhaps most explicit in night schools, which were of three types—those within technical schools, cultural vocational night centers, and community literacy centers. The centers utilized the organization of festivals and choirs, of cooperatives and committees, to develop a spirit of school loyalty designed to stimulate a similar attitude toward the larger society. As in secondary schools, committee structure was hierarchical and subordinate to the school director, who maintained essential decision-making power. In one night school, the Sociedad de Alumnos Fraternidad y Progreso delegated representatives from each class to meet regularly with professors and directors to discuss the economic, moral, and social progress of students and the school. Directors were pleased to report in 1924 that students in this school did not participate in a student protest at the Escuela Nacional Preparatoria although their support had been solicited. Rather, according to the director, the night centers were successfully

> . . . fomenting sentiments of love and respect for the school, of cooperation in its progress and prestige, as well as the dignity of being an honorable member of society.[15]

14. *BSEP* 4, no. 7 (1925): 208.
15. *BSEP* 2, nos. 5 and 6 (1923–1924): 111.

This approach applied to regular classes in vocational schools where more elaborate structures could be built. Here, also, the organization of student government, cooperatives, sports teams, and Boy Scout troops aimed at encouraging cooperation within hierarchy. Classroom instruction stressed habits of work, punctuality, and subordination. Luz Vera said:

> The teacher has no greater satisfaction than the fulfillment of duty and this is made easy when students give all their love to work as the teacher has given to teaching.[16]

One educator explained the relationship between the discipline learned in school and social harmony:

> Student duty must be considered in two aspects: that of punctuality in attendance and that of effectiveness in study . . . and above all, in discipline: discipline of oneself; discipline in relation to others. The man without discipline is a boat without a rudder. . . . In the position we adopt toward ourselves and others, noble harmony ought to dominate. And such harmony is destroyed when deafening our souls, we discard the imperious dictates of our duty, whose voice must be heard. And harmony is broken and disappears also when we forget that we ought to be a coherent social unity and maintain respect for moral hierarchies.[17]

Educators did not lose sight of their goal of social stabilization in the midst of continuing revolutionary upheaval:

> In our effort we count on studious youth . . . and the school . . . a channel for liberating us from the vicissitudes and contingencies of the tumultuous times in which we live.[18]

Within the process of developing a policy of vocational education and an ideology within it, there were important contradictions. Vocational training for modernization coexisted with training in the traditional crafts—a phenomenon illustrating both political contradictions of policy-makers and the facts of Mexico's economic base. Schools for training carpentry, glass-making, tanning, and tailoring coexisted with schools of electricity, mechanics, and construction. In the Vasconcelos period, an effort was made to create several schools for the crafts in the states, especially in central Mexico. As in rural education, the proposed solution for the survival of small production was coop-

16. *BSEP* 4, no. 7 (1925): 208.
17. *BSEP* 8, no. 1 (1929): 88–89.
18. *BSEP* 6, no. 2 (1927): 58.

erativism. An all-embracing cooperative for the sale of products from the technical schools was created in 1925 to provide practical experience with the market and to propagandize for technical education and Mexican-made products. The underlying logic of cooperativism from a radical perspective was articulated by one educator who saw it as a real alternative to privately-owned industry, but his was a minority opinion.[19] The SEP technical school cooperative was in fact an expedient tool for increasing SEP revenues under Calles and a pedagogical means of inculcating market values including those of work, order, and "morality."[20] Rather than undercutting or rivaling private industry, cooperatives were regarded by most educators as a means of preserving small-scale production while simultaneously advancing large-scale production. The vocational school cooperative operated in debt and was unable to purchase raw materials at prices low enough to make its sale prices competitive.[21] Like rural small-holders, traditional craftsmen did not receive the government support necessary to buttress their positions, despite ideological pronouncements of the SEP and other agencies.

Not surprisingly, in the Calles period, greater emphasis was placed on training for modern industry. Many of the crafts and small industries schools in the states were closed down for budgetary reasons. Focus was on the Escuela de Ingenieros Mecánicos y Electricistas, the Escuela de Constructores, and the Instituto Técnico Industrial, created in 1924. New careers were added in advertising, commercial accounting, auto mechanics, radio and telegraph operation and engineering, and oil-well perforating. Together with increased emphasis on specialized training for industry went a decreasing concern for theory. Whereas both Roberto Medellín and José Vasconcelos in the early 1920s had shared John Dewey's hope that educated workers would possess command of both practice and theory in the particular area of production in which they were engaged, this goal was not stressed in the Calles era.

Simultaneously, the relationship between technical education and private industry grew much closer and more specific. The schools received grants from private firms. The Cámara de Comercio (National Chamber of Commerce) sponsored contests for students at the Escuela Superior de Comercio y Administración. Students regularly

19. See, for example, *BSEP* 8, no. 8 (1929): 46–49.
20. *BSEP* 6, no. 2 (1927): 74.
21. *BSEP* 1, no. 4 (1923): 82.

visited private companies producing steel, electricity, oil, copper, sugar, and beer.[22] In 1930, the SEP lobbied to include representatives of the Cámaras de Comercio y Industria in a proposed council for technical and commercial education "in order to achieve a perfect accord between our teachings and the realities of life."[23] Firms in which the students did practice-training were both nationally and foreign-owned. Students, for example, worked in the United States with Allis Chalmers, General Electric, Bethlehem Steel, Baldwin Locomotive, and the Square D Company; a few went to Germany to work for the Krupp and Siemens firms. Thus, a contradiction developed between the educators' hopes that vocational education would stimulate Mexican-controlled industrialization and increasing reliance upon foreign—especially U.S.—firms for machinery and practice-training programs for the vocational schools. This reliance, coupled with the failure to build several technical schools thought to be crucial to nationally controlled industrialization in 1920, mirrored the continued dependent status of Mexico's economy, Calles' compromises with U.S. capital, and the growing influx of U.S. investment in manufacturing.

Although the independent railroad workers' union had criticized the creation of a railroad school on the grounds that it would undercut the power of the union, the government-controlled trade union confederation, CROM, voiced no objection to technical education policy. Because the organization itself came to promote an ideology of class conciliation and worker contribution to industrial development within a capitalist framework, their support for government policy is not surprising. Vicente Lombardo Toledano, director of education for CROM in 1924, spoke in favor of technical education for modernization and the replacement of foreign workers. He argued that technical education should capacitate Mexican workers to one day run Mexican industry. In 1929, however, he came out strongly in favor of Taylorism, or scientific management, as the secret to increased productivity. He may not have understood the extent to which scientific management undermined the power of workers, but he was following a fairly consistent line in favor of capitalist modernization put forward by the dominant organization of the Mexican working class.[24]

22. See, for example, *BSEP* 5, no. 6 (1925): 81–82; 9, nos. 1–3 (1930): 57–58.
23. *BSEP* 9, nos. 1–3 (1930): 59. On donations from private firms, see, for example, *BSEP* 5, no. 2 (1926): 112. On relations with Cámara de Comercio, see BSEP 5, no. 6 (1925): 90–91. On student visits to firms, see, for example, *El esfuerzo* 1: 489–92.
24. Krauze, *Los caudillos culturales*, pp. 307–10.

Vocational Training for Women

Perhaps surprisingly, vocational education in the Mexican Revolution focused heavily upon women.[25] Of thirteen vocational schools in Mexico City in 1926, nine were women's schools. Mexican vocational education in general in the 1920s contributed to a division of labor along sex lines. With the important exception of some training for office work, the trend in women's vocational education was toward removing women from production in the public sector and returning them to the home and petty production. This morally and politically motivated policy probably prejudiced the position of working class women in Mexican society.

With the development of light industry in the second half of the nineteenth century, women began to enter the labor force in relatively large numbers: they came both from migrant rural stock and from artisan families crippled by advancing factory production.[26] In the textile, clothing, hat, and tobacco industries, women workers endured not only low wages, long hours, and unhealthy working conditions but also sexual exploitation at the hands of male employers and managers. Male employers in the garment industry were well known for their economic and personal abuse of women operatives. The Mexican union movement, which before 1906 was dominated by artisans, protested the abuse of women and the disintegration of family life, which was a basic productive and social unit for the artisan sector.[27] The craftsmen, who were anticlerical, argued for women's education to secularize their values, to moralize their behavior, and to

25. Portions of this section on women's vocational education were originally published as "Women, Class, and Education in Mexico, 1880–1928," *Latin American Perspectives* 12–13 (1977): 150–68. The following discussion does not involve women's professional education nor their entry into professions. The latter is an important topic for investigation as statistics indicate significant increases in women's entry into professional schools during the Revolution. Employment in public administration for women increased more than any other single category of women's work in the 1920s. How much of this increase was absorbed in clerical jobs and how much in administrative decision-making remains to be investigated.

26. For background on women in the industrial labor force in the *Porfiriato*, see Margaret Towner, "Monopoly Capitalism in Women's Work during the Porfiriato," in *Women in Latin America: An Anthology* (Riverside: Latin American Perspectives, 1979), pp. 47–61; and Anderson, *Outcasts in Their Own Land: Mexican Industrial Workers, 1906–1911*, pp. 40–41.

27. See, for example, Centro de Estudios Históricos del Movimiento Obrero Mexicana, *La mujer y el movimiento obrero mexicano en el siglo XIX. Antología de la prensa* (Mexico: Centro de Estudios Históricos del Movimiento Obrero Mexicano, 1975), pp. 61–138.

raise their skill level so that they could find better-paying jobs. These goals would presumably help to preserve family life. Their attitudes were based on a conservatism regarding woman's fundamentally subordinate, passive, and domestic role.

A more radical affirmation of women's rights to equality and economic and political participation grew out of the militant organization of industrial workers after 1906. Many women took leadership roles in the development of trade unionism and in political movements—principally in the Casa del Obrero Mundial, anarchist precursor of the CROM, in the Partido Socialista del Sureste, and in the Confederación General de Trabajadores, CROM's militant, independent rival in the 1920s.[28] Their organization was, however, never strong enough to counteract the male orientation of the trade union movement or the ideology of middle-sector women, who came to occupy important posts in the state bureaucracies, including that of education.

In the *Porfiriato*, a few women's vocational schools were geared toward the middle strata, including artisan families wealthy enough to be able to educate their female children. In addition to preparing schoolteachers, these schools trained women for low-level clerical positions and in household or small-shop industries such as sewing, cooking, artificial flower-making, and hairdressing. Some training prepared women for supervisory tasks; some of these women went on to exploit their female employees. Educators were careful to emphasize that this education did not threaten family life but aimed at strengthening it. Training—especially in home economics—sought to make the household at once more economical and moral. The primarily emotional, passive, and subordinate role of women was in no way altered in the minds of educators. Like most men and many women of his time, Justo Sierra viewed feminism as a threat to family life:

In all Mexican schools we are forming men and women for the home: this is our goal. Doing it, we believe firmly that we are performing a service beyond comparison with any to the Republic. . . The educated woman will be truly one for the home; she will be the companion and collaborator of man in the formation of the family. That is what we want and that is what you are being so firmly morally prepared for here. . . You are called to form souls, to sustain the soul of your husband; for this rea-

28. See María Antonieta Rascón, "La mujer y la lucha social," in Elena Urrutía, *Imagen y realidad de la mujer*, pp. 139–74: *Historia Obrera* 2, no. 5 (1975): 4–23.

son, we educate you. *Niña querida*, do not turn feminist in our midst. . . No, you and ourselves are mutually complementary; we form a single personality called to continue the perpetual creation of the nation.[29]

The Porfirian schools produced a small but influential circle of Mexican professional women engaged in education. In the Mexican Revolution, many of these women joined male counterparts in implementing educational policy designed to reshape poor and working women for a primary but subordinate role in the home. As put forward in Mexico City during the years of struggle, one purpose in educating working women was to abate prostitution,

> to aid [*la mujer pobre*] by theoretical-practical training to save her from the dangers which she encounters in life and habilitate her to fully fulfill her social duties as well as her duties as a woman of the home.[30]

In the 1920s, more schools opened to women for training in clerical work, home economics, and domestic-related industries such as sewing, soap- and artificial flower-making, cooking, toy- and shoe-making. These, as well as night centers for working women, were designed explicitly to remove women from factory production—preparing them for household work while providing them with a trade they could practice independently at home such as sewing, embroidery, or candy-making.[31] Wrote Laura Méndez de Cuenca, a leading educator, on the importance of women's education to the stability of family life and the orderly incorporation of children into the social system:

> If we ignore woman leaving her in ignorance we would establish in the Mexican home a regrettable disequilibrium, tending to multiply marital disasters so unfortunately abundant in our society. If someone is in need of education, it is the woman. Her mission is to raise and care for the family and consequently she is the primordial chisel of society. The man sustains the home materially—he represents the physical force of the home—but the woman, wife, and mother nourishes the soul of her children and strengthens that of her husband with wise teachings and prudent advice.[32]

29. Justo Sierra, *Educación*, p. 329.
30. *Boletin de Educación* 1, no. 1 (1914): 126.
31. *BSEP* 1, no. 1 (1922): 243; 1, no. 3 (1923): 236–40, 259–65; 2, nos. 5 and 6 (1923–1924): 111–17, 133–36; 6, no. 6 (1927): 59–62.
32. *Boletín de la Universidad Popular Mexicana* 4 (1918): 188–89.

This trend was an attempt to strengthen women's primary role in the home as a replacer of male labor power on a daily and generational basis while marginalizing her own participation in the labor force. It in fact suggested a return to domestic piecework, a most exploitative form of labor. The trend was further strengthened by limiting participation in skill training for increasingly capital-intensive industry to men.

Women's vocational training reflected and reinforced class-stratified society and women's pervasive subordination within it. Curricula were offered to middle-strata women in homemaking and clerical work, to domestic servants in household labor, and to working-class women in household work and home industries for market sale. The product models and consumer values promoted by the schools reflected those of the wealthy, with the consequence that less affluent women would be encouraged to desire and to subordinate themselves to such models and values. Annual exhibits at women's schools included richly furnished homes replete with crystal flower bowls, Tiffany lamps, fine linen, and contemporary fashions.[33] Further, the industries open to women were usually designed to please men (fashions, cooking, beauty parlors) and so suggested a perpetuation of the subordinate role of women in society. The type of work was often individual or confined to the small shop and thus was not propitious for the development of political consciousness. Because the school emphasized their primary role in the home and defined for them an apolitical and submissive role, women's potential for politicization through work was limited, even if they worked in production.

More than simply returning women to the home, educators saw the need to restructure working-class family life as a unit of sociopolitical stability. Female educators were concerned with increasing the economic efficiency of the workers' home to perform the double function of sustaining a healthy labor force on a low income and internalizing values such as subordination, discipline, and efficiency of time and space, which the worker needed in factory production. In lectures in schools and over the government radio station, home economics professors discussed the function of the housewife:

The head of the household has to be active; if she is lazy, there will never be enough time and her tasks will always be behind, the meals will not be served when they should, the clothes will not be ready, and she will look dirty and disheveled. Nearly always these things arise from laziness and disorder. . . . In the

33. *BSEP* 2, nos. 5 and 6 (1923–1924): 134, 296–302, 305, 310–12.

home the lack of order is failure since without it, it is impossible to develop faculties and to form good habits; if the child is made to wash his face one day and stops doing it for three or four, to ask him again on the fifth day—and if he does not do it again for eight days—means he will not acquire the habit of washing himself.[34]

The wife was a worker who had to balance efficiently the factors of time, work, and money. This would facilitate a regular performance of tasks in the home with appropriate rest periods to avoid exhaustion. Budgeting was not only essential to the economical organization of the home but to the inculcation of proper values among family members:

> Good schedules in the home produce exactitude and punctuality. The child learns to fulfill each of his obligations at the appointed hour and when he comes to govern himself, will be punctual and exact in all his acts. . . . When the schedule of the home does not exist or is badly regulated, the whole family is hurt and it is impossible to form good habits.[35]

As a worker, the housewife had to maintain her health and that of her family:

> To live normally man needs solar light. In darkness, he gets sick, his muscles lose their vitality, his life is altered, his character is modified, and soon anemia sets in. . . . The majority of microbes which breed contagious diseases . . . grow in darkness and produces weakened, depressed individuals, incapable of action.[36]

To allow for "rest," "inspiration," and "tranquility," the home had to be well-decorated, clean, and attractive.[37]

To a degree, the notion of women's work as time-oriented prepared her for her increasing role as a consumer of market-made household goods. The lecturers argued that the housewife should economize her efforts "since if machines become worn out from continual work, the delicate organism of woman is even more affected."[38] Her aids were to be refrigerators, sewing machines, and vacuum cleaners. Since poor women could not afford these, they could purchase ammonia, borax, bicarbonate of soda and other cleaning aids. Above all,

34. *BSEP* 5, no. 6 (1926): 162.
35. Ibid., p. 164.
36. Ibid., p. 171.
37. Ibid., p. 173.
38. Ibid., p. 166.

lecturers insisted on the importance of savings. Poor people could survive on a minimum income if they mended and dyed old clothes, bought vegetables only in season and staples in quantity. Concluded a professor:

Ojalá, Señoras, amas de casa, that my poor suggestions are well taken by some of you that they serve to alleviate the heavy task weighing on heads of families who, looking toward the future, struggle to realize the great task of constructing the nation by bettering the home.[39]

This approach led, on the one hand, to a mystification of household work, which was in fact unpaid labor essential to the reproduction of labor power for industry. It led also to an ideology of the family which attempted to make it the central focus of emotional and social life, in place of class and community. Whereas the working and living conditions of the working class in the period of early industrialization suggested a greater socialization of human relations through collective factory labor and community openness, bourgeois reforms in Mexico and elsewhere saw the revitalization of the private family unit as a corrective to class organization at the level of work place or community. To reformers, family life often appeared to be a morally necessary alternative to the apparent chaos and unhealthiness of working class life, i.e., the saloon, unattended children, crowded streets. Beneath the moral concerns were practical economic and political considerations: rehabilitation of the family as a private unit could act as a catalyst in the formation of a healthy, pliable, and disciplined labor force.

The process of promoting a specific ideology of family life involved a belief in the moral correctness of the bourgeois family model. In Mexico, the idea of transferring this model to the working class reached its highest level of precision and sophistication in a selection of readings assembled by the Chilean poetess Gabriela Mistral. In a deeply patriarchial society, this courageous woman became not only one of the great literary figures of her time but also a committed social activist who cared about the welfare of the exploited and about the independence of Latin America from foreign domination. Nonetheless, she expressed real contradictions in her attitude toward women and, in particular, toward poor women. One of several politically conscious Latin Americans who came to revolutionary Mexico to participate in the educational, cultural, and social reform move-

39. *BSEP* 4, no. 6 (1925): 228.

ment of the Obregón period, she was duly revered for the hours she dedicated to teaching children and women and the books she composed for them. Her book of readings for Mexican women was compiled in conjunction with her teaching in the Escuela del Hogar Gabriela Mistral founded in 1922. Although she was herself an apparently liberated woman in terms of her freedom of movement, intellectual development and creativity, and her political involvement, the readings she edited for Mexican women were deeply traditional and conducive to persistent abnegation, domesticity, and withdrawal from public life.

Her book was dedicated to Mexican women. Its purpose was to "form mothers," which the Chilean writer claimed was the "only reason for women's being on earth."[40] She reprinted John Ruskin, ideologue of the Victorian family, on the home as refuge from a public world of conflict:

> It is a place of peace: the refuge not only against all aggravation, but against all error, doubt, and division. Insofar as it is not this, it is not a home; insofar as the anxieties of exterior life penetrate it, and the society of the inconscient soul, the anonymous and loveless soul of the external world is admitted by husband or wife, it ceases to be a home; . . . it is only a part of the world you have left and where you have lit the fire.[41]

The home became a compensation for the pains and exploitation inflicted by the world of work. If it became the primary focus of love and attention for the male worker—in essence, an extension of his individualized consciousness—it could succeed in divorcing him from politics and, in its solace and authoritarian structure, offer compensation for the humiliation endured in work. Although he lacked control in his paid labor, over his family the man held dominion. This burden fell hard upon children and upon women, from whom it demanded submission and absorption of men's frustrations. Wrote Mistral:

> She ought to be patient, incorruptibly good, instinctive, infallibly wise—wise not for her own advantage, but through self-re-

---

40. Gabriela Mistral, *Lecturas para mujeres* (Mexico: SEP, 1923), p. 8.
41. Ibid., p. 17. For further analysis of the Victorian family model, see Miriam Schneir, *Feminism: The Essential Historical Writings* (New York: Random House, 1972), pp. 162–78, 179–88, and Eli Zaretsky, "Capitalism, the Family, and Personal Life," *Socialist Revolution* 1 (1973): 90–106.

nunciation—wise not with the sin of insolent pride or absence of love, but with the impassioned nobility of modest sacrifice.[42]

The role of mother was to hide conflictive reality by constructing an order within the home which did not exist outside:

> You establish a clear harmony between the chairs, the tables, the buffets . . . simple things . . . nothing disturbs this harmony as nothing disturbs the harmony of the universe.[43]

Like the wife's absorbing her husband's frustrations, the wife and husband together were obliged to hide the conflicts of the adult world from children:

> The disagreements, the discussions, the anger, all this world of inevitable contrarity, you must keep from the eyes of children . . . or you will force them to take sides which is equivalent to breaking the harmony of its effectivity.[44]

Underlying this romanticization was the legitimization of an authoritarian structure replicating a similar structure in the larger society and tending to repress questioning, creativity, critical thought, and conflict. From the woman, this structure required submission, which Mistral mystified in a process of transferring Catholic values to the modern state:

> In as many hours as has the day, you give although it be only a smile, a hand, a word of relief. In as many hours as has the day you seem like Him Who is none but perpetual giving and diffusion. You should fall on your knees before the Father and say unto Him: Thank you because I can give, Father. Never will the shadow of impatience pass over me. Truly, it is worth more to give than to receive.[45]

While modernization coincided with the state's increasing absorption of family functions such as socialization, health, and protection, the particular economic structure of capitalist society required from the family a specific role in the generation of a pliable labor force. At the same time, the state's attempt to define the family's role suggested an effort to limit the family as a source of authority, ideas, and independent thought and action. In so doing, the state acted both to

42. Mistral, *Lecturas*, p. 19.
43. Ibid., p. 24.
44. Ibid., p. 23.
45. Ibid., p. 203.

counteract the ideological influence of the Church on women and family life and to meet the requirements of an expanding market economy. In the extension of schooling in the 1920s, the SEP sought to organize parents to support the school without giving them a say in what took place within the school.[46] While in part the move may have stemmed from the state's fears of Church opposition to the Revolution, the disjunction created between family and school is typical of the effects of expansion of public school systems in capitalist societies. Under the facade of children's rights, the state assumed the right to prescribe the content of the family's socialization of children. Addressing himself to parents in 1926, Puig Casauranc wrote:

> Health, education, and the formation of proper moral criteria are not favors children receive but inalienable rights which their innocence and weakness concedes them.[47]

The teacher was to instruct parents on the proper moral and economic home life for children. In 1927, an effort was made to organize clubs for mothers by identifying their socializing role in the home with patriotism. To be truly patriotic, the mother had to reform herself or "your children will lack this moral formation which will make them useful and vigorous citizens."[48] The content of this reform involved instruction in child care and household organization and confined women's social and political involvement to the formation of choirs, drama clubs, savings associations, and cooperative sewing machine centers. This campaign may be seen as an attempt to secularize the values and interests of Mexican women and to win their loyalties to the state whose representatives saw women as the principal bearers of Church ideology in a period of intense Church-state conflict. It must also be noted, however, that these programs both offered an expansion of female activities beyond the home and also defined limits for such activities.

The process of subordinating the family to the state carries with it a potential for reinforcing a sense of inferiority and inadequacy in economically deprived sectors who are told by the state that they must change their lifestyles and values in order to meet society's standards. This tendency was apparent in Mexico in the extension of other social services by the state. A school health service, otherwise beneficial in disease prevention, intruded upon the home to improve hygienic

46. *BSEP* 4, no. 8 (1925): 24–25.
47. *BSEP* 6, no. 1 (1926): 6; see also *BSEP* 5, no. 5 (1926): 74–76.
48. *BSEP* 6, no. 4 (1927): 180–81.

conditions. In 1925, a Protective Council for Children requested *patria potestad* to secure the integral development of the child.[49] Seeking control over unattended children and the right to place them in day-care centers and special homes, it bid also for the right to intervene in labor contracts negotiated between families and employers to see that the minor had a school certificate, a state medical certificate, and a safe job. The council proposed to introduce to the home the social worker, who, equipped with a knowledge of hygiene, child-care, home economics, psychology, history, and civics, would provide "moral" direction to the family in order to

> ... channel people who need it in the direction of the good, alleviating hardships, helping them to save themselves from frequent hostile situations with others and their relatives by decorous and non-violent means.[50]

The home visitor was to promote an ideology stressing class harmony and self-sacrifice for the benefit of "society":

> To stimulate sentiments of dignity, love for others, and horror of vice, to persuade them of the need to be less concerned with their personal benefit and more with that of society. To develop in them the thought that the most humble work is indispensable to life because it is a factor of progress, a cornerstone in the enormous social fabric, and those who exercise it are as valuable to society as those who dedicate themselves to activities considered higher.[51]

Further, the social worker was to transmit direct information tending to support a specific social order through instruction in history and civics and to focus on the family as the central social unit (the social worker was to teach forms of recreation that could be enjoyed within the home rather than outside it). In short, the extension of social services by the state, although beneficial in many ways, was not a neutral undertaking but an ideologically loaded one which mirrored an existing class structure while at the same time specifying an important but circumscribed role for the family in the reproduction of the social order.

As in other areas of education, the dissemination of a model of family life did not guarantee its effective absorption by masses of people. Such absorption depended on various conditions, i.e., on the

---

49. *BSEP* 4, no. 8 (1925): 140.
50. *BSEP* 4, nos. 9 and 10 (1925): 212.
51. Ibid.

financial capacity of the state to expand its bureaucracies in such a way as to effectively teach the ideology; on the material conditions of masses of people, which determined their ability to implement the model and to see its logic within their own lives; and on the strength of other ideological currents to which people were exposed. For instance, the persistent subordination of women in Mexican society was no doubt influenced by, among other factors, the power of the Church and the absence of a strong feminist movement in the Revolution in general and in the trade union movement in particular.

Between 1900 and 1930, women's participation in Mexican industry declined in absolute numbers by one half—from 211,000 to 104,641. In 1900, women represented 26 percent of the industrial labor force and in 1930, 15.12 percent. Between 1921 and 1930, women employed in domestic service increased from 4,703,973 to 5,336,519, although the proportion of women engaged in domestic service remained about the same: 64 percent of all Mexican women in 1921 and 63 percent in 1930. Perhaps more significantly, the proportion of all Mexican women who were unproductive or whose occupation was unknown rose from 31 to 34 percent in the same period—from 2,297,639 to 2,857,624.[52]

Women's declining participation in industry resulted from a variety of factors. In industry, a simultaneous movement of economic contraction and the trend toward more capital-intensive production limited women's participation, especially given their role as a source of cheap, unskilled labor utilized by marginal firms. The decline had political causes as well. The CROM showed minimal interest in women workers: educational director Vicente Lombardo Toledano believed women should be educated for the home.[53] Insofar as the Revolution fostered a militant women's movement within the trade unions, these women belonged to radical groups like the PSY, the CGT, and the Communist party, which were marginalized in part by state policies. Further, the state itself influenced the trend in women's employment. It is possible that protective labor legislation in the Constitution of 1917 made it more expensive to hire women workers. It is also clear that education at the vocational level limited skilled job training for industry to men and sought to remove women from the factory. There is no doubt that factory labor was exploitative, dangerous, and oppressive for women, as it was for men. For women re-

---

52. *Estadísticas económicas del Porfiriato: fuerza de trabajo y actividad económica por sectores,* pp. 38–40, 45–48, 51, 60; *Anuario estadístico,* 1930, p. 50.
53. Krauze, *Los caudillos culturales,* pp. 27–29.

moved from industrial production, few viable alternatives were put forward. As in other sectors of education in the period, the attempt to encourage petty production was a chimera without massive or effective state support to buoy and protect it. Unprotected by labor unions or labor legislation, petty production, whether in the home or small shop, was extraordinarily exploitative of women's labor. Likewise, female domestic service, without state or union protection, was no alternative to the problems of inadequate remuneration or sexual harassment associated with the factory. In seeking to return women to the home, educators gave inadequate consideration to questions such as low wages for working men or the plight of single mothers. In the final analysis, most working-class women had to work. The Mexican Revolution did not help them to do so in a healthy and rewarding way.

Conclusion

Of incipient but growing interest to educators in the late *Porfiriato*, vocational training became a priority for educators in the Mexican Revolution because of its assumed importance to modernization, industrialization, and national autonomy, i.e., the replacement of foreign skilled workers by nationals. This goal coexisted with a desire among educators to encourage petty production and traditional crafts—a position which reflected the class composition of the Mexican Revolution and the development of Mexico's productive forces. In the Calles period, education for petty production was somewhat eclipsed by training for modern industry. However, the latter area was circumscribed and shaped by the limits of the state and economy within the political-economic trajectory of the Mexican Revolution. Several schools designed to promote economic autonomy could not be built for lack of funds, while those which were developed increased their reliance upon imported foreign technology and practice-training programs in metropolitan countries. The latter corresponded to the government's rapprochement with foreign capital and its increasing penetration into Mexican industry. While independent workers' organizations voiced some objections to vocational education policy, the government-favored and -controlled confederation, CROM, did not. It favored the replacement of foreign by Mexican workers and the idea of class collaboration for purposes of industrialization.

Vocational education contributed to a sexual division of labor in the Mexican economy. It aimed at removing women from factory production and (with the exception of training for office work) returning them to the home and to other forms of petty production (the small shop). This policy corresponded to bourgeois notions of sexual propriety and proper family organization. Reorganization of the working-class family, based upon women's domestic role as the primary producer of labor power on a daily and generational basis, was likewise thought to be a means of politically neutralizing the working class while increasing its productivity. As in so many other areas of Mexican education in the period, the advocacy of petty production in the home was not buttressed by government support adequate to buoy up a declining mode of production. The Mexican Revolution provided few viable employment opportunities to the majority of Mexican working-class women, most of whom had to work in order to survive. While militant, working-class feminist positions were put forward by some radical organizations in the period, they were not strong enough to counteract the official tendencies, which were in fact supported implicitly and explicitly by the CROM.

Chapter 7
Textbooks in Public Schools in the 1920s

When a society experiences a revolution, it can be anticipated that official history will be rewritten to distinguish the past
from the present and future and to reinterpret the events of the past
to conform with new goals and values.[1] On the contrary, Vasconcelos'
editorial department concentrated on editing the European classics
and commentaries on ancient Greece. The single history text published was that of Justo Sierra, whose *Historia patria* had been written
for Porfirian schools. By and large, the prescriptions followed for
writing texts in the years following the Revolution were those laid
down by pre-revolutionary educators. Three of the text writers, Daniel Delgadillo, Gregorio Torres Quintero, and José María Bonilla, had
been important members of the Porfirian school bureaucracy. The
textbooks of the 1920s suggested that the Mexican Revolution
brought about a change in leadership rather than a reorganization of
society with new values and goals. For the writers, the Revolution was
a political struggle for the restoration of democratic liberties such as
freedom of the press and elections. Insofar as they acknowledged the
need for social reform, they interpreted the Constitution of 1917 as
introducing a paternalistic government which would protect the
"weak" from the "strong," while preserving the principles of private
property and open competition. In their concern for order and progress, they tended to undermine the notion of democracy itself by favoring—in a variety of ways—benevolent authoritarianism. They
articulated nineteenth-century anthropological concepts contemptuous of the indigenous component of Mexican society, and, although
the Mexican Revolution had strong anti-imperialist strains, the text
writers of the 1920s were uncritical of foreign participation in Mexico
and explicitly adulatory of the Anglo-Saxon.

Why were the texts not changed? Why were they allowed to articulate values at odds with the nationalism, populism, and pro-indigenous sentiments supposedly emanating from the Mexican Revolution?

---

1. Portions of this chapter were originally published as "History Textbooks in
Mexico in the 1920s," Special Studies Paper No. 53, Council on International Studies,
State University of New York at Buffalo, 1974, and are reprinted by permission of the
Council on International Studies.

Although the reasons are difficult to assess, a variety of factors should be considered. It was not that educators did not understand the importance of texts in the formation of values and attitudes. In the Palavicini period, the education office, for example, had specifically asked for a rewriting of texts to promote patriotism and the work ethic. It was not a question of lack of funds because the editorial department under Vasconcelos published thousands of books. The cause would appear to lie more in the ideology of top educators. For instance, José Vasconcelos was more interested in civilizing his country than he was in publicizing its own history, of which he was in many ways ashamed. Deeply captive to a dependent mentality, Vasconcelos believed Mexico would be educated not by self-analysis but by a dissemination of European and Spanish literature. Further, it is probable that many top officials in the SEP shared values put forward in the older texts and that their own attitudes toward the Mexican Revolution were tentative and confused at best and negative at worst. The overlap between the pre- and post-revolutionary school bureaucracies must not be overlooked. Not only had many top bureaucrats played an important role in the *Porfiriato*, most inspectors and teachers in the capital had been trained in the *Porfiriato*. Many apparently articulated a conservative position on school texts. Thus, in 1925 a new publishing company wrote to President Calles to complain that although the SEP had asked for texts which were not more than five years old, not exclusively reading-oriented, not discouraging spontaneity, without reference to religion, and not lacking in national orientation, the texts chosen had precisely these defects. The SEP responded that the texts were chosen in consultation with inspectors who in turn had consulted teachers. The teachers apparently preferred the texts with which they were most familiar. It is important to note that they probably had little choice, because the SEP did not consider it a priority to direct, guide, and sponsor a rewriting of texts.[2]

The history texts here analyzed would represent the formal historical knowledge of a child who attended primary school in Mexico City in the 1920s. Children in grades three and four read Gregorio Torres Quintero's *La patria mexicana* throughout the 1920s. They also read José María Bonilla's *Evolución del pueblo mexicano*.[3] Longinos Ca-

2. Francisco Román to SEP, 14 Feb. 1925; Puig Casauranc to Francisco Román, 25 Feb. 1925; Roman to Casauranc 25 Feb. 1925; Roman to Calles, 26 Feb. 1925, AGN, Acervos Presidentes, Expediente 121-E-C-55.

3. I was unable to locate the second volume of José María Bonilla's *Evolución del pueblo mexicano*, 2nd ed. (Mexico: Herrero Hermanos, 1923), dealing with the modern

dena's *Elementos de historia general y de historia patria* was required reading in grades five and six throughout the decade. Rafael Aguirre Cinta's *Historia general de México* was used in both primary and vocational schools, especially after 1924. Included in this analysis is also Daniel Delgadillo's *Adelante*, a reader required through 1923 when the introduction of the action school made the use of primary readers optional. The use of history texts continued with the action school and Delgadillo's reader was required again in 1928 and after.[4] Justo Sierra's history text is also examined here as the single history text published by the Secretaría de Educación Pública. Further, it offers an interesting comparison with texts written during the Revolution, for while in ideology and values it is similar to later texts, in some respects it is more open ended.

Text writers in general embraced an ideology which was both liberal and positivist. Positivism is here broadly understood as the materialist philosophy which dominated Mexican intellectual circles in the late nineteenth century. Imported from Europe, it had strong overtones of white racial and European superiority. Mexican text writers saw history as a progressive march from the "warlike" life of the "savage" tribes through theocracy and monarchy to the ultimate state of political-economic development: the modern liberal state based upon principles of private property and competition. Within this interpretation of history, writers tended to suggest that economic modernization was a more important indicator of progress than political democracy. Perhaps this tendency stands out because of the frequent failures of European, Latin American, and Mexican societies, as recorded in the texts, to achieve political democracy. But, beyond this, the historians seemed to have particular preferences for order and progress. Those who brought order and progress to Mexico tended to be authoritarian rulers and an entrepreneurial and scientific elite, including foreigners. The text writers developed their notion of progress within a specific cultural matrix which legitimized social stratification and included characteristics of the dominant class as it emerged in the nineteenth century: adherence to the Christian religion, embellishment in home, dress, and the fine arts, and the sanctity of the nuclear family inclusive of an ethic of moral, sexual,

---

period. His interpretation of the Revolution is analyzed here through his *Derechos civiles* and *Derechos individuales*, which were required reading from 1920 to 1923 and optional thereafter.

4. See *BSEP* 1, no. 1 (1922): 180–81; 2, nos. 5 and 6 (1923–1924): 649; 8, no. 2 (1929): 72–73; *El libro y el pueblo* 2, nos. 1–5 (1923): 86–87; 2, nos. 6–7 (1923): 115.

and economic abstinence. Justo Sierra and José María Bonilla added a specifically Spanish definition of civilization when they defined it as city life or *civitas*. This definition implied that urban culture was civilization: the countryside—and thus the indigenous of Mexico—was barbaric.[5] Urban culture as civilization did not simply mean living in the city: the height of urban culture had been reached by a Europeanized elite in refinement and embellishment. Such a model reinforced class stratification in Mexican society as well as subordination to the foreign model.

The history books represented the formal historical understanding of a child in Mexico City primary school. If the student's family had recently migrated from countryside to city, he or she was at least in part indigenous in background. Generally speaking, the Mexican definition of Indian is cultural. Immigrants to the city who adopt urban ways and customs are usually thought of as *mestizo*, although the process of change is often graded and prolonged. This manner of defining race is important in understanding the attitude toward race in the texts. For all the historians, Mexico was a *mestizo* country. In the light of the texts, *mestizo* implied adopting the goals and criteria of "civilization" and behavior which the school established. To be *mestizo* was to *become*, to adapt, to acculturate. It was a notion grounded in insecurity and contempt for one's roots and for those left behind. This approach was reinforced by the historians' establishment of criteria of behavior which they suggested the Mexican had not yet achieved: civilization had not yet come to Mexico. It would, if all worked hard and obediently.

The nature of race prejudice in the texts was subtle but clear in the treatment of the Indian past. The child would have learned that the pre-Columbian peoples had attained "some degree of civilization," but not a degree comparable with that of the European conqueror.[6] Absorption into the conqueror's civilization was the inexorable out-

5. Gregorio Torres Quintero somewhat mitigated this assertion in his *Patria mexicana*, 4th ed. (Mexico: Herrero Hermanos, 1923). He portrayed Juárez and Morelos as lovers of the clean naturalness of the countryside and the wholesomeness of farm labor. This emphasis reflected at least in part a prescription in the Porfirian educational program that children be taught to love nature. It further reflected both the emphasis on work more apparent in postrevolutionary texts and Torres Quintero's concern, which he shared with other educators, that peasants cease migrating to the cities.

6. Justo Sierra, *Historia patria* (Mexico: SEP, 1922), pp. 26, 27, 31, 33; Longinos Cadena, *Elementos de historia general y de historia patria*, 3rd ed., 2 vols. (Mexico: Herrero Hermanos, 1921), 1: 131, 133, 139; Bonilla, *Evolución*, pp. 26, 37, 38, 44, 49; Rafael Aguirre Cinta, *Historia de México*, 16th ed. (Mexico: Sociedad de Edición y Librería Franco-Americana, SA, 1926), pp. 36–49, 57.

come of progress. The process of imposing a quasi-positivist dogma on the Indian past involved much distortion. Thus as savages live in a constant state of war according to some positivist thinkers, the incidence of war and conquest became the dominant theme in the historians' portrayal of the indigenous past. Cadena defined it as "perpetual antagonism dominated by inextinguishable hatred." Bonilla quoted the French intellectual Lavisse: a barbarous people lived in constant battle dominated by the law of the strongest and ignorant of the principle of justice. The historians were preoccupied with the "bloody" and "cruel" religion of human sacrifice, the logic of which they did not explain. For each, Quetzalcóatl was a white god who preached against human sacrifice.[7]

The historians were mainly concerned with political history. They interpreted Aztec society as one under "absolute monarchy." First, this approach revealed a misunderstanding of Aztec sociopolitical organization which was based in family and clan. The Aztec rulers had limited authority and were never "emperors" as the historians made them; only very late did they begin to act as powerful decision-makers in their city-states. Not only did the historians create an impression of "backward" political development in war-prone absolute monarchy, they tended to portray the people as "almost slaves", in the words of Sierra.[8] For Cadena, the Indians lived in constant fear subject to the tyranny of priests and kings. Bonilla suggested that the pre-Conquest period was one of "decadence" and "corruption" in which tyrant kings and superstitious priests oppressed the "people" who welcomed the Conquest as "salvation."[9] Strikingly similar to the extreme right-wing argument put forward by the Spanish jurist Sepulveda to justify the Conquest in the sixteenth century, this interpretation of Indian society as tyrannical reveals the extent to which nineteenth-century European racist thought reinforced long-standing elite contempt for indigenous culture in Mexico.

A second implication of the writers' imposition of absolute monarchy on the Aztec past was to condone it. With the pre-Columbian ruler who brought "progress" to society began a pattern of valuing benevolent authoritarianism. "Progressive" monarchs like Netza-

---

7. Cadena, *Elementos*, 1: 139; Bonilla, *Evolución*, p. 55. On human sacrifice, see, for example, Sierra, *Historia*, pp. 21, 25, 27; Cadena, *Elementos*, 1: 92, 130–43; Aguirre Cinta, *Historia*, pp. 64, 57, 48; Bonilla, *Evolución*, pp. 22, 27, 58; Gregorio Torres Quintero, *Patria*, pp. 44–45, 53, 74–76. On Quetzalcóatl, see, for example, Sierra, *Historia*, p. 21; Aguirre Cinta, *Historia*, pp. 19–20; Bonilla, *Evolución*, p. 33.

8. Sierra, *Historia*, p. 30.

9. Bonilla, *Evolución*, pp. 137, 32; Cadena, *Elementos*, 1: 130, 192.

hualcóyotl built palaces, temples, gardens, museums, and public works. They sponsored the arts, sciences, and education and encouraged industry and agriculture. They were "civilizers" organizing semi-savage tribes into ordered, embellished, stratified societies.[10] Moctezuma II, on the other hand, became the prototype of the anti-hero, the tyrant who oppressed and finally deserted his people out of cowardice and superstition, i.e., he failed in his responsibilities to guide society on the road of progress.[11]

For each historian, private property and social stratification were signs of progress. Possession of these factors made the Aztecs semi-civilized for Bonilla. Imposing their Europeanized standards, most historians found indigenous art "gross" and the indigenous people physically unattractive. "It was not rare," wrote Bonilla and Aguirre Cinta, "to find some types of beauty" among the Toltecs, because they were reportedly "tall" and "robust."[12] What further distinguished civilization from barbarism was increased embellishment in house architecture, furniture, clothing, and diet—the more elaborate, the more civilized. But the overriding concern was progress in science, technology, and the development of agriculture, industry, and commerce. Insofar as the American peoples advanced from hunters and fishermen to sedentary farmers, manufacturers of textiles, metal workers, monumental builders, traders and rudimentary scientists, they were praised.[13] Valued for their occupational skills, their talent in industry, and their industriousness, the common people in history were confined to the role of worker, subject, and soldier—a pattern which did not change in the course of the texts' interpretation of Mexican history.

Despite the acknowledged avarice and violence of the Conquest, European civilization was the progressive path for Mexico to follow. Only Cadena, out of attachment to a mythical unity of the "human family," was prepared to acknowledge Indian contributions to Europe

10. Sierra, *Historia*, pp. 16, 23–25, 30–32; Aguirre Cinta, *Historia*, pp. 16, 24–31, 37–58; Bonilla, *Evolución*, pp. 35–36, 38, 50–52; Cadena, *Elementos*, 1: 136–42.

11. Sierra, *Historia*, p. 30; Cadena, *Elementos*, 1: 143; Gregorio Torres Quintero, *Patria*, pp. 41–42; Aguirre Cinta, *Historia*, pp. 51–52; Bonilla, *Evolución*, p. 55.

12. Bonilla, *Evolución*, pp. 55, 30; Aguirre Cinta, *Historia*, p. 16. Sierra called Toltec art "horrible" (*Historia*, p. 21). Cadena claimed all indigenous art lacked taste (*Elementos*, 1: 130, 192); it was backward, the painting was imperfect, the music was monotonous, the poetry incipient (*Elementos*, 1: 63).

13. Sierra, *Historia*, pp. 20, 22, 25, 30, 32; Aguirre Cinta, *Historia*, pp. 55, 57, 64, 379–80; Cadena, *Elementos*, 1: 137–38, 140, 143; Bonilla, *Evolución*, pp. 24–26, 31, 33, 58.

in the form of crops, minerals, and commerce. While each of the historians was bound to condemn Spain as an authoritarian monarchy, they, like the sixteenth-century jurist Sepúlveda, also saw Spain as transferring broader European civilization to America in the form of technology, religion, language, customs, writing, and the arts and sciences. "In sum," wrote Cadena, "all which is called civilization."[14] If the Conquest was historically inevitable, the historians felt obliged to justify it on moral grounds. Quoting an unnamed European, Cadena printed a blatant outpouring of uninformed nineteenth-century racist thought:

> There was no idyllic life which civilization destroyed, but existence dominated by the right of the strongest, slavery, tyranny, war, avarice, infanticide, gross superstition: the Discoveries were a sacred duty, since they tended to fill the most imperious needs of life, to extend the dominion of man to the most uncultured regions, to form regular families and friends in countries which until then had known no more than disorder and hostility. They drew men and nations together with the end of dominating nature and exploiting it united.[15]

Noting that the advantages of European civilization were too numerous to list, Bonilla added to the above-mentioned gifts "the promise of progress for all" and the instillation of "vigor, wisdom, and manliness . . . in the Indian."[16] For him, the conquerors were civilizers, the basis of Mexican civilization Iberic, and the Conquest the beginning of Mexican history:

> The History of Mexico begins with the arrival of Cortes . . . because with the Conquest came the benefits of European civilization which we enjoy today.[17]

Children reading the history of the colonial period would emerge with a picture of indigenous culture as backward and bathed in misery and oppression. Bonilla wrote that Aztec culture perished with Cuauhtémoc. Gregorio Torres Quintero, whose history began with the Conquest, wrote that the arrival of the Spaniards wiped out the Indian nobility leaving only the most "backward and ignorant."[18] Sierra pictured the oppressed Indians as

14. Cadena, *Elementos*, 1: 113, see also Bonilla, *Evolución*, p. 67.
15. Cadena, *Elementos*, 1: 118.
16. Bonilla, *Evolucion*, p. 122.
17. Ibid., pp. 117–18; see also Gregorio Torres Quintero, *Patria*, pp. 68, 73, 75–77.
18. Gregorio Torres Quintero, *Patria*, pp. 76, 175–76; Aguirre Cinta, *Historia*, pp. 260–62, 266, 268.

. . . resigned with their religious fiestas in which they spent more than the little they earned and with their pre-Conquest idolatries and superstitions.[19]

Bonilla held fanaticism responsible for fiestas and bullfights, which led to a squandering of savings and a cult of laziness. The Indians, he wrote, degenerated into "beasts of burden" incapable of protesting and without stamina for struggle. Living in "another world," they vegetated in a state of "total ignorance and abandonment." He believed they were bound to disappear because they were inept for the "struggle for life."[20] Cadena believed they could survive if an outside force saved them. They were

. . . waiting for the coming of a Messiah who would take them out of slavery and bring them liberty, culture, and progress, to allow them to sit with other races in the banquet of civilization.[21]

This particular view of the Black Legend of despotic Spain exploiting the Indian was elitist. While it condemned Spanish cruelty, it gave the Indian no dignity. It made him an object rather than an actor responding rationally to a negative situation in which one sought to survive as best one could. There was an exception. Although Bonilla believed the indigenous had no stamina for resistance, he alone treated an Indian rebellion—that led by Canek in Yucatán in 1761. Anticipating a general pattern, he concentrated on the leader of the revolt rather than the people participating in it. He quoted from *México a través de los siglos* which pointed out that Canek was educated. One imagines that Bonilla chose this incidence of revolt to justify his particular view of oppressive Spain.

The heroes of the colonial era were the missionaries, who protected, educated, and "civilized" the Indians, and the "good viceroys," who not only protected the Indians but brought "progress" to the colony in the form of agriculture, industry, commerce, public works, education, architectural embellishment, and the fine arts and sciences. Charity, paternalism, and progressive economic policies were the virtues and accomplishments of these authoritarian figures.

According to the historians, Mexican independence was the effort of *mestizos* and creoles with the directing role usually falling to the creoles. For Cadena, the latter represented the vigor and force of the nation, the property owners and the accomplished in letters and sci-

19. Sierra, *Historia*, p. 63.
20. Bonilla, *Evolución*, pp. 115–16, 152–53, 165.
21. Cadena, *Elementos*, 1: 162.

ences represented "The conscious strength and future leaders in whose heart and brain germinated the ideas of equality and fraternity.[22]" For Sierra, the large landowners, lawyers, intellectuals, and priests directed the independence movement.[23] The heroes were military men of professional background, not the common people. The story of independence was told through these heroes—Hidalgo, Allende, Morelos. The one exception was Pipila, an anonymous member of the crowd who set fire to the granary in Guanajuato. In the treatment of the wars of independence the student of nonelite background would see the common people's role in history as that of an unruly, excessive rabble, more a hindrance than a help to the cause, both in the behavior of Hidalgo's "hordes" and in the crowning of Iturbide, attributed by the historians who disliked him to the bad judgement of the *populacho*.[24] Disapproval of social "fury" was clear in the exaggerated and distasteful terms with which the historians described group action. Aguirre Cinta presented Hidalgo's "following" as

> . . . drunk with vengeance and pillaging in the storming of the Alhóndiga, they assassinated and robbed without compassion. . . . The rebels committed unimaginable cruelties, which Hidalgo punished with severity. . . . Ignorant of the art of war and undisciplined, they could not face a trained army.[25]

Only Sierra was willing to allow that social "fury" had justification in centuries of exploitation.

In their treatment of the nineteenth century, the historians avoided the issue of rich and poor and the distribution of wealth. They did not allude to the social platforms of heroes of independence such as Morelos, whose ideas on land reform were avoided. Only Sierra called the wars of the Reform a struggle against the privileged classes. Almost totally, nineteenth-century history was political history manipulated by an educated elite bent on achieving order and progress. The only positive role the common people played was that of soldier defending the country against foreign invasion. Aguirre Cinta recorded a single instance of social revolt without explaining its causes. He described the Indian invasion of Guadalajara in 1873 led by Manuel Lozada:

22. Ibid., p. 179.
23. Sierra, *Historia*, pp. 69, 84.
24. Ibid., p. 85; Aguirre Cinta, *Historia*, p. 181; Gregorio Torres Quintero, *Patria*, pp. 123–24.
25. Aguirre Cinta, *Historia*, pp. 143–44, 148, 175.

. . . infatuated with his power and influence over the indigenous races, [he led an invasion] of immense hoards of Indians avid for blood and rapine.[26]

The writers universally praised Porfirio Díaz for bringing order, progress, and material well-being to Mexico. Díaz approximated the historians' assessments of both "good" and "bad" rulers. Table 7.1 presents areas of achievement which historians most valued in political leaders and the number of times they were referred to by each author. The categories of accomplishment were deduced through a content analysis in which adjectives used to describe leaders or phrases referring to their achievements were counted for each historian and also combined for the texts as a whole.[27] As the table indicates, the categories of order, national security and aggrandizement, and progress (74, 74, and 108 entries, respectively) were most important for the historians. Sierra's concern for order (5) and national security (8) over material progress (1) reflected his preoccupation with pre-Díaz political anarchy, while his relatively high rating under charity (7), public works (5), education (6), and embellishment (2) referred to the colonial viceroys. Cadena especially emphasized material progress (55), national security and aggrandizement (38), and order (24) in analyzing the progressive march of western civilization. Rafael Aguirre Cinta's preference for order (34) and progress (37) reflected his post-revolutionary admiration for strong-man rule which would guarantee both containment of the lower classes and economic progress. As Bonilla treated only the colonial period, his entries under order (2) and material progress (6) are relatively few, while those referring to charity (12) are relatively more numerous and reflect treatment of the viceroys and missionaries. Gregorio Torres Quintero's order (10) and progress (10) derived both from his treatment of the viceroys and of Porfirio Díaz.

In contrast to the "good ruler," the "bad" ruler was a dictator or

---

26. Ibid., pp. 243–44.

27. To illustrate the method: the Viceroy don Antonio Mendoza was a leader treated favorably by the authors. "Se dedicó al mejoramiento de la colonia," was one of his accomplishments. As this kind of achievement appeared with regularity, it emerged as the category "material progress." To give another example, don Juan Vicente Guemos Pacheco Padilla, segundo conde de Revillagigedo, was described as follows: "Su gobierno fué sin duda el más digno y el más lleño de importancia para México . . . imprimió a la colonia una marcha regular de progreso. Embelleció la ciudad, mandó limpiar las calles y establecer el alumbrado, y, por último, ordenó la formación de un censo." This description merited points for material progress, embellishment of the cities, and public works.

TABLE 7.1
Textbook Content Analysis of Positive Achievements of Political Leaders

Category of Achievement	Aguirre Cinta	Torres Quintero	Sierra	Bonilla	Cadena	Total
Establishment of order and organization	34	10	5	2	24	74
National security and aggrandizement	16	8	8	3	38	73
Material progress	37	10	1	6	55	106
Charity, protection of the poor	24	2	7	12	5	52
Public works	6	5	5		4	19
Education and fine arts	12	1	6	2	17	38
Moralization	18	1	4	2	4	29
Embellishment of cities	24		8		10	42

TABLE 7.2
Textbook Content Analysis of Negative Characteristics of Political Leaders

Category of Negative Characteristics	Aguirre Cinta	Torres Quintero	Sierra	Bonilla	Cadena	Total
Dictatorship, Tyranny	28	12	11		39	90
Abuse of law	4				2	6
Abuse of justice					4	4
Oppression	2				2	4
Terror					3	3
Cruelty	7	4	2	2	18	33
Disregard of public opinion					4	4
Abuse of national security, wealth	23	4	2	8	42	79
Incompetence	11	7	7	12	20	57
Ambition	12		1		19	32

tyrant who failed to fulfill his obligations to the community or to society. Following a similar method to that used in Table 7.1, Table 7.2 indicates negative categories of political behavior and the number of times each writer referred to them. Although tyranny and dictatorship yielded the highest category of negative political behavior (90 entries for the writers combined), what constituted dictatorship and/or tyranny was not well defined. More important than abuse of the laws (6 entries) and the misadministration of justice (4) were political incompetence (57) and self-seeking ambition (32), which resulted often in loss of national security and wealth. The categories would suggest a definition of tyranny drawn from traditional Spanish political theory. The authoritarian leader who failed to honor the needs of the community for survival and growth became a tyrant. Cruelty (32 entries) as an attribute of tyranny is closer to a traditional set of political values than it is to nineteenth-century liberalism. The sense of this argument becomes clearer when one takes into account the historians' off-handed treatment of the electoral process in Mexico. Most Mexican political leaders were not "elected." The historians either ignored the process through which they rose to power or legitimized manipulation of the voting mechanism by power-holders. Thus, some claimed that Díaz was six times elected, when each election in fact represented a heavy-handed manipulation.

Díaz conformed to the image of a "good" ruler, especially in the areas of order (13) and progress (33), as indicated in Table 7.3, which tabulates the writers' references to Díaz' achievements. Gregorio Torres Quintero overlooked the progress of land confiscation from the peasantry and working conditions in factories and mines when he wrote that under Díaz "all social classes felt the pleasure of well-being long dreamed of."[28] However, as Table 7.4 indicates, for each historian, Díaz degenerated into a dictator. Aguirre Cinta regarded this as a "necessary evil."[29] Gregorio Torres Quintero excused it on the grounds that Díaz "was the necessary, the only man who could keep peace in this nation so broken by revolution."[30] Cadena was singular among the writers in criticizing Díaz for oppressing the poor. He identified Díaz with *caciquismo* or bossism and terror, corrupt administration of justice, and unjust distribution of wealth. However, Cadena stated that Díaz was "loved" by the people who "hated" his underlings—thus returning to the old colonial phase, "Long live the

---

28. Gregorio Torres Quintero, *Patria*, p. 174.
29. Aguirre Cinta, *Historia*, p. 259.
30. Gregorio Torres Quintero, *Patria*, p. 174.

TABLE 7·3

Textbook Content Analysis of Díaz' Positive Achievements

Category of Achievement	Aguirre Cinta	Torres Quintero	Cadena	Total
Order	4	5	4	13
National Security	4	5		9
Material Progress	12	10	11	33
Public Works	1	1	1	3
Education		1	1	2
Embellishment	4			4
Moralization		1	1	2

TABLE 7·4

Textbook Content Analysis of Díaz' Negative Characteristics

Category of Negative Characteristic	Aguirre Cinta	Torres Quintero	Cadena	Total
Autocrat	6	3	6	15
Abuse of law			2	2
Abuse of justice			1	1
Disregard of public opinion		1	4	5
Favoritism			3	3
Oppression				
Caciquismo			3	3
Terror			3	3
Unequal distribution of wealth			1	1

King! Down with bad government!" This phrase traditionally upheld the legitimacy of the authoritarian ruler while it protested the corruption of the king's underlings.

Each historian interpreted the causes of the Revolution from a classical liberal point of view. What concerned them was the loss of public democratic liberties and excessive monopolization of wealth, not the social grievances of peasants and workers. The Revolution aimed then at the restoration of the formal democracy.[31] Treating the Revo-

31. Cadena, *Elementos*, 2: 18, 183, 188, 247; Gregorio Torres Quintero, *Patria*, pp. 175–76; Aguirre Cinta, *Historia*, pp. 260–64, 266, 268.

lution briefly, Torres Quintero did acknowledge the existence of exploitation:

> Madero was thought to be the origin of prosperity for the *clases humildes*, who expected economic resurgence capable of alleviating them of their heavy labors in the factories and fields.[32]

But he deplored more deeply the spectacle of renewed disorder. The bloodiest of all revolts, the Mexican Revolution was for him indistinguishable from those which had gone before. "Never had the Mexican family been more divided," he noted.[33] Cadena shared the same misgivings. Díaz, he wrote, "left the country without compass or rudder," with the implication that the singular leader was the responsible agent in Mexican history.[34] Treating Madero and Huerta in a matter of sentences, he jumped to Venustiano Carranza, then president of the country, with no explanation of the social platform of the Revolution or the events which occurred between 1910 and 1918.

Of all the writers, Rafael Aguirre Cinta treated the Revolution in greatest detail. He related it through the exploits of triumphant general-presidents: Carranza, Obregón, and Calles. He glorified leadership rather than the social goals of the Revolution and clearly prized the establishment of order over democratic participation. He portrayed Villa and Zapata as representing no social cause: they were simple obstructors of order. He dismissed Carranza as a "dictator," in accordance with the official political line of the 1920s. His treatment of Obregón and Calles revealed the mission of the leader who would bring progress and instill order by disciplining labor and the peasantry. Obregón, he wrote

> . . . tried to conciliate . . . the interests of owners and workers, who agitated by preaching of false redemption for wage-earners, lost their time and wasted their energy in strikes and impetuous protests without realizing that they would only achieve benefits . . . by educating themselves, preparing for the struggle for life in school; to obtain just compensation for their work, they must support their efforts by increasing their aptitudes through education and by exact fulfillment of their obligations.[35]

Labor had to submit to the needs of capital and the dictates of the states:

32. Gregorio Torres Quintero, *Patria*, p. 178.
33. Ibid., p. 180.
34. Cadena, *Elementos*, 2: 162.
35. Aguirre Cinta, *Historia*, p. 365.

They [the workers] ought to be convinced that capital and labor must march together under the just and equitable rules of government, which anticipates differences and assigns rights and duties.[36]

Likewise, students would learn from this historian that the struggle for land was a false issue. The "so-called agrarian problem," he wrote, existed only in the minds of "some politicians." He praised Obregón for repressing the "so-called *agrarista* leaders, who have prejudiced and made retrograde our nascent agricultural industry with their seditious preachings."[37]

Aguirre Cinta upheld Calles as an "indefatigable worker on behalf of the well-being of the proletarian classes." Calles, he claimed, sought to raise the working classes through education to a "superior moral and material level," but this always through "respecting the rights of others."[38] It is in this treatment of Calles that one understands the additional responsibilities and qualities demanded of postrevolutionary leadership from the point of view of the only historian who treated the subject. Calles was competent, indefatigable, hardworking, efficient, and decisive. Above all, he sought to establish "order," give "work," and encourage the material progress of the country through pacification, government intervention in the economy, and the reestablishment of foreign credit. Further, he was "almost unanimously elected."[39] Such dissimulation about the voting mechanism in Mexico was typical of the historians and raises questions about the extent to which the writers encouraged effective democracy. In fact, Obregón imposed Calles as his successor in an election marred by fraud and forced voting. Text writers were under pressure to legitimize the powers that were if they wanted their texts accepted in the school system. In this case, they had to twist the meaning of democracy. Aguirre Cinta's interpretation of Calles was, for instance, very close to the image Calles himself tried to project.

Like the text of Aguirre Cinta, the civic books of José María Bonilla tended to place initiative and power in the hands of an over-arching, paternalistic state. In explaining the Constitution of 1917, he wrote to persuade Mexicans to fulfill their duties and to respect the law. He defined society as an aggregate of rich and poor, educated and ignorant, who had to live together under rules. Although an adherent of

36. Ibid., pp. 265–66.
37. Ibid., pp. 366, 374.
38. Ibid., p. 370.
39. Ibid., p. 371.

open competition and laissez-faire liberalism, he had to explain the elements of the Constitution which contradicted these. He did so by saying that modern progressive governments legislated in favor of the "strong's protection of the weak." Implicitly he denied independent strength to the "weak" and advocated paternalism.[40]

Equality—and hence inequality—were, he claimed, determined by work or the product of "accumulated wealth" and "merit." In discussing Article 27 on land reform, he stressed the right of property as the product of work and accumulated wealth. Only the state had the right to expropriate property on grounds of public utility and this through due compensation and due process. Although he deplored "the vicious system of territorial property" and envisaged the formation of a nation of small-holders, he specified that action on this issue fell within the sphere of the government only.[41]

In explaining Article 123 on workers' rights, he claimed that the Revolution promised the "emancipation of the proletariat." However, he qualified the article by emphasizing the rights of property and the necessity of capital accumulation. He defined independent workers' action as "excessive" and "criminal." The purpose of the Constitution was to protect workers "without killing the goose that lay the golden eggs, i.e. giving capital guarantees it needs to survive and prosper."[42] He warned against socialism which would have evil results "contrary to the principles of justice."[43] From his interpretation emerged the twin institutions of protected capital and paternalistic government:

> It is a high principle of justice to protect the proletariat against the avarice of the powerful; but we ought not to forget that extremes are always lamentable and that if for the despotism of money we substitute the unbridling of ignorance and low passions, we run the risk of tumbling into an abyss a thousand times worse than what we are trying to avoid.[44]

Thus Bonilla preached worker discipline. Liberty, he wrote, did not mean that one could give oneself to vice, idleness, and dissipation. Liberty involved the obligation to work. "You will eat by the sweat of your brow," he wrote. He preached the inviolability of the individual contract, long a target of labor hostility. Contracts, he wrote, were obligations which could not be broken even if they prejudiced the

---

40. Bonilla, *Derechos civiles*, pp. 10, 13, 98; *Derechos individuales*, p. 13.
41. Bonilla, *Derechos individuales*, p. 98; *Derechos civiles*, pp. 105–6.
42. Bonilla, *Derechos civiles*, p. 193.
43. Bonilla, *Derechos individuales*, p. 142.
44. Bonilla, *Derechos civiles*, p. 193.

workers' welfare. A promise made, he declared, was sacred. He spoke in favor of the right to work, another focus of labor animosity in the period. Strikes which "offended the public interest" were illegal. Although this notion was contained in the Constitution, he emphasized the aspect of restraint rather than the right to strike. He went so far as to criticize Mexican workers' protests against the predominance of foreign workers in particular industries on the grounds that Mexican workers were apathetic, non-punctual, and inexact in their work in comparison with their more productive Anglo-Saxon counterparts.

Bonilla's discussion of democratic liberties revealed some fear of working-class initiative, for while these liberties were limited by the Constitution, he seemed to stress the limitations rather than the rights. The right to free expression was circumscribed by the need for public order. If an individual, he wrote, incited the "masses" to act against the public order, he was a criminal. Such preachings, Bonilla claimed, "have frequently led the criteria of masses astray and have urged them to commit excesses."[45] Freedom of the press was limited by standards of "morality" and "public peace." He explicitly stated that the right of association ought not to be used to form groups bent on "violence, rebellion, or illegal and immoral action."[46]

Text writers then tried to dissuade children from eventually joining militant trade unions and from sympathizing with the *campesinos'* fight for land. In the annals of history, the student of non-elite background could find few examples of positive initiative taken by the class from which he or she came. On the contrary, the writers encouraged students to feel contempt for ignorant Indians, lazy workers, and agitated crowds, and sought to arouse fears at the spectacle of political "agitators" preaching "violence" and "socialism." The writers stressed that only through hard work, the school, and state action would the lot of the poor be improved. The idea that formal education alone promised material betterment was reinforced in the primary reader of Daniel Delgadillo, where the student absorbed such aphorisms as "work and constancy are the parents of abundance," and "work brings profit," and "the work of children is study."

As Delgadillo had been a member of Sierra's brain trust of pedagogues, it is not surprising that his values were those of the Porfirian primary school—obedience, order, respect for authority, and work. His model child was docile, tolerant, and content with what he had. *Envidia*—or envy—he defined as envying the possessions of others.

45. Bonilla, *Derechos individuales*, p. 147.
46. Ibid., p. 39.

"He who has charity and a pure soul," he wrote, "will not talk of the faults of others." Anger and pride he condemned. Heroism he defined as "sacrifice" in service of God, the nation, and one's neighbor.

Table 7.5 indicates the frequency of reference to categories of vices and virtues in *Adelante*. As in previous tables, adjectives, verbs, and nouns indicating approved or negative behavior or characteristics were counted to establish categories of virtues and vices and frequency of reference within them (a more detailed breakdown in Spanish is indicated in Appendix Table A.4).[47] From the content analysis, positive emphasis associated with study and work was strongest. On the other hand, the category of charity had more entries when virtues and vices were combined and it should be noted that those vices—egoism, pride, envy—were those least conducive to obedience and cooperation. The combined categories of charity, order and cleanliness, and truthfulness revealed the educators' concern with making Mexican children sociable—kind, tolerant, complacent, honest, rather than greedy, vengeful, egotistical, dirty, and deceitful. The overwhelming emphasis was upon the correction of these "vices" and reveals a great deal about the way in which Mexican educators regarded Mexican children and the civilizing mission of the school.

The predominant values of obedience to authority, conformity, and hard work were linked in the Delgadillo text to acceptance of class-stratified society. The book focused on the modest urban middle sector—children of low-level state personnel or employees of commercial houses whose wives played traditional domestic roles. Anecdotes about these children were interspersed, however, with stories of richer and poorer children.[48] Differences in social class were carefully pointed out. Children going to school in the morning saw workers, servants, and *"gente pobre"* in the street. It was possible, indeed ligitimizing, for the poor to be good, moral, and even heroic, but the social structure itself was immutable. For example, Emilio, the son of a humble fisherman on the Pacific coast, and Andrés, the son of the owner of the largest fishing boat in the town, were friends although "the social condition of each was very distinct." One day, Andrés became friendly with Pedro, the son of the administrator of the customs office who was more of his social class. Pedro mocked Emilio's clothes

47. To further explain the method: the sentence, "Eugenia, mi compañera de asiento, leía como ninguna," indicates positive approval of study. "Trabaja y vencerás" indicates positive approval of work. "Felipa era una niña muy aplicada, muy obediente, con sus padres y sus maestros," also indicates the importance of work and obedience.

48. See *Adelante*, pp. 22, 39.

TABLE 7.5
Virtues and Vices in Adelante

Virtues		Vices		Total
Work and study	43	Ignorance and laziness	6	49
Order and cleanliness	7	Disorder and dirtiness	5	12
Obedience and respect	23	Disobedience and ingratitude	12	35
Charity	27	Egoism, avarice, anger, cruelty	30	57
Patriotism	5	Bad Mexican	1	6
Truthfulness	3	Falsity	8	11
Other	11		7	18

and told Andrés that the poor boy was interested in his friendship only to use his toys. "He will betray you," Pedro told Andrés. "This class of people have no good sentiments." One day, Pedro and Andrés fought, Andrés fell into the sea, and the poor boy came to his rescue.[49]

Those children who had more material wealth were expected to practice charity on an individual basis while those who had less were to feel no envy. Depicting the modest home of a bureaucrat, his wife and two daughters, Delgadillo delcared: "Surely happiness is not always a question of wealth." It was possible to better one's lot on an individual basis through hard work. Juanito, the son of a poor family, had no new clothes or toys like the other children in school. Shunned, mocked, and blamed for wrongdoing, he was nonetheless industrious and intelligent. He went on to preparatory school, became a lawyer, and eventually a successful judge. When two old schoolmates who had once picked on him were brought before him on charges of robbery, he excused them because they were "companions." Thus, he bore no rancor and exemplified the image of a generous, rich man. Individualism was the only route to betterment in the text. Delgadillo's single reference to workers' associations was negative. He wrote, "as in all guilds, there are envious and disobedient individuals who abuse their more fortunate companions who better apply themselves in their work."[50]

Although Delgadillo's second edition appeared in 1920, it made only one reference to the Mexican Revolution: a town lived in terror of invading revolutionary troops who stood for nothing but violence. A young boy distinguished himself by snuffing out a bomb planted

49. Ibid., pp. 236–40.
50. Ibid., pp. 22–25, 127.

in front of his widowed mother's home by revolutionaries forcibly exacting food.[51] Although scenes such as these had occurred, the Revolution apparently had no larger purpose for Delgadillo. His presentation of the countryside was entirely prerevolutionary and mythologized. For children of *hacienda* administrators and *hacienda* workers, life was peaceful and idyllic. The shepherds and *peones* went off to the fields, the women gracefully carried water jars on their heads, and the countryside basked in the "grandeur of God." There was no misery, no struggle. The *hacienda* was a legitimate institution. Delgadillo recounted a fable of a rat who went to the city in search of food, but, chased by a cat, he returned to the countryside saying, "I prefer to live in my poor but tranquil little house here and not in the houses of the rats of the cities which may be rich but are full of dangers." However, although his presentation of the countryside was idyllic and peaceful, the city in Delgadillo's text remained the source of civilization, education, and culture. The children of *hacienda* administrators went there to continue their studies. That the children of field hands could not do so was implicit but unquestioned.[52]

Mexican texts in history, reading, and civics were written in large part to instill patriotism. Heroes in the history books were highly praised for patriotism and bravery associated with national defense. And yet the form of patriotism put forward in the texts was distorted and skewed by a pervasive elitism on the one hand and subservience to metropolitan European civilization on the other. Text heroes belonged to a power elite above the reach and culture of masses of people: they were political rulers, military chiefs, intellectuals, religious officials, lawyers, and scientists. With rare exception, they were men. Only six of 284 heroes were mentioned as having come from humble origins and of these, only two led revolts against social injustice. In interesting contrast to Sierra's text, later writers tended to stress the humble origins of men like Morelos and Juárez in conjunction with values of hard work and study, apparently to reinforce the notion of individual social mobility.[53] Also, while the texts emphasized science and technology as catalysts of progress, heroes in this field were overwhelmingly European with important implications for Mexican nationalism as it was broadly relayed in the texts. Despite the anti-imperialsim of the Revolution, the texts were uncritical of

51. Ibid., p. 214.
52. Ibid., pp. 43–44, 28, 105.
53. Gregorio Torres Quintero, *Patria*, pp. 87, 109; Aguirra Cinta, *Historia*, pp. 151, 241.

the unequal relationship between Mexico and the metropolitan world, and in fact suggested the necessity of Mexico's imitating the "civilized" countries. The notion of "becoming" functioned not only at the level of an internal Mexican social hierarchy but at the level of an international hierarchy.

Cadena's text on universal history created such a hierarchy of "civilization" consistent with program outlines for history instruction in Porfirian schools. France represented "culture" and symbolic attainment of formal democratic liberties in the Revolution of 1789. England and its offshoot, the United States, represented the pinnacle of democratic liberties and material progress wrought by the inherent "industriousness" of the Anglo-Saxon and the existence of "free institutions," which Cadena defined as formal liberties, the protection of private property, and open competition in the economy. All societies came to be measured against the accomplishments of France, England, and the United States. For its failure to become a rich, capitalist nation, Spain fell to a position of a decadent "second-rate" power: her decadence was attributed to disdain for work, the expulsion of the "industrious" Moors, concentration of wealth in the hands of a nonproductive nobility, and a series of weak and unprogressive monarchs.[54] Russia, too, was a backward appendage of Europe whose progress was determined by the degree to which she absorbed "European civilization."

Nineteenth-century imperialism became the legitimate means of civilizing the world—of forming a "single family" in the European mold.[55] Cadena pointed out that China's contact with the West brought an end to "isolation" and "decadence" and the conversion of a "passive" nation into an "active" one. In 1853, when Japan opened her doors to the West and took European models of development, she effected a "complete transformation" in the assimilation of "civilization." A "persevering and intelligent" people, "apt for industry and the sciences," the Japanese had made "notable progress."[56] Within this hierarchy, Latin America's record was negative. The history of independent Latin America was one of anarchy recently resolved in "order and progress." Cadena's acceptance of European standards led at least implicitly to valuing Latin American authoritarianism as it emerged in figures such as Porfirio Díaz and Pedro II of Brazil.

54. Cadena, *Elementos*, 2: 80–81. On the United States, see ibid., p. 192.
55. Ibid., pp. 175–76, 178–79.
56. Ibid., pp. 178–80. On China, see ibid., pp. 175–76.

Cadena's view led also to an adulation of the Anglo-Saxon. While Mexican liberalism traditionally attacked Spain as a despotic colonizer inhibiting economic development, the imperialism of Great Britain received uncritical praise for having allowed its colonies the formal liberties of press, thought, creed, education, association, and, above all, property. Each of these contributed to "rapid prosperity and economic development." In the United States, this freedom produced a hard-working nation of small proprietors—religious, disciplined, persevering lovers of work and liberty.[57] Elsewhere, claimed Cadena, nineteenth-century British imperialism allowed complete freedom to produce and fabricate, to sell and buy products with no prejudice to the native economy. In this articulation of the ideology of free trade, Cadena demonstrated no awareness of its link with the development of a neocolonial export economy in late nineteenth century Mexico.

While this way of thinking had been challenged by the Mexican Revolution, its continuation in history texts was probably not incompatible with the underlying admiration for the Anglo-Saxon which ran consistently through revolutionary educational thought and policy. Cadena concluded:

> The Anglo-Saxon world is today at the head of the most active, most progressive, most inundating culture. What is the secret of such superiority in a race and their expansive power? We ought to study this to imitate it.[58]

He answered with a paragraph from Samuel Smiles, Salvador Alvarado's favorite author and platitudinous propagandizer of Anglo-Saxonism. The Anglo-Saxons, wrote Smiles, were a great industrial people because of their spirit of enterprise, utility, and hard work. In a further passage distinguishing the North American from the Latin American, Cadena added to these qualities those of respect for order, authority, and property. The Latin, he argued, had a tendency toward public disorder and political disobedience. The North American disdained "dangerous" socialism, which perturbed order, and contemplated social reform only with prudence and measured reflection.

The Latin American paled beside the Anglo-Saxon as Cadena resorted to an articulation of stereotypes associated with nineteenth-century liberal-positivist thought. More theoretical and imaginative

57. Ibid., pp. 70, 61.
58. Ibid., p. 72.

than practical, the Latin American, he wrote, was deficient in aptitude for the "struggle for life." Guilty of laziness and licentious customs, the Mexicans were physically weak, deficient in enterprise, concentration, and a sense of order and economy. They were effeminate insofar as they did not measure up to the Anglo-Saxon standard of masculinity: enterprise and hard work, rugged, profit-seeking individualism. Such self-loathing issuing forth in an imperative to transform behavior had run steadily through educational policy and programs since the nineteenth century. Beneath the anti-imperialism of the Mexican Revolution lay a distorted and ambiguous sense of nationalism which continued to hold the Mexican and Mexico in contempt because the standards of judgement had been and remained those of the metropolitan world, and insofar as they were extended, reinforced, and acted upon, they presented a serious dilemma for those who wished to escape from dependency.

As the Mexican Revolution brought to the fore a more forceful commitment to modernization, Mexican intellectuals were aware in a fragmented sense of the human alienation accompanying this process. Thus, Cadena shared the feelings of many when he argued that while the North American was apt for triumph in the struggle for life, he was cold, egotistical, and insensitive to the fine arts. In their love of art and beauty, the Latin Americans excelled. When Cadena suggested that Mexico be the center for "coordinating the distinctive characteristics of both cultures to achieve a culture which without losing national originality united the good qualities of the Anglo-Saxon with the Latin American," he expressed good intentions shared by other educators. However, his proposal revealed the extent to which imperialist standards operated in the scheme: the potential unity between oppressed nations yielded to the acceptance of an international hierarchy. Cadena saw Mexico as superior to other Latin American countries and destined to lead the continent. Her superiority would result from the degree to which she became Anglo-Saxonized.

In the 1920s, the Mexican Revolution did not produce a systematic change in the orientation of school texts. Despite the nationalist, pro-indigenous, and egalitarian goals espoused by many Mexican revolutionaries, the texts reflected prerevolutionary values and perspectives. They were in many ways racist, authoritarian, supportive of a clearly demarcated social hierarchy, and adulatory of imperialist powers. If they acknowledged the Mexican Revolution at all, they viewed it primarily as a political revolution for the restoration of democratic liberties and tended to accept its social reform goals only when initiative came from the state and when ample guarantees were provided for capital accumulation and private property. Ironically, the writers were so concerned with order and material progress and so opposed to forms of popular mobilization that they consistently condoned authoritarian political rule at the expense of the democratic values for which some of them claimed the Revolution had been fought. This predilection was also in part shaped by their need to support existing governments and official political practices in order to have their books accepted in the schools.

Evidently, alteration of texts was not a SEP priority. While it can be argued that the SEP was more realistically concerned with simply teaching people to read and write, many minds and many pesos were set aside to translate the European classics into Spanish in order to educate and "civilize" the Mexican masses. The gesture reflected the values and priorities of top policy-makers. The choice of texts also probably indicates a degree of bureaucratic autonomy explicable within the context of a fledgling central state in which there was, apparently, a lack of consolidated agreement on the meaning and goals of the Revolution.

Chapter 8
The Movement of Cultural Nationalism

The Mexican educational crusade of the 1920s attracted international attention in part because of the brilliant cultural renaissance orchestrated by José Vasconcelos. The cultural nationalist movement began a process of giving the Mexican Revolution a legitimacy which was eventually transmitted to masses of people through the schools and other media. At the moment of its inception in 1920, this movement brought about a rich flourishing of creativity in music, literature, and the plastic arts. But within the cultural nationalist movement were the same contradictions which characterized education as a whole. The movement revealed preoccupations of an intellectual elite still beholden to metropolitan standards of art and repulsed by much of the real popular culture of Mexico. Related to this was the idea of using art as a mechanism of social control over the working classes. These prevailing tendencies were flamboyantly challenged by the mural artists, who had been exposed to more radical political and artistic trends in Mexico and in Europe. Their identification with the oppressed coupled with the hostility to their art expressed by the mainstream of Mexican intellectuals and educators, revealed the intensity of class conflict in the Mexican Revolution.

The cultural nationalist movement is usually traced to the Ateneo de la Juventud, a group of young Mexico City intellectuals formally constituted in 1909. Among its members were philosophers José Vasconcelos and Antonio Caso, writers Alfonso Cravioto, Alfonso Reyes, Pedro Henriquez Ureña, poets Gómez Robledo, Eduardo Colín and Julio Torri, architects Jesús Acevedo and Fedérico Mariscal, artists Alfredo Martínez, Diego Rivera, and others. To them is attributed a revolt against positivism which in turn opened the way for a discovery of Mexican culture.[1] It has been pointed out that the work of the Ateneo was less than revolutionary.[2] Positivism was considered a dead

1. See, for example, Manuel Gómez Morín,*1915* (Mexico: Editorial Cultura, 1927), pp. 1–4; Patrick Romanell, *The Making of the Mexican Mind* (Lincoln: University of Nebraska Press, 1952), pp. 56–61.
2. Carlos Montsiváis, "Notas sobre la cultura mexicana en el siglo xx," in *Historia general de México*, 4 vols. (Mexico: El Colegio de México, 1976), 4: 325–28; Enrique Krauze, *Los caudillos culturales*, p. 46.

letter in Mexico in the first decade of the century. In burying it, the Ateneistas turned toward fashionable European and North American currents—the anti-intellectual tracts of Bergson, Nietzsche, Schopenhauer, and Boutroux and the pragmatism of William James. Several personalities powerful in the Díaz regime and associated with positivism welcomed the initiative of the Ateneo. Justo Sierra sponsored and attended their lectures, concerts, and art exhibits. For Mexico's centennial Pablo Macedo published an expensive edition of their lectures. Most Ateneistas were in fact products of the Porfirian school system—students or graduates of the Escuela Nacional Preparatoria, the professional and fine arts schools. The Secretaría de Instrucción Pública had sponsored many of them to study art, music, and literature in Europe. Sierra had secured competent faculty to staff the Academía de San Carlos and had fostered the development of the music conservatory, which had formed its own orchestra, gave regular public concerts patronized by the Secretaría de Instrucción Pública, and was producing a generation of skilled musicians and composers. Similarly, it was Sierra's program of bringing European musicians and artists to Mexico which contributed to the flourishing of a cultural milieu in which Ateneo youth matured and thrived.[3]

Nor were the Ateneistas isolated in their pursuit of humanistic studies as an antidote to positivism. These disciplines had never been as absent from the Mexican scene as the Ateneistas liked to suggest. Antonio Caso later acknowledged the importance of Juan de Díos Peza and José María Vigil, teachers in the Preparatoria who taught Spanish, Spanish-American, and Latin poetry. Justo Sierra's classes in Greek history had been inspiring to many. Ateneistas also owed something to the older modernist poets, who had produced fine national literature and who helped to provide a Latin American and European context within which the Ateneo's work unfolded. The journal *Revista Moderna*, edited by the venerable modernist Amado Nervo, served as a bridge between generations. Many of its contributors were young Ateneistas—Caso, Cravioto, Acevedo, Reyes, and Henriquez Uréña. The journal also recognized the growing Hispanist literary movement linking the Spanish Generation of 1898 with Latin American writers of continental vision like the Uruguayan José Enrique Rodó and Manuel Ugarte from Argentina.[4]

3. See José Vasconcelos, *Ulises criollo* (Mexico: Ediciones Botas, 1938), p. 258; Moisés González Navarro, *La vida social*, pp. 770–74. On the Ateneo de la Juventud, see Juan Hernández Luna, *Conferencias del Ateneo de la Juventud* (Mexico: Universidad Nacional Autónoma de México, 1962).

4. On humanistic studies in the Preparatoria, see, for example, Antonio Caso. "1900," *El Universal*, 4 July 1941. The effusive praise of the Ateneo generation for Justo

In its formative years, the Ateneo had little interest in Mexico. In a retreat from the hypocrisy and misery of the late *Porfiriato*, these privileged young men in their readings of Plato's *Republic* and Kant's *Critique of Pure Reason* sought a space for themselves as creative individuals pursuing art for its own sake. "We aspire to the development of personality," they announced in 1906 in the opening issue of their journal, *Sabia Moderna*, in protest against the scholasticism and formalism of the schools and academies.[5] They gravitated toward the mystical expressionism of European artists like Eugene Carrière, and toward outcries against society's assault against the unique individual, such as those issued by Friedrich Nietzsche and Max Stirner. Individual creativity, wrote the young Caso, was the highest expression of mankind—a flowering of essence, uniqueness, and divinity.[6] The cult of the individual as artist emerged in the pages of the literary magazines in the poetry of love, misery, and melancholy, and drawings of tortured souls caught in an atmosphere of decadence and grief. The Ateneistas had no interest in the social revolution brewing around them. Although they often criticized the modernist writers for compromises with the Díaz regime, they retreated from the world of politics altogether in what was generally an attitude of aloof contempt. In 1911, Alfonso Reyes, one of the Ateneo's most promising writers and son of General Bernardo Reyes, unsuccessful vice-presidential contender in 1909, wanted only to be with his books sealed away from the political uproar around him. He was glad to leave for Paris in 1913. Many of the Ateneistas who remained in the capital during the Revolution went into "interior exile": Julio Torri, Atonio Castro Leal and others, for example, rented a house in the suburb of San Angel to learn Greek, "dialogue," and read. Of the original core group, only José Vasconcelos chided the Goethian remoteness of his colleagues and took an active role in the Madero movement in 1910 and the

---

Sierra is well known. See, for example, Alfonso Reyes, *Pasado inmediato y otros ensayos* (Mexico: El Colegio de Mexico, 1941), p. 24; *Justo Sierra: Un discurso* (Mexico: SEP, 1947), p. 13; José Vasconcelos, *Ulises criollo*, pp. 169–70. Ateneistas were also aware of their debt to the modernists. Alfonso Cravioto dedicated an elegant poem to Manuel José Othón in the first edition of *Sabia Moderna* in 1906. On the importance of the modernists to the formation of a national literary culture, see Montsiváis, "Notas sobre la cultura mexicana," pp. 311–13. On recognition of the Hispanist literary movement, see, for example, Miguel de Unamuno, "Don Quixote y Bolívar," *Revista Moderna* 8 (1907): 263–67; Francisco García Calderón, "Las corrientes filosóficas en Latinoamérica," *Revista Moderna* 11 (1908): 150–56.

5. *Sabia Moderna* 1, no. 1 (1906): 1. The editors included Alfonso Cravioto, Antonio Caso, Jesús T. Acevedo, Luis Castillo Ledón, Ricardo Gómez Robledo, Nemesio García Naranjo, Rubén Valenti.

6. *Sabia Moderna* 1, no. 5 (1906): 269–71, 300–303.

Convention of Aguascalientes in 1914–1915. The characterization of the Ateneo as politically aloof, however, can be misleading. Basically very conservative, several Ateneistas were comfortable serving the usurper Huerta as well as Carranza, especially in the field of education. Ateneista Nemesio García Naranjo as Secretary of Education under Huerta was instrumental in moving his colleagues into important positions in institutions of higher education such as the university, the Escuela de Altos Estudios, and the Academía de San Carlos.[7]

Although the Ateneo's interest in Mexico was secondary to its interest in individual artistic expression, the movement developed within the context of a burgeoning Latin American literary current fanned by José Enrique Rodó for whom humanistic endeavors expressed the inherent "spirituality" of Latin American culture in contrast to the materialism and scientism of the Anglo-Saxon world, symbolized for Rodó in the figure of Caliban. Rodó, wrote Alfonso Reyes, "made us understand our mission . . . the notion of an American fraternity . . . and a spiritual reality . . . understood and stimulated by a few at a moment of doubt in reason and in faith."[8] One of the primary accomplishments of the Ateneo was the reinstitution of humanist studies in the Mexican university, especially in the Escuela de Altos Estudios under the leadership of the Dominican writer Pedro Henriquez Uréña during the Huerta regime.[9]

While the literary movement inspired by Rodó stressed the importance of the Latin American artist rather than a Latin American artistic content, cultural nationalism was a logical outgrowth of the former with its incipient criticism of some foreign models. Pedro Henriquez Ureña stimulated an interest in Mexican literature within the Ateneo and in his classes in the Escuela de Altos Estudios. Alfonso Cravioto, Jesús T. Acevedo, and Fedérico Mariscal undertook studies of Mexican colonial architecture. In the education bureaucracy's fine

7. For criticism of the modernists' political compromises, see Ciro Ceballos, "Panorama mexicano, 1905–1910, Costumbres literarios," *Excelsior*, 17 July 1939, 8 Aug., 11 Oct., 14 Nov. 1939. For analysis of Ateneo's attitude toward politics, see Montsiváis, "Notas sobre la cultura mexicana," pp. 326, 330–31. On Reyes' reaction to the Revolution, see Alfonso Reyes, *Diario, 1911–1930*, prólogo de Alicia Reyes (Guanajuato: Universidad de Guanajuato, 1969), pp. 24–28. On the retreat of Torri et al. to San Angel, see Krauze, *Los caudillos culturales*, p. 59. On Vasconcelos' criticism of the Ateneo, see Vasconcelos, *Ulises criollo*, pp. 356–60, 364; Reyes, *Pasado inmediato*, pp. 57–58.

8. Alfonso Reyes, *El cazador*, in *Obras completas* (Mexico: Fondo de Cultura Económica, 1955–1962), 3: 134–36.

9. See Pedro Henriquez Ureña, "La cultura de las humanidades," *Obra crítica* (Mexico, Buenos Aires: Fondo de Cultura Económica, 1960), pp. 597–98; "La influencia de la Revolución en la vida intelectual de México," *Obra crítica*, p. 613.

arts office under Carranza, Cravioto played an important role in improving the renovation and inspection of artistic monuments and in proposing the creation of two colonial museums. In the course of the Revolution, Hispanism developed into something of a cult among those elite intellectuals around Carranza, who, as part of his anti-U.S. foreign policy, made tentative overtures to establish stronger political, cultural, and commercial ties with Latin America and, to a lesser extent, Spain. Palavicini's newspaper *El Universal* introduced a Hispanic section which especially catered to the Spanish colony in Mexico City.[10]

In music in the years preceding the Revolution, composers Julian Carrillo and Manuel Ponce began to utilize Mexican folk themes in classical compositions in a manner befitting European romantic music. In the plastic arts around 1906, students at the Academía de San Carlos and those pensioned in Europe launched a critique of the formalism and precepts of academic art. In what was essentially a belated and eclectic adaptation and combination of impressionism and expressionism in painting, they favored a return to nature and exalted the artist's intuitive creativity. Wrote the young painters associated with the Ateneo in 1906: "The work of art is nothing but a state of the soul to which exterior things lend expressive elements."[11] With the exception of Jorge Enciso, whose Mexican landscapes reflected his provincial training, and Saturnino Herrán, who was too poor to study in Europe, the young artists were more interested in European content and styles than they were in Mexico. Early exhibits by Diego Rivera, Alfredo Ramos Martínez, and Roberto Montenegro consisted largely of European landscapes, ports, and peasant scenes.[12] In 1910, when Justo Sierra sponsored an exhibit of Spanish painting in conjunction with the centennial celebrations, students at the Academía de San Carlos set up a counter exhibit of their own painting. In 1911, they went on strike against the academy for its restrictions on their creativity. The prolonged protest was favorably resolved in 1913 when the old director was removed and replaced by Ramos Martínez, one of the foremost spokesmen of the return to nature and cult of intuition. In imitation of French impressionism, Ramos Martínez

10. See Pedro Serrano, *Los hispanistas mexicanos*, 2 vols. (Mexico: Imprenta Nacional, 1920), 1, for descriptions of intellectuals allegedly espousing Hispanism. For development of official ties between the government and Latin American intellectuals and students, see, for example, *Excelsior*, 25 Feb., 3, 4 April 1920.

11. *Sabia Moderna* 1, no. 2 (1906): 147; 1, no. 4 (1906): 223–26.

12. Jean Charlot, *The Mexican Mural Renaissance* (New Haven and London: Yale University Press, 1963), pp. 57–60; *Revista Moderna* 1, no. 9 (1906): 41–42.

opened Mexico's first open-air painting school in the suburb of Santa Anita. Although emphasis at Santa Anita was still on self-expression rather than on objective content, almost by default if young painters were to paint outside the studio, they would paint Mexico—landscapes and hired indigenous models. Interest in Mexican content deepened as the Revolution and World War I cut the country off temporarily from European currents. In music as well, Pedro Henriquez Ureña recalled that the inability to contract European opera companies led to the development of Mexican performers and composers.[13]

In a formal sense, the Ateneo de la Juventud dissolved in the Mexican Revolution. It maintained some cohesion through the Universidad Popular, Mexico's first university extension program. Although the Universidad Popular provided some skills training and quite succinctly stressed a disciplining of the working class in its lectures on hygiene, alcohol, sexual mores, savings, the work ethic, and sanctity of the nuclear family, one of its primary purposes was to bring art to the masses as a means of civilizing them. The Universidad Popular's altruism in this task has received much praise.[14] However, it is important to emphasize the conservatism of the Universidad Popular and the fact that its approach was not new in Mexican history. The idea that art formed part of the state's educational responsibility and that it had a moralizing purpose had been clear to the first Mexican liberals who created the Dirección General de Educación Pública in 1833. In the *Porfiriato*, Sierra and other educators had been aware of the "refining" and civilizing aspects of art forms like music, drama, and literature, and had upon occasion suggested these as a substitute for taverns and bullfights. In the last years of the regime, Sierra sponsored the creation of workers' choirs and low-cost performances of European opera for the poor—partly to draw them away from drink.[15]

The idea that art civilized and domesticated the masses was also central to the thought of José Enrique Rodó. Rodó's Caliban was not

---

13. Manuel Gómez Morín, *1915*, pp. 7–8; Krauze, *Los caudillos culturales*, p. 65; Pedro Henriquez Ureña, "La influencia de la Revolución en la vida intelectual," p. 614. The impact of the Revolution on Mexican music is treated in the survey by Robert Stevenson, *Music in Mexico: A Historical Survey* (New York: Thomas Y. Crowell, 1952), pp. 224–70. See also Julián Carrillo, *La revolución musical mexicana del Sonido 13, expuesta brevemente en tres capítulos en forma de conferencias, dedicadas al señor ministro plenipotenciario de México en Quito, Ecuador, quien las transmitió por radio del capital bello país hermano* (Mexico: n.p., 1936).

14. See Krauze, *Los caudillos culturales*, pp. 48–50.

15. *El Imparcial*, 5, 8, 11, 16, 17 Dec. 1903; 26 Feb. 1904; 2 July 1907.

simply an invasion of North American materialism. Caliban was also in evidence in the working class which burgeoned with modernization. As Rodó watched Italian and Spanish immigrants flood the port of Montivideo at the end of the century, he recalled an image from Charles Morice: "The falange of ferocious Prudhommes, bearing the standard of mediocrity and marching animated with hatred for everything extraordinary.[16] To privileged Latin America youth, Rodó had not only recommended a Greek cultivation of beauty and personality in the salon, he had spoken of the need for heroic action. He posited the idea of an aristocracy of merit in which the Greek sentiment of beauty cultivated in humanistic studies would link with the Christian heritage to awaken the spirit of the redeemer, missionary, and philanthropist. An intellectual elite, preserving taste, art, and delicate customs, could educate the barbarous mass. It would mitigate passions with art and moral directives. In short, it would civilize. All the while, the Greek spirit of hierarchy would maintain sentiments of order and place and an "aristocratic disdain for the humble and weak."[17] A very real contempt for democracy pervaded the thought of Rodó as it did that of the Ateneo and the Universidad Popular.[18]

The Universidad Popular set out to "raise the intellectual and cultural level of the *clases humildes*" on the assumption that "the condition of the people only improve with the culture of the same."[19] In all likelihood, lectures on Socrates, Wagner, Edgar Allan Poe, and Rodin had little appeal to a working class in the midst of organizing and concerned with locating enough tortillas and charcoal in a city periodically invaded by revolutionary armies. Lectures on colonial Church architecture would have had limited interest to people whose anticlericalism led them to pillage the sanctuaries. In fact, Pedro Henriquez Ureña later wrote that the lectures on hygiene were for the workers while the important lectures were for the *"público culto."*[20]

In 1915, Antonio Caso presented a series of lectures in the Universidad Popular which provided a philosophical justification for the civilizing role of art and the tasks of an aristocracy of knowledge and

---

16. José Enrique Rodó, *Ariel* (Monterrey: Talleres Modernos de Lozano, 1908), p. 44.

17. Ibid., p. 54.

18. Ibid., pp. 46–47; see also Montsiváis, "Notas sobre la cultura mexicana," p. 33.

19. Alfonso Pruneda, *Universidad Popular Mexicana en el segundo año de sus labores, 1913–1914. Informe del Director* (Mexico: Imprenta Stefan y Torres, 1915), pp. 3–13.

20. Pedro Henriquez Ureña, "La influencia de la Revolución en la vida intelectual de México," p. 613.

virtue.[21] Caso argued that a scientific explanation of the universe with its alleged social corollaries of egotism and maximum profit with minimum effort formed only one aspect of human life—the bestial and lowest sphere. Culture represented a higher level which separated man from beast and made men human. In Kantian terms, art was disinterested pleasure, the intermediary through which man passed from the biological to the spiritual realm. Disinterested contemplation, or Rodó's ancient idle time, was the forerunner of moral behavior. Art awakened the depths of the human spirit. Through contemplating or creating it, men became moral. Art civilized the masses. Like Rodó, for Caso the essence of morality was Christian doctrine.[22] Their spirit awakened through art, men were moral out of enthusiasm—Rodó's evangelical fervor. What was moral was heroic sacrifice and altruism or the greatest effort for the least profit.

To the privileged Mexican youth whom he taught in the preparatory school and university, Caso preached the need for heroic action. An unabashed elitist, he once quipped:

> *No me gustan ni las misas, ni las masas;*
> *Prefiero las mozas y las musas.*[23]

As Alfonso Reyes noted, it was difficult for the Ateneo generation (or their students) to recognize heroes in the ignorant *rancheros* or striking workers who made the Mexican Revolution.[24] Caso's heroes were his students and erudite colleagues. They formed the virtuous aristocracy of genius with a civilizing mission. In this period of his life, Caso had lifted the notion of "art for art's sake" into a holistic philosophy. For him, "culture" had an existence independent of society, history, and social class. Its content and civilizing potential did not have to be questioned. By implication, "culture" had only to be taken to society in order to purify it.

Scholars have pointed out that Caso's philosophy operated in a self-defined historical vacuum. A disciple of the individualism of anti-intellectual thinkers like Nietzsche and Stirner, Caso denied any relationship between the individual and the state, economy, social

21. These were published as Antonio Caso, *La existencia como economía y caridad* (Mexico: Editorial Porrua, 1916); see also *Boletín de la Universidad Popular Mexicana* 2, no. 2 (1916): 49–51.

22. Antonio Caso, "La perennidad del pensamiento religioso," *Revista Moderna* 8 (1909): 67–72; "La psicología del cristianismo," *Boletín de la Universidad Popular Mexicana* 2, no. 2 (1916): 49–51.

23. Patrick Romanell, *The Making of the Mexican Mind*, p. 70.

24. Alfonso Reyes, *Pasado inmediato*, pp. 7–8, 62.

class or history. That he did not wish to confront these factors is clear from his Universidad Popular lectures on Christian evangelism. For him, Tolstoy represented the correct Christian rejection of the powerful, the world, and social institutions. For Tolstoy, it was equally vile to command or to obey.[25] It can be argued that there was reason for Caso's evasions. For him, the First World War had buried not only positivism but industrialism, militarism, and mercantilism—in short, a "century of egotism."[26] The overthrow of Díaz and the unfolding of the Mexican Revolution added to this sense of finality. However, as Manuel Gomez Morín, a Caso student, pointed out a decade later, the new world which was to take the place of the old was clouded in mysticism and romanticism. A vague sense of good will toward mankind—perhaps even what Gomez Morín called a sentimental kind of socialism—ran through Caso's thought but it coexisted with a profound arrogance toward Mexico and toward those making the Revolution, both the generals and the troops.[27] Those who took Caso's mission seriously were to discover that culture was not independent of historical time, national context, economics, social class, or individual socialization. As historical actors they had to face questions of political power and class loyalties. Most also were to come to terms with the idea that the Revolution did not destroy positivism, but refined it in the form of technocracy applied in the interests of national capitalism.[28]

Caso captured an important initial and enduring sentiment among many Mexican educators—the notion of art as civilizing, a mechanism of restraint rather than liberation. In 1914, the plastic arts movement began to take a different, more populist direction. In that

---

25. *Boletin de la Universidad Popular Mexicana* 2, no. 2 (1916): 51. For a cogent argument on Caso's idealism and failure to take history and societal institutions into account, see Enrique Florescano, "Antonio Caso y la historia," *Historia Mexicana* 12 (1963): 358–78.

26. Manuel Gómez Morín, *1915*, pp. 14–15; Krauze, *Los caudillos culturales*, p. 69.

27. Manuel Gómez Morín, *1915*, pp. 14–15, pp. 19–20.

28. Manuel Gómez Morín wrote *1915*, in which he emphasized the importance of technique, to criticize the idealism and lack of intellectual discipline and direction typical of elite intellectual circles during the Revolution. As the architect of the national bank and the agricultural credit bank in the Calles period, he was the prototype of the neo-positivist statesman created by the Revolution. It is also interesting to note that Daniel Cosío Villegas pointed out that the generation of 1915 produced no writers in the strict sense of the term. Rather, most became involved in one way or another in service to the revolutionary governments—many of them, of course, in teaching. See Daniel Cosío Villegas, "La justificación de la tirada," *Ensayos y notas* (Buenos Aires and Mexico: Editorial Hermes, 1966), p. 26.

year, Gerardo Murillo, known as Dr. Atl, replaced Alfredo Ramos Martínez as head of the Academía de San Carlos. An eccentric schooled in Europe and Mexico outside academic circles and a provocateur of the student strike of 1911, Atl objected in 1914 to the exclusivity and individualism of Ramos Martínez' Santa Anita school. Art should be for the "people" and by them.[29] He wanted architects to design and artists to paint and decorate public buildings rather than devote their time to easel portraiture for self-gratification and the pleasure of reduced audiences. He wanted the art schools opened to the broader public. His tenure at the academy was brief, however, because his Carrancista backers were temporarily forced out of the capital in late 1914. Atl was instrumental in securing the support of the workers' organization, the Casa del Obrero Mundial, for the Constitutional cause.

As he went to war with the Red Batallions of workers in 1915, Atl took with him the artists David Alfaro Siqueriros and José Clemente Orozco. These artists actually participated in the Revolution. Siqueiros entered combat under General Manuel Diéguez. By 1918, his drawings were different from the picturesqueness typical of Santa Anita, where he had studied. Not only had armed peasants entered his repertoire, but the question of social class and cultural distance emerged. In 1918, he drew "Sugar Skulls," in which a bourgeois girl skipped rope beside a squatting Indian woman selling skeletons on the Day of the Dead.[30] Although José Clemente Orozco had studied at the Academy of San Carlos, his artistic roots were in Mexican popular culture, in the tradition of broadsheet engravings typified by Manuel Posada. In the *Porfiriato*, Posada had illustrated the sensational and mundane aspects of popular life—floods and epidemics, women protesting merchants' price increases, men tricked into signing contracts to labor on jungle plantations. Orozco, who earned his living as a newspaper cartoonist etching political satire, illustrated for *La Vanguardia*, journal of the Red Batallions and organizing tool for the Casa del Obrero Mundial as it began to recruit workers nationally. It was in the trenches and battlefields of Veracruz that Orozco observed what he would later paint—the peasant and workers in the tragedy of warfare. How could anyone, inquired the elegant Ramos Martínez, want to paint an Indian with a cartridge belt and pistol, when it was more like Millet to paint him holding a vase?[31]

29. Charlot, *The Mexican Mural Renaissance*, p. 47. For background on Atl, see Raquel Tibol, *Arte mexicano, Época moderna y contemporánea* (Mexico: Editorial Hermes, 1963), p. 133.

30. Charlot, *The Mexican Mural Renaissance*, p. 196.

31. Ibid., p. 166.

These approaches to art and culture reflected different, dynamic, and changing relations within the context of a social revolution. In 1920, Vasconcelos called all of these individuals together to join in a crusade for national culture, which had as its unifying principle Mexican artistic expression. David Alfaro Siqueiros and Diego Rivera were called back from Europe. Ramos Martínez returned to direct the academy of fine arts and opened a new painting school in the suburb of Coyoacán. Poets—former Ateneistas like Julio Torri, who had retreated to San Angel during the Revolution, and students of Caso like Carlos Pellicer and Antonio Castro Leal—moved into the editorial department to edit the classics of Greece and Latin American literature. Julian Carrillo became director of the music conservatory. Alba Herrera y Ogazón, the pianist who had once played Beethoven at the conferences of the Ateneo, took a leading role in the development of a music program for the masses. Pedro Henriquez Ureña directed the university's extension department, which replaced the Universidad Popular. Roberto Montenegro accompanied Vasconcelos on his tours of the states where he familiarized himself with techniques of indigenous ceramicists. José Clemente Orozco recalled the moment:

> Artists and intellectuals were summoned to collaborate and painters had such an opportunity they had not known in centuries. . . . It liquidated a whole epoch of brutalizing Bohemianism, of frauds who lived the life of a drone in their ivory towers . . . their fetid dens where drunkenly strumming on guitars, they kept up a pretense of absurd idealism, beggars in a society that was already rotten and close to extinction.[32]

In conceptualizing his cultural program, Vasconcelos attributed major influence to Anatoli Lunacharsky, first commisar of education and the fine arts in revolutionary Russia, but, in their approach to art and culture, the two men were markedly different. A cursory overview of Lunacharsky's policy provides a model for what Vasconcelos' program was not. As a Marxist, the Russian did not believe in creativity independent of social circumstance but saw the artist as expressing feelings and emotions stemming from his particular psychological makeup within a particular class situation functioning in a specific socioeconomic milieu. Lunacharsky saw the fin-de-siècle art for art's sake movement as an evasion of social problems in the bourgeois world. For him, art had a commitment to deal with social problems,

---

32. José Clemente Orozco, *Autobiography*, trans. Robert C. Stephenson (Austin: University of Texas Press, 1962), pp. 82–83. See also Daniel Cosío Villegas, "La justificación de la tirada," p. 20.

the future lay in the working class, and the role of art was to express the feelings and aspirations of that class—to depict class struggle, to define class, and to paint a vision of the future toward which men would strive. Lunacharsky did not accept all spontaneous expressions of the working class as legitimate art. He believed the working class should be educated to appreciate art. Art education would raise the level of culture so as to enable workers to utilize their own skills in creating art and organizing a new society. Lunacharsky believed the artist should seize upon the psychological moment of change in the outburst and enthusiasm of revolution to propel men into action affirming their role as makers of history. Not only the masses, but the artists required education. Although he sponsored artists of aristocratic and bourgeois origin, he urged them through systematic criticism to change their world view and attitudes. He encouraged them to understand the revolution from a popular perspective, to describe everyday life in the workplace, home, and community, to probe the problems posed by revolution, to deepen the understanding of the cultural, socioeconomic, and political tasks, and to assist the working class in creating a new ethic.[33]

Lunacharsky sought to use the art of the past not to civilize and restrain people but to form a proletarian culture which in turn would stimulate historical initiative. His approach to the past was selective. In preserving historical monuments, he aimed at giving Russians a sense of their history to motivate them toward creating their future. In choosing works of art from the past, he selected those of social protest and criticism. When he edited a series of the classics to correct the preference of the unsophisticated for banal art, he chose his classics to instill a sense of heroism which would motivate action and change. Dramas by contemporary Russian artists were set in revolutionary periods to capture the heroism of struggle. Mass spectacles portrayed the great episodes of the Russian Revolution.[34]

In contrast to the Russian educator, José Vasconcelos had no clear theory of the relationship between art and social reality. As a child of the Ateneo, he was grounded in the movement of art for art's sake. That art was for him an escape from his social surroundings came out in his law thesis, completed in 1905. He wrote:

> We accept the present epoch: we receive this vulgar industrialism as a grievous and necessary transition which prepares for a

33. Howard Holter, "Anatoli Lunacharsky and the Formulation of a Policy toward the Arts" (Diss., University of Wisconsin, 1967) p. 154.
34. Ibid., pp. 159, 169.

better future. Our sympathies are not with it, but it does not strangle everything. Although work and machines invade the earth, there will always remain in the heavens a space which preserves ideals. Our Latin race, little adapted to the coarse task, will not go to the head of peoples waving the triumphal standard in these almost niggardly struggles. It will continue resigned to a movement which it sees as necessary and will conserve its vigor for a time when the ideal flowers, when the industrialists have put all riches to capacity and life is a long dream of contemplation of the infinite.[35]

Derivative of Rodó's concept of Latin beauty, Vasconcelos' cult of art was at its root a profound expression of alienation from his own environment, resulting at least in part from his class background and his Europeanized education, which enhanced his separation from and contempt for Mexican realities. What he perceived to be the squalor, the dirt, and the violence surrounding him in Mexico was a constant source of anguish, which increased with the Mexican Revolution. He resolved the problem in part through preoccupation with aesthetics and a utopian vision of Latin American civilization. In the 1920s, he articulated his theory of the cosmic race—a vision of Latin America as a future paradise without racism, egotism, or greed.[36] In its time a popular antidote to European theories of white racial superiority which had so dominated Latin American intellectual circles in the late nineteenth century, the theory of the *Raza Cósmica* in fact established the Spanish and white creole as the superior and integrating elements of Latin American culture and its link with civilization. In the cosmic race, the other peoples of Latin America were acceptable only in aesthetic and stereotypic stylizations synthesized in an artificial symphony composed apparently out of no concrete historical process. This race would, according to Vasconcelos, capture:

> the abyss of the Indian soul, the Negro's eagerness for sensual happiness; the Mongol whose oblique eyes make him see everything in unexpected perspectives; the Judaic strains in the Spanish blood; the melancholy of the Arab; and the [rationality] of the white whose thought is as lucid as his skin.[37]

35. José Vasconcelos, "Teoría dinámica del derecho," in *Obras completas*, 1: 35.

36. José Vasconcelos, *Raze cósmica*, in *Obras completas*, 2: 918–23; *Indología*, in *Obras completas*, 2: 1123–25; *Discursos*, pp. 59, 116. Vasconcelos first presented his vision of an American utopia in *Prometheo vencedor*, in *Obras completas*, 1: 239–86. Written in 1918, it developed themes similar to Caso's, i.e., that the First World War had demolished positivism and discredited the ethic of greed and accumulation. Latin America would elaborate a utopia based upon Christian ethics and refined aestheticism.

37. José Vasconcelos, *Raza cósmica*, p. 923.

Underlying this metaphysical construct was the notion that what was civilized was European and that the highest expression of civilization was art or aesthetic beauty. In terms of policy, the latter implied that an artistic movement in Mexico would attempt to demonstrate to an unbelieving world (specifically a metropolitan world) that Mexico was indeed civilized. A deep sense of cultural dependence underlay Vasconcelos' own motives. At one of the many cultural festivals he sponsored in Chapultepec Park, he told President Obregón as he watched Mexican children dance the *jarabe* that he would not be satisfied until he saw them dancing to the strains of Rimski-Korsakov.[38] He was anxious to tell a North American audience that he had created a national symphony orchestra which performed classical music.[39]

A major thrust of the art movement was to provide Mexican musicians with training and forums in European classical music which continued to prevail in concerts, cultural festivals, and the government radio station. In editing the classics of European literature, Vasconcelos sent large numbers of them abroad to make known Mexico's civilizing crusade.[40] He relied on the applause of European intellectuals like Romain Rolland, Henri Barbusse, and Miguel de Unamuno. Latin rather than Anglo-Saxon, they were still part of the metropolitan world he wanted to impress. His stand before them was revolutionary. He was proud of overcoming the notion that a nation of halfbreeds was unredeemable.[41] While one cannot overlook the political importance of this cultural movement to the Obregón government boycotted for its nationalism and social reform proposals by the imperialist countries, the cultural movement carried in it a deep and persistent sense of inferiority and dependency inherent in the national bourgeois revolution.

Unlike Anatoli Lunacharsky, Vasconcelos was not particularly interested in the content of art. He was more interested in "beauty." His program emphasized the nonideational forms of music and dance rather than drama. No mass spectacles depicting episodes of the Mexican Revolution—indeed of Mexican history—formed part of the Vasconcelos program. More typical were Mexican schoolgirls dressed in Greek togas dancing in the style of Isadora Duncan. It was

38. José Vasconcelos, *El desastre*, in *Obras completas*, 1: 1374.

39. José Vasconcelos, "Educational Aspirations," *Survey Graphic* 52, no. 3 (1924): 169.

40. These classics actually reflected the eclectic interests of Vasconcelos in oriental mysticism as well as European literature. See, for example, chapters on Buddha and the Upanishads in *Lecturas clásicas para niños* (Mexico: SEP, 1924–1925), chapters 11, 12.

41. *BU* 1, no. 4 (1921): 329; *BSEP* 1, no. 3 (1923): 5–6.

not a question of propelling the masses into action as historical actors. Rather, it often seemed that Vasconcelos' cultural festivals were an attempt to channel energies unleashed by revolution into a perfect construct of pure beauty. At the inauguration of the national stadium in 1923, he watched children dance the *jarabe* and sing Mexican folk songs while athletes performed in the style of the "German infantry." The stadium he called a church (a collective expression of the good and holy) and a school (a place where human behavior could be channeled and purified). The stadium would witness great collective works, patriotic dances, choral performances, symbolic religious rites, accompanied by "cosmic music." "Strange revelations in sound, rhythm and voice" would burst forth "in color and image," he claimed in a flow of aesthetic rhetoric:

> A gleam born in the depths of the Cosmos will shine forth in the sun . . . A race will speak, will dance, will sing. Splendid, joyful, wise, and strong, indulge in divine joy. Pure, clean, new Mexico, surge forth and glitter, throw off the shadows! Advance![42]

"Purified in beauty," all would be able to "ascend." For Vasconcelos, art not only civilized, it was an end in itself—a path to the divine.[43]

It followed that the cultural festivals may have had popular content in Mexican folk dances and songs, but they had no revolutionary content. The level of cultural dependency which many Mexican intellectuals felt expressed itself in an intense preoccupation with demonstrating the beauty of Mexican "civilization" in contrast to the violence and squalor, which obsessed and repulsed them. In choosing songs for schools, workers' centers, and cultural festivals, the policy of the fine arts department was to "firmly channel the disposition ours have for the beautiful and aesthetic."[44] As Ruben Campos, former Ateneista and fine arts program official, stated, the most "beautiful" songs were chosen to prove "the Mexican soul is not blood and death but exquisite sensitivity, tenderness, and passion." "The gentle songs of the fatherland," which expressed the "collective soul," were to capture "all the tenderness of a race worthy of elevating itself to the destinies of the privileged races."[45] The songs chosen for the cul-

42. José Vasconcelos, *Discursos*, pp. 115–16.

43. Ibid., pp. 42, 58, 78; José Vasconcelos, "De Robinson a Odiseo," in *Obras completas*, 2: 1559. Vasconcelos' philosophy is well synthesized in Haddox, *Vasconcelos of Mexico*, and Blanco, *Se llamaba Vasconcelos*.

44. *BSEP* 1, no. 2 (1922): 208. See also pp. 215–20.

45. Rubén Campos, *El folklore y la música mexicana: investigaciones de la cultura musical en México, 1525–1925* (Mexico: SEP, 1928), pp. 152–54.

tural festivals were lyrics of unrequited love, of nostalgia for the countryside, and of the rustic beauties of the land enjoyed by a romanticized poor.[46]

Cultural nationalism often became a means of creating a sense of community which obfuscated class conflict and real sources of exploitation and oppression. The effort to use art forms to create a sort of popular "folk" nationalism grew out of the class perspective of the educators. Almost totally ignored was the *corrido* of the Revolution, a rich expression of a people affirming their daily culture, their loves and hopes, hatreds and weaknesses. The *corrido* very often expressed political protest. As one balladeer portrayed the tyranny of Porfirio Díaz:

> You were the sublime protector of the brave *hispanos*. The fearsome stepfather of the Mexican *indios*.[47]

The avoidance of the political *corrido* was in part deliberate, for the *corridos* were known to intellectuals.[48] Their absence from the school program probably also reflected class isolation and insensitivity, which sometimes reached great proportions. In the midst of the widespread misery which had just provoked thousands of people to take up arms, Elena Landazuri wrote for a North American audience:

> Our life carries a flavor of languor, of well-being, of sensuousness, but also a spirit of peace, serenity, a depth of feeling, almost of mysticism. We tend toward the metaphysical in our philosophy and in our literature, which is almost always lyrical, we tend toward the mystical. Even our houses, built around ample patios, filled with growing plants and trees, with fountains which murmur quietly, influence us to leave action and to indulge in quiet and contemplation.[49]

The images chosen reflected a particular class experience while the pretension to Latin American soulfulness in contrast to North American materialism and aggressiveness had become more an elite literary

46. These are the major themes in the published texts of Vicente T. Mendoza, *La canción mexicana. Ensayo de clasificación y antología*, vol. 1 of *Estudios de folklore* (Mexico: Instituto de Investigaciones Estéticas, Universidad Nacional Autónoma de México, 1961); see also BSEP 1, no. 2 (1922): 12; 1, no. 4 (1923): 327–30.

47. Merle E. Simmons, *The Mexican Corrido as a Source for Interpretative Study of Modern Mexico, 1870–1950* (Bloomington: Indiana University Press, 1957), p. 78.

48. See Katherine Anne Porter, "Corridos," *Survey Graphic* 52, no. 3 (1924): 157–58. Diego Rivera used *corridos* in his murals in the SEP.

49. Elena Landazuri, "Why We Differ," *Survey Graphic* 52, no. 3 (1924): 160.

theme rather than a reflection of social realities. The approach, which was widespread among intellectuals, contrasted with the underlying drive of education to make Mexicans more pragmatic and hardworking following a North American model. But in fact this contradiction was more apparent than real. Vasconcelos and other educators believed the two aspects of human behavior should be combined in the Mexican: Vasconcelos spoke of forming "cultured" workers.

What Rodó and Caso had tentatively suggested became emphatic politics for Vasconcelos: art should reach beyond privileged circles to the masses. Following a theme of the Ateneo, he further held that art should not compromise itself with corrupt political power.[50] Like Rodó and Caso, he accepted the idea that an aristocracy of virtue civilized the masses through art. Hence, in contrast to Lunacharsky, there was no question of changing the artists' perspective or the content of art. There was rather an emphasis on the artist and creativity and an emphasis on bringing art to the masses to rescue them from unruly behavior. Such was the underlying theme of the SEP journal, *El Maestro*. Intended for workers, teachers, and intellectuals, the magazine's cover stated:

> Workers, *campesinos*, employees, all workers who know it avails them nothing to better their wages if they do not know how to give good use to them, that to every increase in wages corresponds a new need in life which perfects its comforts and approximates the simple and healthy existence of the civilized man. Let wages and salaries not increase if they serve only to foment vice and to assure the slothfulness of their children.[51]

El Maestro reflected the contradictions of the cultural nationalist movement. On the one hand, it provided a forum through which aspiring young Mexican poets of the *clase media* could publish their work for European and Latin American audiences. This poetry, expressing introspective themes of loneliness, unrequited love, nature, doubt, and suffering, was probably somewhat removed from Mexican popular culture and certainly not conducive to unified mass social action.[52] However, it also reflected a primary purpose and consequence of the cultural nationalist program: it provided a legitimate and affirmative form of cultural expression for Mexico's emerging

---

50. José Vasconcelos, *Discursos*, p. 11.

51. Policy statement was on the back of each issue of the magazine *El Maestro*, published irregularly by the SEP in the Vasconcelos period.

52. *El Maestro* 1, no. 2 (1921): 203–6; 1, no. 3 (1921): 317–19; 1, no. 4 (1921): 425.

national bourgeoisie. In so doing, *El Maestro* expressed class attitudes contemptuous of the working class and peasantry. Social philosophy and children's stories were translated primarily from French and English. The journal contained very few pieces on indigenous culture. Those it did publish were often derogatory. In an article condemning the use of *pulque*, Vasconcelos blamed the invention on the Aztecs. In a poem, Alfonso Cravioto articulated familiar stereotypes which had some basis in truth but had come to constitute a total picture of the pre-Hispanic past: the Aztecs were a warlike race practicing human sacrifice; Moctezuma was a cowardly despot. A tendency to attribute problems of Mexico to the oppressed themselves was reiterated by the modernist poet, José Juan Tablada, who blamed them for deforesting the country. In a singular article on the popular classes in Latin America, Venezuelan writer Blanco Fombona continued the penchant for blaming the victim: he attributed the failure of democracy in Venezuela to the *llaneros'* ignorance of civilized political process and their preference to work out disputes through violence.[53] Writers were sometimes transparent in revealing their class fears. Ezequiel Padilla, later Minister of Education, described the culture of Mexico's poor as

> . . . the dark cryptic of the social inferno haunted by the demons of alcoholism, prostitution, and pauperism . . . a culture of despair, hatred, contempt, and crime and grief.[54]

To be sure, there was confusion and divergence in *El Maestro's* attitude toward the masses. No one expressed this confusion better than José Vasconcelos. On the one hand, he wished to straightjacket barbarous Mexico. He once detailed to teachers in the literacy program how Mexican workers should spend their time: all had the obligation to work diligently during job hours; on Saturday afternoons, they should bathe and exercise; on Sunday morning, they should read and study; on Sunday afternoon, they should go to the countryside where in joining choirs they would refresh their souls.[55] On the other hand, Vasconcelos sincerely wanted social reform and an equalization of wealth, although it is doubtful that he wished to see this transformation initiated and carried out by the masses themselves. Similarly, in

53. On Vasconcelos' essay on pulque, see *El Maestro* 1, no. 3 (1921): 215. On Cravioto's interpretation of the Aztecs, see ibid., 1, no. 2 (1921): 207–8. See José Juan Tablada's essay in ibid., 1, nos. 5 and 6 (1921): 521–22. Blanco Fombona's statements are in ibid., 1, no. 3 (1921): 245–50.

54. *El Maestro* 3, no. 3 (1923): 185–86.

55. José Vasconcelos, *Discursos*, p. 32; *BU* 4, no. 1 (1920): 38.

elaborating upon the mission of the aristocracy of virtue, Pedro de Alba, a Caso student and member of the younger generation, wrote in *El Maestro* that the redemption of the masses involved support for material social reform.[56] What Gomez Morín had called a "vague and sentimental socialism" permeated the pages of *El Maestro* in articles by H. G. Wells, Henry George, and Tolstoy.[57] *El Maestro* also served as a mouthpiece for the Partido Agrarista, which took a more militant position on social change than did the majority of Mexico City educators, and it is probable that their articles had a radicalizing impact on rural teachers, for whom the magazine was in part intended. However, a strong tendency ran through the magazine to support the principle of structural reform while simultaneously attempting to restrain mass action and dull the edge of class conflict. The journal counseled workers in agitation to "reflect on the prudence of our middle class, to say nothing of the passivity of millions of *campesinos*."[58] To the *campesino* as well, *El Maestro* preached passivity. Stories by Tolstoy suggested that power, accumulation, and greed were evils. The simple work of the hands was virtue. Although Tolstoy claimed that it was immoral to eat the bread which others had labored to make without due compensation, he offered no retribution against the rich who did not work because he believed in nonviolence and the Christian ethic of turn-the-other-cheek.[59]

In certain aspects of the cultural nationalist program, the pacifying role of art became explicit. The notion of art as civilizing underlay the establishment of workers' cultural centers, which were modeled after the Universidad Popular. In the centers, musicians developed a theory of the pacifying role which music could play especially in the formation of bands, orchestras, and workers' choirs. In an article in the SEP bulletin, one educator stated that music had the disciplinary purpose of "calming . . . agitation."[60] While the process of bringing music to the workers was difficult because of the state of "disunion, apathy, and lack of sociability and discipline among them," it was necessary because cultural centers, which took people away from "slothfulness and vice," gave them honest recreation and corrected "rude struggles of violence, . . . the tendency for disorder, and the lack of

56. *El Maestro* 1, nos. 5 and 6 (1921): 535–39.

57. Enrique Krauze aptly chooses the phrase "socialismo de honradez," which he attributes to Vasconcelos: Krauze, *Los caudillos culturales*, p. 110.

58. *El Maestro* 1, no. 1 (1921): 100.

59. See *El Maestro* 1, no. 1 (1921): 41–53; 1, no. 2 (1921): 137–44; 1, no. 3 (1921): 257–62; 1, no. 4 (1921): 357–62.

60. *BSEP* 1, no. 3 (1922): 414.

respect in society." According to Aristotle and Shakespeare, the writer argued, a man without music was "liable to betrayals, deceit, and robbery." Music would awaken aspirations for the "eternal, the fatherland, the family, and the good."[61]

Music became important to the overall work of incorporation into a social hierarchy. Alba Herrera y Ogazón noted that it would halt the "growing invasion of ill-omened egotism" and the "separatism of groups" to establish "currents of sympathy in the collectivity."[62] Just as the concept of egotism had been used to criticize the rich and powerful, so had it become for many a euphemism for workers' demands for higher wages. She continued:

> The man or woman who cries when listening to an inspired verse or a deep melody has many probabilities, perhaps securities of escaping from delinquency and perversion. The work of social redemption purifies. It is much more effective than politicians' platforms and the illusory preachings of doctrinaire groups.[63]

Initially created for literacy training, the workers' centers taught skills in small industries and in their total program aimed at creating disciplined and docile workers. As José María Bonilla, former Porfirian pedagogue now working in the SEP, said, they would be transformed into "elements of production and cooperation."[64] This training involved athletics to further physical fitness and group discipline, hygiene to improve conditions in the home, and civics instruction to "awaken and ennoble civic and moral sentiments for the good exercise of rights and exact fulfillment of social obligations." As elsewhere, the program advised against labor agitation and encouraged the use of state arbitration in conflicts. In general, the centers were to teach workers how to "conserve joy in life by maintaining constant good humor and perseverance in work."[65] The university's extension department, headed by former Ateneista Pedro Henriquez Ureña, preached a similar ideology in courses given in night schools, union halls, and factories. It mixed skills training and basic science courses with a disciplining approach to workers reflected in discussions of the consequences of robbery; the positive values of work, hygiene, perseverance, gratitude, punctuality, and savings; the per-

61. Ibid., p. 415, 413.
62. *BSEP* 1, no. 1 (1922): 337–38.
63. Ibid., p. 339.
64. *BSEP* 2, no. 2 (1922): 368.
65. *BSEP* 1, no. 1 (1922): 150, 162, 164.

nicious influence of alcohol and tobacco; the importance of correct domestic organization and the influence of the home in children's education. Despite the fact the Henriquez Ureña was reportedly an advocate of Fabian socialism in this period, available lecture outlines for university extension courses indicate no politics aimed at improving the material conditions of the working class through self-actuation.[66]

Clearly, all aspects of the cultural program were not intended to discipline the poor. The music conservatory created a free night school where people from different social classes could learn guitar, other popular and classical instruments, and choral singing. As part of the artistic free-for-all which Vasconcelos encouraged, these courses seemed closer to the spirit of the plastic arts movement, freer of social control motives although characterized at first by a definite elitism. When Ramos Martínez inaugurated a new open-air painting school in Coyoacán in 1921, he still acted upon tenets of the Ateneo. Old theories and scholastical structure and stricture destroyed, he asked students to commune with the only source of truth—nature.[67] In 1921, this communion with nature also meant a communion with Mexican customs and daily life—especially the lyrical and picturesque. Upon his return from Paris in 1918, Roberto Montenegro also discovered the Mexican scene. Accompanying Vasconcelos on trips to the states, he and Jorge Enciso observed native potters and in September 1921 in the capital, Montenegro and Adolfo Best Maugard opened a show of their own Mexican folk art, which they had somewhat Europeanized. José Clemente Orozco recalled how quickly capital fashion became inundated with *rebozos, serapes,* and *huaraches* accompanied by painting of *charro* and *china* dancing the *jarabe.*[68] Adolfo Best Maugard introduced Aztec design motifs to art classes in Mexico City public schools. In the ex-Church of San Pedro and San Pablo, Montenegro, commissioned by Vasconcelos, executed the Revolution's first mural. His Dance of the Hours portrayed elegant ladies dancing around an armored knight leaning against a Persian tree of life, under which the artist incongruously inscribed a motto of Goethe: "Action is mightier than fate. Conquer!"[69] The gesture was, in fact, quite Rodó-esque. Although some Mexican content entered

66. On university extension program, see *BSEP* 1, no. 3 (1923): 294–303. On alleged socialism of Pedro Henriquez Ureña, see Krauze, *Los caudillos culturales,* p. 157.

67. See description by Charles Michel of the Escuela de Pintura in Coyoacán in *BSEP* 1, no. 4 (1923): 347–49.

68. Orozco, *Autobiography,* p. 82.

69. See Charlot, *The Mexican Mural Renaissance,* pp. 97–98.

the plastic arts, it was often bathed in European modes and styles, and compatible with the emphasis upon aesthetics. At most, it captured an unthreatening decorative and lyrical strain of cultural nationalism.

It was not Montenegro who produced the great art of the Mexican Revolution but the group of artists who in 1923 formed the Syndicate of Revolutionary Painters—Diego Rivera, José Clemente Orozco, David Alfaro Siqueiros, Jean Charlot, Ramon Alva de Canal, Fernando Leal, and others. While the three major muralists, Rivera, Orozco, and Siqueiros, had trained in the Mexican academy, much of their artistic and ideological development had taken place outside this milieu. José Clemente Orozco, heir of Posada, newspaper cartoonist, illustrator for *La Vanguardia*, had exhibited drawings of prostitutes in his first show in Mexico City in 1918. In 1919, he worked in a doll factory in New York City while trying to establish himself as an artist. A declared enemy of decorative folk nationalism, he sought an art which would address the emotional intensity of reality. Siqueiros, who left the trenches of Mexico to study in Paris, carried news of the Revolution to Diego Rivera, who was also in touch with Russian enthusiasts of socialist art.[70] At the time, Rivera was deeply immersed in Cubism which had restored construction to art as a corrective to the formlessness exalted by impressionism and expressionism. Both Rivera and Siqueiros felt the need not only to return to classical and academic art as a means of restoring structure, but also to recreate monumental art of historical content, akin to David's classical representations of the French Revolution and to the Roman, Byzantine, medieval, and Renaissance traditions of Italy, which they toured in the early 1920s.[71] Unashamed in their appreciation of the skills and knowledge of academic painters, intent upon an "objectification" of art as an antidote to the convolutions of impressionism and expressionism, they were also willing to face the future directly. Unlike so many Mexican intellectuals who, in their revulsion against modern society, sought refuge in spiritual utopias or dreams of artisan communes, Siqueiros and Rivera looked to contemporary technology, architecture, and engineering in creating their art.[72]

The turn toward a definitive Mexican content and toward the

70. MacKinley Helm, *Modern Mexican Painters* (Freeport: Books for Libraries Press, 1968), p. 40.
71. Charlot, *The Mexican Mural Renaissance*, p. 126; see also Tibol, *Arte mexicano*, p. 141.
72. Charlot, *The Mexican Mural Renaissance*, p. 73.

Revolution as a source of art came not from Paris, however, but from within Mexico. Recalled Fernando Leal who was painting scenes of a *Zapatista* camp at the open-air school in Coyoacán, "I was the first to paint a revolutionary theme to everybody's disgust . . . especially that of Ramos Martínez."[73] Although José Vasconcelos was no friend of *indigenismo*, he understood the importance of certain aspects of folk nationalism. When Rivera returned from Paris in 1921, Vasconcelos was reluctant to give him a wall to paint because of his immersion in Cubism, so he took him on a trip to Yucatán where Rivera witnessed not only the revolutionary politics of the Partido Socialista de Yucatán but also the Mayan temples of Chichen Itza.

Formed in 1923 when Siqueiros returned from Europe, the Syndicate of Revolutionary Painters in characteristic flamboyance declared war on "bourgeois individualism" and repudiated "easel painting and any other form of art emanating from ultra-intellectual and aristocratic circles." They would revive the collective guild tradition of the Middle Ages in their creation of a truly public art. Carrying the nationalist movement to its radical conclusions, they committed themselves to Mexican history and to the Revolution. They proposed the creation of a monumental art for and about the Mexican people which would capture "the moment of transition from a decrepit order to a new one." In contrast to the delicacy, lyricism, and nostalgia of the dominant movement, the muralists conceived of beauty "which would suggest struggle and arouse it." Rather than civilizing Mexico, they would seize upon her barbarism as their primary subject matter.[74] Rather than seeking to control the masses through art, they would express the people's aspirations.

The murals provoked a storm of outrage in Mexican intellectual circles. Although Rivera's first murals in the Escuela Nacional Preparatoria, completed in 1923, were not explicitly political, their portrayal of a nude and of unadorned indigenous people led the press to question spending public money on what was not art but bad taste.[75] Rivera was accused of corrupting art in his love for "ugliness." One intellectual declared, "I would rather sweep the streets than paint like that." The painters' syndicate, on the other hand, defended the new

---

73. Ibid., p. 166.

74. Helm, *Modern Mexican Painters*, p. 32; Tibol, *Arte mexicano*, pp. 147–50; Montsiváis, "Notas sobre la cultura mexicana," p. 354.

75. *El Demócrata*, 5 July 1923; *El Universal*, 10 March 1923; *BSEP* 1, no. 4 (1923): 371; Diego Rivera, "The Guild Spirit in Mexican Art," *Survey Graphic* 52, no. 3 (1924): 175–76.

art as "purely organic Mexicanism, free of unhealthy and fatal picturesqueness."[76]

Other artists began to paint the walls of the Preparatoria with pictures still more unpopular. In the allegorical representation of creation, David Alfaro Siqueiros chose an Indian woman, a worker, in red skirt and *rebozo* to symbolize tradition. When José Clemente Orozco began to reconstruct the Revolution in the agony and strength of a worker displaying the stumps of his arms mutilated in battle and in the anger of Christ burning his cross, the *gente decente* raged. Students slashed the frescoes with knives and sticks and covered them with graffiti; Catholic ladies railed against the new art. The press and intelligentsia thundered that Orozco's work was not art but propaganda. It was "degrading to Mexico, representative only of peons, Indians, laborers—the dregs of society." Where, they asked, were the beautiful and cultured people?[77] The writer Salvador Novo called the pictures repulsive and designed to awaken in the viewer not an aesthetic emotion but "an anarchistic fury if he is penniless or, if wealthy, to make his knees buckle with fright."[78] When the carpenters' union asked Ezequiel Chávez, then rector of the university, to stop the student vandalism, he replied that he doubted the murals were art and that the students were justified in protesting the attempt to "make their school ugly."[79] Artists and workers took matters into their own hands when one morning the sculptor Ignacio Asúnsolo entered the patio of the Preparatoria with a band of sixty stonecutters armed with machetes and knives. Asúnsolo opened fire shouting "Death to the students who resist beauty!"[80] The campaign escalated. The federation of Mexican students defended the destruction of the murals on principles of honor, dignity, education, and civilization. The press supported them: the students, the press claimed, were justly fed up with hearing day after day "Where is the beauty in these paintings which breed terror?"[81]

In his panels in the Secretaría de Educación Pública, Diego Rivera, who had joined the fledgling Communist party, took further steps in the direction of a more Mexican and political art. The panels began with an affirmation of pre-Columbian cultures and scenes from contemporary indigenous life. They reflected in part a recent trip he had

76. Bertram Wolfe, *Diego Rivera, His Life and Times* (New York: Knopf, 1939), p. 155.
77. Ibid., p. 223.
78. *El Universal*, 3 July 1924.
79. Ezequiel Chávez to SEP, 8 May 1924, AEC.
80. Orozco, *Autobiography*, p. 166.
81. *El Universal*, 26 June 1924; *Excelsior*, 10 July 1924.

taken to Tehuantepec. The elite shuddered at these renditions, as Indian civilization represented to them little more than bloodthirstiness and sacrifice. In the Court of Labor, Rivera painted the history of production in Mexico from its primitive beginnings to its industrial stage culminating in proletarian revolution—women weaving, dyeing, selling, men gathering bundles of cane, sugar refiners pouring molasses into huge vats, stirring them, churning the wheels of the mill. The exploitative organization of work emerged in the figures of armed overseers on tropical plantations and the weighing of peasants' grain by an armed *mayordomo*. In the iron foundry, a worker stirred a vat of molt while others propelled wheels and cylinders. Miners entered pits at the command of foreign foremen or relentlessly dug their picks into stone quarries. Here, Rivera inscribed a poem by Gutierrez Cruz urging miners to shape the metal they extracted into daggers and to seize the mines for themselves. The poem provoked a new storm of rage. Vasconcelos asked him to remove the poem. He did and painted in its place a portrait of peasant and worker embracing.

Not surprisingly, intellectual opinion was somewhat neutralized when foreign critics enthusiastically received the new art.[82] Rivera grew bolder. The Court of Fiestas celebrated the collective spiritual activities of the Mexicans: the Tehuana dance, the Yaqui deer dance, the corn harvest festivals, the Day of the Dead, the Christmas festival of Jalisco. The Revolution surged forth in the Court of Corridos in a chain of bullets weaving through a pyramid of advancing soldiers. Armed masses mocked the words of gentlemen reformers sitting on tomes of Spencer, Comte, and Mill. Foreign owners—Fords, Morgans, Rockefellers—gorged at a table beside a mechanized vault with a dollar sign in an electric lightbulb, symbolizing the sterility of a society in which technology was introduced for private gain rather than for social purposes. In the "twilight of the bourgeoisie," Rivera painted a rich man with a dollar sign on his coat emerging from a vault to be hit on the head by a worker's hammer. The people swept the garbage of luxury and the head of a priest from the street. Zapata and Felipe Carrillo Puerto were portrayed as martyred saints in long, white robes, flanked by women. These saints were not the traditional macabre figures of Mexican Catholicism and the women did not weep. Affirming the people's right to inherit the Revolution they made, women bore ears of rich corn, men harrowed the fields with modern tractors, commanded the oil wells and the steel mills. In the

82. Charlot, *The Mexican Mural Renaissance*, pp. 285–86.

celebration of May Day, battle-worn and battle-strengthened peasants and workers, their faces now individualized, carried the banner. "The true civilization will be the harmony of men with the land and of men among themselves."

Completed in 1928, Rivera's panels were hardly well-received. Alvaro Pruneda wrote in *El Universal* on his viewing of the murals:

> I did not want to suffer more. With bowed head I continued my climb but—oh, wonder!—on the last step I had to stop, attracted by an impression still more disagreeable: the self-portrait of the painter forms part of a group of workers and adopts the sad situation of an imbecile.[83]

Student defacement of the murals, Catholic protests, and intellectual hostility persisted. In 1929, the governor of Durango called for the removal of the murals. The locus of artistic opposition was the school of architecture: here, the students' work flowed more easily into the paradigm of President Calles in their designing of public buildings, tourist facilities, and middle-class and luxury private homes. These projects were linked with the lucrative building contracts of the rising class of Mexican entrepreneurs close to Calles. The architects claimed in 1930 that they would exercise no further direct action against the murals as the paintings were deteriorating because of the inadequacy of the encaustic process in which they were done.[84]

The development of mural painting must be understood within a dialectical process of ongoing revolution. Vasconcelos allowed the muralists to paint because of his hypersensitivity to art as a mark of civilization, his desire to promote Mexican artists, and his basic respect for individual creativity. Besides, the artists were of his own class and no matter how outrageous their behavior, they were part of the artistic milieu which Vasconcelos could tolerate within his own conception of a Mexican Renaissance. He did not like the content of the murals. He had anticipated that Diego Rivera would paint beautiful female figures representative of each state of Mexico in the SEP panels within the genre of lyrical folk nationalism.[85] At one point, he walked into the Ibero-American library in the SEP building where Emilio Amero was painting and told him to stop. He said he was tired of seeing so many Indians and wanted more important subjects like Homer's *Iliad*, or *Don Quixote*.[86] After Vasconcelos left office, he

83. *El Universal Ilustrado*, 5 March 1925.
84. Wolfe, *Diego Rivera*, p. 228.
85. José Vasconcelos, *Discursos*, p. 40.
86. Charlot, *The Mexican Mural Renaissance*, p. 271.

claimed that Rivera's panels had "degenerated into abjection of covering the walls with portraits of criminals."[87] But, in fact, Vasconcelos had been a vigorous defender of the muralists. Not coincidentally did the campaign against the Preparatoria murals come in the midst of his resignation from office. The SEP stopped the mural painting and fired all the artists with the exception of Rivera who went on to complete the SEP panels.[88] Several artists went off to Jalisco to paint under the protection of Governor Guadalupe Zuno. Siqueiros went on to organize miners. Orozco took a minor post in the SEP editorial department illustrating government publications. Rivera's privilege aroused the jealousy of other artists and criticism of his service to a bourgeois government.

The latter criticism had some validity. Rivera's murals in a sense provided the emerging Mexican state with illustrations of the kind of populism which flowed heavily from politicians' rhetoric. Most murals were strategically placed in government buildings, thus ostensibly reflecting a government ideology and in effect helping to provide one. Further, there was little systematic effort to educate the public about mural art and its meaning from the perspective of the artists in this period of the Revolution. It was not reproduced in texts in the 1920s. It was not discussed over the government radio station. It was not explained in SEP pamphlets or workers' cultural centers.

In conclusion, the cultural nationalist movement reflected the contradictions of the Mexican Revolution. With roots in nineteenth-century liberalism, Porfirian educational policy, and the Ateneo de la Juventud, a strong tendency in the movement advocated the use of art as a method of social control over the masses of people who were perceived by intellectuals to be in need of pacification and civilization. On the other hand, the mural artists embraced the popular Revolution and its aspirations and attempted to propel it forward in a period of ongoing political mobilization and class conflict, which both informed the murals and was reflected in them. In the 1930s as the Revolution moved briefly leftward, the mural movement achieved greater legitimacy just as the more conservative elements of the cultural nationalist movement in the 1920s were momentarily marginalized and forced to come to terms with a form of populism which endured. In the final analysis, within the context of Revolution as a whole, the cultural nationalist movement provided the national

---

87. Wolfe, *Diego Rivera*, p. 232.
88. Orozco was also kept on so that he could restore his murals which had been destroyed by students in the Preparatoria.

bourgeoisie with an ideology affirmative of Mexico and the Mexican which was both an impetus and channel for their own self-expression and self-actuation as well as a mechanism of social control over the working class and peasantry. However, because the working class and peasantry were principal actors in the struggle, they not only affirmatively entered the official cultural ideology of the Mexican Revolution, as the murals demonstrate, they also gained in consciousness and integration from the articulation of this ideology.

Chapter 9
Conclusion

In the *Porfiriato*, educators understood the importance of public schooling to political stability and economic growth and were more concerned with these factors than they were with education's promotion of democracy, social mobility, or individual betterment. The failure to develop fully a primary school system was not a question of the dictatorship's negligence or malevolence. Obstacles to the development of mass schooling related to the dependent, transitional character of the Mexican economy and to the incipiency of the capital accumulation process. The latter, within a context of neocolonialism which determined a considerable export of capital, meant that public funds for development were scarce. Primary education was not a spending priority because in the transitional economy in which precapitalist modes of production persisted, not all entrepreneurs and politicians agreed on its importance. Despite occasional expressions of cynicism about the indigenous peoples being irredeemable, among the most articulate proponents of public schooling were the positivists, who were modernizers. The positivists functioned not only within a capitalist paradigm, they accepted in varying degrees a dependent capitalist model. In Europe and North America in the nineteenth century public schooling was considered, in part, a means of disciplining the working class. In Mexico this view was expanded to include also a desire to transform the behavior of an entire society judged to be backward by policy-makers whose dependent mentality expressed itself in adulation of European civilization, contempt for Mexico, and anxiety about societal transformation. To these preoccupations must be added an obsession with instilling political order after decades of anarchy. These concerns reinforced the authoritarianism and rigidity inherent in the dominant European pedagogy and curriculum which educators adapted to Mexico.

Porfirian educational policy promoted uneven development in the school system mirroring uneven development in the economy. Despite the centralizing tendency of the state, the latter provided no financial aid to the states for education. The federal government spent more money per capita on schools than did the states. The capital had the best primary schools, highest enrollments, and best-developed system of post-primary schooling. Those regions experiencing economic growth could afford to expand public school systems more readily than those with lower growth rates. Further, the primary school system developed best in the northern states where capitalist modes of production were dominant; these state governments had progressive school policies. Even in the north, the Porfirian school system tended to reflect uneven development between urban commercial centers and rural areas. Rural schools, where they existed, had reduced programs, inferior equipment, and untrained teachers who were poorly paid.

The incipient bureaucratization of public schooling gave rise to contradictions. The process of centralization involved only informal central control over state school bureaucracies. State governments absorbed control over schools from municipalities and introduced skeletal inspection systems to monitor teachers and programs. While the teaching profession grew more rapidly than any other in the *Porfiriato*, primary teachers were not well enough trained, remunerated, or controlled to perform as loyal civil servants. The situation encouraged absenteeism and apathy on the one hand, and political insubordination on the other as teachers used their classrooms to organize against the dictatorship within the context of a growing opposition movement in the first decade of the century.

Although policy-makers wished to reach the urban and rural working class, schools were nonexistent in many rural areas, and in both rural and urban situations, the increased rate of exploitation accompanying growth intensified the use of child labor. Those who benefited most from the schools were probably the middle strata, made up of people associated with precapitalist modes of production (artisans and small merchants) and administrative, technical, and professional personnel linked with the growth of the state and modern economy. The school system was a hierarchical one corresponding to the transitional nature of the economy and the financial limitations of the budget within the context of incipient, dependent growth. Few people could afford to pursue education beyond primary school, nor were they supposed to do so. The school system tended to reinforce existing class relations while offering some mobility to the middle strata.

In the Mexican Revolution of 1910, different social classes protested the oppressive conditions affecting them. The struggle was early brought under control of leadership of middle-sector origin. In retrospect, it is clear that the Revolution operated consistently within a capitalist framework: it aimed at eliminating precapitalist obstacles to modernization such as debt peonage, inefficient landed estates, ideological domination by the Church; it sought more national control over the economy, especially in the export sector; it was committed to social reform in order to neutralize mobilized workers and peasants while at the same time using them to force changes upon the old owning class, including its foreign component and the Catholic Church. Although the Revolution took place within a capitalist framework, there was a variety of political opinion among middle-sector revolutionaries ranging from conservative to radical. Much of their thinking was a response to the mobilization of masses of oppressed people in defense of their basic needs. The Revolution's strong commitment to public education reflected, on the one hand, the demand of the Mexican masses, and, on the other, the desire of middle-sector leadership for swift economic growth, modernization, and political domination.

In this study, three illustrations of middle-sector educational thought and practice in the years of struggle (1910–1920) were chosen to demonstrate the interplay between the popular forces and middle-sector revolutionaries in the evolution of an ideology of schooling: the classically liberal, the developmentalist, and the quasi-socialist approaches to schooling. The classically liberal and developmentalist approaches supported education for increased productivity, individual well-being, and the practice of democracy within a capitalist framework. Both were willing to acknowledge the need for some structural reform benefitting labor and the peasantry. Contradictions in educational thought revolved around notions of private property and social order. While most middle-sector educators envisioned a society based upon small property, they often overlooked the fact that competition would lead to a reconcentration of wealth. Most acknowledged the need for large-scale private industry and the subordination of labor to capital. The latter potentially limited the educators' hope that schooling would increase material well-being for all in an equitable manner. This problem was aggravated by the country's low level of capital accumulation and persistent economic dependency, which educators understood inadequately. Many educators further recognized the need for social control over the insurgent peasantry and working class and so contradicted their own commitment to democracy in their implicit and often explicit support for a strong state capable of controlling the masses and establishing social order. In a variety of ways, support for renewed authoritarianism was to make its way into school policies, programs, and methods after 1920. An alternative approach to education from a populist, quasi-socialist perspective was put forward between 1918 and 1924 by the Partido Socialista de Yucatán, which sought to utilize state power for the explicit benefit of workers and peasants and put forward a pedagogy designed to encourage class consciousness and militancy in an ongoing struggle for structural reforms. This educational experiment anticipated the Mexican socialist school of the 1930s.

Each of these political positions was represented at the Constitutional Congress in Querétaro in 1916–1917 where debates on education focused almost entirely upon the role of the Church, whose influence in schooling many delegates wished to eliminate. In defense of principles of federalism and the free municipality, the Constitution dismantled the Secretaría de Instrucción Pública and returned responsibility for schooling to states and municipalities. In view of the modernizing thrust of the Revolution and the broad mandate for public education, most politicians came to recognize the incorrectness of this move and supported the creation of a new federal ministry with national jurisdiction in 1921.

In the 1920s under the presidencies of Obregón and Calles, the Mexican revolutionary state began to take shape: a strong developmentalist state which would promote nationally-controlled economic growth while providing social reform. The state sought to control the subordinate classes through the formation and/or co-optation of their organizations and the creation of government bureaucracies in labor, agriculture, education, and health. However, the state operated in a context of weakness vis-à-vis internal and external forces. In 1920, power was more effectively lodged in the states. Although the central government gained considerable control over the regions in the course of the decade, this control was incomplete and was wrested at some expense to the treasury in the suppression of military rebellions.

The persistence of the dependent export economy further constrained Mexican development. Its bourgeoisie dislodged by the Revolution and alienated from it, the Mexican state looked to foreign capital for assistance. The price demanded by foreign capital—notably the United States—was repayment of the Mexican foreign debt, which limited the domestic options of the revolutionary government, and Mexico's agreement not to implement clauses of the 1917 Constitution prejudicing foreign holdings. The latter concession made by Obregón in 1923 compromised the revolutionary commitment to national autonomy.

The restrictions placed upon the revolutionary project by dependency became more apparent under Calles. Initially, he took an aggressive position against foreign domination and in favor of worker and agrarian reform. However, depression in the world oil and silver markets in 1926 as well as growing hostility from U.S. oil producers and the State Department caused him to abandon nationalism and social reform. In 1927, the United States sent Dwight Morrow to Mexico as ambassador. Calles' mentor in most areas of policy, Morrow advised a reduction in social expenditures. External factors alone did not determine the abandonment of nationalist and reform goals. The government's rapprochement with the Porfirian owning class and the growth of a neocapitalist class among the revolutionaries influenced the direction of policy. Because in the 1920s the central government had not secured full control over the regions, the working class, or the peasantry, popular forces mobilized as the government's commitment to reform ebbed.

The Secretaría de Educación Pública, created in 1921, had a centralizing capacity greater than that of its predecessor. Through contracts with state governments, the federal government built and controlled schools in the states, especially in rural areas. In retrospect, schooling as a state function appears to have been designed to establish order, further national integration, and increase productivity. In relation to the latter, Dewey's techniques were adopted in 1923 in the pedagogy of learning by doing. Major priorities were the expansion of primary education, intensification of teacher training, increase in technical schooling, and orientation of university education toward the applied sciences and social sciences. As the federal government extended aid and control over schools in the states, it altered the Porfirian tendency for primary school expansion to reflect increased state income: the majority of federal primary schools in the states in the 1920s were rural and were located in central and southern Mexico. However, due to limited federal funds, the discrepancies of the *Porfiriato* remained. Financial responsibility for rural schools rested with the villages themselves. Teachers wages' remained low. Their training was highly inadequate especially in relation to their task of improving local economic conditions. Education beyond the primary level continued to be biased in favor of urban centers and especially the capital. Technical training for modern industry was almost exclusively confined to Mexico City. Public education beyond the primary level required the payment of fees and tuition.

A centralizing tendency was discernible in primary education as federal schools and enrollments increased at a faster rate than those of the states and municipalities. The federal government introduced mechanisms of bureaucratic control over personnel in the states. However, given the instability of the state, its meager resources, and the enduring strength of the regions, the SEP created a structure for bureaucracy rather than the effective functioning of the same. Teachers and inspectors enjoyed considerable liberty. In a situation of continuing class conflict, teachers became a political force, organizing into unions, pressing for social reforms for their constituents, or resisting reforms of any sort.

Ideologically, the SEP reflected diverse middle-sector approaches to education within a context of class conflict. Upper level personnel in the Secretaría de Educación Pública who were engaged in urban primary and technical education, the cultural program, the writing of texts and definition of rural pedagogy, tended to be former Porfirian bureaucrats or urban intellectuals who identified little or not at all with the popular revolution. In contrast, rural education at the base and middle levels of the bureaucracy attracted the innovative and reform-minded. Urban educators viewed the school as a means of economic betterment but were less committed to and/or in agreement with the need for structural reforms which would correct unequal resource distribution. Many stressed the disciplining aspects of education and were alarmed by working class agitation. School text writers often articulated Porfirian values of obedience, docility, and respect for social hierarchy, while expressing negative views or at best tentative support for the social reform goals of the Revolution. Many leaders in the cultural nationalist movement wished to use art to calm class agitation. Many reacted with disgust to the portrayal in mural art of indigenous culture and popular protest.

Because top policy-makers tended to see the causes of rural poverty in human character rather in than socioeconomic and political structure and because they were often ignorant of rural conditions, they underestimated the need for structural reforms in the countryside. Although educators often stated that they wished to create a nation of small-holders, they underestimated the need for supportive mechanisms of credit, technical assistance, and marketing institutions to sustain what was in fact a disappearing mode of production. Neither were these mechanisms forthcoming on an effective scale from other government ministries. Many rural teachers recognized the contradictions in policy and used the school to organize communities for structural change—often to the dismay of the SEP hierarchy.

Perhaps because of the organizational hegemony of CROM which increasingly supported class conciliation and the development of privately-owned national industry, there was less opposition to SEP vocational education policy. Although an ambivalence persisted here also as to whether training should focus upon small- or large-scale production, the trend was toward supplying national and foreign entrepreneurs with personnel. While offering mobility to some, vocational education duplicated a process of increasing hierarchization in the division of labor within production. Although CROM spokesmen claimed vocational training would capacitate workers for eventual control over the means of production, actual program content suggested a strengthening of relations of hierarchy and subordination.

Mexican vocational education also encouraged a sexual division of labor. Training for skilled work in industry was limited to men. Except for clerical training, women's vocational education aimed at removing them from factories and returning them to domestic craft production. Although educators' motives were benign, women's vocational training probably contributed to the marginalization of women as wage-earners and seems to have been designed to strengthen the nuclear family model in the working class as a means of producing a healthy and disciplined labor force. While the family unit was theoretically to absorb the costs of the reproduction of labor power, its authoritarian structure mirrored and thus implicitly helped to legitimize a similar structure in the larger society. The attempt to strengthen the private family unit and women's traditional role in the home coincided with the state's increasing absorption of family functions such as socialization, health, and protection, which suggested a curtailment of the family's role as a source of authority, ideas, and independent thought and action. The process of subordination of family to state carried with it a potential for reinforcing a sense of inferiority and inadequacy in economically deprived sectors of society who were told by the state to alter their behavior in order to meet society's standards. However, this process was far from complete in the 1930s owing to the level of economic growth, the limits of state power and expenditures, and the strength of competing ideologies.

In 1928, the assassination of president-elect Obregón by a clerical fanatic produced a crisis in the transfer of power to which Calles responded by forming the Partido Nacional Revolucionario, which brought together major military and civilian power-holders and interest groups under the leadership of civilian representatives of the state. Although the creation of the party signified a further consolidation of state authority, Calles used it between 1928 and 1934 as a personal instrument through which he chose presidents whom he controlled.[1] These regimes were characterized by a further deterio-

---

1. Tzvi Medin, *Ideología y praxis política de Lázaro Cárdenas* (Mexico: Siglo Veintiuno Editores, SA, 1974), pp. 20–25.

ration of reform policy and falling away of the mass base. No longer favored by the government, the CROM fell into disrepute and separate, more militant rank and file groups emerged. *Campesinos* had become ideologically sophisticated and organizationally quite independent of the central government, although an important sector of their leadership after 1930 belonged to the radical wing of the PNR. The strength of this wing within the PNR grew as the Depression hit Mexico and grass-roots mobilization surged in the form of land invasions, hunger marches, and worker strikes.

It was this situation which brought Lázaro Cárdenas to the presidency in 1934. A sincere social reformer as well as a loyal and accomplished general, Cárdenas initiated the most radical phase of the Revolution. An extensive land reform was carried out; workers' militancy was encouraged; foreign policy was more vigorously anti-imperialist than it had been in the past. Although impressed by collective production in the Soviet Union, Cárdenas was not a socialist. He appears to have envisioned a highly interventionist state simultaneously promoting growth and justice—a vision understandable given the worldwide crisis of capitalism which had given the rise to experiments in state intervention.[2] He promoted the organizational unification of workers into the Confederación de Trabajadores de Mexico (CTM) and of peasants into the Confederación Nacional Campesina (CNC) as a means of carrying out reforms and providing these sectors with the strength to bargain with ownership over time. But, like his predecessors, he sought state control over these organizations. He was not opposed to foreign capital, although he wished to subject it to state regulation. Nor was Cárdenas averse to foreign investment in the manufacturing sector, provided Mexican laws were respected.[3] The targets of Cárdenas' reforms were precapitalist enclaves, especially in agriculture, and the foreign-dominated export sector. The expropriation of oil in 1938 climaxed his presidency.

Under Cárdenas, socialist education was introduced to Mexico. Analysis of this experience is beyond the scope of the present study. It is clear that the roots of the socialist school lay in the dynamics of education from 1910 onward. Not surprisingly, teachers formed an important part of the national reform movement. The linkage between the rural school and structural reform in the 1930s has been

2. Nora Hamilton, "The Mexican State: Cárdenas and State Autonomy" (Ph.D. diss., University of Wisconsin, 1978), III-14, 15, 21; Anatoli Shulgovski, *México en la encrucijade de su historia* (Mexico: Ediciones de Cultura Popular, SA, 1968), p. 84.

3. Hamilton, III-16.

well documented by recent scholarship.[4] As workers and peasants mobilized and the state responded, significant changes took place in Mexican education, some of which endured. It was in this period rather than in the 1920s that the ideology of the Mexican Revolution took root in schooling. The heroism of Emiliano Zapata, the social reform goals, the affirmation of indigenous culture, the worker and peasant as agents of Mexican history and development, nationalism and anti-imperialism as part of revolutionary ideology are legacies of the socialist school of the 1930s.[5] However, the Cárdenas government deepened the centralization and bureaucratization process in Mexican schooling which, along with other measures of co-optation and repression, contributed to the political domestication of education after 1940.

In conclusion, public education is a function of the modern state which filters out a labor force and acts as a mechanism of social control. The Mexican case suggests that effective implementation of the social control function of education may depend upon the development of the bureaucracy and the level of political mobilization in the society. The study also suggests that the economic base of society determines the nature of the school system; it determines what is required from the school system. It limits or advances the possibilities for social mobility through education. School systems in capitalist societies tend to reflect the class structure. This phenomenon may be particularly true of school systems in dependent capitalist societies. Finally, while this study has stressed the continuity between the Porfirian and post-revolutionary states, it also confirms that there was a social revolution in Mexico. Schooling and pedagogy were deeply affected by political mobilization and the conflicting interests and demands of different social classes in the Mexican Revolution.

4. The practice of socialist education is best captured by David Raby in his study of rural schoolteachers in the 1930s, *La educación y la revolución social en México 1921–1940*.

5. See, for example, Raby, *La educación*; Shulgovski, *México en la encrucijada de su historia*, pp. 146–64; A. Bremauntz, *La educación socialista en México* (Mexico: n.p., 1943); Arnaldo Córdova, "Los maestros rurales en el cardenismo," *Cuadernos Políticos* 2 (1974): 77–92. For texts, see, for example, SEP, Comisón Editora Popular, *Escuelas primarias urbanas. Lectura oral. Primer año; Segundo año* (Mexico: SEP, 1938); G. Lucio, *Simiente. Libro primero para las escuelas rurales; Libro segundo; Libro tercero* (Mexico: SEP, Comisión Editora Popular, 1935); Luis Chávez Orozco, *Historia patria. Tercer año*, 8th ed. (Mexico: Editorial Patria, SA, 1949); Rafael Ramos Pedrueza, *Sugerencías revolucionarias para la enseñanza de la historia* (Mexico: Universidad Nacional Autónoma de México, 1932).

Appendix

TABLE A.1

Combined State and Municipal Revenue, 1888–1906 (Mexican Pesos)

State	1888	1900	1906
Aguascalientes	143,259	225,819	486,282
Campeche	275,424	454,815	627,948
Chiapas	170,126 [a]	697,826	1,008,329
Chihuahua	642,251	1,760,039	2,649,921
Coahuila	502,562	1,010,715	2,270,802
Colima	151,509	198,527	328,075
Durango	272,643 [b]	1,063,131 [b]	1,103,988 [b]
Guanajuato	1,562,241	1,991,558	2,165,809
Guerrero	519,450	572,321	697,874
Hidalgo	1,020,846	1,605,521	1,445,491
Jalisco	1,261,742 [a]	2,268,946	3,019,644
México	986,399	1,612,891	2,854,067
Michoacán	962,027	1,435,185	1,522,931
Morelos	451,448	570,795	701,543
Nuevo León	339,017	962,824	1,171,143
Oaxaca	616,788 [c]	1,360,802	1,616,028
Puebla	1,780,554 [a]	2,062,951	3,929,203
Querétaro	295,298 [a]	461,838	590,605
San Luis Potosí	1,429,466	1,271,490	1,550,803
Sinaloa	894,051	1,291,709	1,465,110
Sonora	537,311	1,034,368	1,650,455
Tabasco	366,462	668,083	958,231
Tamaulipas	252,705 [a]	790,872	1,359,211
Tlaxcala	165,668	291,626	377,872
Veracruz	2,909,419	3,817,040	4,396,092
Yucatán	682,207	1,874,746	3,772,206
Zacatecas	1,153,197	1,844,552	1,815,448

Notes:

(a) Municipal revenue figure not available and therefore estimated by averaging the proportion of state to municipal revenue for the years 1888–1894.

(b) Municipal figures for Durango are not available for any years.

(c) State revenue figure not available and estimated by averaging the proportion of state to municipal revenue for the years 1888–1894.

Sources: *Anuario estadístico*, 1897, 1907.

TABLE A.2

Federal Rural School Effort, 1923

	Mission-aries	Rural Teachers	Rural Schools	Enroll-ment
Aguascalientes	—	—	—	—
Campeche	1	2	2	115
Chiapas	7	32	30	1,530
Chihuahua	2	15	15	840
Coahuila	0	9	9	630
Colima	1	8	8	448
Durango	6	2	2	180
Guanajuato	3	11	10	610
Guerrero	5	30	30	2,160
Hidalgo	5	50	50	3,050
Jalisco	3	22	21	714
México	7	54	54	2,268
Michoacán	9	30	30	2,970
Morelos	2	13	12	744
Nuevo León	1	10	10	480
Oaxaca	9	72	72	5,400
Puebla	10	63	63	4,664
Querétaro	2	15	15	510
San Luis Potosí	5	21	20	1,580
Sinaloa	1	13	13	719
Sonora	4	16	16	832
Tabasco	1	3	3	239
Tamaulipas	1	14	14	913
Tlaxcala	1	4	4	240
Veracruz	8	37	37	1,480
Yucatán	—	—	—	—
Zacatecas	4	13	13	546

Note: Table does not include statistics for former territories of Baja California, Quintana Roo, or Tepic.

Source: *Boletín de la Secretaría de Educación Pública* 1, no. 4 (1923).

TABLE A.3
Federal Schools in the States, 1925–1928

	Rural 1925	Primary 1928	Urban 1925	Primary 1928	Normal 1925	Normal 1928	Professional 1925	Professional 1928	Technical 1925	Technical 1928
Aguascalientes	27	26	3	6					1	1
Campeche	28	42	32	16						1
Chiapas	77	151	21	20						
Chihuahua	51	161	3	6						
Coahuila	27	55	9	8						
Colima	36	26	18	8						
Durango	19	58	4	4				1		
Guanajuato	99	162	13	13				1	5	1
Guerrero	80	182	7	12		1				
Hidalgo	88	195	9	13		1		1	1	1
Jalisco	121	129	4	2					1	1
México	177	316	17	—				2	1	—
Michoacán	118	175	9	13	3	1		1		
Morelos	31	57	14	12		1				
Nuevo León	81	140	35	21						
Oaxaca	98	157	4	16		1				
Puebla	125	214	12	14	1	1				3
Querétaro	33	60	11	12		1				
San Luis Potosí	109	201	17	14					1	—
Sinaloa	48	75	6	5				1	1	1
Sonora	30	92	1	2					2	2
Tabasco		45		4						
Tamaulipas	1	63	5	4						
Tlaxcala	34	55	8	6		1				
Veracruz	44	175	1	3				1	1	1
Yucatán		3								
Zacatecas	96	134	7	6						

Note: Table does not include statistics for former territories of Baja California, Quintana Roo, and Tepic.
Source: *Anuario estadístico*, 1930.

TABLE A.4

Frequency of Reference to Virtues and Vices in Delgadillo's Adelante

Virtues			Vices			Total
Work and Study			*Ignorance and Laziness*			
Inteligencia	4		Ignorancia	2		
Talento	1		Tontería	1		
Trabajo	9		Pereza	1		
Aplicación	6		Torpeza	2	6	
Ahinco	1					
Estudio	7					
Amor a la escuela	1					
Laboriosidad	2					
Constancia	4					
Voluntad	1					
Paciencia	4					
Resolución	1					
Destreza	1					
Exactitud	1	43				49
Order and Cleanliness			*Disorder and Dirtiness*			
Arreglo	1		Descuido	2		
Aseo	3		Desaseo	3	5	
Robustez	1					
Salud	2	7				12
Obedience and Respect			*Disobedience, Disrespect*			
Obediencia	6		Discólo	3		
Respeto a los padres	10		Travieso	3		
Respeto a los otros	1		Disobediencia	4		
Docilidad	1		Caprichoso	1		
Silencia	1		Ingratitud	1	12	
Paciencia	4	23				35
Charity			*Egoism, Avarice, Anger*			
Caridad	10		Maltrato a los otros	4		
Bondad	8		Maltrato a los animales	5		
Tolerancia	2		Envidia	6		
Complacencia	1		Egoísmo	1		
Abnegación	3		Avaricia	3		
Perdon sin rencor	1		Rencor	1		
Amabilidad	1		Vanidad	4		
Dulzura	1	27	Venganza	2		
			Cólera	2		

TABLE A.4 (cont.)

Frequency of Reference to Virtues and Vices in Delgadillo's Adelante

Virtues			Vices			Total
			Orgullo	1		
			Crueldad	1	30	57
Patriotism			*Bad Mexican*			
Patriotismo	5		Mal Mexicano	1	1	6
Truthfulness			*Falsity*			
Sinceridad	1		Mentir	3		
Decir la verdad	1		Falsedad	1		
Cumplir promesa	1	3	Embustero	1		
			Tramposo	1		
			No cumplir con las promesas	1		
			No cumplir con el deber	1	8	11
Other						
Juicioso	3		Pasión	1		
Justicia	2		Glotón	1		
Amor al terruño	1	6	Blasfemía	1		
			Robar	1	4	10

Bibliography

Archives

Archivo don Ezequiel Chávez. Universidad Nacional Autónoma de México.
Archivos de Francisco I. Madero. Instituto Nacional de Antropología.
Archivo General de la Nación. Acervos Presidentes, Ramo Presidentes Obregón-
  Calles.
Archivo General de la Nación. Fondo de la Secretaría de Instrucción Pública y
  Bellas Artes.
Archivos de la Secretaría de Educación Pública.

Mexican Government Publications

Congreso de los Estados Unidos Mexicanos. *Iniciativa de ley sobre educación
  integral rudimentaria, presentada por la diputación del estado de Oaxaca.*
  Mexico, 1912.
Congreso de los Estados Unidos Mexicanos. Cámara de Diputados. *Diario de
  los debates del Congreso Constituyente.* 2 vols. Mexico, 1922.
Crónica y debates de las sesiones de la soberana convención revolucionaria. 3 vols.
  Mexico: Talleres Gráficos de la Nación, 1964–1965.
Departamento de Aprovisionamientos Generales. Fernando González Roa.
  El aspecto agrario de la Revolución. Mexico, 1919.
Departamento de Aprovisionamientos Generales. Alberto Pani. *On the Road
  to Democracy.* Translated by J. Palomo Rincón. Mexico, 1918.
Dirección General de Educación Pública. *Informe rendido al C. Venustiano Car-
  ranza, Primer Jefe del Ejercito Constitucional encargado del Poder Ejecutivo,
  por el Prof. Andrés Osuna, Director General de Educación Pública, referente
  a los labores del año escolar de 1916.* Mexico: Departamento Editorial de
  la Dirección General de Educación Pública, 1917.
Dirección General de Estadísticas. *Anuario estadístico de la república mexicana.*
  Mexico: 1893, 1900, 1906, 1907.
Departamento de Estadística Nacional. *Anuario estadístico.* Mexico: Talleres
  Gráficos de la Secretaría de Agricultura y Fomento, 1930.
Departamento Universitario y de Bellas Artes. *Boletín de la Universidad.*
  Mexico, 1919–1920.
Ley sobre la instrucción primaria en el Distrito Federal y territorios federales. Mexico:
  Imprenta del Gobierno Federal en el ex-Arzobispado, 1888.
Quiroz Martínez, M. *La educación pública en el estado de Sonora.* Mexico: Tall-
  eres Gráficos de la Nación, 1920.
Secretaría de Agricultura y Fomento. Manuel Gamio. *Programa de la Dirección
  de Estudios Arqueológicos y Etnográficos.* Mexico, 1918.
Secretaría de Economía. Dirección General Estadística. Moisés González Na-

varro et al. *Estadísticas sociales del Porfiriato, 1877–1910.* Mexico. 1956.
Secretaría de Educación Pública. Antonio Mediz Bolío. *Salvador Alvarado.* Mexico, 1968.
Secretaría de Educación Pública. *Apuntes sobre algunos temas de geografía e historia de México y los Estados Unidos; sugestiones de clase para uso de los maestros en relación con los proyectos de amistad infantil internacional.* Publicaciones de la Secretaría de Educación Pública, 19, no. 10 (1928).
Secretaría de Educación Pública. *Bases para la organización de la escuela primaria conforme al principio de la acción.* Publicaciones de la Secretaría de Educación Pública 1, no. 8 (1925).
Secretaría de Educación Pública. *Boletín de la Secretaría de Educación Pública.* 1921–1930.
Secretaria de Educación Pública. Rafael Ramírez. *Campaña pro-cálculo en las escuelas rurales. Consejos metodológicos.* Mexico, 1928.
Secretaría de Educación Pública. *La Casa del Estudiante Indígena. 16 meses de labor en un experimento psicológico colectivo con indios. Febrero de 1926 a junio de 1927.* Mexico, 1927.
Secretaría de Educación Pública. Katherine M. Cook. *La Case del Pueblo, un relato de las escuelas nuevas de acción de México.* Mexico, 1933.
Secretaría de Educación Pública. *Cinco años de labor educativa del gobierno de México.* Mexico, 1929.
Secretaría de Educación Pública. Francisco Manuel Alvarez. *Consideraciones y datos sobre la enseñanza técnica en México y en el extranjero.* Mexico, 1920.
Secretaría de Educación Pública. *Contribución al V. Congreso Panamericano del Niño en la Habana, Cuba, 1927.* Publicaciones de la Secretaría de Educación Pública 21, no. 17 (1929).
Secretaría de Educación Pública. Charles Gide. *La cooperación y la educación primaria.* Mexico, 1929.
Secretaría de Educación Pública. Jumberto Tejara. *Crónica de la escuela rural mexicana.* Mexico, 1963.
Secretaría de Educación Pública. Ezequiel Padilla. *La cruzada de los maestros misioneros.* Publicaciones de la Secretaría de Educación Pública 20, no. 5 (1929).
Secretaría de Educación Pública. José Manuel Puig Casauranc. *La cuestión religioso en relación con la educación pública en México.* Mexico, 1928.
Secretaría de Educación Pública. *Edificios construidos por la Secretaría de Educación Pública en los años de 1921 a 1924.* Mexico, 1924.
Secretaría de Educación Pública. *La educación pública en México.* Mexico, 1922.
Secretaría de Educación Pública. *La educación pública en México a través de los mensajes presidenciales desde la consumación de la independencia hasta nuestros días.* Prólogo de J. M. Puig Casauranc. Mexico, 1926.
Secretaría de Educación Pública. Max Miñano García. *La educación rural en México.* Mexico, 1945.
Secretaría de Educación Pública. Moisés Sáenz. *La educación rural en México.*

Publicaciones de la Secretaría de Educación Pública 19, no. 20 (1928).
Secretaría de Educación Pública. *Educación rural y programa de la escuela rural. Cómo son y porqué son así nuestras escuelas rurales. Plática del Dr. J. M. Puig Casauranc, Secretario de Educación Pública a los miembros de las misiones culturales, del 25 de febrero de 1927.* Publicaciones de la Secretaría de Educación Pública 17, no. 5 (1928).
Secretaría de Educación Pública. Rafael Ramírez. *La escuela de la acción dentro de la enseñanza rural.* Mexico, 1942.
Secretaría de Educación Pública. *La escuela de comercio.* Mexico, 1926.
Secretaría de Educación Pública. *La escuela industrial Gabriela Mistral.* Mexico, 1926.
Secretaría de Educación Pública. Gregorio Torres Quintero. *La escuela por la acción y el método de proyectos.* Publicaciones de la Secretaría de Educación Pública 6, no. 18 (1925).
Secretaría de Educación Pública. *La escuela rural.* Vols. 5, 6. Mexico, 1926.
Secretaría de Educación Pública. *Las escuelas al aire libre en México.* Mexico, 1927.
Secretaría de Educación Pública. *Escuelas federales en la sierra de Puebla; informe sobre la visita a las escuelas federales en la sierra de Puebla realizado por el C. Subsecretario de Educación Prof. Moisés Sáenz.* Publicaciones de la Secretaría de Educación Pública 15, no. 5 (1927).
Secretaría de Educación Pública. *El esfuerzo educativo en México, 1924–1928.* 2 vols. Mexico, 1928.
Secretaría de Educación Pública. Rubén Campos. *El folklore y la música mexicana; investigaciones de la cultura musical en México, 1525–1925.* Mexico, 1928.
Secretaría de Educación Pública. Rafael Ramírez. *Formación y capacidad de los maestros rurales para hacer eficaz la acción de la escuela en los pueblos indígenas.* Mexico, 1935.
Secretaría de Educación Pública. Ignacio Ramírez López. *Genésis de la escuela rural mexicana.* Mexico, 1947.
Secretaría de Educación Pública. *Informe del C. Presidente de la República al ramo de la educación pública, septiembre de 1928.* Publicaciones de la Secretaría de Educación Pública 18, no. 19 (1928).
Secretaría de Educación Pública. Moisés Sáenz. *Escuelas federales en San Luis Potosí. Informe de la visita practicada por el Subsecretario de Educación Pública en noviembre de 1927.* Publicaciones de la Secretaría de Educación Pública 18, no. 6 (1928); also published in *Boletín de la Secretaría de Educación Pública* 7, no. 2 (1928).
Secretaría de Educación Pública. Gabriela Mistral. *Lecturas para mujeres.* Mexico, 1923.
Secretaría de Educación Pública. *El libro y el pueblo.* Mexico, 1923–1928.
Secretaría de Educación Pública. *El maestro.* Mexico, 1921–1924.
Secretaría de Educación Pública. *Memoria del Segundo Congreso del Niño.* Pub-

licaciones de la Secretaría de Educación Pública 2, no. 1 (1925).

Secretaría de Educación Pública. *Memoria que indica el estado que guarda el ramo de educacion al 31 de agosto de 1925 para conocimiento del G. H. Congreso de la Union.* Mexico, 1925.

Secretaría de Educación Pública. *Memoria que indica el estado que guarda el ramo de educación pública el 31 de agosto de 1926.* Mexico, 1926.

Secretaría de Educación Pública. *Memoria que indica el estado que guarda el ramo de educación pública el 31 de agosto de 1927.* Mexico, 1927.

Secretaría de Educación Pública. *Memoria de los trabajos realizados en la Junta de Directores de Educación Federal, verificada en la ciudad de México del 24 de mayo al dos de junio de 1926.* Mexico: Talleres Gráficos de la Nación, 1926.

Secretaría de Educación Pública. *Las misiones culturales en 1927. Las escuelas normales rurales.* Mexico. 1928.

Secretaría de Educación Pública. *Las misiones culturales, 1932–1933.* Mexico, 1933.

Secretaría de Educación Pública. *Monografía de las escuelas de pintura al aire libre.* Mexico, 1926.

Secretaría de Educación Pública. *El movimiento educativo en México. Resumen de trabajos, 1920–1922.* Mexico, 1922.

Secretaría de Educación Pública. *Noticia estadística sobre la educación pública en México correspondiente al año de 1927.* Mexico: Talleres Gráficos de la Nación, 1928.

Secretaría de Educación Pública. *Noticia estadística sobre la educación pública en México correspondiente al año de 1928.* Mexico: Talleres Gráficos de la Nación, 1930.

Secretaría de Educación Pública. Luis Alvarez Barret. *La obra educativa de don Rafael Ramírez.* Mexico, 1959.

Secretaría de Educación Pública. *Organización técnica de los departamentos de "Antropología" y de "Educación rural e incorporación cultural indígena" y de "Investigación psico-pedagógica e higiene."* Mexico, 1924.

Secretaría de Educación Pública. José Manuel Puig Casauranc. *El papel de la escuela de acción en la república.* Mexico, 1925.

Secretaría de Educación Pública. *Plan de trabajo de las escuelas rurales.* Mexico, 1925.

Secretaría de Educación Pública. Manuel Gamio. *La población del valle de Te-noch-Teotihuacán. El medio en que se ha desarrollado. Su evolución étnica y social. Iniciativa para procurar su mejoramiento.* 2 vols. Mexico, 1922.

Secretaría de Educación Pública. *Primer Congreso Nacional de Instrucción, 1889–1890.* Mexico, 1975.

Secretaría de Educación Pública. Moisés Sáenz. *Reseña de la educación pública en México en 1927.* Mexico, 1928.

Secretaría de Educación Pública. *Resultados morales del cooperativismo.* Publicaciones de la Secretaría de Educación Pública 6, no. 14 (1925).

Secretaría de Educación Pública. Alfonso Reyes. *Justo Sierra. Un discurso.* Mexico, 1947.

Secretaría de Educación Pública. Salvador Novo. *El sistema de escuelas rurales en México.* Mexico, 1927.

Secretaría de Educación Pública. Carlos Basauri. *La situación social actual de la población indígena de México y breves apuntes sintéticos sobre antropología y etnología de la misma.* Publicaciones de la Secretaría de Educación Pública 16, no. 8 (1928).

Secretaría de Educación Pública. Moisés Sáenz. *Visión de una escuela rural.* Mexico, 1926.

Secretaría de Fomento. Manuel Gamio. *El gobierno, la población, y el territorio.* Mexico, 1917.

Secretaría de Justicia y Instrucción Pública. *Memoria que el Secretario de Justicia y Instrucción Pública Joaquín Baranda presenta al Congreso de la Unión comprende desde el 1er de diciembre de 1892 hasta el 30 de noviembre de 1896.* Mexico, 1899.

Secretaría de Instrucción Pública y Bellas Artes. *Anuarios escolares de la Secretaría de Instrucción Pública, Educación primaria, 1910–1911.* Mexico, 1911.

Secretaría de Instrucción Pública y Bellas Artes. *Boletín de Educación, 1914–1916.*

Secretaría de Instrucción Pública y Bellas Artes. *Boletín de Instrucción Pública, 1903–1911.*

Secretaría de Instrucción Pública y Bellas Artes. *Congreso Nacional de Educación Primaria. Antecedentes, actas, debates, y resoluciones.* Mexico: Tipografía Económica, 1910.

Secretaría de Instrucción Pública Bellas Artes. *Congreso Nacional de Educación Primaria. Informes presentados al Congreso Nacional de Educación Primaria por las delegaciones de los estados, del Distrito Federal, y territorios en septiembre de 1910.* 3 vols. Mexico: Imprenta de A. Carranza e Hijos, 1911.

Secretaría de Instrucción Pública y Bellas Artes. *Decreto que establece en todo la república escuelas de instrucción rudimentaria independientes de las escuelas primarias existentes. Expedido el 30 de mayo de 1911 y promulgado el 18 de junio del mismo.* Mexico, 1911.

Secretaría de Instrucción Pública y Bellas Artes. Alberto Pani. *Una encuesta sobre la instrucción rudimentaria en la república.* Mexico, 1912.

Secretaría de Instrucción Pública y Bellas Artes. Gregorio Torres Quintero. *La instrucción rudimentaria en la república. Estudio presentado en el Primer Congreso Científico Mexicano, por el Sr. Prof. Gregorio Torres Quintero, jefe de la Sección de Instrucción Rudimentaria en la Secretaría de Instrucción Pública y Bellas Artes.* Mexico, 1913.

Secretaría de Instrucción Pública y Bellas Artes. Alberto Pani. *La instrucción rudimentaria en la república. Estudio presentado por vía de información al C. Ministerio del Ramo por el Ing. Alberto J. Pani. Subsecretario de Instrucción Pública y Bellas Artes.* Mexico, 1912.

Secretaría de Instrucción Pública y Bellas Artes. *Programas de enseñanza formados con aprobación de la Secretaría de Instrucción Pública y Bellas Artes por los señores profesores de los departamentos respectivos.* Mexico, 1914.

School Textbooks

Aguirre Cinta, Rafael. *Historia de México.* 16th ed. Mexico: Sociedad de Ediciones y Librería Franco-Americana, SA, 1926.

Bonilla, José María. *Derechos civiles.* Mexico: Herrero Hermanos, 1918.

——. *Derechos individuales.* Mexico: Herrero Hermanos, 1918.

——. *Evolución del pueblo mexicano.* 2nd ed. Mexico: Herrero Hermanos, 1923.

Cadena, Longinos. *Elementos de historia general y de historia patria.* 3rd ed. 2 vols. Mexico: Herrero Hermanos, 1921.

Chávez Orozco, Luis. *Historia patria. Tercer año.* 8th ed. Mexico: Editorial Patria, SA, 1949.

Delgadillo, Daniel. *Adelante.* 2nd. ed. Mexico: Herrero Hermanos, 1920.

——. *La república mexicana. Geografía elemental.* Mexico: Herrero Hermanos, 1911.

Lucio, G. *Simiente. Libro primero para las escuelas rurales.* Mexico: SEP, Comisión Editora Popular, 1935.

——. *Simiente. Libro segundo para las escuelas rurales.* Mexico: SEP, Comisión Editora Popular, 1935.

——. *Simiente. Libro tercero para las escuelas rurales.* Mexico: SEP, Comisón Editora Popular, 1935.

Nervo, Amado. *Lecturas mexicanas.* Mexico: Librería de la Vda. de Ch. Bouret, n.d.

Ramos Pedrueza, Rafael. *Sugerencías revolucionarias para la enseñanza de la historia.* Mexico: Universidad Nacional Autónoma de México, 1932.

Rébsamen, Enrique. *Método para la enseñanza de la historia en las escuelas primarias elementales y superiores de la república mexicana.* Mexico: Librería de la Vda. de Ch. Bouret, 1898.

Secretaría de Educación Pública, Comisión Editora Popular. *Escuelas primarias urbanas. Lectura oral. Primer año.* Mexico: SEP, 1938.

Secretaría de Educación Pública, Comisión Editora Popular. *Escuelas primarias urbanas. Lectura oral. Segundo año.* Mexico: SEP, 1938.

Secretaría de Educación Pública. *Lecturas clásicas para niños.* Mexico: SEP, 1924–1925.

Sierra, Justo. *Historia patria.* Mexico: SEP, 1922.

Torres Quintero, Gregorio. *Patria mexicana.* 4th ed. Mexico: Herrero Hermanos, 1923.

Newspapers and Periodicals

Boletín de la Universidad Popular Mexicana. 1914–1916. 4 vols. Mexico City.

Bulletin of the Pan-American Union. 1920–1927. Washington, D.C.

El Demócrata. 1923–1924. Mexico City.

Excelsior. 1920–1928. Mexico City.

El Imparcial. 1897–1908. Mexico City.

La Libertad. 1883. Mexico City.
El Monitor. 1914. Mexico City.
Revista Moderna. 1906–1910. Mexico City.
Revista Positiva. 1901. Mexico City.
Sabia Moderna. 1906. Mexico City.
El Sol. 1914. Mexico City.
El Universal. 1923–1924. Mexico City.
El Universal Ilustrado. 1925. Mexico City.

Other Documents, Memoirs, and Contemporary Articles and Books

Alessio Robles, Miguel. *Mi generación y mi época.* Mexico: Editorial Stylo, 1949.
Alessio Robles, Vito. "La Convención de Aguascalientes." *Todo,* 7 December 1950.
———. *Mis andanzas con nuestro Ulises.* Mexico: Ediciones Botas, 1938.
Alvarado, Salvador. *A dónde vamos. Las cinco hermanas.* Mérida: Imprenta de Novela, n.d.
———. *Actuación revolucionaria del General Salvador Alvarado en Yucatán.* Mexico: Costa Amic, 1965.
———. *Breves apuntes acerca de la administración del General Salvador Alvarado como gobernador de Yucatán.* Mérida: Imprenta del Gobierno Constitucionalista, 1916.
———. "Carta al pueblo de Yucatán publicada en *La Voz de la Revolución,* 5 de mayo de 1916, aniversario de gloria para la patria mexicana." In *La cuestión de la tierra, 1915–1917. Colección de folletos para la historia de la Revolución mexicana, dirigida por Jesús Silva Herzog.* Mexico: Instituto Mexicano de Investigaciones Económicas, 1962.
———. *Problemas de México.* San Antonio, Texas: n.p., 1920.
Aviles, Hildardo F. *En pro del libro mexicano. Artículos de crítica, comunicaciones oficiales de gobernadores, directores generales, y presidentes municipales, cartas y adhesiones de particulares en favor de la adopción en las escuelas primarias de libros de texto nacionales.* Mexico: Imprenta Francesa, 1919.
Barreda, Gabino. "La educación moral." *Revista Positiva* 1, no. 5 (1901): 169–79.
———. "La instrucción pública." *Revista Positiva* 1, no. 8 (1901): 257–340.
———. *Opúsculos, discusiones y discursos. Coleccionados y publicados por la Asociación Metodofía Gabino Barreda.* Mexico: Imprenta del Comercio de Dublán y Chávez, 1877.
Beals, Carleton. "The Obregón Regime." *Survey Graphic* 52, no. 3 (1924): 135–37, 188–89.
Best-Maugard, Adolfo. *A Method for Creative Design.* New York: Alfred A. Knopf, 1927.
Bojorquez, Juan de Dios [pseud. Djed Borquez]. *Crónica del Constituyente.* Mexico: Ediciones Botas, 1938.

Campbell, Evan Fraser. "The Management of Mexican Labor." *Engineering and Mining Journal* 91 (1911): 1104–5.

Carrillo, Julián. *La revolución musical mexicana del Sonido 13, expuesta brevemente en tres capítulos en forma de conferencias, dedicadas al señor ministro plenipotenciario de México en Quito, Ecuador, quien las transmitió por radio del capital del bello país hermano*. Mexico: n.p., 1936.

Carrilo Puerto, Felipe. "The New Yucatán." *Survey Graphic* 52, no. 3 (1924): 138–42.

Caso, Antonio. "1900." *El Universal*, 4 July 1941.

———. *La existencia como enómia y caridad*. Mexico: Editorial Porrua, 1916.

———. "Nietzsche: su espíritu y su obra." *Revista Moderna* 8 (1907): 348–58.

———. "La perennidad del pensamiento religioso." *Revista Moderna* 12 (1909): 67–72.

———. "La psicología del cristianismo." *Boletín de la Universidad Popular Mexicana* 2, no. 2 (1916): 49–51.

Chávez, Ezequiel. "Don Justo Sierra y Antonio Caso." *Abside* 27, no. 1 (1963): 89–101.

———. "Recuerdos de mi vida profesional." *Excelsior* 13 August 1945.

Chávez, Leticia. *Los programas de educación de las escuelas primarias del Distrito Federal*. Mexico: Imprenta Victoria, 1919.

Colección de leyes y decretos del estado de Morelos formada por acuerdo del ejecutivo por el Lic. Cecilio A. Robelo. Vols. 12, 13. Cuernavaca: Imprenta del Gobierno del Estado, 1895.

Coloca, Lauro. "Exposición de motivos de las bases del Congreso de Misioneros que se celebrará en el capital." *Etnos* 1, no. 1 (1922–1923): 63–68.

Cosío Villegas, Daniel. *Ensayos y notas*. Buenos Aires and Mexico: Editorial Hermes, 1966.

Dewey, John. *Democracy and Education*. New York: The Free Press, 1966.

———. "From a Mexican Notebook." *The New Republic* 48 (1926): 239–41.

———. *Impressions of Soviet Russia and the Revolutionary World: Mexico, China, and Turkey*. New York: New Republic, 1929.

———. "Mexico's Educational Renaissance." *The New Republic* 48 (1926): 116–18.

———. *School and Society*. Chicago: University of Chicago Press, 1963.

———. "The School as Social Center." *Proceedings of the National Education Association*, 1902, pp. 373–83.

———. "Teaching Ethics in the High School." *Educational Review* 6 (1893): 313–21.

Dewey, John, and Evelyn Dewey. *Schools of Tomorrow*. New York: E. P. Dutton, 1962.

Dublán, Manuel, and José M. Lozano. *Legislación mexicana o colección completa de las disposiciones legislativas expedidas desde la independencia de la república ordenada por los licenciados*. Vols. 1–11. Mexico: 1876–1908.

Elwes, Hugh G. "Points about Mexican Labor." *Engineering and Mining Journal* 90 (1910): 662.

Escuelas laicas. Textos y documentos. Mexico: Empresas Editoriales, SA, 1948.

Fabela, Isidro. "A mi maestro Justo Sierra." *El Nacional*, 29 January 1948.

Ferrer Guardia, Francisco. *La escuela moderna*. Barcelona: Imprenta Elseveriana-Borras Mestres y Ca., 1912.

Freeman, Frank. "Sorting the Students." *Educational Review* 68 (1924): 169–74.

Gamio, Manuel. *Forjando patria*. Prólogo de Justino Fernández. Mexico: Editorial Porrua, 1960.

———. "The New Conquest." *Survey Graphic* 52, no. 3 (1924): 192–94.

García Calderón, Francisco. "Las corrientes filosóficas en Latinoamérica." *Revista Moderna* 11 (1908): 150–56.

Gómez Morín, Manuel. *1915*. Mexico: Editorial Cultura, 1927.

Gruening, Ernest. "Felipe Carrillo Puerto." *The Nation* 118, no. 3054 (1924): 61.

———. "The Mexican Renaissance beneath the Battle of Politics." *The Century Magazine* 107 (1924): 520–39.

———. "Up in Arms against Ignorance." *Collier's* 72 (December 1923): 8.

Guiza y Acevedo, Jesús. *Me lo dijó Vasconcelos*. Mexico: Editorial Polis, 1965.

Guzmán, Martín Luis. "Una manera de gobernar." *El Universal*, 8 April 1928.

———. "Un ministro de guerra." *El Universal*, 25 March 1927.

Hammond, John Hays. *The Autobiography of John Hays Hammond*. New York: Arno Press, 1972.

Henriquez Ureña, Pedro. "La cultura de las humanidades." *Obra crítica*. Mexico and Buenos Aires: Fondo de Cultura Económica, 1960, pp. 595–603.

———. "La influencia de la Revolución en la vida intelectual de México." *Obra crítica*. Mexico and Buenos Aires: Fondo de Cultura Económica, 1960, pp. 610–17.

———. "Profesores del idealismo." *Revista Moderna* 14 (1910): 213–16.

———. "The Revolution in Intellectual Life." *Survey Graphic* 52, no. 3 (1924): 166–68.

Hernández Luna, Juan. *Conferencias del Ateneo de la Juventud*. Mexico: Universidad Nacional Autónoma de México, 1962.

Ingenieros, José. "En memoria de Felipe Carrillo Puerto." *Historia Obrera* 1, no. 4 (1975): 2–7.

Inman, Samuel Guy. *Intervention in Mexico*. New York: George H. Doran Co. 1919.

Kelley, Francis G. *Blood-Drenched Altars*. Milwaukee: Bruce Publishing Co., 1935.

Lamb, Mark R. "Tales of Mountain Travel in Mexico." *Engineering and Mining Journal* 90 (1910): 676.

Landazuri, Elena. "New Tendencies in the Public Instruction of Mexico." *Bulletin of the Pan-American Union* 55, no. 5 (1922): 462–76.

———. "Why We Differ." *Survey Graphic* 52, no. 3 (1924): 160–63.

Lima, Salvador, and Marcelino Rentería. "La escuela de acción." *Educacion* 2, no. 4 (1923): 241–49, 285–99.

Lombardo Toledano, Vicente. *Puntos de vista y proposiciones del Comité de Edu-*

cación de la CROM presentados por el presidente del Comité Vicente Lombardo Toledano ante la 60. Convención de la CROM, celebrada en Ciudad Juárez, Chihauhua, en el mes de noviembre de 1924. Mexico: Editorial Cultura, 1924.

Ludlow, Edwin. "The Coalfields of Las Esperanzas, Coahuila, Mexico." *Transactions of the American Institute of Mining Engineers* 32 (1902): 140–45.

Lumiss, Charles F. *The Awakening of a Nation: Mexico of Today.* New York and London: Harper and Brothers, 1898.

de la Luz Mena y Alcocer, José. *La escuela socialista, su desorientación y fracaso, el verdadero derrotero.* Mexico: n.p., 1941.

de la Luz Mena y Alcocer, José, et al. *Informe de la delegación del estado de Yucatán al Congreso Nacional de Maestros.* Mexico: n.p., 1920.

Machorro Narvaez, P. *La enseñanza en México.* Mexico: Imprenta de Manuel León Sánchez, 1916.

Madero, Francisco. *La sucesión presidencial.* Mexico: Librería de la Viuda de Ch. Bouret, 1911.

Malcolmson, James W. "Mining Development in Mexico during 1902." *Engineering and Mining Journal* 75 (1903): 35–39.

———. "Mining in Mexico." *Engineering and Mining Journal* 75 (1903): 210.

———. "Mining in Mexico." *Engineering and Mining Journal* 77 (1904): 21–22.

Mariscal, Federico. *La patria y la arquitectura nacional.* Mexico: Imprenta Stefán y Torres, 1915.

Martínez, Maximino. *El estado actual de la educación pública en México.* Mexico: Talleres Gráficos de la Escuela Industrial de Huérfanos, 1919.

Memoria del Primer Congreso del Niño. Mexico: El Universal, 1921.

Memoria leido por el C. Gobernador del estado libre y soberano de Yucatán General Octavio Rosado. En el solemne instalación de la décima legislatura constitucional verificada el 1 de enero de 1884. Mérida: Imprenta de Echanove y López, 1884.

Memoria que el cuidadano General Bernardo Reyes, gobernador de Nuevo León, presenta al XXIV legislatura del mismo y corresponde al período transcurrido del 4 de octubre de 1903 al 3 de octubre de 1907. Monterrey: Tipografía del Gobierno del Estado, 1907.

Mendieta de Nuñez Mata, Esperanza. *Carta a una maestra rural.* Oaxaca: Talleres Tipográficos del Gobierno, 1931.

Menéndez, Rodolfo. *Reseña histórica del Primer Congreso Pedagógico de Yucatán, 1915.* Mérida: Imprenta del Gobierno Constitucionalista, 1916.

"Mexico's Educational Progress." *The Nation* 115 (August 1922): 192–93.

Murillo, Gerardo. *Las artes populares en México.* Mexico: Editorial "Cultura," 1922.

Obregón, Alvaro. *Discursos.* Mexico: Biblioteca de la Dirección General de Educación Militar, 1932.

Orozco, José Clemente. *Autobiography.* Translated by Robert C. Stephenson. Austin: University of Texas Press, 1962.

Palavicini, Felix F. *Historia de la Constitución de 1917.* 2 vols. Mexico: n.p., 1938.

———. *Mi vida revolucionaria.* Mexico: Ediciones Botas, 1937.

———.*Palabras y acciones.* Mexico: n.p., 1919.

———. *La patria por la escuela.* Mexico: Linotipografía, 1916.

———. *Pro-patria. Apuntes de sociología mexicana.* Mexico: Tipografía La Ilustración, SA, 1905.

———. *Problems de la educación.* Valencia: F. Sempere y Compañia, Editores, 1910.

Porter, Katherine Anne. "Corridos," *Survey Graphic* 52, no. 3 (1924): 157–58.

Portes Gil, Emilio. *Quince años de política mexicana.* Mexico: Ediciones Botas, 1941.

Primer almanaque de la Universidad Popular Mexicana. Mexico: Imprenta Victoria, 1919.

El Primer Congreso Feminista de Yucatán, convocado por el C. gobernador y comandante militar del estado, Gral. don Salvador Alvarado. Mérida: Talleres Tipográficos del "Ateneo Peninsular," 1916.

Primer Congreso Obrero Socialista celebrado en Motul, estado de Yucatán. Mexico: Centro de Estudios Históricos del Movimiento Obrero Mexicano, 1977.

Proyecto de reformas a la ley vigente de instrucción pública en el Distrito Federal que por acuerdo de la Secretaría de Justicia formulan los profesores de la Escuela de Medicina Rafael Lavista, Francisco de P. Chacón y Eduardo Liceaga. Mexico: Eduardo S. Dublán, Impresor, 1895.

Pruneda, Alfonso. *La Universidad Popular Mexicana en el segundo año de sus labores, 1913–1914. Informe del director.* Mexico: Imprenta Stefán y Torres, 1915.

———. *La Universidad Popular Mexicana en el tercer año de sus labores, 1914–1915.* Mexico: Imprenta Stefán y Torres, 1915.

Reyes, Alfonso. *El cazador.* In *Obras completas*, vol. 3. Mexico: Fondo de Cultura Económica, 1955–1962, pp. 85–215.

———. *Diario, 1911–1930.* Prólogo de Alicia Reyes. Guanajuato: Universidad de Guanajuato, 1969.

———. *Pasado inmediato y otros ensayos.* Mexico: El Colegio de México, 1941.

Rico, Juan. *La huelga de junio.* Mérida: n.p., 1922.

Rivera, Diego. "The Guild Spirit in Mexican Art," *Survey Graphic* 52, no. 3 (1924): 174–77.

———. *My Art, My Life: Autobiography.* (As told to Gladys March.) New York: Citadel Press, 1960.

Rodó, José Enrique. *Ariel.* Monterrey: Talleres Modernos de Lozano, 1908.

Rogers, Allen H. "Character and Habits of the Mexican Miner." *Engineering and Mining Journal* 85 (1908): 700–702.

Romero, Matías. *Geographical and Statistical Notes on Mexico.* New York and London: G. P. Putnam's Sons, Knickerbocker Press, 1898.

———. *Mexico and the United States.* New York and London: G. P. Putnam's Sons, 1898.

Sáenz, Moisés. *Carapán.* Morelia: Departamento de Promoción Cultural del Gobierno de Michoacán, 1970.

Salazar, Rosendo. *Las pugnas de la gleba. Los albores del movimiento obrero en México.* Mexico: Comisión Nacional Editorial, PRI, 1972.

Salinas, Duclos. *The Riches of Mexico and Its Institutions.* St. Louis: Nixon Jones Printing Co., 1893.

San Luis Potosí. *Programa detallado de estudios para las escuelas primarias de San Luis Potosí.* San Luis Potosí: n.p., 1906.

Segundo Congreso Obrero de Izamal. Mexico: Centro de Estudios Históricos del Movimiento Obrero Mexicano, 1977.

Serrano, Pedro. *Los hispanistas mexicanos.* Vol. 1. Mexico: Imprenta Nacional, 1920.

Sierra, Justo. *La educacíon nacional. Artículos, actuaciones y documentos.* In *Obras completas,* vol. 8. Edición ordenada y anotada por Agustín Yañez. Mexico: Universidad Nacional Autónoma de México, 1948.

———. *Evolución política del pueblo mexicano.* In *Obras completas,* vol. 12. Edición establecida y anotada por Edmundo O'Gormán. Mexico: Universidad Nacional Autónoma de México, 1948.

———. *México. Su evolución social.* Mexico: J. Ballesca y Compañia, 1900–1902.

———. *México social y político.* In *Obras completas,* vol. 9. Edición ordenada y anotada por Agustín Yañez. Mexico: Universidad Nacional Autónoma de México, 1948.

———. *Periodismo político.* In *Obras completas,* vol. 4. Edición ordenada y anotada por Agustín Yañez. Mexico: Universidad Nacional Autónoma de México, 1948.

Sol, Hugo. *La reacción de privilegio.* Mexico: Imprenta I. Escalante, SA, 1918.

Tannenbaum, Frank. "Mexico—A Promise." *Survey Graphic* 52, no. 3 (1924): 129–32.

———. "The Miracle School." *The Century Magazine* 106 (August 1923): 499–506.

Tays, E. A. H. "Present Labor Conditions in Mexico." *Engineering and Mining Journal* 84 (1907): 621–24.

Ugarte, Manuel. "Las nuevas tendencias literarias." *Revista Moderna* 12 (1909): 273–75.

de Unamuno, Miguel. "Don Quixote y Bolívar." *Revista Moderna* 8 (1907): 263–67.

Urzaiz, Eduardo. *Congreso Nacional de Maestros.* Mérida: Talleres Tipográficos del Gobierno del Estado, 1921.

U.S. Senate. *Investigation of Mexican Affairs,* 66th Congress, 2nd Session, 1919–1920. 2 vols.

Vasconcelos, José. *La caída de Carranza: de la dictadura a la libertad.* Mexico: Murguía, 1920.

———. *Cartas políticas.* Primera series. Con un preámbulo y notas de Alfonso Taracena. Prólogo de José Ignacio Vasconcelos. Mexico: Clásica Selecta, 1950.

———. *De Robinson a Odiseo.* In *Obras completas,* vol. 2. Mexico: Libreros Mexicanos Unidos, 1958, pp. 1495–1720.

————. *El desastre.* In *Obras completas*, vol. 2. Mexico: Libreros Mexicanos Unidos, 1958, pp. 1215–1800.

————. "El Día del Maestro en América." *Repertorio Americano* 8 (June 1924): 225–28.

————. *Discursos.* Mexico: Ediciones Botas, 1950.

————. "Educational Aspirations." *Survey Graphic* 52, no. 3 (1924): 169-70

————. "La educación en México." *Repertorio Americano* 105 (March 1923): 376–78, 386–89.

————. "Freedom or Imperialism." *The Nation* 119 (August 1924): 212–13.

————. *Indología.* In *Obras completas*, vol. 2. Mexico: Libreros Mexicanos Unidos, 1958, pp. 1069–1304.

————. "Intellectual Progress in Mexico." *Bulletin of the Pan-American Union* 49 (July 1919): 54–61.

————. "Latin America: An Interpretation and a Prophecy." *Living Age* 329 (May 1926): 233–38.

————. "Programme for Spanish Americans." *Living Age* 321 (June 1924): 1185–88.

————. *Prometeo vencedor.* In *Obras completas*, vol. 1. Mexico: Libreros Mexicanos Unidos, 1958, pp. 239–86.

————. *Raza cósmica.* In *Obras completas*, vol. 2. Mexico: Libreros Mexicanos Unidos, 1958, pp. 903–1068.

————. "El secreto del Ateneo." *Todo*, 25 July 1946, p. 11.

————. "Teoria dinámica del derecho." In *Obras completas*, vol. 1. Mexico: Libreros Unidos Mexicanos, 1958, pp. 13–36.

————. *La tormenta.* In *Obras completas*, vol. 1. Mexico: Libreros Mexicanos Unidos, 1958, pp. 723–1214.

————. *Ulises criollo.* Mexico: Ediciones Botas, 1938.

————. *Los últimos cincuenta años.* Mexico: n.p., n.d.

————, and Manuel Gamio. *Aspects of Mexican Civilization.* Chicago: University of Chicago Press, 1926.

Vaughan, Kenelm. "What Catholics Have Done for Education in Mexico." *The Catholic World*, 59 (1894): 120–29.

Velazquez Andrade, Manuel. *La educación rural. Nuevos puntos de vista en su doctrina, organización y plan de estudios.* Mexico: Imprenta Franco-Mexicana, 1919.

Velazquez Bringas, Esperanza. "The Educational Missionary." *Survey Graphic* 52, no. 3 (1924): 172–73.

Vera Estanol, Jorge. *Carranza and His Bolshevik Regime.* Los Angeles, Calif.: Wayside Press, 1920.

Weyl, Walter E. "Labor Conditions in Mexico." *U.S. Labor Department Bulletin* 7 (1902): 1–94.

Woodbridge, Dwight. "Labor Data on a Northern Mexican Mine." *Mexican Mining Journal* 17, no. 1 (1913): 348–49.

Yucatán. Departamento de Educación Pública. *Ley de educación primaria.* Mérida: 1918.

————. Departamento de Educación Pública. *Reglamento interior de la ley de educación primaria*. Mérida: 1918.

Zarco, Francisco. *Historia del Congreso Extraordinario Constituyente de 1856–1857*. Mexico: El Colegio de México, 1956.

Secondary Sources

Aguilar Camín, Hector. *La frontera nomada: Sonora y la Revolución mexicana*. Mexico: Siglo Veintiuno Editores, 1977.

——, et al. *Interpretaciones de la Revolución mexicana*. Mexico: Editorial Nuevo Imagen, 1979.

Alba, Victor. "Julián Carrillo, Los primeros pasos." *Mañana*, 25 July 1953.

Almada, Francisco R. *Diccionario de historia, geografía, y biografía chihuahuenses*. Chihuahua: Talleres Gráficos del Gobierno del Estado, 1927.

Althusser, Louis. *Lenin and Philosophy and Other Essays*. New York: Monthly Review Press, 1975.

Alvear Acevedo, Carlos. *La educación y la ley: La legislación en materia educativa en el México independiente*. Mexico: Editorial Jus, 1962.

Anderson, Rodney D. "Díaz y la crisis laboral de 1906." *Historia Mexicana* 19 (1970): 513–35.

——. *Outcasts in Their Own Land: Mexican Industrial Workers, 1906–1911*. Dekalb: Northern Illinois University Press, 1976.

Araiza, Luis. *Historia del movimiento obrero mexicano*. Mexico: Editorial Cuauhtemoc, 1965.

Aries, Philippe. *Centuries of Childhood: A Social History of Family Life*. New York: Vintage, 1965.

Arnáiz y Freg, Arturo. "Alamán en la historia y en la política." *Historia Mexicana* 3 (1953): 241–60.

"El asesinato de Felipe Carrillo Puerto." *Historia Obrera* 1 (March 1975):9.

Bailey, David C. "Alvaro Obregón and Anti-Clericalism in the 1910 Revolution." *The Americas* 26 (1969): 183–98.

——. "Obregón: Mexico's Accommodating President." In *Essays on the Mexican Revolution: Revisionist Views of the Leaders*. Edited by George Wolfskill and Douglas Richmond. Austin: University of Texas Press, 1979, pp. 82–99.

——. "Revisionism and the Recent Historiography of the Mexican Revolution." *Hispanic American Historical Review* 58 (1978): 62–79.

——. *Viva Cristo Rey! The Cristero Rebellion and the Church-State Conflict in Mexico*. Austin: University of Texas Press, 1974.

Baldwin, Deborah Jo. "Variation in the Vanguard: Protestants in the Mexican Revolution." Ph.D. dissertation, University of Chicago, 1979.

Bar-Lewaw, Mulstock. *José Vasconcelos, vida y obra*. Mexico: Clásicas Selectas Editoras Libreras, 1966.

Barta, Roger. "La revolución domesticada: del bonapartismo pequeñoburgués a la institucionalización de la burguesía." *Historia y Sociedad* 6 (1975): 13–29.

Basave Fernández del Valle, Agustín. *La filosofía de José Vasconcelos. El hombre y su sistema.* Madrid: Cultura Hispánica, 1958.

Bassols Batalla, Narciso. *El pensamiento político de Alvaro Obregón.* Mexico: Ediciones El Caballito, 1967.

Basurto, Jorge. *El proletariado industrial en México (1850–1930).* Mexico: Instituto de Investigaciones Sociales, Universidad Nacional Autónoma de México, 1975.

Bazant, Jan. *Alienation of Church Wealth in Mexico: Social and Economic Aspects of the Liberal Revolution, 1856–1857.* Cambridge: Cambridge University Press, 1971.

Bernstein, Marvin D. *The Mexican Mining Industry, 1890–1950: A Study in the Interaction of Politics, Economics, and Technology.* Albany: State University of New York, 1964.

Biasutto, Carlos. *Educación y clase obrera.* Mexico: Editorial Nuevo Imagen, 1978.

Blanco, José Joaquín. *Se llamaba Vasconcelos. Una evocación crítica.* Mexico: Fondo de Cultura Económica, 1977.

Booth, George C. *Mexico's School-Made Society.* Stanford: Stanford University Press, 1941.

Bourdieu, Pierre, and Jean Claude Passeron. *La reproducción. Elementos para una teoria del sistema de enseñanza.* Barcelona: Editorial Laia, 1972.

Branch, H. N. "The Mexican Constitution of 1917 Compared with the Constitution of 1857." *Annals of the American Academy of Political and Social Sciences* (Supplement) May 1917.

Braverman, Harry. *Labor and Monopoly Capital: The Degradation of Work in the Twentieth Century.* New York and London: Monthly Review Press, 1974.

Bravo Ugarte, José. *La educación en México.* Mexico: Editorial Jus, 1966.

Bremauntz, A. *La educación socialista en México.* Mexico: n.p., 1943.

Britton, John A. "Indian Education, Nationalism and Federalism in Mexico, 1910–1911," *The Americans* 32 (1970): 445–58.

———. "Moisés Sáenz, nacionalista mexicano." *Historia Mexicana* 22 (1972): 79–98.

Bustillos Carillo, Antonio. *Yucatán al servicio de la patria.* Mexico: Casa Ramírez Editores, 1959.

Callahan, Raymond. *Education and the Cult of Efficiency.* Chicago: University of Chicago Press, 1962.

Cardoso, Fernando Henrique, and E. Falleto. *Dependencia y desarrollo en América Latina.* Mexico: Siglo Veintiuno, 1969.

Carmona, Fernando, et al. *Reforma educativa y "apertura democrática."* Mexico: Editorial Nuestro Tiempo, 1971.

Carnoy, Martin, and Henry M. Levin. *The Limits of Educational Reform.* New York: David McKay Co., 1976.

Carr, Barry. *El movimiento obrero y la política en México, 1910–1929.* 2 vols. Mexico: SepSetentas, 1976.

———. "Las peculiaridades del norte mexicano," *Historia Mexicana* 22 (1973): 320–46.

Castillo, Isidro. *México y su revolución educativa.* Mexico: Editorial Pax-Mexicana, Librería Carlos Cesarman, SA, 1965.

Ceballos, Ciro. "Panorama mexicano, 1905–1910, Costumbres literarios." *Excelsior,* 17 July; 8 August; 11 October; 14 November 1939.

Córdova, Arnaldo. *La ideología de la Revolución mexicana: la formación del nuevo régimen.* Mexico: Ediciones Era, 1973.

――――. "Los maestros rurales en el cardenismo." *Cuadernos políticos* 2 (1974): 77–92.

Cosío Villegas, Daniel, ed. *El Porfiriato: La vida económica.* Historia moderna de México. 2 vols. Mexico: Editorial Hermes, 1965.

――――. *El Porfiriato: La vida social.* Historia moderna de Mexico. Mexico: Editorial Hermes, 1957.

Costeloe, Michael. *Church Wealth in Mexico: A Study of the "Juzgado de Capellanías" in the Archbishopric of Mexico, 1800–1856.* Cambridge: Cambridge University Press, 1967.

Counts, George S. *Education and American Civilization.* New York: Teachers College Press, Columbia University, 1952.

Cumberland, Charles C. *Mexican Revolution: The Constitutionalist Years.* Introduction by David C. Bailey. Austin: University of Texas Press, 1974.

David, Joe Edward. "The Development of Justo Sierra's Educational Thought," Ph.D. dissertation, University of Texas, 1951.

Dulles, John W. F. *Yesterday in Mexico: A Chronicle of the Revolution, 1919–1936.* Austin: University of Texas Press, 1961.

Durán, Mario Antonio. *El agrarismo mexicano.* Mexico: Siglo Veintiuno, 1975.

Ebaugh, Cameron Duncan. *The National System of Education in Mexico.* Baltimore: Johns Hopkins University Press, 1931.

Estrada, Dorothy T. "Las escuelas lancasterianas en la ciudad de México, 1822–1842," *Historia Mexicana* 22 (1973): 494–513.

――――. "The 'Escuelas Pías' in Mexico City, 1786–1820." *The Americas* 31 (1974): 51–71.

Falcón, Romana. "El surgimiento del agrarismo cardenista: Una revisión de las tesis populistas." *Historia Mexicana* 27 (1978): 333–86.

Fernández, Justino. *El arte moderno de Mexico. Breve historia. Siglos XIX–XX.* Prólogo de Manuel Toussaint. Mexico: Talleres Cultura, 1937.

――――. *Roberto Montenegro.* Mexico: Universidad Nacional Autónoma de México, 1962.

Ferrer Mendiolea, Gabriel. *Historia del Congreso Constituyente de 1916–1917.* Mexico: Biblioteca del Instituto Nacional de Estudios Históricos de la Revolución Mexicana, 1957.

Figes, Eva. *Patriarchal Attitudes.* New York: Fawcett World Library, 1971.

Fischer, Ernest. *The Necessity of Art: A Marxist Approach.* New York: Penguin, 1963.

Florescano, Enrique. "Antonio Caso y la historia." *Historia Mexicana* 12 (1963): 358–78.

Flower, Elizabeth. "The Mexican Revolt against Positivism." *Journal of the History of Ideas* 10 (1949): 115–29.

Fowler Salamini, Heather. *Agrarian Radicalism in Veracruz, 1920–1938*. Lincoln: University of Nebraska Press, 1978.

Fox-Riven, Frances, and Richard A. Cloward. *Regulating the Poor: The Function of Public Welfare*. New York: Random House, Vintage Books, 1971.

Franco, Jean. *The Modern Culture of Latin America: Society and the Artist*. London: Penguin Books, 1970.

Gil, Mario. *Los ferrocarrileros*. Mexico: Editorial Extemporáneos, 1971.

Gilly, Adolfo. *La Revolución interrumpida. México, 1910–1920. Una guerra campesina por la tierra y el poder*. Mexico: Ediciones El Caballito, 1974.

Gintis, Herbert, and Samuel Bowles. *Schooling in Capitalist America*. New York: Basic Books, 1976.

González, Gilbert G. "The Relationship between Progressive Educational Theory and Practice and Monopoly Capital." Occasional Papers No. 1, Program in Comparative Culture, University of California at Irvine, California, 1976.

González y González, Luis. "El agrarismo liberal." *Historia Mexicana* 7 (1958): 469–96.

———. "El liberalismo triunfante." In *Historia General de Mexico*, vol. 3. Mexico: El Colegio de Mexico, 1976, pp. 163–282.

———. *San José de Garcia: Mexican Village in Transition*. Austin: University of Texas Press, 1974.

González Flores, Enrique. *Chihuahua de la Independencia a la Revolución*. Mexico: Ediciones Botas, 1949.

González Navarro, Moisés. "Educación y trabajo en el Porfiriato." *Historia Mexicana* 6 (1957): 620–25.

———. *El Porfiriato: La vida social*. Historia moderna de México. Edited by Daniel Cosío Villegas. Mexico: Editorial Hermes, 1957.

———. *Raza y tierra: La guerra de castas y el henequén*. Mexico: El Colegio de México, 1970.

Graham, Patricia Albjerg. *Community and Class in American Education, 1865–1918*. New York: John Wiley and Sons, 1974.

Graña, Cesar. "Cultural Nationalism: The Idea of Historical Identity in Spanish America." *Social Research* 29 (1962): 395–418; 30 (1963): 37–52.

Green, Thomas F. *Work, Leisure, and the American Schools*. New York: Random House, 1968.

Greer, Colin. *The Great School Legend*. New York: Basic Books, 1972.

Gutelman, Michel. *Capitalismo y reforma agraria en México*. Mexico: Ediciones Era, 1974.

Haddox, John. *Antonio Caso, Philosopher of Mexico*. Austin: University of Texas Press, 1971.

———. *Vasconcelos of Mexico: Philosopher and Prophet*. Austin: University of Texas Press, 1967.

Hale, Charles A. "José María Luis Mora and the Structure of Mexican Liberalism." *Hispanic American Historial Review* 45 (May 1965): 196–227.

———. *Mexican Liberalism in the Age of Mora*. New Haven: Yale University Press, 1968.

———. "The War with the United States and the Crisis in Mexican Thought." *The Americas* 14 (1957): 164–71.

Hall, Linda B. "Alvaro Obregón and the Politics of Mexican Land Reform, 1920–1924." *Hispanic American Historial Review* 60 (1980): 213–38.

Hamilton, Nora. "Mexico: The Limits of State Autonomy." *Latin American Perspectives* 2 (1975): 81–108.

———. "The Mexican State: Cárdenas and State Autonomy." Ph.D. dissertation, University of Wisconsin-Madison, 1978.

Hanson, Roger. *The Politics of Mexican Development.* Baltimore: Johns Hopkins University Press, 1971.

Harris, Richard L. "Marxism and the Agrarian Question in Latin America." *Latin American Perspectives* 19 (Fall 1978): 2–26.

Hart, John M. *Los anarquistas mexicanos, 1860–1900.* Mexico: SepSetentas, 1974.

de la Helguera, Alvaro. *Enrique C. Creel. Apuntes biográficos.* Madrid: Imprenta de Ambrosio Pérez Asensio, 1910.

Helm, McKinley. *Modern Mexican Painters.* Freeport, New York: Books for Libraries Press, 1968.

Hernández Luna, Juan. "La imagen de América en José Vasconcelos." *Filosofía y Letras* 16 (1948): 101–12.

———. "Primeros estudios sobre el mexicano en nuestro siglo." *Filosofía y Letras* 20 (1950): 327–53.

———. "La universidad de Justo Sierra." *El Nacional,* 14 September 1947.

Hilton, Stanley E. "The Church-State Dispute over Education in Mexico from Carranza to Cárdenas." *The Americas* 21 (1964): 163–83.

Historia Obrera 5 (June 1975).

Holter, Howard, "Anatoli Lunacharsky and the Formulation of a Policy toward the Arts." Ph.D. dissertation, University of Wisconsin-Madison, 1967.

Hu-Dehart, Evelyn. "Development and Rural Rebellion: Pacification of the Yaquis in the Late Porfiriato." *Hispanic American Historial Review* 54 (1974): 72–93.

Hughes, James Monroe. *Education in America.* New York: Harper and Row, 1970.

Huizer, Gerrit. "Peasant Organization in Agrarian Reform in Mexico." In *Masses in Latin America,* edited by Irving Louis Horowitz. New York: Oxford University Press, 1970, pp. 445–502.

Innes, John S. "La Universidad Popular Mexicana." *The Americas* 30 (1973): 110–50.

Issel, William. "Modernization in Philadelphia School Reform. 1882–1905." In *Education in American History,* edited by Michael B. Katz. New York: Praeger Publishers, 1973. pp. 187–98.

Johnson, John. *Political Change in Latin America.* Palo Alto, Calif.: Stanford University Press, 1958.

Joseph, Gilbert. "Mexico's 'Popular Revolution': Mobilization and Myth in Yucatán, 1910–1940." *Latin American Perspectives* 22 (1979): 46–65.

Karier, Clarence J. *Shaping the American Educational State, 1900 to the Present.* New York: Macmillan Free Press, 1975.

———, et al. *Roots of Crisis.* Chicago: Rand McNally, 1973.

Katz, Friedrich. "Labor Conditions on Haciendas in Porfirian Mexico: Some Trends and Tendencies." *Hispanic American Historial Review* 54 (1974): 1–47.

Katz, Michael. *Class, Bureaucracy and the Schools.* New York: Praeger Publishers, 1971.

———. *Education in American History.* New York: Praeger Publishers, 1973.

———. "Origins of the Institutional State." *Marxist Perspectives* 1 (1978): 6–23.

Keesing, Donald B. "Structural Change in Early Development: Mexico's Changing Industrial and Occupational Structure from 1895 to 1950." *Journal of Economic History* 29 (1969): 716–38.

Keremitsis, Dawn. *La industria textil mexicana en el siglo XIX.* Mexico: Sep-Setentas, 1973.

———. "Women Workers in the Mexican Revolution, 1910–1940: Advance or Retreat?" Unpublished Paper, Valley Community College, Saratoga, California, n.d.

Kneller, George. *The Education of the Mexican Nation.* New York: Columbia University Press, 1952.

Krause de Kolteniuk, Rosa. "Antonio Caso y el positivismo." *Filosofía y Letras* 31 (1957): 113–29.

Krauze, Enrique. *Los caudillos culturales de la Revolución mexicana.* Mexico: Siglo Veintiuno, 1976.

———. *La reconstrucción económica.* Historia de la Revolución mexicana. 23 vols. Vol. 10: Período 1924–1928. Mexico: El Colegio de México, 1977.

Krug, Edward A. *The Shaping of the American High School, 1880–1920.* New York: Harper and Row, 1964.

Labarca, G., et al. *La educación burguesa.* Mexico: Editorial Nuevo Imagen, 1977.

Laffey, John. "Auguste Comte: Prophet of Reconciliation and Reaction." *Science and Society* 29 (1965): 44–65.

Larguía, Isabel, and John Dumoulin. "Aspects of the Condition of Women's Labor." *NACLA's Latin America and Empire Report* 9 (Sept. 1975): 4–13.

Larroyo, Francisco. *La historia de la educación comparada en México.* Mexico: Universidad Nacional Autónoma de México, 1948.

Lazerson, Marvin. *Origins of the Urban School: Public Education in Massachusetts, 1870–1915.* Cambridge, Mass.: Harvard University Press, 1971.

———, and W. Norton Grubb. *American Education and Vocationalism.* New York: Teachers College Press, Cornell University, 1974.

Leal, Juan Felipe. *La burguesía y el estado mexicano.* Mexico: Ediciones El Caballito, 1974.

———. "The Mexican State, 1915–1973: A Historical Interpretation." *Latin American Perspectives* 2 (1975): 49–79.

Lee, Gordon C. *An Introduction to Education in Modern America.* New York:

Holt, Rinehart and Winston, 1953.

Lieuwin, Edwin. *Mexican Militarism: The Rise and Fall of the Revolutionary Army, 1910–1940.* Albuquerque: University of New Mexico Press, 1968.

List Arzubide, Germán. "La rebelión constituyente." *Historia Mexicana* 1 (1951): 227–50.

Lombardi Satriani, L. M. *Apropriación y destrucción de la cultura de las clases subalternas.* Mexico: Editorial Nuevo Imagen, 1978.

Manrique, Jorge Alberto. "El proceso de las artes, 1910–1970." *Historia General de México*, vol. 4. Mexico: El Colegio de México, 1977, pp. 285–302.

Martínez Jiménez, Alejandro. "La educación elemental en el Porfiriato." *Historia Mexicana* 22 (1973): 514–52.

Medin, Tzvi. *Ideología y praxis política de Lázaro Cárdenas.* Mexico: Siglo Veintiuno Editores, 1974.

Mendoza, Vincente T. *La canción mexicana. Ensayo de clasificación y antología.* Estudios de folklore. vol. 1. Mexico: Instituto de Investigaciones Estéticas, Universidad Nacional Autónoma de México, 1961.

———. *El corrido de la Revolución mexicana.* Mexico: n.p., 1956.

Meyer, Jean. *La cristiada.* 2 vols. Mexico: Siglo Veintiuno Editores, 1973.

———. *Estado y sociedad con Calles.* Historia de la Revolución mexicana. 23 vols. Vol. 11: Período 1924–1928. Mexico: El Colegio de México, 1977.

———. *Problemas campesinos y revueltas agrarias en México, 1821–1910.* Mexico: SepSetentas, 1973.

Meyer, Lorenzo. "Historial Roots of the Authoritarian State in Mexico." In *Authoritarianism in Mexico*, edited by José Luis Reyna and Richard S. Weinert. Philadelphia: Institute for the Study of Human Issues, 1977.

———. *Mexico and the United States in the Oil Controversy, 1917–1942.* Austin: University of Texas Press, 1977.

Meyer, Michael C. *Huerta: A Political Portrait.* Lincoln: University of Nebraska Press, 1972.

———, and William Sherman. *The Course of Mexican History.* New York and London: Oxford University Press, 1979.

Meyers, William K. "Politics, Vested Rights, and Economic Growth in Porfirian Mexico: The Company of Tlahaulilo in the Comarca Lagunera, 1885–1911." *Hispanic American Historical Review* 57 (1977): 425–54.

Michaels, Albert C. "El nacionalismo conservador mexicana desde la Revolución hasta 1940." *Historia Mexicana* 16 (1966): 219–38.

Monroy Huitrón, Guadalupe. *Política educativa de la revolución, 1910–1940.* Mexico: SepSetentas, 1975.

Montsiváis, Carlos, "Notas sobre la cultura mexicana en el siglo XX." In *Historia general de México*, vol. 4. Mexico: El Colegio de Mexico, 1976, pp. 303–476.

Morales, María Dolores. "La expansión de la ciudad de México en el siglo XIX en caso de los fraccionamientos." In *Investigaciones sobre la historia de la ciudad de México.* Seminario de Historia Urbana, Mexico: Cuadernos de Trabajo del Departamento de Investigaciones Históricas,

Instituto Nacional de Antropología e Historia, 1974, pp. 77–104.

Morales-Gómez, Daniel. *La educación y el desarrollo dependendiente en América Latina.* Mexico: Ediciones Gernika, 1979.

Niblo, Stephen. "Progress and the Standard of Living in Contemporary Mexico." *Latin American Perspectives* 5 (1975): 109–24.

Niemeyer, E. V. *Revolution at Querétaro: The Mexican Constitutional Convention of 1916–1917.* Austin: University of Texas Press, 1974.

Nuñez Mata, Efrén. "Salvador Alvarado y la educación nacional." *Historia Mexicana* 11 (1962): 422–36.

Olivera Sedano, Alicia. *Aspectos del conflicto religioso de 1926 a 1929. Sus antecedentes y consecuencias.* Mexico: Instituto Nacional de Antropología e Historia, 1966.

Oritz Peralta, René. "Las posiciones ideológicas de la Convención Radical Obrera." *Historia Obrera* 1, no. 2 (1974): 10–16.

Ortega, Fidel. *Política educativa.* Mexico: Editorial Progreso, 1967.

Paoli, Francisco, and Enrique Montalvo. *El socialismo olvidado de Yucatán.* Mexico: Siglo Veintiuno, 1974.

de la Peña, Sergio. *El modo de producción capitalista: teoria y método de investigación.* Mexico: Siglo Veintiuno, 1978.

Perry, Laurens Ballard. "La reforma liberal y la política práctica en la república restaurada, 1867–1876." *Historia Mexicana* 23 (1974): 646–94.

Pike, F. *Hispanismo: 1896–1936: Spanish Conservatives and Liberals and Their Relations with Intellectuals in Spanish America.* South Bend, Ind.: University of Notre Dame Press, 1971.

Ponce, Anibal. *Educación y lucha de clases.* Mexico: Editorial América, 1937.

Powell, T. G. *El liberalismo y el campesinato en el centro de México, 1850–1876.* Mexico: SepSetentas, 1974.

———. "Mexican Intellectuals and the Indian Question, 1876–1911." *Hispanic American Historical Review* 48 (1968): 19–36.

Presley, James. "Mexican Views on Rural Education, 1900–1910." *Americas* 20 (1963): 379–403.

Pugh, William Howard. *José Vasconcelos: el despertar de México moderno.* Mexico: Editorial Jus, 1938.

Quirk, Robert E. *The Mexican Revolution and the Catholic Church, 1910–1929.* Bloomington, Ind.: Indiana University, 1973.

Raat, William D. "Ideas and Society in Don Porfirio's Mexico." *Americas* 30 (1973): 32–53.

———. "Positivism in Díaz's Mexico, 1867–1910: An Essay in Intellectual History." Ph.D. dissertation, University of Oregon, 1969.

———. "Leopoldo Zea and Mexican Positivism: A Reappraisal." *Hispanic American Historical Review* 48 (1968): 1–18.

Raby, David. *Educación y revolución social.* Mexico: SepSetentas, 1974.

———. "Los maestros rurales y los conflictos sociales en México, 1931–1940." *Historia Mexicana* 18 (1968): 190–226.

———. "Los principios de la educación rural en México: el caso de Mi-

choacán, 1915–1929." *Historia Mexicana* 22 (1973): 553–81.
Ramírez, Rafael, et al. *La enseñanza de la historia en México.* Mexico: Talleres de la Editorial Cultura, 1948.
Ramos, Samuel. *Historia de la filosofía en México.* Mexico: Imprenta Universitaria, 1943.
———. *Veinte años de educación en México.* Mexico: Imprenta Universitaria, 1941.
Rascón, María Antonieta. "La mujer y la lucha social." In Elena Urrutía, *Imagen y realidad de la mujer.* Mexico: SepSetentas, 1975, pp. 139–74.
Reed, John. *Insurgent Mexico.* New York: Simon and Schuster, 1969.
Reinhardt, Kurt. "Facets of Mexican Thought: José Vasconcelos." *The Americas* 3 (1946): 332–34.
———. "A Mexican Personalist: Antonio Caso, 1883–1946." *The Americas* 3 (1946): 20–30.
Reyes Herola, Jesús. *El liberalismo mexicano.* 3 vols. Mexico: Universidad Nacional Autónoma de México, 1957–1961.
Reyna, José Luis, and Richard S. Weinert, eds. *Authoritarianism in Mexico.* Philadelphia: Institute for the Study of Human Issues, 1977.
Reynolds, Clark. *The Mexican Economy: Twentieth-Century Structure and Growth.* New Haven: Yale University Press, 1970.
Richmond, Douglas. "Factional Political Strife in Coahuila, 1910–1920." *Hispanic American Historical Review* 60 (1980): 49–68.
Robles, Martha. *Educación y sociedad en la historia de México.* Mexico: Siglo Veintiuno, 1977.
Romanell, Patrick. "Bergson in Mexico: A Tribute to José Vasconcelos." *Philosophy and Phenomenological Research* 21 (June 1961): 501–13.
———. *The Making of the Mexican Mind.* Lincoln: University of Nebraska Press, 1952.
Ruíz, Ramón Eduardo. *Mexico: The Challenge of Poverty and Illiteracy.* San Marino, Calif.: Huntington Library, 1963.
———. *The Great Rebellion: Mexico, 1905–1924.* New York: W. W. Norton and Company, 1981.
———. *Labor and the Ambivalent Revolutionaries: Mexico, 1911–1923.* Baltimore: Johns Hopkins University Press, 1976.
Ruiz Gaytán, Beatriz. "Justo Sierra y la Escuela de Altos Estudios." *Historia Mexicana* 16 (1967): 541–64.
Salmerón, Fernando. "Los filósofos mexicanos del siglo XX." *Estudios de la filosofía en México.* Mexico: Universidad Nacional Autónoma de México, 1963, pp. 269–322.
Sandels, Robert. "Silvestre Terrazas and the Old Regime in Chihuahua." *The Americas* 28 (1971): 191–205.
Santiago Sierra, Augusto. *Las misiones culturales.* Mexico: SepSetentas, 1973.
Schmidt, Henry C. *The Roots of Lo Mexicano: Self and Society in Mexican Thought, 1900–1934.* College Station, Texas: Texas A and M University Press, 1978.
Schmitt, Karl M. "Catholic Adjustment to the Secular State: The Case of Mexico, 1867–1911." *Catholic Historical Review* 482 (1962): 182–204.

———. "The Díaz Conciliation Policy on State and Local Levels, 1876–1911." *Hispanic American Historical Review* 40 (1960): 513–32.
———. "The Mexican Positivists and the Church-State Question, 1876–1910." *Journal of Church and State* 8 (Spring 1966): 200–213.
Schneir, Miriam. *Feminism: The Essential Historical Writings.* New York: Random House, 1972.
Schoenhals, Louise. "Mexico's Experiment in Rural and Primary Education, 1921–1930." *Hispanic American Historical Review* 44 (1964): 22–43.
Scholes, Walter V. *Mexican Politics during the Juárez Regime, 1855–1872.* Columbia, Missouri: University of Missouri Press, 1957.
Semo, Enrique. "La hacienda mexicana y la transición del feudalismo al capitalismo." *Historia y Sociedad* 5 (1975):63–81.
Sennett, Richard, and Jonathon Cobb. *The Hidden Injuries of Class.* New York: Random House, Vintage Books, 1973.
Shields, James J., and Colin Greer. *Foundations of Education: Dissenting Views.* New York: John Wiley and Sons, 1974.
Shulgovsky, Anatoli. *México en la encrucijada de su historia.* Mexico: Ediciones de Cultura Popular, SA, 1968.
Simmons, Merle. *The Mexican Corrido as a Source for Interpretative Study of Modern Mexico, 1870–1950.* Bloomington, Ind.: Indiana University Press, 1957.
Simon, Walter. *European Positivism in the Nineteenth Century.* Ithaca, N.Y.: Cornell University Press, 1963.
Simpson, Eyler. *The Ejido: Mexico's Way Out.* Chapel Hill, N.C.: University of North Carolina Press, 1937.
Sims. Harold D. "Espejo de caciques: Los Terrazas de Chihuahua." *Historia Mexicana* 18 (1969): 299–379.
Sinkin, Richard N. "The Mexican Constitutional Congress, 1856–1857: A Statistical Analysis." *Hispanic American Historical Review* 53 (1973): 1–26.
Sizer, Theodore. *Secondary Schools at the Turn of the Century.* New Haven: Yale University Press, 1964.
Smith, Peter H. "La política dentro de la revolución: El Congreso Constituyente de 1916–1917." *Historia Mexicana* 22 (1973): 363–95.
Smith, Robert Freeman. *The United States and Revolutionary Nationalism in Mexico, 1916–1932.* Chicago: University of Chicago Press, 1972.
Sommers, Joseph. *After the Storm: Landmarks of the Modern Mexican Novel.* Albuquerque: University of New Mexico Press, 1968.
Spring, Joel. *Education and the Rise of the Corporate State.* Boston: Beacon Press, 1972.
Stabb, Martin S. "Indigenism and Racism in Mexican Thought, 1857–1911." *Journal of Inter-American Studies* 1 (1959): 405–43.
———. *In Quest of Identity: Patterns in the Spanish-American Essay of Ideas, 1890–1960.* Chapel Hill, N.C.: University of North Carolina Press, 1967.
Stevenson, Robert. *Music in Mexico: A Historical Survey.* New York: Thomas Y. Crowell, 1952.
Stone, James C., and Frederick W. Schneider. *Readings in the Foundations of*

Education: Commitment to Teaching. 2 vols. New York: Thomas Y. Crowell, 1971.

Tibol, Raquel. *Arte Mexicano, Época moderna y contemporánea.* Mexico: Editorial Hermes, 1963.

Tischendorf, A. *Great Britain and Mexico in the Era of Porfirio Díaz.* Durham, N.C.: Duke University Press, 1961.

Towner, Margaret, "Monopoly Capitalism and Women's Work during the Porfiriato." *Women in Latin America: An Anthology from Latin American Perspectives.* Riverside, Calif.: Latin American Perspectives, 1979, pp. 47–61.

Turner, Frederick C. *The Dynamics of Mexican Nationalism.* Chapel Hill, N.C.: University of North Carolina Press, 1968.

Tyack, David B. *The One Best System: A History of American Urban Education.* Cambridge, Mass.: Harvard University Press, 1976.

Ulloa, Bertha. *La revolución escindida.* Historia de la Revolución mexicana. 23 vols. Vol. 4: Período 1914–1917. Mexico: El Colegio de México.

Vaughan, Mary Kay. "Education and Class in the Mexican Revolution." *Latin American Perspectives* 2 (1975): 17–33.

———. "History Textbooks in Mexico in the 1920s." Special Studies Paper No. 53, Council on International Studies, State University of New York at Buffalo, 1974.

———. "Women, Class, and Education in Mexico, 1880–1928." *Latin American Perspectives* 12–13 (1977): 150–68. Reprinted in *Women in Latin America: An Anthology from Latin American Perspectives.* Riverside, Calif.; Latin American Perspectives, 1979, pp. 63–80.

Vázquez, Josefina Zoraida. "Le educación socialista en los años treinta." *Historia Mexicana* 18 (1969): 408–23.

———. *Nacionalismo y la educación.* Mexico: El Colegio de México, 1970.

———. "Los primeros tropiezos." In *Historia general de México*, Vol. 3. Mexico: El Colegio de México, 1976, pp. 1–69.

Villa, Manuel. "Discusión de algunas categorías para el análisis de la Revolución mexicana." *Revista Mexicana de Ciencias Políticas* 70 (1972): 25–38.

Villarello Vélez, Ildefonso. *Historia de la Revolución mexicana en Coahuila.* Mexico: Talleres Gráficos de la Nación, 1970.

Villaseñor, José. "El Gran Círculo de Obreros de México." *Historia Obrera* 1, no. 4 (1975): 25–32.

Villegas, Abelardo. *La filosofía de lo mexicano.* Mexico: Fondo de Cultura Económica, 1960.

Warman, Arturo. *Los campesinos, hijos predilectos del régimen.* Mexico: Editorial Nuestro Tiempo, 1972.

Wasserman, Mark. "Oligarquía e intereses extranjeros en Chihuahua durante el Porfiriato." *Historia Mexicana* 22 (1973): 279–319.

Weinstein, James. *The Corporate Ideal in the Liberal State, 1900–1918.* Boston: Beacon Press, 1968.

Weyl, Nathaniel, and Sylvia Weyl. *The Reconquest of Mexico: The Years of Lázaro Cárdenas.* New York: Oxford University Press, 1939.

Wiebe, Robert H. *The Search for Order, 1877–1920*. New York: Hill and Wang, 1967.

Wilkie, James W. "The Meaning of the *Cristero* Religious War against the Mexican Revolution." *Journal of Church and State* 8 (1966): 214–33.

———. *The Mexican Revolution: Federal Expenditure and Social Change since 1910*. Berkeley: University of California Press, 1967.

Wilson, Irma. *Mexico: A Century of Educational Thought*. New York. Hispanic Institute of the United States, 1941.

Wolfskill, George, and Douglas Richmond. *Essays on the Mexican Revolution: Revisionist Views of the Leaders*. Austin: University of Texas Press, 1979.

Womack, John. *Zapata and the Mexican Revolution*. New York: Alfred A. Knopf, 1968.

Zaretsky, Eli. "Capitalism, the Family, and Personal Life." *Socialist Revolution* 1 (1973): 90–106.

Zea. Leopoldo. *El positivismo en México: Nacimiento, apogeo, y decadencia*. Mexico: Fondo de Cultura Económica, 1978.

Index